D1094919

Stanley Kubrick

To Stanley Kubrick, for obvious reasons,
and to Nicole, for reasons less obvious

Stanley Kubrick

Seven Films Analyzed

Randy Rasmussen

McFarland & Company, Inc., Publishers
Jefferson, North Carolina, and London

ALSO BY RANDY RASMUSSEN

Children of the Night:
The Six Archetypal Characters of Classic Horror Films
(McFarland, 1998)

Library of Congress Cataloguing-in-Publication Data

Rasmussen, Randy.
    Stanley Kubrick : seven films analyzed / Randy Rasmussen.
       p.   cm.
    Includes bibliographical references and index.
    ISBN 0-7864-0870-7 (library binding : 50# alkaline paper) ∞
    1. Kubrick, Stanley — Criticism and interpretation.   I. Title.
PN1998.3.K83R37   2001
791.43'0233'092 — dc21   00-68719

British Library cataloguing data are available

Manufactured in the United States of America

McFarland & Company, Inc., Publishers
  Box 611, Jefferson, North Carolina 28640
    www.mcfarlandpub.com

Contents

Acknowledgments

My thanks to Michael and Jeanne Anderegg and to Donald and Joann McCaffrey for their many years of encouragement and conversation about Kubrick. Also thanks to Barb Hobart, for helping me cope with a temperamental computer, and to Renee Twite, for being a friend. And a special thanks to my father, Loren, and my sister, Terri, for their love and support.

Introduction

You can start with a game plan but depending on where the ball bounces and where the other side happens to be, opportunities and problems arise which can only be effectively dealt with at that very moment.
— Stanley Kubrick (Ciment, 175)

Stanley Kubrick made the above comment while comparing filmmaking to a sporting contest, but it could just as easily apply to any of the major characters in his films. Each of them struggles to master the conditions of his or her life — to impose a pleasing order on the world. And in doing so each character encounters a kaleidoscope of circumstances which present a confusing, ever-changing series of "opportunities and problems."

One historical paradigm for the quest of mastering one's self and one's environment is Napoleon Bonaparte, about whom Kubrick once hoped to make a movie. Considered from a variety of perspectives, the French emperor yields contradictory impressions. Destroyer of whatever shreds of idealism remained to revolutionary France, he nevertheless left Europe with a legacy that eroded opposition to those ideals. As a military leader, he was a genius at capitalizing on opportunities that presented themselves and at creating opportunities where conventional military wisdom saw none. But, as time marched on, his battlefield tactics became a definable system, subject to imitation and calculated counterattack.

Kubrick's fictional universes too are places of constant change. Environments change. The cast of characters changes. And individual characters change: physically, emotionally, and intellectually. In the course of seven meticulously wrought films, from *Dr. Strangelove* through *Eyes Wide Shut*, Stanley Kubrick passionately dramatized the complexity and mutability of human struggle, in settings and situations so diverse that some of his critics fail to see the common threads in his works. The goal of this book is to trace some of those threads — to describe the shifting patterns of strategic, moral, and aesthetic relationships among the characters (individual and collective)

1

and environments (natural and artificial) that Kubrick sets in motion. Like chess, one of Kubrick's favorite pastimes, each move by one piece can alter relationships among all other pieces involved in the action, as well as change our understanding of all previous moves.

Few artists are as thorough in their delineation of character and environment, or in their orchestration of complex events, as Kubrick. In order to preserve some sense of the dramatic flow he generates, I chose to explore each of the films in this book scene by scene instead of organizing the discussion by thematic categories. One of the joys of viewing a Kubrick film is to experience the intense lyricism of precisely sculpted impressions that *build* on one another. The risk of my approach to Kubrick's lyricism is that of lapsing into pointless synopsizing, which I have tried to avoid. Yet it is remarkable how much viewers can disagree about the details of what they saw and heard in a given film.

Kubrick's camera acts as a roving participant/observer, slipping into and out of intimate alignment with the various perspectives of his characters. In *The Shining*, for example, it tracks members of the Torrance family through the maze of corridors in the Overlook Hotel, functioning alternately as purely subjective double, partly subjective companion, detached observer and occasionally even metaphorical predator. Kubrick's use of sound, especially music, is equally dynamic, sometimes reinforcing and sometimes contradicting visual impressions. Kubrick's cinematic universe is an endless lyrical dance featuring multiple partners in constant movement. By infusing each of these partners with its own dramatic integrity while not allowing any one of them to completely dominate the story, Kubrick strives for a comprehensive perspective that eludes his characters.

Anthropologist Germaine Tillion wrote about the dilemma of objective versus subjective points of view in her study of Nazi atrocities during World War II. Speaking as both a victim of the Holocaust and a professional student of people and their institutions, she notes:

> The pervasive element of bias will always affect interpretation, of course, and it is almost impossible to dislodge. But conversely, a total absence of emotional "involvement" amounts to almost unbelievable incomprehension. There is a very narrow line between bias and incomprehension, and this narrowness is one of the most basic problems of humanity and history [Tillion, 201].

Journalist Thomas L. Friedman, reporting on Middle Eastern affairs during the 1980s, described a similar tension in his job: "Intimacy without disinterest lapses into commitment to one side or another; disinterest without intimacy lapses into banality and misunderstanding" (Friedman, 69).

Kubrick's films are juggling acts in which he tries to bring many ingredients vividly to life without losing track of their interaction. Narrative film is an abstract *representation* of reality that bridges the gap between "bias" of the moment and "total absence of emotional involvement." The audience gets to have its cake and eat it too. Perhaps for that reason Kubrick is sensitive to film's capacity for deception, often drawing comparisons between film and the various abstract visual filters of his characters. In *2001: A Space Odyssey*, for example, the widescreen film frame parallels numerous examples of artificially contained or modified perspective within it. Sometimes we see subjectively *with* and other times objectively *beyond* what the characters see. In *Dr. Strangelove*, General Turgidson's beloved Big Board is a glorified movie screen that provides him with a simplified, abstract, and manageable impression of nuclear war quite different from the messy realities we encounter outside its borders. Alex, in *A Clockwork Orange*, comments on the intoxicating clarity of movies: "It's funny how the colors of the real world only seem really real when you viddy them on the screen." Kubrick frequently reminds us that the vantage point of a film audience is both artificial and privileged. It can illuminate or it can deceive.

Short of Alex's tightly controlled Ludovico viddy sessions in *Clockwork*, no film audience (or *any* audience, for that matter) can be manipulated down to the last detail. Even a serious student of film, who is supposedly more attentive to nuances than the average viewer, will latch on to a work and maneuver it in directions he or she wants it to go, which never exactly match the filmmaker's original vision. And the act of interpretation inevitably serves a purpose distinct from the artist's. But that fact does not discount the possibility of sympathetic understanding or insight. Kubrick's films are full of characters who, for one reason or another, try to redefine each other. Only when that process gets out of hand does it become grotesque and reprehensible, and a target for Kubrick's sometimes savage satire.

Most of Kubrick's films have been adapted from novels. The creative process by which one work of art is transformed into another potentially involves the same conflict of interest portrayed *in* his films. An ambitious filmmaker employs a literary work as raw material, to be broken down and remade into something of his own choosing. Likewise, screenwriters collaborating on a script bring different perspectives to bear. Under the best of circumstances this interaction enriches the final product. Stimulating dialog between partners may even yield *separate* products, each benefiting from a kind of creative cross-pollination. Such interplay between Kubrick and Arthur C. Clarke, for example, paid off handsomely for both. Yet *2001* the film is very different from *2001* the novel, which was written concurrently with rather than before the script. Analogous working relationships are portrayed in many of Kubrick's films, where they are subjected to dramatic scrutiny. In *2001* the initially cooperative relationship between astronauts Bowman and Poole and computer HAL falls apart under the strain of their Jupiter Mission. In *Clockwork* a perverse alliance between convicted murderer Alex and the government's Interior Minister breaks down in the chaos of Ludovico's political fallout, then is patched up with an unholy bargain that neatly serves their separate needs.

A detailed comparison of Kubrick's films and their source novels could easily fill a book and already has. In this study I am concerned primarily with shifting patterns of perspectives and forces within the films, and only incidentally with their literary roots. However, I begin most chapters with a few introductory comments about important changes made by Kubrick in constructing one narrative out of the fragments of another, partly because that process is similar to processes so vividly depicted in his films.

Practical considerations of space prompted my decision to limit this study to Kubrick's last seven films, which represent his most mature and least compromised work. *Spartacus*, though an interesting work in its own right, was dominated by its star and writer. Even *Paths of Glory*, a beautiful film, plays somewhat to the prestige of its lead actor by making his character heroic (though not infallible). But it is after *Lolita*, another fine work, that Kubrick was really able to cut loose and make films the way *he* wanted to make them.

CHAPTER 1

Dr. Strangelove:
Failed-Safe

The military machine ... is in fact simple, and appears on this account easy to manage. But let us reflect that no part of it is in one piece, that it is composed entirely of individuals, each of which keeps up its own friction in all directions.
— Carl von Clausewitz, *On War* (164–65)

Early in Peter George's novel *Red Alert*, from which *Dr. Strangelove* was adapted, the crew of an American B-52 bomber performs a seemingly trivial act of propriety. One of them is about to relate an amusing sexual anecdote when over the radio arrives an order to attack the Soviet Union. The anecdote is left untold because the crew tacitly agrees that it would no longer be funny. The novel as a whole is built around a tacit agreement between author and reader of what would and would not contribute to a dignified if chilling portrait of men at war. Deviant behavior by an American Air Force base commander who orders an unauthorized nuclear attack on Russia is quasi-legitimized by his impressive argument for doing so. And the same character retains his capacity for self-criticism and cogent debate into the heart of the nuclear darkness he triggers. Many characters in violent opposition to each other talk pretty much alike, never straying too far into the language of irrationality no matter how desperate their situation and never allowing their personal biases and subconscious motivations to dictate their professional decisions. Nor do emotional stress, misunderstanding, and lack of information overwhelm officials charged with preserving peace. Names like Clint Brown, Andrew Mackenzie, or Generals Quinten and Franklin suggest a stereotypically American brand of integrity, sensibility, and determination that surely must triumph over disaster. In a story that questions the value of nuclear weapons as instruments of foreign policy, the myth of disinterested and harmonious collective effort is preserved, thanks in part to some carefully arranged luck. *Red Alert* concludes with a euphoric, two-pronged leap of faith: in the power of a new technology, intercontinental ballistic missiles, to guarantee the deterrent logic of Mutual Assured Destruction, and in the enduring moral lesson of a close call with nuclear obliteration. Presumably no one who has such an experience could ever again wish for war. Some of the survivors of World Wars I and II harbored similar delusions.

Dr. Strangelove rejects the novel's optimistic conclusion and its sense of propriety. Kubrick's film zealously explores the possibility of a *failure* to contain the technological and psychological forces involved in such a conflict. Emotional turmoil sufficient to inspire a S.A.C. base commander to launch an unauthorized nuclear attack just might deprive him of his capacities for self-examination and rational debate. Cracks in various collective structures of containment result, under extreme pressure, in eruptions of *private* interest, including the sexual passions so discreetly sidestepped in *Red Alert*. The burdens of professional responsibility, misunderstandings, inaccurate information, and irreconcilable differences among various points of view coalesce to trigger the chain-reaction breakdown of a fragile peace. The dignity of man at war is one of the first casualties. Kubrick and his co-screenwriters, Terry Southern and Peter George, echo this change by rechristening the novel's characters, giving them symbolic names denoting the narrow concerns and inclinations that eventually dominate and defeat them. The epitome of this breakdown is Dr. Strangelove, a character never glimpsed in *Red Alert*, yet one that grows out of the weaknesses in characters common to both novel and film.

Dr. Strangelove is a satiric odyssey through the labyrinth of one of modern civilization's most elaborate creations: military deterrence in the nuclear age. The struggle for power and security within that structure is fought by numerous, overlapping identities: nation versus nation, one military service versus another within the same political organization, organization versus individual, individual versus individual, and individual versus himself. Within this increasingly chaotic interplay of identities the definitions of Self and Other become blurred, subject to sudden, radical, and sometimes absurd change.

* * *

Dr. Strangelove is a battlefield right from the start. In the prologue we hear a dispassionate, disembodied narrator, whose voice could have been culled from any Pentagon documentary of the early 1960s, convey official Western concerns about a secret new Soviet weapon threatening the nuclear standoff of Mutual Assured Destruction. What we *see*, meanwhile, are fog-shrouded mountain peaks along Russia's Arctic coast, or Nature employed by the Soviets to conceal their new weapon from N.A.T.O.

Unlike traditional film credits, which are formal and tidy in appearance, *Dr. Strangelove's* are scrawled across the screen as if by the hand of a child. Already the private intrudes on the collective. Odd proportions, too, distort conventional perceptions. Trivial words are inflated far beyond their grammatical worth, while more important information appears in tiny print. A different kind of distortion gives preponderance to professional titles over personal names, implying that the power and personality quirks of individual characters are magnified by their collective positions of authority. The most spectacular example of that phenomenon is Strangelove, whose rank as science advisor to the President of the United States is echoed by a bloated "DR.," an official title that both masks and facilitates the grandiose fulfillment of his misanthropic vision.

Paralleling the opening credits as a battleground between private and collective perspectives is the midair refueling of a B-52 bomber by a tanker aircraft. Taken from documentary footage, this imagery is a visual extension of the narrator's dispassionate tone of voice in the prologue. But now the soundtrack switches gears to intrude a *private* sensibility which, by juxtaposition, alters our impression of what we see. The normal whine of jet engines is displaced by the romantic ballad, "Try a Little Tenderness." Lilting violins transform the refueling maneuver into a stratospheric sexual rendezvous of gargantuan proportions. The tanker's nozzle becomes a ludicrously detailed penis while the undulating movement of the disembodied camera imposes a sexual choreography on the two mechanical giants. Sex and the capacity for mass destruction become intertwined and confused.

Caught up in the rivalry between nations during the prologue, Nature now blindly lends itself to the aesthetics of a struggle between private and collective man. Glimpses of land miles below, through gaps in velvet clouds, generate a sense of ethereal detachment from mundane, earthbound realities. Sunlight gleams off metal flanks. Grotesquely ironic though it is, the "mating" of two warplanes is strangely beautiful. Considered in more general terms as products of human creativity, like a beautifully designed building or bridge, the two aircraft are astonishing achievements which empower man far beyond his natural abilities. Thomas Nelson, one of the director's most astute critics, notes the duality of the director's attitude towards technology. "Kubrick implies that this merger of madness and machine originates as much in a human passion for beauty as it does in a primal darkness of the Id" (Nelson, 97).

The refueling scene in *Dr. Strangelove* is reminiscent of the beginning of Leni Riefenstahl's *Triumph of the Will* (1936), in which the landing of Adolf Hitler's airplane at Nuremberg is fashioned into a Wagnerian descent from the heavens by a German god. In both films documentary footage is infused with extrinsic meaning by music. But Riefenstahl placed no ironic signposts in or around her composition. We can appreciate its lyrical fusion of disparate ingredients (machine, Nature, and music) into a passionate new whole, while criticizing its moral shortcomings. Kubrick, by contrast, gives us *overlapping* impressions, celebrating man's technological genius while satirizing his susceptibility to aesthetic intoxication and sublimation. It remains to be revealed specifically *who* is redefining and corrupting the institutional instruments shown on screen.

When the camera cuts to Burpleson Air Force Base, all traces of private distortion disappear, for awhile. Subjective music is washed from the soundtrack. Exterior shots of the base depict a relatively peaceful routine of military vigilance. This impression of efficient, rationally controlled power carries over into the base command center: an uncluttered, evenly lit realm of computers, graphs, maps, and uniformed personnel calmly going about their appointed, coordinated tasks. Even Captain Lionel Mandrake, a British Air Force officer serving temporarily as Burpleson's executive officer, seems more an extension than a wielder of official power. In his first appearance, he steps out from behind a computer printout that neatly defines his view of the world. He is virtually an appendage of that machine and its institutional programming. His Dickensian name refers to a plant root once thought to resemble a human being. His conformity to social norms, even under conditions which render them irrelevant, will occasionally make him seem less human than automaton. In a shot of him speaking on the telephone with his superior, Mandrake's head is bracketed by rotating computer tapes visible in the background, while his service cap sits on a S.A.C. procedure manual. His outlook and the organization's are virtually the same. Behind him also is a sign featuring the official S.A.C. motto, "Peace Is Our Profession," printed in tidy, modest letters. With the diffident Captain as its implied spokesman, that motto is believable. But at the other end of the phone line is a character who belies the motto and instead exemplifies the base's odd name, Burpleson — a comic reference to a purely *private*, if trivial, outburst.

Unlike Mandrake's command center, General Jack D. Ripper's office reeks of personality. A single overhead fluorescent light creates a gothic effect of shadow and glare. Metaphorically the light is a measure of the intense pressure Ripper puts on himself. On the wall behind the General are pictures of a World War II American superfortress dropping bombs on an invisible target and a S.A.C. propaganda poster proclaiming "Peace Is Our Profession" over an armored fist clutching lightning bolts and an olive branch. Ripper's version of the S.A.C. motto is an unconvincing marriage of peaceful intent and destructive capacity. It compares to Mandrake's version as the film's scrawled opening credits would to a more conventional display.

The General himself is a big block of a man, filling out his heavily decorated uniform to imposing proportions. Mandrake, by contrast, makes his

R.A.F. uniform look like a well-pressed business suit. But if Ripper and his office are a bold celebration of S.A.C.'s capacity for destruction, his phone conversation is not. For strategic reasons, he conceals from his executive officer the fact that his activation of Wing Attack Plan R was unauthorized, letting Mandrake assume that the order to attack the Soviet Union was issued by Washington.

Captain Mandrake's reaction to the prospect of a nuclear war is curiously divided. Repressing his anxiety, he utters a profanity so mild he could just as well be protesting the loss of a parking spot. Conflicting institutional loyalties pull him in opposite directions. To a man who believes in the official policy of MAD as a credible deterrent to war, a Soviet attack on the United States makes no sense. But to challenge General Ripper's declaration would be an act of insubordination. So Mandrake conjures up a safe interpretation of Ripper's disturbing announcement, reconciling the contradictory fragments of collective order. S.A.C. must be conducting a harmless loyalty *test*.

By limiting our understanding of General Ripper's pronouncement to what Mandrake can see, Kubrick lays ironic groundwork for revelations to come. Misleading impressions of the crisis make us better aware of the handicaps faced by the characters involved in it. Security measures ordered by Ripper seem to follow established S.A.C. procedure. Only in retrospect can his order to seal off the base be seen as an act that replaces Burpleson's official mission with his own. Confiscation of privately owned radios closes off contact between base personnel and the outside world, including the military chain of command above Ripper. Through the instruments of an organization to which they all belong, base personnel become extensions of the General's private will. Base sirens wail. S.A.C.'s mechanical cry of alarm has become Ripper's personal battle cry. But even as he extends his power over all base resources, the General is a man of divided vision. What initially appear to be expressions of compassionate concern by a commander leading his troops into combat can be seen, in retrospect, as symptoms of self-doubt about triggering that combat. Alone in his office, General Ripper rubs his forehead as though fighting off self-doubt. Then he closes the Venetian blinds on windows overlooking the base, as if to avoid facing the consequences of his deviant actions. The General is at war with the Soviet Union, with S.A.C. and, most of all, with himself.

For the third time running, Kubrick begins a scene by juxtaposing elements of institutional and private perspective. For the second time running, he depicts those disparate points of view first before and then after the onset of a crisis. Bland, matter-of-fact narration describes the destructive power of a B-52, while on screen we see documentary footage of such bombers in flight. That each aircraft carries a nuclear payload equal to sixteen times the total force of all the bombs and shells exploded in World War II no doubt accurately reflects twenty years of technological progress. But it conveys little of what such destructive power would mean to the world if unleashed, or, for that matter, what one-sixteenth of it meant to the world when unleashed during World War II. The narrator conceals as much by his choice of language and neutral tone of voice as the Soviets do beneath the fog of their Arctic islands.

Inside the cockpit of one particular B-52, individual man appears to be in tune with the narrator's dispassionate description of S.A.C.'s power and mission. In a tight frontal shot, pilot T. J. "King" Kong seems attentive to his assigned task of guarding America against foreign attack. Then a reverse zoom reveals that he is instead preoccupied with a copy of *Playboy* magazine, satisfying personal interests while ostensibly performing his institutional task.

A hand-held camera tours the aircraft and introduces the rest of the crew. Again, the impression is of private and collective perspectives intermixed. In the tradition of Hollywood war movies celebrating America as a melting pot, the crew is a classic cross section of American male society. Shown at a random moment of their fail-safe routine, Kong and his men form a curious portrait of solidarity and isolation. In the midst of their collective duty, several of the men have slipped back into their private cocoons. Some are eating. One reads a book. Another amuses himself with card tricks. Kong looks at his magazine. But as the man responsible for the overall performance of the aircraft, the Major does not slip back entirely into himself. Before indulging in a short nap, he casts a wary glance at the autopilot mechanism next to him. The absent copilot's flight helmet sits atop the controls, hinting at the encroachment of technology into the role played by individual man in his increasingly complex collective endeavors. Major Kong is the pilot of this B-52, but not literally at all times. Just as the positioning of Captain Mandrake's service cap atop a S.A.C. manual implied a perspective largely shaped by institutional training, Kong shares his symbol of command with a machine of collective design. The autopilot is a precursor to *2001*'s HAL, the sophisticated computer which renders individual man almost superfluous in the execution of complex missions.

The B-52 is an engineering maze of dials, gauges, and switches. Suddenly one of those micromechanisms springs to life. The camera zooms in on that tiny fragment of the bomber's vast electronic network. A formerly anonymous piece of a much larger system suddenly looms large and important. The disproportion in the opening credits metaphorically foreshadows events such as this. A coded message arrives over the aircraft's radio. The crew's only contact with most of the outside world is limited to radio messages and an official code book by which those messages are deciphered. In this way S.A.C. isolates and ensures itself control over the flawed individuals who operate its weapons. General Ripper aimed for a similar measure of control over Burpleson personnel by sealing off the base and confiscating private (i.e., *un*coded) radios. But if the coded message received aboard the B-52 is institutional in outward appearance, it carries the seed of a private agenda within it. The message translates into "Wing Attack Plan R"—"R" for "Romeo," which in this case ironically echoes the sexual motivation of the officer who irresponsibly sent it.

Acceptance of nuclear war comes slowly to Major Kong and his crew, as it did to Captain Mandrake. Individual man is not easily roused from pleasant diversions (*Playboy*, food, games) or, in Mandrake's case, from ingrained presumptions (the deterrent validity of MAD). Radio Operator Goldberg continues to eat as he relays the attack order to Kong. Chewing and talking at the same time prove to be an awkward combination of desire and duty. Major Kong, like Mandrake before him, seeks out alternate, safe explanations of the attack command. He first accuses Goldberg of playing a practical joke — in other words, of appropriating parts of S.A.C. (the radio and the code book) for a selfish purpose. He is correct, but he has the wrong person in mind. Though that explanation is discounted, Kong nevertheless remains skeptical: "I've been to a World's Fair, a picnic and a rodeo and that's the stupidest thing I ever heard..." The folksy examples by which he illustrates his vast experience of life's oddities are rooted in his private life outside the Air Force. Later he will draw upon that same resource to bolster his *support* for nuclear war. But for now he employs it to *dispute* the war message received over the radio. He is not by inclination a warmonger.

Major Kong meticulously (a very Kubrickian trait) verifies the attack order as best he can. Other crew members pop up from other areas of the aircraft, looking to their leader for clarity, reassurance, and direction. The previous mood of self-absorption evaporates in the face of a collective crisis. One of the men offers up the same, safe explanation of the attack order that Mandrake mentioned earlier. Perhaps S.A.C. is merely conducting a loyalty test. The battle lines in *Dr. Strangelove* are clearly not limited to national and ideological differences. Imbedded within those broader conflicts is the distrust between collective and individual man. There is some question in the minds of the B-52 crew whether their adversary is the Soviet Union or S.A.C. Unable to discredit the radio message, Major Kong finally accepts it, concluding that the "Rooskies" have launched a sneak attack on the United States. For an American patriot there can be no other explanation. Kong manufactures the rational and morally unambiguous scenario he needs in order to execute his grim duty unencumbered by doubt. Most war films would supply the objective facts to match his vision of a world at war. Instead, *Dr. Strangelove* depicts a series of limited, contradictory, and interlocked perceptions of reality.

Girding himself for battle, Kong personalizes his institutional mission. From out of an aircraft safe he pulls both official instructions for the implementation of Plan R and a white cowboy hat. The latter he substitutes for his flight helmet, thereby incorporating the mission into his broader, civilian sense of identity, just as S.A.C. has incorporated him into *its* mission. Recostumed and primed for action, Kong tells his crew, "Well, boys, I guess this is it. Nuclear combat toe to toe with the Rooskies." His strength of purpose is equaled by the obsolescence of his language. Nuclear combat is not fought toe to toe. Technology has made direct contact between opponents unnecessary, at least on the level of a nuclear exchange.

Subjectively flowing from Kong's cultural storehouse, like his cowboy hat and colorful speech, is the background music emerging on the soundtrack. The American Civil War song, "When Johnny Comes Marching Home," recollects patriotic passions of a bygone military conflict. As employed in *Dr. Strangelove*, it both echoes and comments on the passions of an unrelated war fought a hundred years later. Presented in an instrumental version, it is abstracted from its historical origins just enough to make it an effective *new* battle song. It is ironic that a *Yankee* song from the Civil War is used to reflect the fervor of a man whose sympathies would probably have been for the Confederacy. And like Kong's "toe to toe" comment, the notion of a soldier "marching" home does not quite fit with a *flight* crew involved in *intercontinental* combat. Yet, in another context, the song's Civil War roots fit the current situation. Major Kong unwittingly participates in an updated conflict within the American political system. His B-52 is the spearhead of an unauthorized secession by General Ripper from the established power structure in Washington, D.C.

Kong returns to his seat and relieves the autopilot of its temporary command. This is a job for a human being, not a machine. And part of that job is to buck up morale among the crew. To that end, Kong supplies moral justification for the mass destruction they are about to unleash. He and the crew have a sacred institutional trust to avenge the folks back home, many of whom are presumably dead or dying. Later revelations expose this reasoning as a mirage. Yet Kong's misinterpretation of the facts is understandable, given his background and his restricted access to the outside world. Only when he segues from sincere if stilted rhetoric about sacred duty to promises of future promotions and citations does his logic become inherently absurd. Attempting to bolster morale with an appeal to self-interest, Kong betrays the inadequacy of his own imagination. How likely is it that total nuclear war will leave S.A.C. protocol and ritual intact, or that it will be a profitable career opportunity? Kong's expectations seem rooted more in the experiences of earlier, nonnuclear wars.

Major Kong doubles back to a collective point in order to sweeten his appeal to self-interest. There is a crude nobility about his rigorous attention to society's rules of fair play. Rewards for combat service will be distributed in a democratic manner, "regardless of yer race, color or yer creed." Jewish and African-American members of his crew are perhaps the intended beneficiaries of this amendment. Judging by their rapt attention, Kong's efforts to bolster his crew's team spirit are both necessary and effective. And though his reasoning is based on false assumptions about the nature of the crisis and of probable conditions in a postwar world, Kong emerges from this scene as a man of emotional resilience, strong will, and leadership ability — virtues unfortunately detached from any capacity for objectivity. Like Colonel "Bat" Guano, his comic double on the ground, the Major combines certain narrow strengths with pronounced weaknesses that are exposed and inflated by circumstances beyond his control.

General Buck Turgidson, a member of the Joint Chiefs of Staff, is the senior officer of the Strategic Air Command. Yet, like Kong and his crew, he is preoccupied with private matters when first drawn into the nuclear crisis triggered by General Ripper — so much so, in fact, that we don't even see him when the camera transports us to his apartment bedroom in Washington, D.C. Walls in that room are lined with mirrors that turn vision back upon itself. A sunlamp substitutes for the real thing. The General's secretary, Miss Scott, serves her boss as both a mistress and a telephone screening device. And the telephone itself is set to ring softly. Kubrick shoots this scene in a single take and without camera movement, emphasizing the static, closed, constipated nature of the General's perspective. Turgidson, meanwhile, is removed from even the self-indulgent micro-universe of his bedroom. He is satisfying a more urgent and private need in the bathroom off screen. Only under protest does he emerge to attend to professional matters. He is dressed in shorts and an open shirt, aesthetically lacking whatever aura of authority and competence his Air Force uniform would have provided, as it did for General Ripper. Stripped of his costume, he is a middle aged, pot-bellied man with pallid skin. While speaking on the phone, he casually thumps his prominent stomach. Thomas Nelson interprets that slap as a sign of primitivism (Nelson, 91). Alexander Walker describes it as a man "sounding his own war drum" (Walker, 177). I see it instead as an expression of contentment from a monarch barricaded in his small but well-stocked kingdom and reluctant to leave it for the annoying call of duty.

The telephone that brings Colonel Puntridge's disturbing message is a grudging compromise of the General's privacy. Lines of communication among the characters in *Dr. Strangelove* are fragile, tentative, and often confusing. Miss Scott, for example, serves as a communication filter in both directions, fielding the Colonel's call in order to spare her boss the annoyance of doing so himself, yet also softening Turgidson's rude responses to Puntridge's statements. She is both a transmitter and a diplomatic translator. She also pursues a *personal* as well as a professional agenda over the telephone.

Employing the same, soothing tone of voice with which she tempers communication between the Colonel and the General, she conceals from each man the fact that she is having or has had a romantic relationship with the other. The professional exchange of information contains an undercurrent of private emotional baggage.

Finally coaxed out of his pleasure den by disturbing news from the outside world, General Turgidson leaves his passionate mistress with a promise to return soon and satisfy her sexually. Perched over her on the bed, he makes a sexual boast couched in the metaphor of a rocket launch — one of the film's many verbal and visual links between sexuality and military hardware. The camera cuts immediately to the image of a machine gun barrel tilted upward on its jeep mount. In the context of the General's remark, the weapon becomes phallic, just as the midair refueling scene was imbued with sexual meaning by romantic background music. Turgidson, of course, is unaware of the link he forges between sex and weapons. And that is one of the core problems in *Dr. Strangelove*, where most characters, lacking insight into their own motivations, confuse their personal concerns with their professional duties.

From inside his ivory tower, General Ripper imposes his fictional view of the outside world on all base personnel through the mechanism of an intercom. His voice rings godlike throughout Burpleson while subordinates execute his instructions. They are dwarfed by the instruments of war around them and, implicitly, by the sense of duty instilled in them. The gospel according to Ripper is a hodgepodge of American right-wing rhetoric. Ripper's private motivations remain concealed behind patriotic clichés. "Today the nation is counting on us and we are not going to let them down" is almost the same thing Major Kong said to bolster the courage of *his* crew. But Ripper's call for commitment to duty is more extreme than Kong's. He offers no promotions or pay raises to soften the prospect of self-sacrifice.

While General Ripper infects the entire base with his false vision of a Soviet invasion, Captain Mandrake, true to form, methodically closes down his temple of S.A.C. rationality. Deterrence has failed. Machines associated with the routine maintenance of deterrence are switched off. But the exercise of power is never absolute in a Kubrick film. There are always leaks, oversights, and accidents to consider. Mandrake's discovery of a radio hidden inside the same printout machine (by now a symbol of S.A.C. rationality) from which he visually emerged earlier breaches the outer layer of Ripper's deception. Through that otherwise trivial device, Mandrake catches a true glimpse of the outside world. Always attuned to conventional wisdom and expectations, Mandrake finds the presence of normal civilian broadcasting inconsistent with the image of national emergency projected by Ripper. As the scene ends, he rushes off to tell his commander the good news.

Major Kong's B-52 is locked into an attack mode. "When Johnny Comes

Marching Home" pounds out its martial enthusiasm like a defective record-ing that keeps repeating itself. Unlike Mandrake, Kong and his crew are in no position to question the validity of Ripper's order. An aircraft safe once again yields a mixture of private and collective material. Photographs of semi-nude women are juxtaposed with official instructions for the implementation of Plan R. Like Kong's cowboy hat, the pictures both corrupt and humanize the crew's appointed mission. Not even the most guarded recesses of institu-tional policy and power are free from the taint of personal desire.

Settling into a well-rehearsed S.A.C. scenario, Major Kong reads aloud the Plan R attack profile in the manner of a commercial airline pilot describ-ing a flight plan to his passengers. The profile itself is an eloquent example of the institutional mind's detachment from the physical and emotional real-ities of war. A hydrogen bomb is referred to as a "thirty megaton device," making it sound more like a surgical implant than a weapon of mass destruc-tion. Following that is a lot of military jargon both technically precise and chillingly lacking in moral substance. It is easy to criticize the shortcomings of such language, but it is equally important to appreciate the rationale for it. By rendering its instructions in such a dry matter-of-fact manner, S.A.C. attempts to douse rather than inflame emotions which might impair the per-formance of its soldiers. Ironically, the dispassionate language of Major Kong's attack profile now serves the *excessively* passionate, deviant goals of General Ripper rather than S.A.C.'s original, peacekeeping mission.

Activation of the bomber's CRM 114 radio circuits, originally intended by S.A.C. to insulate the crew from false enemy instructions, in this case insu-lates them from S.A.C. and ensures their obedience to General Ripper's ille-gal command.

Captain Mandrake is such a slave to decorum that, while rushing to his commander's office to relay the happy news that there is no war, he pauses to drop some trash in a wastepaper basket. Not even a nuclear crisis is an excuse for untidiness. Inside General Ripper's lair, he continues to behave in an exceedingly courteous manner. The wonderful discovery that nuclear war has not broken out is relayed as, "Something rather interesting has just cropped up." Nearly everything the Captain perceives, says, and does passes through a filter that reduces it to something emotionally remote and manageable. On the basis of continuing civilian radio broadcasts, he speculates that the attack order is merely a test, then meekly criticizes Washington leadership for "tak-ing things a bit too far." Obviously he is uncomfortable challenging higher authority.

We hear on Mandrake's radio, which he plays for Ripper, an American-ized, jazz rendition of the old English tune, "Greensleeves." In *The Merry Wives of Windsor*, William Shakespeare referred to the same song as the *mod-ern* half of an anachronistic pairing (Act II, Scene 1, lines 55–57). In *Dr.*

Strangelove "Greensleeves" is the *ancient* component blended with modern jazz. In similar fashion the diffident Englishman seems out of place in the domain of the egomaniacal American. While Mandrake follows on his heels like a puppy, eagerly explaining his safe interpretation of the attack order, Ripper calmly walks around the room locking doors, trapping the Englishman inside, and plugging the leak caused by Mandrake's discovery of normal civilian broadcasting. Mandrake seeks reassurance from a leader who simultaneously maneuvers to deprive him of it. They speak two different languages, with the General's silent actions as eloquent as Mandrake's words. Of course, their ironic duet can only be appreciated in retrospect, after Ripper's intentions become known to us. Until then, we share Mandrake's ignorance

Ripper's reaffirmation of the attack order defies Mandrake's optimistic interpretation of the crisis. The Captain recognizes an ominous new pattern of meaning in a succession of little surprises and reassessments rather than a single, shocking revelation. His ponderous, careful method of ferreting out the truth is typical of his personality. Even when the ugly truth dawns on him, Mandrake is reluctant to face it directly. "I would say, sir, that there were something dreadfully wrong somewhere" maintains a formal appearance of respect for the General and avoids naming Ripper as the source of the problem.

Because he can distinguish between devotion to an organization and obedience to a superior officer within that organization, Mandrake is able to choose sides in a conflict between the two. But that choice is emotionally difficult for him. Courageous and foolish at the same time, he tries to do the right thing but gets bogged down in the trivialities of a military decorum that is still second nature to him. Snapping to attention, he displays formal submission to Ripper even as he challenges him. Seeking collective sanction for his uncomfortable defiance of a superior officer, Mandrake calls on his allegiance to the government of Great Britain, which predates his assignment to S.A.C. but which has no authority over the General. Also, Mandrake is naively forthright about his intention to issue the recall code and bring back the bombers on his own initiative. His very proper demand that Ripper give him the code is almost apologetic and predictably in vain. And by continuing to address the General as "sir," Mandrake absurdly tries to serve two severed halves of the same organization, repairing damage done to the whole while remaining respectful of the officer responsible for that damage.

When his half-hearted, ill-conceived challenge to the outlaw General fails, Mandrake panics. His sense of decorum, along with his voice, momentarily cracks. "Then I must insist that you give them to me!" he tells Ripper — no longer to the representative of Her Majesty's government, which *had* been his excuse for defying a superior officer, but to "*me!*" If General Ripper's monstrous preversion of S.A.C. is the principle target of Kubrick's satire here, a secondary target is Mandrake's reluctance to dump the military protocol which hinders his attempt to restore S.A.C. integrity. What the General has too much of, the Captain sorely lacks.

When Mandrake's verbal challenge shows signs of potency, Ripper replies with a far more potent *show* of force by shifting a pile of loose papers on his desk and uncovering a pistol. The Englishman is duly humbled. And it is appropriate that Ripper's weapon was concealed beneath a stack of paperwork that is both a product and a symbol of institutional due process. Like Kong's cowboy hat and nudie pictures in the B-52 safe, Ripper's gun lurks deceptively within the trappings of his professional duty.

Confident of his strategic advantage over Mandrake, Ripper reveals some of the motive behind his illegal appropriation of S.A.C. bombers. Borrowing and twisting the logic of former French leader Georges Clemenceau, who among others presided over the military mistakes of World War I, he argues that today's politicians "have neither the time, the training, nor the inclination for strategic thought." That observation is borne out by subsequent events in the Pentagon War Room. But when Ripper substitutes his own leadership and strategic thought for that of President Muffley, he fails to realize that he, too, is ignorant of some aspects of the military situation: specifically of the Doomsday Machine, which invalidates the idea of a victorious first strike.

Shown in a low-angle close-up and lit harshly from above, General Ripper presents an image of forceful determination. The cigar jutting straight out from his face seems like an aggressive extension of his will. But it does not yet connect with the blatantly phallic image of an aircraft fuel nozzle shown during the opening credits. The nature of the military crisis and the nature of general Ripper's psychological disturbance are revealed to us in bits and pieces, each contributing to our understanding of those revealed before. Under Kubrick's direction, Sterling Hayden plays Ripper with such conviction that the character becomes more than a simple caricature of militarism gone mad. Ripper's deviant theory of war in the nuclear age is granted limited credibility before being undercut by the General himself. His professed world view is shot through with repressed, ulterior motivations. At the end of his formal argument, he tacks on a few words that radically alter our impression of it. America's struggle for survival against Communism is, in Ripper's mind, a last-ditch effort to stop a red conspiracy to "sap and impurify all of our precious bodily fluids." Ideological conflict on an international scale is reduced to one man's biological fixation. Nothing in *Dr. Strangelove* can be viewed in the same way after a line like that. And Kubrick maximizes its shock value by cutting immediately to the next scene without showing Mandrake's reaction, which is surely the same as our own.

From high overhead the Pentagon appears as a massive, symmetrical fortress — an abstract impression of collective containment unblemished by any visible evidence of individual man or private interest. But far below that facade is the War Room, occupied by a group of very human, very flawed individuals. Visually dwarfed by their cavernous environment, government and military leaders sit around a huge conference table. Their separate voices ring thin and hollow. An enormous circle of fluorescent lights hangs suspended over them, like an omnipresent halo, casting an aura of importance and legitimacy over their debates and decisions. But, at best, the halo provides an ironic state of grace. It looms over everyone like the expanding shock wave of a nuclear explosion, placing a tremendous burden of responsibility on the men under it.

At once mammoth and claustrophobic, the War Room is both a giant, artificial window on the outside world, with a vast array of communication and information resources, and a shield against the more immediate physical and emotional realities of war. Impressions of the outside world reach its occupants via giant images projected on a wall referred to as the Big Board. Luminous maps of the United States and the Soviet Union reduce both countries to a series of abstract strategic highlights. In contrast to the wall of mirrors in General Turgidson's bedroom, these images turn attention outward rather than inward, and with a range far beyond the senses of individual man. But they also redefine the outside world in very selective, simplistic terms that can be as deceptive as they are revealing.

Projected images make the War Room a kind of movie theater — another location where people get caught up in an abstract representation of reality. The War Room's Big Board and underground location are institutional means of insulating, regulating, and in some respects improving the perceptions of government officials gathered there. Barriers erected to simplify or limit perspective are not always evil. Insulation from the horrors of war is to some extent vital to the effective performance of vulnerable and flawed leaders charged with coordinating a vast collective effort. But such ivory tower detachment can also promote gross ignorance of the consequences of one's actions.

Kubrick stages and shoots the first War Room scene as a closed affair around the closed shape of the conference table. Relatively few camera placements are used again and again, while camera movement is kept to a minimum. A uniformly sedate tone of voice and a methodical approach to problem solving characterize the initial proceedings. And the character who best personifies that calm deliberation is President Merkin Muffley, who, like Captain Mandrake, is a rational man governed largely by a refined sense of decorum. When first shown up close, he is discreetly tucking a soiled handkerchief up his sleeve. Unlike Ripper, who *imposes* his private life on the collective world, Muffley *conceals* his private concerns.

The first War Room session is a seriocomic inventory of the shortcomings of both private and collective vision. No master plan, including one as sophisticated as nuclear deterrence, can anticipate every contingency. Most of President Muffley's top advisors are out of the country on various missions. Sitting in for them are a number of *under*secretaries of this and that, who for the most part look sober and attentive but contribute nothing. They remain anonymous players in the game, swaying to and fro in breezes stirred up by a few bolder though not necessarily more intelligent characters. One of these officials asks what the President thinks of Civil Defense. The question is so broad and casually offered that its author might be preparing for a congressional hearing months in the future rather than addressing an immediate crisis. As with Mandrake, Kong, and Turgidson, he is slow to appreciate the seriousness of the situation.

Since the bedroom scene, General Turgidson has undergone a reversal of perspective and appearance. Now wearing his uniform, he appears every inch a soldier instead of a half-dressed civilian. His demeanor and priorities, too, have shifted from informal and private to formal and professional, though he retains many of the mental habits he exhibited previously. He is bombastic, closed minded, and inconsistent. He changes his mind several times during the film, embracing contradictory viewpoints without even realizing it. He is a fictional example of what historian and political philosopher Hannah Arendt called the "banality of evil" (Arendt). Writing about Nazi bureaucrat Adolf Eichmann at his 1961 trial in an Israeli court, Arendt describes a man part monster and part clown, unable to view events from outside his narrow self-interest, relying on platitudes to clarify his thoughts and justify his actions, and oblivious to his factual and moral contradictions in doing so. General Turgidson is more outspoken than Eichmann, and he operates in a different political setting. But as the crisis in *Dr. Strangelove* deepens, he proves equally capable of rationalizing the most outrageous, undemocratic, and brutal solutions.

More than anyone else in the War Room, General Turgidson is a disciple of the official S.A.C. view of the world. He is mesmerized by the Big Board. Two S.A.C. guidebooks, entitled *World Targets in Megadeaths* and *War Alert Actions Book*, lie on the table in front of him. No doubt magnificently detailed products of collective research and logic, they define for Turgidson the unalterable realities of nuclear war. A title like *World Targets in Megadeaths* combines the topic of mass annihilation with the objective tone of a textbook, while the book's thickness indicates the depth to which its narrow thesis is pursued. Besides Turgidson, nearly everyone at the conference table has an institutional guidebook of some sort within reach. And the General himself serves as President Muffley's guide through the labyrinthian complexities of S.A.C. This first War Room scene is essentially a debate between General Turgidson, whose personal identity is wrapped up in S.A.C. and who sees the crisis through the filter of its war scenarios, and President Muffley, who has a broader vision but a poorer understanding of the nuclear forces under his command.

As commander in chief of America's military establishment, President Muffley is responsible for supervising S.A.C. In this role he is a failure, though few situations test his mastery to the limit. Unfortunately, the crisis precipitated by General Ripper does exactly that. His deficient understanding of and control over weapons of war theoretically under his command are revealed bit by bit in a conversation with General Turgidson. The limited capacities of individual man prove a disastrously weak link in the collective chain of command, from which he has not been entirely weeded out (as will nearly be the case in *2001: A Space Odyssey*). Muffley operates under the false assumption that only he, as President, is empowered to launch a nuclear strike. Turgidson reminds him that under the provisions of Emergency War Plan R, which Muffley himself approved, America's deterrent credibility is "safeguarded" by granting base commanders the authority to launch retaliatory strikes on their own initiative if unable to contact higher authority. The separate institutional goals of limiting access to the nuclear launch button and discouraging a Soviet sneak attack on Washington, D.C., are incompatible — resolved by an imperfect compromise. Though he is emotionally stable, determined, and innovative during most of the crisis, President Muffley cannot possibly comprehend or coordinate all of the resources under his command.

A struggle between institutional and individual man has preceded the impending war between nations. Extensive human reliability tests of base commanders, the results of which an inexpert and overtaxed Muffley accepted on faith, were supposed to guard against the breakdown of authority made possible by Plan R. Furthermore, the President was unaware that S.A.C. bombers routinely patrol at their fail-safe points. He assumed fail-safe was an *additional* safeguard against false alarms. He also did not realize that Plan R mandates sealing off bombers from radio contact with everyone except their base commanders, who alone possess the code to unlock that barrier. In other words, those aspects of S.A.C. of which the President was either unaware or misinformed performed as designed, whereas those aspects of which he *was* aware (the human reliability tests) failed miserably.

As its chief spokesman, General Turgidson defends S.A.C. against Muffley's criticism: "Well, I don't think it's quite fair to condemn a whole program because of a single slip-up." His choice of words and tone of voice downplay the importance of that "slip-up." And ordinarily his argument would be sound. No man-made system passes all tests all the time. But, in this instance, institutional man has aimed at a perfection of control required by the forces involved. The single "slip-up" of General Ripper is sufficient to free the nuclear genie from its bottle. Designed to circumvent the fallibility of President Muffley, Plan R ends up serving a far worse flaw in General Ripper.

One by one, General Turgidson erects walls around the President's power to defuse the crisis. In fact, Turgidson merely points out those barriers in a conversation the two men should have had long before Ripper's outlaw action. As the bearer of unpleasant news, Turgidson takes the heat for his leader's frustration and guilt. Searching for leverage *outside* S.A.C., Muffley calls on General Faceman of the United States Army to help him bulldoze a path out of an institutional maze in which he seems trapped. He employs a strategy of divide and conquer against a military system that has lost internal integrity. General Ripper and Burpleson are to be forcibly brought back into line by soldiers belonging to an allied service. Predictably, General Turgidson is too deeply committed to the Air Force to follow Muffley's radical lead. He and the equally provincial General Faceman indulge in verbal chest-thumping over whose soldiers will prevail when Army troops go up against Ripper's base security forces. Normally commendable, their paternal devotion to their "boys" is out of sync with a larger crisis that plays havoc with conventional perceptions.

Challenging President Muffley's unorthodox proposal for avoiding war with the Soviets, Turgidson outlines the strategic imperatives *for* all-out commitment to such a war. A limited nuclear attack on the Soviet Union would, he reasons, trigger a retaliation that would destroy the United States. Though neither sharing in nor comprehending General Ripper's bizarre rationale for war, S.A.C.'s highest-ranking officer makes a pitch for fulfilling Ripper's mad dream. Ripper's deviant action is thus incorporated into and quasi-legitimized by the presumably orthodox outlook of a superior officer. A crisis can make for strange bedfellows. Turgidson refers to an "unofficial" S.A.C. study which anticipates and provides a remedy for the failure of the official study that produced Plan R. But the recommendation of that unofficial study flatly contradicts the goal of the official study, which was to preserve the peace. And General Turgidson seems oblivious to this grotesque discrepancy.

Attempting to sway the President to his way of thinking, Turgidson employs contradictory tactics and betrays his lack of understanding of the consequences of what he advocates. To make war sound more palatable, he minimizes the cost. "We stand a good chance of catching them with their pants down" is his folksy description of the obliteration of Russia, while the prospect of ten to twenty million Americans killed by Soviet retaliation is reduced to "modest and acceptable civilian casualties." Yet while making his stand on this philosophical high ground, he unwittingly betrays an almost infantile motivation lurking behind it. His sly grin and the conspiratorial raise of his eyebrows turns the prospect of total nuclear war into the emotional equivalent of a boyhood raid on an enemy's snow fort. With his shameless enthusiasm for war thus exposed, his dispassionate appeal to higher military strategy loses some credibility.

President Muffley's reluctance to accept the total war option prompts Turgidson to reverse tactics. Now emphasizing rather than trivializing American casualties, the General transforms what had been a liability into an advantage. In a clear, firm voice, and with eyes slightly upturned in a trademark Kubrick portrait of aggression, he confronts Muffley with the unavoidable choice of "two admittedly regrettable but nevertheless distinguishable post-war environments: one where you've got twenty million dead and the other where you've got a hundred and fifty million dead." The burden of minimizing potential damage to America is lifted from Turgidson's shoulders and dumped on the President's. When Muffley rejects the total war option on the grounds that it would render him in the eyes of history another Adolf Hitler, the General again presses his advantage, charging his opponent with blatant self-interest. Incredibly, the self-centered Turgidson is able to paint the nearly selfless Muffley in his own image. And the President acknowledges the sting of Turgidson's criticism by arbitrarily ending a debate that had turned against him. Muffley is not yet aware that his best argument against Turgidson's total war option lies hidden in Soviet territory. The General's moral victory is an illusion based on his faulty assessment of the enemy's nuclear arsenal.

Clutching his articles of faith (the S.A.C. guidebooks) to his chest, pointing to the sacred Big Board, and complaining about a violation of security, Turgidson protests President Muffley's unorthodox attempt to circumvent S.A.C. by enlisting the Soviet Ambassador as an ally in preventing war. The General fails to recognize that Ripper's appropriation of S.A.C. bombers has already breached American military security from the *inside*. Muffley, though a failure in his performance as overseer of S.A.C., nobly tries to regain control of that hijacked organization rather than agree to its total war option. As long as the President can improvise his way around that option, his irrational alter ego, Dr. Strangelove, remains an anonymous figure on the fringes of the action. Thomas Nelson describes Muffley as an "ineffectual man of reason" (Nelson, 85). Norman Kagan and Gene D. Phillips are more generous in their assessment of the President's peacekeeping skills (Kagan, 141, and Phillips, 115). Though sometimes too mindful of propriety, like Captain Mandrake, Muffley is not "ineffectual" until the end of the film, when he runs out of innovative ideas to ward off Doomsday.

Miss Scott's ill-timed phone call to General Turgidson reveals his radical shift in perspective from private to collective. In the splendid isolation of his bedroom, he promised to give his mistress sexual fulfillment after dealing with a minor, annoying professional matter. In the War Room, overwhelmed by the setting and the situation, his priorities change. Miss Scott's interruption is now an embarrassment to him. Speaking quietly so as not to be heard by other officials, he cuts their conversation short. And before hanging up, he urges her to say her prayers and promises to marry her some day. From naked lust to respectable piety, the General's priorities have flip-flopped without him being aware of it. But his newfound sense of propriety will prove shallow and brief.

Back aboard Major Kong's B-52, a routine inventory of crew survival kits reveals S.A.C.'s paternalistic effort to address the many and varied needs of individual soldiers trapped behind enemy lines. Labeled "All Purpose," the kits are identical because S.A.C. planners have neither the time nor inclination to delineate the strengths and weaknesses of each soldier. A pistol, ammunition, Russian money, food rations, vitamins, antibiotics, and morphine cover basic material requirements. But to the medicinal drugs are added pep pills, sleeping pills, and tranquilizers — a catalog of modern society's remedies for various stresses encountered by the fragile individual.

Also deemed important to the well-being of American soldiers shot down behind enemy lines is chewing gum. This may seem a trivial choice but, judging from the behavior of several characters in *Dr. Strangelove*, the physical and often oral manipulation of some inanimate object can help an individual cope with unwanted tension. The more frustrated General Turgidson becomes in his debate with President Muffley, the more vigorously he chomps on his gum. And General Ripper's cigar is as much a pacifier as it is a symbolic penis. In emotionally shattered and materially deprived Europe just after World War II cigarettes became, for a time, the principle currency of exchange for goods and services (Botting, 234). The war movie cliché of a soldier smoking a cigarette rings true no matter what nonsense surrounds it. But apparently nothing soothes the stress of soldiering better than sex. S.A.C. packs condoms, lipsticks, and nylon stockings in its survival kits. The second and third items assist the men in getting it (offense), the first in not getting something unwanted in return (defense).

The most absurd item in the survival kits is a combination miniature Bible and Russian phrase book. It is S.A.C.'s attempt to address spiritual and practical needs in a single, extremely condensed stroke. Overall, the kits are a wonderfully comic statement of the mass of contradictory needs and urges that is individual man. Major Kong sums up their value nicely: "Shoot, a fella could have a pretty good weekend in Vegas with all that stuff" — except that, according to his earlier, misinformed speculation, Las Vegas is probably a radioactive ruin by now. At thirty thousand feet, it is easy to lose sight of reality on the ground.

The obvious overdubbing of "Vegas" for "Dallas" may have been a concession to public decorum after the assassination of President Kennedy shortly before *Dr. Strangelove* was released. Too bad. Major Kong is more a Texas cowboy than a Vegas playboy. But the discreet substitution of one city for another is an actual example of the collective masking that is frequently the subject of dramatic scrutiny in Kubrick's work.

A Kremlin Bolshevik in President Muffley's court, Russian Ambassador Alexei de Sadesky strides into the War Room as a self-contained projection of Communist rhetoric and arrogance. No less than General Turgidson's, his personal sense of identity is wedded to an institution, at the cost of all critical detachment from it. Examining tables piled high with food, which in themselves are a measure of the War Room's splendid isolation from the frontline realities of war, de Sadesky haughtily objects to the cuisine on two distinct counts. First, it does not suit his patrician Russian palate (the name "de Sadesky" evokes sensual indulgence). Second, it is ideologically tainted, according to his Soviet moral standards. When these separate criteria clash, the ambassador condescends to accept food of which his taste buds approve, even though it is "the work of imperialist stooges." Like everyone else in the film, de Sadesky is a man of multiple allegiances, private and collective. An American officer challenges de Sadesky's Marxist sensibilities with a comment about "*commie* stooges," which pretty well illustrates the barriers to communication President Muffley must overcome if he is to unite Soviets and Americans in the cause of peace.

In symbolic as well as pragmatic terms, the President breaks out of America's closed circle of strategic thought by leaving the conference table to greet the Soviet ambassador. An outraged General Turgidson, still clutching his beloved S.A.C. notebooks, trails after his errant leader in protest. American General and Soviet diplomat share no common ground on which to base an understanding. What they do share is a mutual hatred for each other and all that their opposing countries represent. Describing the Ambassador's national leader as "a degenerate atheistic communist," Turgidson's attack is emotionally equivalent to one immature boy challenging another by insulting his father. Morality, religion, and political affiliation are all brought to bear to distinguish *us* from *them*. President Muffley tries to mediate between the two men, but when he is momentarily distracted, the verbal battle between Turgidson and de Sadesky degenerates into a wrestling match. Muffley returns to scold his two reluctant allies: "Gentlemen! You can't fight in here! This is the War Room!" He is right, of course. The War Room was not designed as a stage for hand-to-hand combat. But if it is something of a temple to dispassionate thought, the War Room is also part of a collective network which amplifies violence far beyond that of a pathetic brawl between two middle-aged men. Muffley's words are at least as anachronistic as are Turgidson and de Sadesky's actions. Nevertheless, in a larger sense, the President is trying to prevent a war. By addressing the General and the Ambassador as "gentlemen," he appeals to one set of collective sensibilities to override another — the latter fueled by private passions.

That Turgidson is not a total idiot is confirmed when he exposes de Sadesky as a spy carrying a hidden camera, in violation of diplomatic propriety. The General and the Ambassador are both unimaginative men whose perceptions of the world are ruled by their shallow political allegiances and their sensual desires. Together they feed off each other's prejudices and perpetuate each other's paranoia. A kindred soul of sorts, Turgidson is better able to assess de Sadesky's character than is the President. But under the bizarre circumstances created by Ripper, the unmasking of de Sadesky as a spy is of little strategic value to the United States. Resolving the nuclear crisis peacefully depends, or at this point in the film *appears* to depend, on Muffley's ability to lift the Ambassador above ideological bias so that he can help forge an alliance between their two governments.

The farcical and pointless battle of the hidden camera is interrupted by an attempt to contact Soviet Premier Dmitri Kissoff over the Hot Line. Turgidson and de Sadesky, who have fought each other into a pose ludicrously suggestive of sexual intimacy, are shocked out of their small-minded feud by the sobering prospect of a confrontation between their institutional fathers. Jolted into a spirit of cooperation, de Sadesky proves his value to the President's cause by redirecting the American search for Kissoff to a *private* telephone number. Through the Ambassador we learn that Muffley will be dealing with a Soviet counterpart whose perceptions are divided between collective duty and personal desire, just like everyone else's.

The attack by General Faceman's soldiers on Burpleson security forces is at first presented subjectively from the latter's point of view. Kubrick again employs a hand-held camera to help convey the disorientation of frontline combat troops. From inside the base perimeter, the camera views approaching motorized columns at far range, framed by branches and leaves in the foreground. This framing effect gives the image a visual sense of containment similar to that of the Big Board in the War Room or to a movie screen. The soldiers' perception is shaped and contained by General Ripper, who informed them of the devious form a Soviet attack might take. His security troops cannot help but notice, through evidence gathered by direct sight and therefore not censored by Ripper, their foe's convincing disguise. They are uneasy about firing on American uniforms and equipment. Such is the aesthetic power of collective identification. But the rule of obedience to a superior officer binds them to Ripper's will and overrides the aesthetic factor. The soldiers rationalize away their doubts by speculating that the enemy obtained their disguises from United States Army surplus. Morally reassured by an illusion, they open fire on American soldiers.

If Burpleson security troops look out at the world through a distorted lens, courtesy of their commanding officer, General Ripper in turn is even more insulated inside his office. Shielded from invading U.S. Army forces by

President Muffley (Peter Sellers, right) tries to talk General Turgidson (George C. Scott, left) and Ambassador de Sadesky (Peter Bull) out of a petty ideological squabble so they can tackle a crisis that threatens to destroy both of their countries.

his security troops, and from the ordeal of his troops by the blinded windows, he is able to sustain his illusion of a justified nuclear war. He stands in a silent pose of exaggerated masculinity, cigar jutting aggressively out of his mouth. Captain Mandrake, meanwhile, sits helplessly on the other side of the room, pacifying himself by neatly reconstructing an empty gum wrapper, folding and flattening until it resembles its original form. But the gum, like Major Kong's B-52, is already out of its container (fail-safe). Mandrake's action is just a metaphorical phantom of the power (to recall the bombers) he does not possess. Distant sounds of combat through shaded windows and locked doors signal the painfully slow approach of forces which could help him acquire that power.

The War Room returns to its original, symmetrical appearance of order, with discussion once again contained within the circle of the conference table. The President has expanded that circle to include two Soviet voices. Though still pouting over his uncordial reception, Ambassador de Sadesky accepts a seat on Muffley's right and helps facilitate a conversation with Premier Kissoff. He is, for the present, the President's right-hand man. A burly Nikita Khrushchev look-alike, de Sadesky is an example of a lesser bureaucrat whose importance, like some of the trivial words in *Dr. Strangelove*'s opening credits, is suddenly inflated by circumstances. He proves his worth again by warning the President that Kissoff is drunk. Most of the officials gathered around the table listen to the conversation between Muffley and Kissoff on their own phones. They are silent, passive, visually frozen spectators rather than shapers of this great event. General Turgidson, however, registers his frustrated disapproval of Muffley's efforts by chewing his gum furiously.

The dialog between President Muffley and Premier Kissoff, whose volatile temperament is perhaps modeled after Nikita Khrushchev's, is a comic masterpiece of conflicting styles and concerns. Muffley faces a wide range of obstacles in his quest for an American-Russian alliance to thwart General Ripper's apocalyptic initiative. Beginning at a Dick-and-Jane first-grade-primer level of communication, the two leaders try to negotiate their way out of a scenario to which their respective governments have devoted vast financial, technological, intellectual, and emotional resources to render it as automated as possible. Even their salutation is labored, with both leaders finally agreeing that "It's great to be fine." When Muffley tries to steer conversation towards the crisis at hand, he finds himself talking at cross-purposes. His calm voice and euphemistic words are meant to anesthetize the Premier's patriotic sensibilities but are too subtle for the drunken Russian to comprehend. Compelled, for the sake of clarity, to call a hydrogen bomb a hydrogen bomb, Muffley nevertheless again steps back from a frank discussion of the crisis, reducing General Ripper's potentially catastrophic action to "He went and did a silly thing" as a result of "going a little funny in the head." This is almost baby talk, absurdly ill matched to the larger reality of events. His description of Ripper's state of mind as "funny" is accompanied by a sickly facial expression implying the opposite. But Kissoff's delicate state of mind, plus the equally delicate state of Soviet-American relations, compel the President to approach the problem with extreme caution. He is tiptoeing through an emotional minefield.

While drunk, Premier Kissoff is subject to a short attention span and rapid mood swings. In addition to making an effort not to anger the head of the Soviet state, President Muffley also has to contend with his counterpart's inability to focus on the matter at hand. When told point-blank that his country is under nuclear attack by American bombers, the Premier is understandably furious. But moments later, reacting to Muffley's mild irritation at that anger, Kissoff veers off into irrelevance. The chief defender of the communist faith and the Soviet state gets sidetracked by the worry that Muffley doesn't like him. Intoxication robs him of a sense of proportion, and for a few moments he sucks the President of the United States into his weird orbit.

Reluctantly dragged by Muffley back to higher matters of State, Premier Kissoff, like de Sadesky before him, becomes a vital link in the President's improvised network of containment, providing the Americans with the telephone number of the Soviet Central Air Defense headquarters. The Russian civilian telephone system is now added to Muffley's alliance. As that patchwork arrangement expands, so do the chances of a breakdown within it. And the piecing together of parts of different systems potentially violates the internal integrity of one or more of those separate parts. Muffley's alliance with the Soviets involves turning over to them classified information about the flight plans and defensive capabilities of American bombers. General Turgidson, still emotionally committed to S.A.C., is outraged by this action.

The first Hot Line discussion should conclude at this point so that new opportunities can be acted upon. Unfortunately for President Muffley, Premier Kissoff's private concerns rise to the surface again and demand attention. Distracted from the larger crisis, Muffley allows himself to get bogged down in what is, under the circumstances, a puerile matter of pride. They bicker pointlessly over who feels more sorry about the situation, finally agreeing that they are equally sorry. Indeed they are, but not in the sense *they* mean.

For a second time, the scene reaches a logical point of conclusion. But, in a Kubrick film, there are always loose threads which threaten (or promise, as the case may be) to unravel the most elaborate plans. After a brief conversation with Kissoff, Ambassador de Sadesky drops a bombshell on the proceedings. He reveals the existence of a "Doomsday Machine," a device which theoretically would destroy all human and animal life on earth. General Turgidson pounces on this new development as a chance to reinsert himself into the debate. If it exists, the Doomsday Machine invalidates the logic of Turgidson's precious S.A.C. scenarios and further dims the prospect of Muffley agreeing to an all-out attack on the Soviet Union. So the General tries to drive a wedge between the President and his new Soviet partners by claiming the Doomsday Machine is a bluff to intimidate the United States.

As he did after General Ripper's bizarre declaration about communist corruption of America's "precious bodily fluids," Kubrick cuts away from the War Room scene almost immediately after an unexpected revelation reshapes, or *apparently* reshapes, everything that has occurred before it. If Ripper's comment transformed a fairly rational argument about military strategy in the nuclear age into a strange obsession with personal health, word of the Soviet Doomsday Machine hints darkly of a logic superceding all others, private and collective, heard so far.

The silent impasse between General Ripper and Captain Mandrake deep inside Burpleson is suddenly broken. Frightened by the gunfire of enemy soldiers laying siege to his private fortress, the General reaches out to Mandrake for understanding and support. Building on his earlier claim, Ripper paints a picture of communist infiltration out of the coincidental fact that both the Cold War and government-enforced fluoridation of water began in 1946. He clumsily embraces the reticent Englishman as he explains the threat. Trapped between Ripper's intimate bid for coalition and the threat of harm symbolically implied by the General's gun collection, visible on the wall behind them, Mandrake is extremely uncomfortable. Folding his empty gum wrapper into ever tighter configurations, he struggles to suppress laughter, which under less dangerous circumstances would be a normal reaction to the General's bizarre logic. Mandrake is rescued from this tight spot by gunfire smashing through the blinded windows of Ripper's office. The advance troops of his American double, President Muffley, are getting closer.

Though it signals the approach of an ally, Mandrake recognizes that gunfire places him in mortal danger, so he cowers on a couch. Ripper, in contrast, rises boldly to meet the challenge to his power. From out of his innocuous golf bag, the harmless plaything of a peacetime officer, Ripper pulls a large machine gun. Like Major Kong retrieving his cowboy hat from a S.A.C. safe, Ripper's action illustrates the presence of private concerns within all things institutional. He sweeps aside stacks of official paperwork (tokens of collective due process) as he sets up his weapon to defend his rebellion against higher authority. The machine gun's phallic appearance, like Ripper's rather cozy approach to Mandrake earlier in the scene, has yet to fully connect with our understanding of the General's motives for launching an attack on Russia. But it is obvious that Ripper's capacity for making associations is out of control. Calling on Mandrake to help him operate the machine gun, General Ripper conjures up two ill-matched historical references to bolster his appeal. "In the name of Her Majesty and the Continental Congress" is hardly a juxtaposition of devoted allies. And "The Redcoats are coming" makes even less sense. The British *were* the Redcoats and, as long as Mandrake remains loyal to Her Majesty's government rather than to his American commander, there can be no true alliance with Ripper.

When President Muffley left the War Room conference table to greet Ambassador de Sadesky, he broke out of a bankrupt institutional arrangement in order to improvise something better. By introducing the Doomsday factor, the Russian nullifies that progress. *He* now leaves the table, spouting gloom and doom about the secret Soviet device. General Turgidson, who earlier trailed after Muffley to protest the President's unorthodox action, now trails after de Sadesky to debunk the Doomsday claim. Both Muffley's improvised alliance with the Soviets and de Sadesky's revelation about Doomsday upset the General's orthodox, S.A.C. world view. The Big Board visible behind Turgidson no longer tells the whole military story. Turgidson's Air Force jacket is unbuttoned, reflecting a partial breakdown of the S.A.C. self-confidence with which he began the War Room strategy sessions. President Muffley now leaves the conference table in hopes of re-integrating the Ambassador and his disturbing news into the collective effort to avoid war.

The Doomsday Machine is the Soviet government's solution to the unreliability of individual man, as well as to economic and social problems caused by the arms race with the United States. It is a deceptively simple, relatively inexpensive, and apparently foolproof nuclear deterrent. A series of massive and very dirty hydrogen bombs are buried in strategic locations and linked to a complex of computers programmed to detonate them automatically if Russia is attacked or if any attempt is made to untrigger the system. Such a weapon is at once an act of desperation and a leap of faith in the ability of collective man to foresee the future. It is a perpetual motion device and a scorched-earth policy beyond anything the Soviets employed against the Germans during World War II. In a single brilliant, yet absurd, stroke, the Russians have erected an impenetrable barrier to enemy sabotage or sneak attack. By eliminating all of the system's middlemen, they have apparently solved a huge managerial problem. Soviet leaders have designed even *themselves* out of the MAD equation by precluding any future change in the conditions under which Doomsday will trigger itself. Or, to look at it another way, by making the machine's programming unalterable, they have deified their own predictions about all potential future military situations.

Unfortunately for nearly everyone, the Russians could no more anticipate all possible circumstances under which their country might be attacked than were their American counterparts able to plug all of the leaks in their more cumbersome Plan R. There are prices to be paid for both rigidity and flexibility. Ambassador de Sadesky concedes that the present situation renders the triggering of Doomsday an insane decision. But that decision was irrevocably made before the present situation arose. The insanity of one American S.A.C. base commander is matched by the insanity of a Soviet deterrent suddenly removed from its anticipated strategic context. The two sides have merely approached madness from opposite directions.

Attempting to discredit Doomsday and woo President Muffley back into the S.A.C. fold, General Turgidson stumbles, falls, rolls over, and leaps back up like a dog doing tricks to get its master's attention. But de Sadesky counters with a convincing argument in support of Doomsday's existence. It was from America's own revered free press, specifically the *New York Times*, that the Soviets learned of America's work on a Doomsday Device before beginning theirs. The suspicions of Western leaders noted by the narrator in the film's opening scene were evidently preceded by identical suspicions in the Soviet camp. In the paranoid atmosphere of Cold War nuclear strategy, every suspicion and every rumor looms large in the thinking of officials responsible for their country's defense. The loudly trumpeted if dubious "fact" of Russia's missile superiority in the early 1960s was sufficient to trigger a massive military buildup in the United States. In *Dr. Strangelove*, those roles are reversed. The Ambassador speaks of a "Doomsday Gap" fueling the Soviet desire for a Doomsday Machine. Incidentally, the term "Doomsday Gap" is an oxymoron. "Doomsday" implies annihilation of both the United States and the Soviet Union, while "Gap" suggests the possibility of a winning edge for one side or the other. The technology of destruction has outgrown the language of superpower competition, or so it seems for the moment.

Ambassador de Sadesky delivers his moral justification for building the Doomsday Machine with smug satisfaction. By citing the *New York Times*, he employs one of America's own vaunted resources against the President. Yet the larger crisis that threatens to engulf both countries renders de Sadesky's personal victory pointless and ironic. Another failure, though of a different kind, belongs to President Muffley, who, by denying any knowledge of the American Doomsday project, once more demonstrates his inadequate grasp of the military forces under his command. How could he anticipate and plan for a Russian Doomsday response to an American Doomsday initiative of which he was unaware? General Ripper's earlier accusation that modern politicians have neither the time nor the inclination for strategic thought has proven correct. But neither did Ripper anticipate the Russian Doomsday Machine, which reduces to nonsense his deviant scheme to defeat the Soviets with a sneak attack.

Typically, President Muffley summons an aide to tell him what he should already have known. His chief science advisor, Dr. Strangelove, emerges like a gothic specter from out of the largely anonymous circle of government officials around the conference table. Confined to a wheelchair, he rolls slowly out onto center stage to enter the discussion. General Turgidson's discreet inquiry about the new player reveals that Strangelove is a former Nazi scientist now assimilated into the high government echelons of a former enemy. His original name was "Merkwverdigichliebe," suggesting a psychological disturbance predating General Ripper's deviant action and even the Cold War. "Strangelove" is at best a thin disguise of the original. Yet his name, his former political affiliation, and his increasingly bizarre behavior will become less and less visible to War Room officials as they look to him for the means to their salvation.

Dr. Strangelove and President Muffley are Mr. Hyde and Dr. Jekyll variations on a single character. By casting Peter Sellers in three of the film's pivotal roles, and originally intending more, Kubrick makes of the actor an Everyman, spanning a wide range of personality traits and institutional positions. Muffley's balding head, transparent eyeglasses, and tranquil voice are superficially suited to a person of emotional detachment, propriety, and reason. Strangelove's flaring, bleached blond hair, dark glasses concealing hysterical eyes, tense voice, and mouth clenched in a mirthless smile betray lurking, violent passions. His black-gloved right hand seems alien even to himself. The symbolic center of subconscious forces, it often acts independently

of his will. Strangelove also appears to be a chain smoker, employing cigarettes to vent frustrated emotions, in the manner of Turgidson chewing gum
and Mandrake refolding gum wrappers. Dr. Strangelove is the crippled legacy
of Adolf Hitler, one of history's most extreme examples of an individual
infiltrating an institution and using it to serve his private whims. The fall of
Nazi Germany left Strangelove's warped desires in a state of involuntary sup-
pression. But if the former Third Reich scientist appears physically fragile as
he wheels into his first close-up, the monstrous institutional halo above his
head implies the potentially great power he can wield through his affiliation
with the United States government.

A consecration of individual man by collective order, the halo recalls the
floating circles of light that form around False Maria in the creation scene of
Fritz Lang's *Metropolis* (1926). Like the robot made in the image of a woman,
Strangelove wields influence in relation to how other people perceive him. As
their passions overflow conventional moral boundaries, his power to shape
events grows. But Dr. Strangelove is more than a product of collective perception. He is also an egotistical manipulator operating behind the scenes
while ostensibly serving a higher authority. His gloved right hand and overall appearance recall *Metropolis*'s Rotwang, the mad scientist who creates False
Maria at the request of his desperate political boss, Jon Frederson. Strangelove's
Jon Frederson is President Muffley, with False Maria equivalent to the bizarre
plan for postapocalyptic survival that Strangelove will reveal to his superiors
at an opportune moment.

As Director of Weapons Research and Development, Strangelove has
found a satisfying if limited outlet for his peculiar passions. He confirms
Soviet suspicions of an American Doomsday initiative. The Doomsday idea
is Strangelove's variation on Hitler's Final Solution, neatly disguised behind
the facade of the Bland Corporation, whose name implies emotional detachment. A sound-alike for a key firm involved in the development of American nuclear strategy in the 1960s, Bland is the Merkin Muffley of defense
industries. Through it and the President, Strangelove ascends to power. Yet
he can barely pry his addictive cigarette from his impulsive gloved hand.
Weakness and power, at different levels, merge in the same character.

Strangelove explains the peculiar beauty of his Doomsday concept: "The
technology required is easily within reach of even the smallest nuclear power.
It requires only the *will* to do so." Power once limited to the largest, richest,
and most technologically advanced nations is now available to ever smaller
organizations. Potentially, more and more would-be tyrants will possess the
means to destroy the world. The Soviets build Doomsday presumably to deter
a growing U.S. nuclear threat. The device, insists Dr. Strangelove, must be
designed to trigger itself automatically if it is to inspire in the enemy a *fear*
of attacking. His emphasis on the words "will," "fear," and "human meddling"

betray his preverse attraction to the Doomsday concept. He cares little about deterring attack or preserving peace. He cares about power and domination. And Doomsday is the institutional means by which he can impose himself on the whole world, present and future.

Nudged off center stage for the time being, General Turgidson expresses to a colleague his admiration for Strangelove's ingenious device which he does not feel for the scientist himself. He is like a child looking at toys in a store at Christmas. Each new one seems better than the last. Strangelove's toy is desirable to Turgidson only when possessed by a collective "we" (the United States), that for him translates emotionally into an "I." When possessed by the Soviets it is an undesirable thing. Yet the logic of Doomsday implies equal annihilation for both countries, regardless of who owns it. Overlooked by the myopic General is the fact that Doomsday negates the idea of a winnable nuclear war, which was the foundation of his argument in favor of launching an all-out attack on Russia in support of General Ripper's outlaw initiative. In one particularly revealing camera shot, Turgidson's head and upper body overlap the map of Russia on the Big Board behind him. Lines representing American bombers closing in on Soviet targets figuratively close in on the General too. *Our* nuclear attack would trigger *their* Doomsday Device, which would presumably kill everyone on *both* sides, including Turgidson.

As for Doomsday's conceptual father, Dr. Strangelove, General Turgidson exhibits the same accidental insight into character that he did in his assessment of Ambassador de Sadesky. "A Kraut by any other name," he muses, his judgment based on nothing more than a cultural stereotype. Strangelove will indeed live down to that stereotype, but, by the end of the film, the self-righteous General will be his greatest advocate.

If Strangelove's Doomsday concept makes some strategic sense within the narrow context of MAD, the Soviet application of it is fatally flawed. The device's existence must be made known to the enemy if it is to deter him from attacking. But, as de Sadesky sheepishly confesses, national policy is sometimes captive to personal whim. Premier Kissoff delayed public announcement of the Soviet device in order to spring it as a surprise at a Communist Party Congress to be held in a few days. In this instance the element of secrecy, so highly prized during the Cold War, yields no strategic advantage. With the revelation about a weapon whose development arose from tenuous crosscurrents of Soviet and American perceptions, every strategic scenario introduced in the film thus far is thrown off kilter.

When Dr. Strangelove joins the discussion, he is initially framed looking rather small and subordinate between Muffley and de Sadesky, who are closer to the camera. Officially, he is the President's right hand-man, as are, in various capacities, Turgidson, Faceman, and de Sadesky. In another sense, however, Strangelove is to the President what his gloved right hand is to himself—a renegade. Muffley's inadequate supervision of Strangelove's research at the Bland Corporation is equivalent to the scientist's difficulties managing the actions of his own right hand. The problems of individual and collective power are both similar and intertwined.

If President Muffley loses ground on one front of the battle to prevent war, he appears to gain ground on another. Fighting at Burpleson has progressed to inside base perimeters. General Ripper's outer defenses are crumbling. Kubrick's hand-held camera has switched points of view and now sees events through the eyes of the invader. Ripper's inner sanctum, meanwhile, is again riddled with bullets. The General returns fire with his machine gun. His courage in the face of danger contrasts with the behavior of Captain Mandrake, who in his terror seeks shelter near the General. He moves to Ripper's side and helps feed ammunition to the machine gun, until incoming gunfire becomes so intense that he deserts his post and absurdly seeks protection behind a flimsy chair with a gaping hole in it. In terms of appearances, this is not the Englishman's finest hour.

Mandrake's opportunity to resume his efforts to preserve peace comes during a brief pause in the chaos of battle. General Ripper, warming to his only companion as the hostile world outside his office closes in, elaborates on his weird vision of a communist plot to corrupt the bodies of individual Americans and, by extension, the American body politic. For the first time, he reveals the role of sex in his political theories. The idea of biological warfare through fluoridation came to him while making love with a woman. "A profound sense of fatigue, a feeling of emptiness, followed. I can assure you it has not recurred." Suddenly the sexual metaphors that have abounded in the film thus far find a point of origin, in Ripper. Whatever the nature of his problem with women (it really doesn't matter to the larger point of the film), he compensates for it in spectacular fashion. His fear of women translates, via institutional channels, into a fear of communism. But he is quick to point out that his refusal to give them his "life essence" does not mean he avoids women altogether. Any hint of homosexuality would be intolerable to a man so steeped in the aggressively masculine traditions of military life.

At one point during the General's explanation, Mandrake mutters under his breath, "Good Lord." Ripper perceives it as a sign of the Captain's awakening to the grim truth about the communist conspiracy. We, however, understand it to express Mandrake's astonishment at the monumental absurdity of Ripper's logic. Ironically, the surrender of Burpleson's security forces to General Faceman's invaders destroys the mood of confidentiality between Ripper and Mandrake, precluding any further revelations by the General, who emotionally withdraws into himself. Mandrake resumes in vain his earlier effort to reason the General out of his deviant plan. He persists in attacking the *fringes* of an ideology based ultimately on unresolved *internal* conflicts.

Despite the absurdity of Ripper's intensely subjective view of the world, Kubrick and Hayden invest the character with enough passion to command grudging respect and enough self-doubt to color his madness with a hint of tragedy. This scene contains a particularly vivid close-up of the General's haunted face, his jutting, now obviously phallic, cigar out of sync with his eroding confidence. Ripper is a man under assault on two fronts. While invading soldiers overwhelm his outer defenses, doubt and remorse plague him from within. After previously expressing disappointment that his "boys" failed in their assignment to defend the base, Ripper reverses himself and describes their effort as a noble sacrifice, in order to bolster his own flagging sense of purpose.

When Ripper confesses that he fears revealing the recall code if tortured, Mandrake seizes on it as a strategic opening. He encourages the General's fear by describing his own experience of torture by Japanese soldiers during World War II. In the course of doing so, he notes that the soldiers who tortured him seemed inspired more by personal and sadistic than by patriotic and pragmatic motivations. And yet the Japanese "make such bloody good cameras." It strikes him as odd that a nation of people who could indulge such violent and selfish interests could also be capable of great organizational and manufacturing genius. For such comparatively restrained men as Captain Mandrake and President Muffley there is a fundamental contradiction between brutish behavior and civilization, which perhaps accounts for their failure to anticipate the emergence of a General Ripper or a Dr. Strangelove within the ranks of a civilized organization such as S.A.C.

The purpose of Mandrake's reminiscence about World War II is to nudge General Ripper onto a precipice of self-doubt and encourage him to share the recall code with a loyal ally. But the strategy backfires. Assured by Mandrake that no one can stand up under torture, the General retreats completely and irrevocably into himself, where he confronts another of his internal demons. In a beautiful close-up that conveys the poignancy as well as the banality of his perspective, Ripper ponders the ultimate moral ramifications of his actions. "I happen to believe in a life after this one. And I know I'll have to answer for what I've done. And I think I can." Mandrake's claim to be a religious man too sounds insincere by comparison, generating a conflict between our aesthetic and moral perceptions of the two characters. Kubrick does not simply strip the General of an external world which might justify his views and actions. That would merely replace one narrow vantage point (unquestioning patriotism) with another (absolute contempt for patriotism). Ripper's decision to sacrifice his own life for his horribly misguided cause earns him a degree of preverse dignity, especially when contrasted with Mandrake's less than courageous behavior in much of this scene.

General Ripper's decision to commit suicide in order to ensure the success of his crusade against communism is in one respect analogous to the

Soviet Union's Doomsday defense. Both plans attempt to eliminate unreliable individual man from the strategic equation.

Ripper kills himself in the privacy of his bathroom, which in a different context of self-absorption was also the preferred sanctuary of General Turgidson. Failing miserably to appreciate the passion of his commander's strange faith, Captain Mandrake misinterprets the General's profound withdrawal into himself as a simple desire to freshen up. Likewise, when the Englishman takes possession of the machine gun Ripper discards, it no longer seems a potent thing. Mandrake carries it around limply, with no intention of using it for his cause. In aesthetic terms, he is a less impressive character than the General. But because Mandrake's cause is the cause of peace, he *must* be our hero.

The crumbling of General Ripper's physical and emotional defenses makes him a more sympathetic character than he was earlier, in spite of the danger he poses to the world. The same holds true for Major Kong and his crew when their B-52 is attacked by a Soviet antiaircraft missile. They become a model of disciplined, coordinated effort. Equally impressive is the multilayered defensive system S.A.C. has provided the aircraft. The Russian missile is detected on radar at a distance of sixty miles. As it approaches, the B-52's defense mechanisms go into operation, one by one. Finally, at a distance of ten miles, the missile veers off track. It explodes and damages the aircraft but does not destroy it. The sheer density of S.A.C. forethought is quite beautiful — Kubrick's tribute to the engineering genius of weapons design. But that very beauty endangers the larger cause of peace. How could S.A.C. engineers have anticipated a situation in which the survival of a B-52 in combat would be *detrimental* to the overall survival of the United States?

When the Russian missile explodes and severely damages the aircraft, the brilliance of S.A.C. engineering gives way to the courage and ingenuity of the crew as they struggle to restore the B-52's mechanical integrity. Electronic distortion of Lieutenant Kivel's voice over the intercom and a handheld, partly subjective camera careening through the aircraft interior give us a visceral feel for the chaos. Individual crew members are glimpsed in fitful images, the most striking of which is a silhouette of Major Kong, still wearing his cowboy hat as he improvises repairs. He has abandoned his pilot seat because it is no longer a position of power, just as President Muffley temporarily abandoned the War Room conference table in order to improvise a solution to *his* crisis. Ironically, the two displays of courage and skill serve opposite causes. Displaced for a time by the sounds of explosions and alarms, "When Johnny Comes Marching Home Again" resumes on the soundtrack as the bomber, under control again, shakily continues on its misappointed way.

In a subjective overhead close-up from Captain Mandrake's point of view, we see General Ripper's hand-drawn recall code, cast in the form of a crossword puzzle featuring two repeated and interlocked phrases. "Purity of Essence" is derived from the General's private sexual fixation, while "Peace on Earth" ties in with S.A.C.'s antiseptic image of itself, "Peace Is Our Profession." Like the contents of the safes on board Kong's B-52, like Miss Scott's dual performance on the telephone (as General Turgidson's secretary and as a woman concealing affairs with both the General and Colonel Puntridge) in the bedroom scene, and like the Soviet Doomsday Machine, General Ripper's crossword puzzle is an irreducible mix of private and collective perspectives.

Expanding our view beyond Mandrake's narrow interest, the camera slowly reverse zooms to reveal a ring of doodles surrounding the crossword puzzle. By simply altering the camera frame within a single shot, Kubrick juxtaposes two separate dramatic entities, the second adding meaning to the first. The doodles furnish a hint of Ripper's personal history, which has had so great an impact on current international events. Among the drawings is one of a rather prim, dour-looking woman. Ripper's mother? The word "scour" is highlighted inside a box. Possibly these are veiled clues to Ripper's antagonistic relationship with women and his obsession with purity. In *Citizen Kane*, Rosebud serves as a gateway into the private life of Charles Foster Kane. But *Dr. Strangelove* is not a biography of Jack D. Ripper. Mandrake, unlike *Kane*'s reporter, Thompson, is less interested in the man himself than in the terrible legacy he has left to the world. The doodles are tantalizing glimpses into the General's mind — nothing more. The point made so succinctly by the reverse zoom is that the private concerns of one person can, under certain circumstances, greatly influence the shape of institutional events.

On the verge of breaking Ripper's recall code, Mandrake is interrupted by the violent entrance of Colonel "Bat" Guano, United States Army. Technically, the two men are allies. Circumstances, however, dictate otherwise. A rugged, glowering combat soldier with hand grenades on his chest (mother's milk to a man in his hazardous profession) and a rifle in his hand, the Colonel is President Muffley's instrument of policy by way of General Faceman. Mandrake, standing behind Ripper's desk, literally and figuratively occupies the former base commander's position of authority. But breakdowns in communication prevent cooperation between the two men. Mandrake, believing he has the recall code and annoyed by interference with his efforts to implement it, vents his anger on the Colonel and the Colonel's men. Guano, understandably defensive after the ordeal he and his troops have just been through, retaliates, using the tools at his command. As distrustful of foreigners as are Turgidson, Kong, and Ripper, he regards the stranger in the funny-looking "suit" as a prisoner. Considering his rude greeting by Mandrake, the limited information he was given by his superiors in Washington, and his unfamiliarity with Ripper's bizarre behavior, his skepticism of Mandrake's story about the General committing suicide is not unreasonable. Like Kong, Guano is a man of flawed, biased, and often unimaginative perspective. But he is also a very competent combat soldier whose shortcomings are wildly inflated by the crisis which engulfs him.

As viewed by a camera subjectively aligned with the Colonel, Captain Mandrake is a contradictory portrait of power and weakness. His possession of the recall code (or three possible variants) and his position behind Ripper's desk suggest an elevation of his status. The wall behind him has been swept clean of Ripper's personal relics of command. Unfortunately for the Captain, the military phone links to Washington are severed, and he is threatened by Guano's rifle, pointing at him from the foreground. Guano refers to Mandrake as "Charlie," a nickname given to the enemy by American soldiers during the Korean War, which is evidently the Colonel's point of reference for defining friend and foe. Guano unwittingly serves as General Ripper's agent rather than President Muffley's. Captain Mandrake, at the moment of his greatest triumph since the crisis began, gets bushwhacked by a poorly timed and ill-informed "rescue" mission.

Like many others in the film, the name "Bat" Guano is a comic reduction of individual man to something either base or narrowly obsessive. Such names forecast the absurdity to which the characters are driven by extreme conditions acting upon their human frailties. Captain Mandrake is the only character to question this intrusion of blatant stylization into the story by challenging the validity of Guano's name. In effect, he reaches across the artificial barrier separating character from filmmaker to debunk Kubrick's comic approach to the subject of nuclear war. He *rationally* questions "Bat" Guano's *ir*rational name.

Surviving the Soviet missile attack, Major Kong's B-52 hurtles over Arctic land and seascapes at extremely low altitude. This is a far cry from our first view of such an aircraft, gliding serenely through the stratosphere, its tremendous speed disguised by the lack of nearby objects against which to measure its progress. In a way, the flight of Kong's bomber progresses from sublime detachment to intense, then hysterical, involvement. Eventually, man is expelled from the aircraft altogether, exposing him directly to the chaos of Nature and of his collective technology.

Order is restored inside the aircraft, but significant changes have occurred since the missile attack. A zoom-in on the radio reveals a charred wreck, its CRM 114 designation burned off. A crew member's comment about the radio's auto destruct mechanism getting hit and blowing itself up sums up the internal contradiction of the mechanism's design. In its attempt to preserve a communication link between bomber and command center yet simultaneously guard against enemy exploitation of that link should the electronic censor

(CRM 114) malfunction, S.A.C. created CRM 114 and then equipped it with a self-destruct device. The radio's self-destruction, as an indirect result of the missile attack, retroactively negates the significance of Washington's victory at Burpleson and Mandrake's solution of the recall code, though none of the characters as yet realizes it. *Dr. Strangelove*'s three principle arenas of action are out of strategic sync with each other. In retrospect, Mandrake's argument with "Bat" Guano now seems pointless. But, at the time it began, it seemed very relevant to the outcome of the crisis.

If the CRM 114 development reflects *back* on other events, the navigator's computation of the aircraft's fuel leakage rate bears on *future* events we cannot as yet see. That rate would allow the B-52 to reach both its primary and secondary targets, but at the cost of a safe return to base. The crew become concerned for their personal safety. Again, however, S.A.C. foresight proves its value. An alternative sanctuary for the crew is available in the form of a weather ship. The men are reassured, and the mission proceeds. Major Kong's bullish determination to complete that mission is, for the moment, General Ripper's greatest ally and President Muffley's greatest enemy. And by only *half* succeeding, the Soviet missile attack that Muffley helped arrange both destroys all hope of a recall and forces the aircraft to fly at low altitude, where radar cannot detect it.

Part Two of Captain Mandrake's debate with Colonel "Bat" Guano continues in the same manner as Part One, except that the intervening scene nullifies its strategic significance. Mandrake, after failing to intimidate his liberator with tough talk, desperately probes for a new angle of attack. "I must know what you think has happened!" is a cry for new material to work with. The American obliges, though in a spirit of contempt rather than cooperation: "I think you're some kinda deviated prevert [sic]. I think General Ripper found out about your preversions [sic] and that you were organizing some kinda mutiny of preverts [sic]." Though hostile, Guano's expression of suspicion eventually provides Mandrake with two valuable pieces of information: that Guano knows nothing about the American attack on Russia, and that his orders are to forcibly put Burpleson's commander in contact with the President. No doubt for security reasons, the higher authorities that sent him on his mission gave him very little background information. And so, in the wake of General Ripper's death, the Colonel is rudderless, drifting this way and that according to his personal inclinations. Mandrake takes control of that rudder and gives him direction. Guano is supposed to connect Ripper with the President. Ripper is dead. Mandrake is Ripper's executive officer. Therefore the President will want to speak with him. But this simple, clear, institutional logic runs smack into the Colonel's monumental thickheadedness, which finds it almost inconceivable that an individual, let alone a foreigner, of such modest military rank has any business talking to the highest government authority in the land. However, Mandrake's reasoning harmonizes with the Colonel's orders and is therefore sufficient to overcome Guano's resistance. Yet, even in defeat, the American's lingering, *private* suspicions make themselves felt. If the Englishman attempts any "preversions" in the phone booth, he'll get his head blown off— the shortest way with dissenters and perverts.

Captain Mandrake's close encounter with the public telephone system, through which he attempts to circumvent disrupted military phone lines, is an absurd clash of hopelessly mismatched perspectives. This time it is private innovation that must deal with institutional ignorance instead of the other way around. Just as Premier Kissoff's drunkenness complicated his Hot Line conversation with President Muffley, Mandrake's call to the White House is endangered by the telephone operator's stubborn fidelity to company (i.e., institutional) rules. Mandrake does not have enough coins to pay for the call. The operator is unaware of the nuclear crisis and probably would not believe the Captain if he told her about it. Ever resourceful, Mandrake finds a path around this obstacle. He orders the Colonel to shoot off the lock of a Coca-Cola vending machine and appropriate money from its coin box. "Bat" Guano, in possibly the most hilarious reaction shot in film history, deadpans, "That's private property." His shock that Mandrake would even think of such an idea illustrates his pathetic inability to rise above a collective habit of perception in order to address a far more serious matter. The telephone operator can be excused her ignorance, but the Colonel has at least an inkling of how desperate the situation is. The inviolability of private property is an American tradition he accepts without reflection or qualification, the same way General Turgidson cleaves unreservedly to S.A.C. Coca-Cola is the corporate epitome of private property. Only Mandrake's direct order overcomes the Colonel's reluctance to break into the vending machine. One institutional perception (the military chain of command) overrides another (the sanctity of private property). Guano does as he is told, but not before issuing an apocalyptic warning to the superior officer who would commit such a sacrilege. If Mandrake fails to get through to the President, he will have to answer to the Coca-Cola Company — no doubt a fate as grim as nuclear incineration. And sure enough, private property takes its revenge. Guano gets squirted in the face by soda pop gushing from the hole he blasts in the machine. He glances accusingly at Mandrake as if to say, "I told you so." Kubrick's satirical target here is not the concept of private property, but rather the degree of blind commitment to any idea which leaves no room for flexibility.

Disproportion is the key factor in yet another of this scene's portraits of the relationship between private and collective man. A public-service poster on the wall outside the telephone booth reads, "Civil Defense Is Your Business," and features a giant institutional finger (equivalent to the War Room's giant halo light) pointing at a group of tiny individuals. All along the military chain of command, from President Muffley to Major Kong, the collective sense of duty places great burdens on the individual, who too often proves inadequate to the task. Captain Mandrake, in his final appearance, shoulders that burden quite well. He does his best to restore integrity to S.A.C. Unfortunately his efforts were rendered irrelevant by prior events onboard Major Kong's B-52.

Mandrake's phantom victory is echoed by the Big Board in the War Room. B-52 attack tracks retreat from the map of the Soviet Union. Jubilation reigns among government officials reliant on electronic abstractions for knowledge of the crisis they are charged with managing. To paraphrase the protagonist from Kubrick's *A Clockwork Orange*, the end of the crisis seems really real only when you viddy it on the Big Board. Liberated from the conference table deliberations, all the President's men stand around in loose solidarity, exchanging relieved congratulations. General Turgidson, predictably, is moved to express this relief in conventionally pious terms. He whistles for attention, assumes a posture of self-importance, and solemnly intones a prayer of thanks to God, garbling scripture in the process. His comrades submissively bow their heads and silently attend to his words: "Lord, we have heard the wings of the Angel of Death fluttering over our heads in the Valley of Fear, and you have seen fit to deliver us from the forces of evil." He conveniently forgets his own unwitting embrace of Death when he advocated an all-out American attack on Russia in support of General Ripper's limited strike. President Muffley's rejection of that option has, apparently, brought Turgidson to the state of grace for which he now gives thanks. Shedding his Air Force jacket, Turgidson has also, for the moment, shed his passionate commitment to S.A.C.'s obsolete, hardline attitude towards the Soviet Union.

During Turgidson's prayer, the camera cuts away to Dr. Strangelove, sitting in the shadows, apart from the celebrants. The Angel of Death is still alive, though not exactly flying high. His wire-rimmed glasses and metal wheelchair glisten in the half-light. They are the technological tools of a physically frail, emotionally repressed individual who bides his time until circumstances are more congenial to the fulfillment of his desires. He shares with the late General Ripper a desire for nuclear war, though their motivations are not the same. Projections on the wall near the Doctor no longer convey a military situation to his liking. The fingers of his gloved right hand, the symbolic center of his frustrated passions, work in agitation. His bare left hand rises to tame its unruly brother. Clasped together they give him the ironic appearance of a prayerful pose equivalent to that of his peace-loving companions off screen. But if Strangelove prays to any god, that god is Chaos, which would disrupt the precarious peace and free the Doctor from his rational alter ego, President Muffley. Twenty years earlier, Strangelove found personal fulfillment through a national leader more like himself—Adolf Hitler.

In the present scene, his silent "prayer" is answered. Premier Kissoff calls on the Hot Line and is furious. The fabric of international cooperation, hastily stitched together by Muffley, is about to unravel from an unexpected loose end.

The image of Major Kong's B-52 flying over Russian Arctic air space completes the destruction of the Big Board's illusion of peace restored. General Ripper's unauthorized attack proceeds unchecked, with one critical exception. The navigator reports an increase in the rate of fuel loss. The consequences of that new development are not yet in sight, but in retrospect we can recognize that it renders obsolete the actions which will be taken by President Muffley and Premier Kissoff in the next scene. As with the confrontation between Captain Mandrake and Colonel "Bat" Guano, Kubrick has altered the strategic context of a scene by introducing an element prior to and apart from it which changes the terms of conflict. We are encouraged to perceive each scene as an isolated drama, defined by its own rules *and* by the rules of a larger whole.

The once symmetrical order of the War Room gets jumbled by the strain of events. Caught off guard in their moment of premature celebration, government officials find themselves in new positions. President Muffley, conferring on the telephone with Kissoff, occupies what had been General Turgidson's place at the conference table. The now pointless *World Targets in Megadeaths* lies ignored on the table in front of him. Various advisors, from pipe smoking, scholarly civilians to military officers laden with medals, stand in loose formation around the President, passively looking to him for deliverance from the revived Angel of Death.

Only Kong's B-52 remains operational and hostile, but it is enough to endanger the fragile Soviet-American alliance. Muffley is inclined to believe the Premier's story about one American bomber being unaccounted for, but Turgidson, a late convert to the alliance, is quick to break ranks with a policy that only moments earlier he characterized as a gift of mercy from God. Regressing to former habits, he accuses the communists of deception, interpreting Kissoff's message as an excuse for Russian retaliation instead of an appeal for more help. But he has no strategy to offer against either Soviet counterattack or Doomsday. President Muffley has no choice but to stick with the Russians. When asked to confirm the identity of the surviving B-52's primary and secondary targets, Turgidson does so with a helpless nod of his head. He stands frozen in a Neanderthal-like pose, torn between conflicting loyalties. Unwittingly he contributes to the eventual defeat of the alliance he both clings to and rejects. Relying blindly on Turgidson's confirmation of the remaining B-52's targets, Muffley advises Kissoff to concentrate all Soviet air defense forces into those two sectors, where "you can't miss."

For the first time in the film, though for different reasons, President

Muffley and Major Kong desire the same course of action. The pilot, with his fierce determination to drop his bombs on their primary targets, is now the President's greatest ally. Unfortunately for Muffley, the navigator's disclosure that the aircraft's increasing fuel loss rate puts the primary targets out of reach destroys that harmony. Kong reluctantly agrees to an alternate target provided by S.A.C. contingency plans. Once again, S.A.C. flexibility proves to be as big a problem for the Soviet-American alliance as does the *in*flexibility of the Russian Doomsday Machine.

For the first time since the attack order came through, there is divided opinion between Major Kong and his crew. While reporting the aircraft's revised fuel loss figures, the navigator makes repeated references to the life-saving weather ship. Obviously he wants to abandon the mission, head for the weather ship, and survive. Bombardier Lothar Zogg silently expresses his anxiety by chewing his gum furiously, like General Turgidson in the War Room. But Kong will not abort the mission. That determination, which was the Soviet-American alliance's greatest ally when the target was one of the primaries, becomes its greatest threat in the wake of a new target selection.

"Keep our fingers crossed," "We're all in this together," and "We're with you all the way" are President Muffley's attempts to reinforce the Soviet-American alliance with well-worn clichés. The flimsiness of the last of those clichés becomes evident when Muffley asks General Turgidson if the renegade B-52 is capable of reaching its primary target in spite of massed Soviet air defenses. Turgidson, though aware that the bomber's success would presumably doom himself as well as the rest of the world, cannot help slipping back into his former, Cold War mode of perception. The result is an absurd display of divided allegiance. He insults the Russians grossly, arousing indignation in Ambassador de Sadesky. Then he tries to cover up the insult, instead making it worse. He loses sight of the President's original question until Muffley angrily reminds him of it. As always, the President must drag his subordinate back into the light of a broader reality. Chastened, Turgidson returns to the subject of the rogue bomber's chances of survival. But he veers off again, waxing eloquent about the evasive capabilities of a B-52 in the hands of a skilled pilot. He practically takes flight himself in a burst of childlike empathy for Major Kong: "Has he got a chance? Hell yes!" Then, suddenly, he recognizes the grotesque irony of his joy, glances around in embarrassment, and covers his big mouth with his hand.

In dramatic terms, the approach of Major Kong's B-52 to its revised target is similar to the missile attack scene. The viewer is caught between empathy for the crew's effort to complete their mission and an objective recognition of the catastrophe that will result if they do.

S.A.C.'s divided vision is never more evident than during Major Kong and the bombardier's long checklist of electronic devices surrounding the hydrogen bombs. Official strategy (MAD) is to make use of those weapons unnecessary and difficult yet also possible. Four separate "bomb fusing master *safeties*" stand guard over "bomb *fusing* circuits," which are in turn tested for viability. And the actions of *three* crew members are required in order to execute the process. And what exactly is a "primary switch override?" Is it designed to compensate for a trigger that fails or to protect *against* a trigger that activates by mistake? Finally the bombs are ready for use. But the lengthy process of activating them has been an institutional tug of war between the need for access to nuclear weapons and a fear of giving that access to individual man. The same contradictory priorities motivated S.A.C. to institute a launch option for base commanders, in case the President is incapacitated by a Russian sneak attack, yet also mandate human reliability testing to weed out unstable base commanders who could execute that option.

As Kong and his crew run down their checklist, the camera zooms in on essential components involved, juxtaposing them with shots of well-trained soldiers performing their coordinated tasks with mechanical precision and external shots of the B-52 racing towards its target. This contrapuntal editing, aurally held together by the martial strains of an old Civil War song, generates an intoxicating sense of purpose and sophisticated control — until a note of dissonance intrudes.

Of all the aircraft's electronic systems, the bomb bay doors must be the least complex. Yet their failure threatens the success of Kong's mission and creates some hope for the success of the alliance. Even S.A.C.'s remarkable powers of foresight fail here, as four redundant back-up systems all prove inoperative. Zogg speculates that the Soviet missile attack might have severed cables carrying electronic signals to the bomb bay doors. A whole sequence of prior events is reshaped by that revelation. Cooperation between American and Soviet air forces, which caused the CRM 114 to self-destruct (nullifying Captain Mandrake's solution of the recall code) and created a progressive fuel leak that changed Kong's target selection (nullifying Soviet air defense efforts around the primary targets), finally appears to have done the alliance some good. But just as President Muffley stepped outside conventional wisdom in order to improvise the Soviet-American alliance, Major Kong now improvises a way to complete his misguided mission. Employing colorful, colloquial language to fortify his courage, Kong personally descends into the bomb bay to open the doors manually. His bravery and ingenuity, which would be celebrated in so many other war movies, works *against* the survival of his country and the world in this instance.

When Major Kong mounts one of the hydrogen bombs in the bomb bay in order to reach the faulty door mechanism, the visual impression of bloated male sexuality takes its meaning from the late General Ripper's perception of things rather than from Kong, who has the misfortune to carry his

Major Kong (Slim Pickens) improvises repairs so he can drop his hydrogen bombs, each bearing contradictory messages from private and collective man, on a Soviet target.

commander's strange banner into battle. In *Red Alert*, the bombs are given the emotionally neutral nicknames "Bim" and "Bam" (Bryant, 30). In *Dr. Strangelove*, the weapons each have two inscriptions: one a ludicrously understated, dispassionate, neatly printed (like the "Peace Is Our Profession" sign in Captain Mandrake's headquarters) warning from S.A.C. to the bomb's handlers, the other a handwritten (like the film's opening credits), mock-romantic message from those handlers to Russia, their appointed target: "Nuclear Warhead: Handle With Care" shares space with "Hi There!" and "Dear John." Once again, collective and private perspectives are joined in the same enterprise. Traditional opening and closing lines in a romantic relationship between two individuals, "Hi There!" and "Dear John," become, by juxtaposition with weapons of war, the prelude and coda to an international rendezvous of unimaginable violence. The B-29 that dropped the atomic bomb on Hiroshima at the end of World War II bore the nickname of its pilot's mother. But that private act of appropriation remained subordinate to the authority and goals of institutional man. In *Dr. Strangelove*, General Ripper reduces S.A.C. and its weapons to his personal messenger. He makes literal the inscriptions Kong and his crew scribbled on the bombs in jest and violates the collective admonition, "Handle With Care."

Major Kong's attempt to repair the damaged bomb door circuits unfolds in classic Hollywood style, like a commando squad racing to repair a loose wire on an explosive charge strapped to a strategically vital bridge over which a Nazi armored column is about to pass, or some such scenario. Navigator Kivel counts down the miles to the target while Kong employs a simple pair of pliers to circumvent broken circuits. When the moment of truth arrives, one of the crew calls out, "Where the hell is Major Kong?" "Hell" is an accurate description of Kong's whereabouts. His improvisation opens the bomb bay doors, exposing him to the infernal roar of frigid air and a terrifying view of the target area below. No longer sheltered by the artificial environment of his aircraft, Kong finds himself face to face with the prospect of imminent death. Overwhelmed and stripped of all professionalism, he takes refuge in a comforting memory from his civilian past. Like *2001*'s Dave Bowman retreating to the tranquillity of his genteel apartment, Kong transforms his death plunge into something familiar and manageable. Waving his cowboy hat and yelling like a rodeo star, he rides an H-bomb down to ground zero as though it were a bucking bronco. A partly subjective camera accompanies his wild descent, giving us a taste of his hysteria. But it also gives us a different perspective. The giant cylinder clasped between the pilot's legs looks outrageously phallic because we see Kong's ride through the filter of General Ripper's sexual obsession, which triggered Kong's mission in the first place.

Thomas Nelson interprets the nuclear explosion that follows as the fulfillment of the Soviet Doomsday strategy (Nelson, 97). I disagree. The Doomsday Machine was designed as a nuclear *deterrent*. Its triggering signals the *failure*, not the fulfillment, of its mission. And even if that mission were the eradication of all human and animal life on earth, Doomsday is still a failure, as the film's final scene demonstrates.

As though sensing Major Kong's success, and the consequent irrelevance of the Big Board from which he turns away, Dr. Strangelove wheels around to confront his hapless War Room companions. He too, like Muffley and Kong before him, has an improvised plan to turn defeat into victory. Emerging from the shadows and back out under the institutional halo, he is unable to suppress a little chuckle of delight as he outlines a plan to "preserve a nucleus of human specimens" in mineshafts far below the radioactive wasteland. "Human specimens" should betray his misanthropic attitude towards his fellow man. But the promise of escape from Doomsday blinds other officials to his increasingly obvious motives. They crowd around him like moths to a flame, lashing their hopes to him. Facing him, as though in skeptical opposition, are President Muffley, General Turgidson, and a civilian adviser, seated on the same bench where Turgidson and Ambassador de Sadesky once wrestled over a spy camera. Strangelove now challenges Muffley's bankrupt thinking the way the President once challenged the pointless bickering between Turgidson and de Sadesky. But Strangelove has no constitutional authority over his opponents, and he must therefore seduce rather than scold them into acquiescence.

The vulnerability of the three men on the bench is obvious. President Muffley clings to a drink for emotional support. General Turgidson clings to the President for the same reason. Their civilian colleague, never a major player in this crisis, remains passive and silent. Diabolically clever, Dr. Strangelove launches a two-pronged attack on these tenuously allied power brokers, tailoring each prong to a specific target. He soothes the President's concerns about the well-being of mineshaft survivors, but he also insidiously capitalizes on Muffley's reluctance to decide who would and would not be allowed to occupy the mineshafts. By suggesting that a computer program of his own design could be used to make that decision, Strangelove bids to usurp the President's abdicated authority. And he would expand on that authority by the *absolute* subordination of survivors to a social order of his own design.

General Turgidson offers a different and simpler challenge to Strangelove's powers of persuasion. Correctly assessing the true nature of Turgidson's expressed concern about the elimination of monogamy in a postwar environment, Strangelove offers the prospect of a male sexual fantasy disguised as a selfless, patriotic sacrifice. The General's arm gradually loosens its grip on President Muffley as his allegiance shifts to Strangelove, who in a beautiful close-up leans forward and announces in conspiratorial fashion to his entire audience, "Of course it would be absolutely vital that our top government and military men be included to foster and impart the required principles of leadership and tradition." It is the perfect combination of appeals: one to the desire for personal survival and sensual gratification, the other to a sense of civic responsibility. Captivated by Dr. Strangelove's mineshaft scheme, General Turgidson untethers himself physically and emotionally from President Muffley, who appears less enamored of the plan. Without so much as a backward glance at the promise of marriage he made to Miss Scott, Turgidson follows the scent of polygamy like a dog. Even Ambassador de Sadesky, who is not likely to be among the chosen few, is attracted to Strangelove's plan. He compliments the Doctor, who reacts with seeming respect and humility. Once again a crisis makes for strange bedfellows. Representatives of one of the most bitter international conflicts in history (Nazi Germany versus Communist Russia), Strangelove and de Sadesky find common ground in their *private* desires. But General Turgidson's subsequent grumbling about possible Soviet plans to use their own mineshafts as shelters bursts de Sadesky's bubble. The Ambassador silently withdraws from his foreign hosts and sneaks off to photograph the Big Board with his camera. Falling back on old habits of perception, like Turgidson, he executes a spy mission which under present circumstances is no longer of strategic value to his country.

The more power Dr. Strangelove acquires on an institutional level, the more he loses control over his own passions, which are inflamed by the prospect of fulfillment. His gloved right hand leads the way in this self-betrayal. Subconsciously motivated, the hand reflects back on such film characters as Rotwang in *Metropolis*, Inspector Krogh in *Son of Frankenstein* (1939), and Dr. No in *Dr. No* (1962), and forward to Luke Skywalker in *Return of the Jedi* (1983). During a climactic struggle with his evil father, Darth Vader, Luke almost yields to his baser emotions, symbolically rooted in his gloved, artificial hand. He successfully resists temptation. Dr. Strangelove, on the other hand, has long since given in to his "dark side." It is his rational alter ego, President Muffley, who yields to temptation in this scene.

During the course of his triumph over American democracy, Dr. Strangelove's gloved hand becomes increasingly unruly: refusing to release its grip on a chemical chart, periodically jutting out in an inappropriate Nazi salute, turning his wheelchair and therefore him away from his audience, punching him in the chin, rising out of his lap like a rampant penis, and finally trying to strangle him. His desperate efforts to suppress these involuntary eruptions are both hilarious and unsuccessful. But what does it matter? Not one of his rapt listeners (except for actor Peter Bull, who cannot quite hide the amusement his and the other characters *should* be feeling) recognizes or cares about Strangelove's blatantly selfish, undemocratic, and sadistic motives.

Exhausted by his internal battle and slumped in his wheelchair, Dr. Strangelove overcomes President Muffley's resistance to his plan from what looks like a position of weakness. He transforms the President's lingering doubts about the emotional ordeal of mineshaft survivors into a "bold curiosity for the adventures ahead," whereupon he falls victim himself to another spastic Nazi salute.

Swallowing the bait dangled in front of him by Strangelove, General Turgidson in turn adapts the Doctor's mineshaft scheme to his original, "unofficial" S.A.C. plan for winning a nuclear war, which had seemed invalidated by the advent of Doomsday. Garnering support from his civilian counterpart seated on the other side of the President, Turgidson rapidly constructs a scenario of renewed Soviet-American hostility extending indefinitely into the future. His argument takes shape out of a chain reaction of separate contributions. Turgidson suggests the Russians might stash a nuclear bomb for use against the United States after Doomsday survivors emerge from their underground sanctuaries. Another official adds that the Soviets might even plot to take over American mineshaft space. Turgidson then appropriates and expands on *that* idea. Surely the Russians *will* try to steal our mineshaft space, breed more prodigiously than Americans and, upon emerging, conquer America with superior numbers. General Ripper's sexual paranoia is reborn, through Turgidson, as an integral part of the government's defense strategy.

Rejuvenated by the enthusiastic support of General Turgidson (George C. Scott) and the reluctant acquiescence of President Muffley (Peter Sellers), Dr. Strangelove (Peter Sellers) rises in triumph from his wheelchair.

Outmaneuvered by President Muffley throughout most of the crisis, Turgidson now traps his commander in chief in a variation of the "missile gap" myth.

In a high-angle shot taking in nearly all of the War Room occupants, General Turgidson stands, turns, and confronts Muffley. "Mr. President, we must not allow a mineshaft gap!" is his updated Cold War battle cry. Visually, the General now stands at the right hand of Dr. Strangelove, serving the scientist just as the scientist at first *appeared* to serve the President. Both empowered and emotionally overcome by his triumph over the democratic order of a former enemy, Strangelove stiffly rises out of his wheelchair, his left and right hands at last performing in harmony. Positioned near center screen, with all of the other officials gathered in orbit around him, he is now the focus of collective authority. His institutional battlecry, "I have a plan!" mixes with his joyful cry of resurrection to power as an individual and as the standard bearer for a Third Reich crippled by the Soviet-American alliance of World War II. "Mein Führer! I can walk!" No longer bound by physical or political restraints, Strangelove exults in victory, much as as Adolf Hitler revelled, to the point of dancing a jig over the destruction of the railroad car where Germany surrendered to the Allies at the end of World War I. Strangelove Über Alles; Or, How a Peace Loving Democracy Learned to Stop Worrying and Love the Bomb.

Dr. Strangelove's rebirth into power is visually confirmed by a lyrical montage of nuclear explosions — the Soviet Doomsday Machine triggering itself and coincidentally bringing about a future social order of Strangelove's nightmarish design. Consisting of documentary footage dating back to the 1940s, the montage is a capsule review of United States nuclear testing. This collection of *separate* episodes is redeployed by Kubrick as a *single* lyrical unit. Every character who should know better has learned to stop worrying and love the bomb, or at least love the hedonistic future the bomb promises them. The sexual coupling depicted in the film's opening credits reaches nuclear orgasm in the film's final scene. General Ripper's *private* metaphor has become, thanks to Dr. Strangelove, a *collective* reality.

"Try a Little Tenderness" returns with a vengeance as "We'll Meet Again," a popular *British* (yet another Nazi foe appropriated and transformed into an ally) World War II song that in the present context echoes Strangelove's triumph. Lead singer Vera Lynn is accompanied by a chorus, just as Strangelove brings America's leaders into harmony with *his* voice. "We'll Meet Again" is a song about lovers reunited at the end of a long separation caused by war. But the "lovers" reunited at the end of *Dr. Strangelove* are the United States and the Soviet Union. And they are reunited in mutual suspicion and hate, not love. General Turgidson's declaration, "We must not allow a mineshaft gap!" implies a perpetuation of the Cold War. The logic of Doomsday, which for awhile seemed to validate MAD and to render nuclear war obsolete, has been eclipsed.

"We'll Meet Again," as used in *Dr. Strangelove*, is not a cynical embrace of nuclear Armageddon as the fitting end of an insane species. It is a satiric *lament* over the fact that even the mighty hydrogen bomb apparently cannot bring about a revolutionary change in old habits of perception.

In *Dr. Strangelove*'s closing credits, individual man's twisted scrawl from the opening credits is replaced by tidy institutional lettering. A return to normalcy? Not quite. That tidy lettering forms a vertical column suggestive of both sexual arousal (a private concern) and a nuclear explosion (collective technology). The private preoccupations of General Ripper and Dr. Strangelove have been monstrously elevated to the status of public policy. Fail-safe has failed in more ways than one.

CHAPTER 2

2001: A Space Odyssey:
The Face in the Machine

Man is a rope, fastened between animal and Superman — a rope over an abyss.

— Friedrich Nietzsche, *Thus Spoke Zarathustra* (43)

2001: A Space Odyssey developed concurrently as a film and a novel, with Stanley Kubrick and Arthur C. Clarke exchanging ideas for a story about man's evolution, exploration of outer space, and possible encounter with extraterrestrial intelligence. Each then pursued those ideas to his own dramatic end. Clarke's nine-page story, "The Sentinel," served as a starting point for the collaborators. But their separate results, film and novel, are very different from one another in narrative style and in the depiction of man, technology, and extraterrestrial life.

Unlike narration in several Kubrick films, the narrator in Clarke's novel is nearly omniscient, passing into and out of the minds of various human characters and speculating freely on the nature and intentions of extraterrestrials. *2001*, the film, dispenses with narration. Instead, Kubrick juxtaposes detailed impressions of immediate reality, as experienced by the characters, with more abstract impressions that place localized events into a broader dramatic context of which the characters are largely unaware. Consider, for example, Heywood Floyd. In the novel, he is a virtual spokesman for Clarke, thrilling to the experience of space travel and keenly aware of humanity's struggle to attain such freedom of movement. Clarke reinforces Floyd's poetic sensibilities by making him a widower whose passions are more than commonly channeled into his work. In the film, he is more a creature of his time, experiencing space travel as routine, even tedious. And against this portrait of complacency, Kubrick projects images of wonder and awe. The mundane mixes with the extraordinary in a lyrical synthesis that highlights both.

Clarke makes it clear that the benevolent intervention of godlike aliens rescues humankind at perilous moments during his odyssey. Apeman is saved from starvation and predation by the gift of technology. Spaceman is saved from his dependence on machines and from the harsh conditions of outer space by the gift of biological adaptation. In *2010: A Space Odyssey*, Clarke's 1982 sequel, this cosmic paternalism is pushed even further. Unseen aliens act as stern though generous landlords to the solar system's inconsiderate human tenants. Kubrick's *2001* depicts the crucible of human evolution in different terms. His apeman is mired in static routine, disrupted by moments of great uncertainty but not necessarily on the verge of extinction. The origin of his technological skills is ambiguous, as are their moral ramifications. As to the state of human affairs on Earth circa *2001*, Kubrick postulates an era of international cooperation and the peaceful use of technology. The ghosts of *Dr. Strangelove* are mostly, though not entirely, exorcised. In Clarke's novel, Earth civilization in 2001 is on the verge of apocalyptic self-destruction.

The novel leaves little doubt that HAL, the supercomputer on board spaceship *Discovery*, is a conscious entity. The film, on the other hand, is more ambiguous on that point, toying with the idea of artificial consciousness while providing a possibly mechanical explanation for its human-like responses. Aesthetics and ethics clash as HAL both outperforms and threatens man.

The biggest discrepancy between film and novel is in their depictions of the monolith's role in human development. Clarke's monolith is clearly a function of benevolent alien intervention, teaching Moonwatcher about crude technology and transforming Dave into the Star Child. Kubrick's monolith is, for the most part, an inert artifact of unknown origin that alters man less by acting upon him than by man's emotional and intellectual responses to its mystery. It is a veritable symbol of the ever-promising and often overwhelming Unknown, forever enticing humankind to the next horizon. Astronaut Dave Bowman, at the end of the film, becomes a child of the stars not by alien manipulation while he sleeps but through the conscious act of reaching out for the monolith from his deathbed.

Lyricism in *Dr. Strangelove* is focused to an ironic pinpoint through the narrow filter of a specific time, place, and situation. Absurdity and horror dominate the efforts of individual and collective man to trigger and avert nuclear war. Released from those claustrophobic dimensions, *2001: A Space Odyssey* plays like an antidote to its predecessor. Pursuing the same general topic of human creativity from the first technological innovation to the sophisticated endeavors of the foreseeable future, Kubrick throws his dramatic aperture wide open. Beauty and irony mix on more or less even terms. Dramatic impressions cross enormous boundaries of time and space, linking separate events in a more abstract, generalized manner than in *Dr. Strangelove*. But differences between the two films should not obscure their deeper stylistic similarities. Both exhibit a passion for environmental detail. In *2001* that passion expands to include Nature as well as man-made environments.

* * *

Following the pattern set by *Dr. Strangelove* and *Lolita*, *2001* opens with a striking dramatic impression and then steps away from it in order to work back to a similar impression under modified circumstances. The screen fills with the image of a lifeless Moon. The camera then tilts up to reveal the Earth directly behind that Moon. From behind the Earth then appears the Sun. All three celestial bodies are in perfect linear alignment. The dead Moon is in eclipse, while the Earth, a bright crescent of sunlight crowning its upper edge, is in a period of dawning, or ascendancy. Even before his first appearance, man's odyssey begins here, over the horizon of a dormant Moon.

As bold a metaphorical statement of the advent of man as the bright crescent around Earth are the opening bars of Richard Strauss's *Thus Spoke Zarathustra* on the soundtrack. Like "Try a Little Tenderness" in *Dr. Strangelove*, *Zarathustra* redefines what appears on screen. Strauss's musical interpretation of Friedrich Nietzsche's philosophical poem begins with a glorious evocation of sunrise, which Kubrick visually reworks into Earthrise. Written in a burst of creative joy after years spent attacking society's most cherished beliefs, Nietzsche's *Zarathustra* was an attempt to restore some sense of purpose and beauty to human existence. *2001* offers a similar change of pace from the delusion-bashing satire of *Dr. Strangelove*. As employed in the film, *Zarathustra* is an ecstatic herald of human progress. Yet the scenes that immediately follow it challenge the music's celebratory spirit.

The title *2001: A Space Odyssey* implies an epic of the future, but the film begins surprisingly in a primeval setting, tracing the roots of human technological ingenuity far back in time for the purpose of comparison and contrast with the potential future. Employing the first of many blackouts that separate widely dispersed events in *2001*, Kubrick takes us back to "The Dawn of Man" on Earth. This dawn is both a logical and an ironic parallel to the one before it. The sublimely remote image of Earthrise indirectly portrayed the advent of man. It is displaced by and juxtaposed with a closer, more direct view of the same phenomenon. A series of extreme long shots depict sunrise over a rugged, uninhabited landscape. Unlike the linear alignment of Moon, Earth, and Sun in the previous shot, the natural order in "The Dawn of Man" appears more random. Asymmetrical impressions of emptiness and stasis replace a symmetrical impression of progressive change. And silence replaces *Zarathustra*.

The ten-shot montage that opens "The Dawn of Man" is really two scenes in one, portraying the slow-moving sunrise of a single prehistoric day while simultaneously implying the passage of countless sunrises between

Earth's formation and the appearance of human-like creatures. Billions of years of terrestrial development are summed up in a few seconds of visual shorthand. *One* sunrise viewed from numerous camera angles is also a *series* of sunrises over a landscape that changes very little over time. On the soundtrack the muted noise of insects yields to muted bird calls as primitive life forms make way for those more complex.

During the tenth shot the camera finally moves, in tandem with the sound of a light breeze. These modest signals of change ironically bring with them evidence of death and decay. We see the bleached bones of animals far more biologically advanced than the insects we first heard. Figuratively speaking, the Earth is coming to life. In evolutionary terms, the stage is set for the arrival of man. His sudden appearance is both impressive, by juxtaposition with the absence of higher life forms in previous shots, and rather comical, in view of what the film's futuristic title led us to expect. The camera, meanwhile, establishes itself as a neutral observer. The pattern of events is established primarily through editing, which creates a unified impression out of otherwise unconnected images.

Apeman is a medium-sized, fragile-looking, semisociable creature competing irritably but not savagely for food with a group of dull-witted tapirs grazing alongside him. We see early man without speech, without tools, and firmly entrenched in behavioral habits passed down over countless generations. Often framed by the camera to appear below the ground level of surrounding terrain, he is, in effect, trapped in the geological layers of time. He seems, at first glance, a fairly well-adapted outgrowth of the natural world that surrounds and has preceded him. Then, suddenly, this complacent impression is shattered. Caught off guard and apart from his companions, one of the apemen is pounced upon by a leopard. The predator's eyes, reflecting natural light, glow with pure, undiluted instinct. Unable to fend off a creature far better endowed by Nature for combat, the apeman dies in terror and pain. Members of his tribe cannot rescue him and are not inclined to try. Not burdened by feelings of guilt or a sense of duty, they flee the scene. "The Dawn of Man" is for early man a time of alternating routine and lethal uncertainty. The emotionally detached camera discreetly fades to black before the leopard completes its kill, concluding scene one of the human drama. So far there is no indication of progressive change in apeman's existence.

In a scene that could be taking place later that same prehistoric day, or a few years or many generations later, the second episode of "The Dawn of Man" expands on and modifies impressions from the first. A group of apemen groom each other. But displays of intimidation determine which of them gets priority at the life-sustaining waterhole. Conflicts between individuals occur within a tenuous framework of social cooperation. To this duality is then added collective rivalry when a second tribe takes possession of the waterhole from the first. Territoriality and leadership become definable features of apeman's social existence. As always, the human drama plays out in a natural environment that aesthetically overwhelms and remains indifferent to it.

The rival tribe duplicates the role of the leopard, but without the bloodshed. The battle between tribes is more a contest of shouts and gestures than a struggle to the death. The first tribe retreats in disarray while the invaders take control of the waterhole. In the scene's final shot, the victorious leader looks directly into the camera, subjectively aligned with the defeated rival, and roars his triumph and contempt. Though strictly a function of camera angle and not of the character's intent, the victorious apeman appears to defy us and all of our modern, civilized sensibilities. Kubrick rubs our noses in the fact that apeman is, after all, *our* ancestor. And his aggressive behavior is not much different from what we see in *Dr. Strangelove*. As was frequently the case in that film's War Room scenes, leaders set the example for their subordinates. After the victorious apeman leader utters his roar of conquest, one of his followers apes him, so to speak.

Night on primeval Earth relegates apeman to an emphatically inferior rank in the biological order of things. Darkness erodes his already meager power to control the circumstances of his life. The only sound disturbing the dead quiet of night is not made by apeman. Employing a staggered revelation that is one of his trademarks, Kubrick first lets us hear that sound, then a few moments later reveals its source. It is the rumbling sound of animal breathing coming from a leopard lying regally atop its zebra kill. The big cat's eyes shine in the moonlight. Supremely adapted to and virtually an extension of blind natural forces, this consummate predator is at once a powerful declaration and destroyer of life in a largely inanimate world. Its muscular frame and loud breathing stand out sharply against an incomparably vaster Nature surrounding it, yet its instinct-driven behavior is a reflection of that Nature. Its weapons, food, motivations and, above all, limitations are all accidents of evolution rather than products of its will.

Higher up on the evolutionary ladder yet still dominated by the leopard, apeman sleeps fitfully in the security of a cave, which first appears as a puny, natural fortress set against an immensity of moonlit clouds and sky. From inside this cramped sanctuary, one of the apemen growls defiantly at the distant roars of the leopard. But it is an empty challenge. The big cat rules the night. Apeman's eyes reflect the same light of natural instinct as does the leopard's, but from the other side of the predator/prey equation.

Though essential to his survival, the cave is a compromise for apeman. His sociability, always tenuous, becomes strained in tight quarters. Token verbal defiance of the unseen leopard quickly degenerates into raucous bickering with a neighbor over a piece of food. This, in turn, triggers a chain reaction of grumbling among all the cave dwellers. But this, too, passes, giving way to a beautiful close-up of the tribal leader's face, tense with concentration as he ponders, to the extent he can, the mysteries of the terrifying, alien realm outside his sanctuary. If only for a moment, his bright eyes reflect curiosity as well as fear. Apeman appears to us both contemptible and curiously noble as he takes scarcely comprehended steps beyond his narrow confines. Outside the cave, a blood-red dawn lightens the horizon. Nature red in tooth and claw (or a Strangelovian dawn of nuclear fire, if we telescope far into the future) awaits apeman at the start of a new day.

As a second dawn breaks over apeman, background music returns to the soundtrack for the first time since the opening credits. But *Zarathustra* was a gloriously generic expression of progress and purpose. Gyorgy Ligeti's *Requiem* generates a very different effect. Subjectively linked to a specific character, it conveys to us the wonder but also the uncertainty and terror of an encounter with the unknown.

The tribal leader awakens from a fitful night's sleep to discover something entirely new in his world. His is both a literal awakening from routine rest and the metaphorical awakening of early man as a species from the mental and physical habits that have dominated him for generations. Rousing his companions with a cry of alarm, the leader sniffs the air and stomps his foot — a mixed reaction of curiosity and fear. His companions imitate him. Do they sense the approach of the leopard? By not first revealing to us the object of their anxiety, Kubrick draws our attention to apeman's *reaction*.

The focus of apeman's agitation is a large, gray-black, rectangular monolith standing in a pit outside the tribe's cave. Though inert, it appears unmistakably artificial and unique. Fighting an internal battle between furtive curiosity and hysterical fear, the apemen advance and retreat, advance and retreat, reaching out tentatively towards the monolith, then pulling back from it. Finally the leader makes and maintains physical contact. Curiosity conquers fear, but the process is agonizingly slow, as Kubrick effectively conveys by not rushing it. As the apemen grow more comfortable with the strange object in their midst and gather around its base, their agitated yells are displaced by the music of *Requiem*, signaling a shift in perspective from undiluted terror to a kind of religious awe.

Like the leopard and the rival tribe, the monolith challenges apeman's security. But because that challenge is passive it is also largely intellectual. The camera, which had remained a detached observer of apeman's earlier experiences, now follows the soundtrack's lead into a more subjective mode. It cuts closer to the monolith, which as a result appears less earthbound and more imposing. Then it becomes completely subjective from the vantage point of the tribal leader. He has carried out tests of touch and taste on the object, but the test of sight proves the most inspirational. As viewed from an extremely low, reverential angle, the monolith "directs" his/our gaze skyward towards a linear alignment of the Sun and a crescent Moon, with the monolith's top edge forming a horizon. Thanks to this artificially altered perspective, a sense of harmonic order enters apeman's consciousness. The monolith-Moon-Sun imagery parallels the Moon-Earth-Sun imagery from the opening credits. But the emergence of a crescent Earth from behind a lifeless Moon took us from an inanimate cosmos to the biological evolution of one planet. Now, following the upward thrust of the monolith, apeman looks *away* from his terrestrial origins, towards the Moon and beyond. That will be the direction of his future journeys.

In Arthur C. Clarke's novel of *2001*, the monolith is clearly an alien device for promoting higher awareness among primitive life forms throughout the galaxy. In the film, however, the monolith's origin and purpose are more ambiguous. In visual terms, it stands out magnificently from the surrounding landscape and from apeman himself, its contours smooth and regular. On a symbolic level, it stands in for all of the unrecorded events, the interactions of mind and matter, that trigger progressive change in man. An idealized embodiment of mystery, it sums up everything unfamiliar to us at any given moment in our existence. What the monolith is to prehistoric apeman is not necessarily what it will be to man in the year 2001. Nor does it perform in the same manner for both. The monolith appears to apeman, particularly the tribal leader, after a night of fitful sleep, contemplation and perhaps dreaming. Did subconscious disturbance surface in the morning as conscious inspiration? Interestingly, the monolith is rooted in the same hollow as the cave in which the tribal leader kept his night vigil and perhaps dreamt of better worlds. He is the one member of the tribe who is ready to profit from this strange encounter. Something in his mental makeup renders him receptive to the monolith's passive "message." By virtue of that receptivity, he becomes Moonwatcher. Thomas Nelson insightfully describes the monolith as "an emblem, more than an artifact, of the Mystery Beyond" and "an otherworldly vision of such artifacts and extensions as bone, fountain pen, satellite, spaceship, computer, eighteenth century room, and crystal glass" (Nelson, 116, 105).

The fact that music accompanying this scene comes from a requiem, or hymn for the dead, foreshadows the irony of the action to come. Moonwatcher's enlightenment triggers a host of morally paradoxical consequences. Apeman's encounter with the monolith is a secular variation on the Biblical story of Adam, Eve, and the Tree of Knowledge, except that primeval Earth, as depicted in "The Dawn of Man," is no Paradise, and apeman's liberation from his natural limitations is both a fall and an ascent.

A direct cut links the fourth and fifth episodes of "The Dawn of Man," indicating no major time lapse between them. The apeman who led the approach to the monolith is clearly the protagonist again. There has been no generational leap during the scene transition, as there might have been earlier. The preponderance of Nature is reestablished in a series of shots depicting an unchanged landscape. The camera resumes its detached perspective. The music of *Requiem* has disappeared. The tribe has resumed its routine foraging for food, apparently unaffected by their encounter with the monolith. But something *has* changed. The camera cuts to a frontal shot of Moonwatcher, a camera angle often employed by Kubrick to convey strong emotion in a character.

Moonwatcher crouches and ponders over a pile of sun-bleached tapir bones. The camera cuts away briefly to a subjective shot of his recollection of the monolith-Sun-Moon alignment from the previous scene. Displaying remarkable sophistication, Moonwatcher consciously employs a memory, as opposed to merely *reacting* from memory, to interpret something immediately at hand. He clumsily fiddles with one of the longer bones. Invention and accident work hand in hand as he jostles other bones with it, producing an amplified version of the effect he would get by using his hand alone. Moonwatcher translates the linear reinforcement of monolith-Sun-Moon into the linear reinforcement of hand-bone-target, with spectacular results. Gradually he recognizes the potential expansion of his power which this little experiment brings about. *Zarathustra* builds to a crescendo on the soundtrack, matching the character's ecstasy over this revolutionary event. Music associated earlier with the emergence of Earth as the birthplace of humanity now echoes the passion of one apeman's emergence as a technologically creative being. Moonwatcher's mastery of the bone club is a strangely beautiful example of physical movement becoming more and more controlled and harmonic. It is a creative act bringing order to chaos, but also, judging from the tapir skull he smashes to pieces, chaos to order. As a secular Tree of Knowledge, the monolith bears mixed fruit.

At the start of the scene, Moonwatcher is framed by the camera to appear lower than a rocky ledge in the background. As he masters the bone club, the camera cuts to a low-angle close-up of his hairy arm upraised against the sky, his hand now *firmly* clutching his new tool. In effect, he has crawled out of the geologic layers of time and escaped absolute subservience to Nature. He is now capable of dictating some of the terms of his own existence. A jump cut juxtaposes different stages of his mechanical skill, from tentative to confident. Slow motion cinematography further abstracts the action, emphasizing, along with the music, its broader significance in the evolution of humankind. In an extreme low-angle shot, Moonwatcher stands nearly erect, his face contorted with pleasure as he employs *both* hands to wield his club against the pile of bones. By cutting closer to him at an ever lower angle, the camera duplicates its approach to the monolith in the previous scene. But, in that earlier scene, the camera aligned itself more and more with Moon-watcher's point of view. In the present scene, we see the action more and more from the perspective of the potential victims of his aggression. Brief, cutaway shots of a tapir collapsing to the ground are purely subjective images from Moonwatcher's imagination. Drawing on the recent past (the monolith-Sun-Moon alignment) to reshape the present (the invention of bone technology), he now projects the revised present onto the potential future (the killing of tapirs).

Moonwatcher's invention of bone technology is a thing of grotesque beauty, yielding impressions of liberation *and* enslavement. The intense plea-sure he experiences as a result of his increased power over the world around him can of itself be incapacitating. Unable to contain his joy, Moonwatcher flings the bone club away in the scene's final shot. He is reduced from an imposing figure of muscular coordination to one of spastic hysteria. *Dr. Strangelove* exhibited a similar loss of self-control during his exhilarating ascent to power.

Another direct cut leads to the sixth episode of "The Dawn of Man." *Zarathustra* is gone. The pervasive stillness of Nature returns. But we are not back to square one. Moonwatcher enters the film frame and, glancing suspi-ciously all around him, greedily consumes the fruit of his revolutionary labors. The fantasy of tapirs falling before his new weapon has been realized. A for-mer competitor for food has now become food. Wider shots reveal that, despite his self-absorption, Moonwatcher's boon is shared by his tribal com-panions. The leader's invention has altered the routine of the entire commu-nity. Infants play with bones stripped of meat, beginning a tradition of learned technological skills. Meanwhile, tapirs continue to graze nearby. They have not yet adjusted to the lethal change in *their* environment.

Night returns, with the same visual and aural dominance as before. But this time *apeman* has changed. Instead of hiding inside their cave, a few mem-bers of the tribe venture outside, near the entrance. Fear of night's lurking dangers, real and imagined, is slowly being overcome. And that newfound confidence carries over, via another direct cut, into yet another variation on a previous scene.

We are transported into the middle of another screaming, gesticulating battle between two tribes of apemen for possession of the waterhole. But this time one of the tribal leaders clutches a bone club in his hand and stands a bit more erect than his rival. As it did during the invention of bone technol-ogy, progress occurs in a fitful rather than a smooth manner. Not yet fully confident in the use of his new tool, Moonwatcher refrains from attacking with it until his foe lunges at him and forces the issue. Startled, Moonwatcher delivers a disabling blow to his rival's head, followed by a furtive sequence of retreat and attack reminiscent of his initial approach to the monolith. His tribal students then join in on what is by now overkill. Members of the fallen leader's tribe cower nearby, then flee in terror, just as they would from a leopard. They are, if quicker to appreciate the danger than were the tapirs, baffled by the mysterious force confronting them. Moonwatcher's invention of bone technology transforms what had been a shouting contest into a lethal encounter. Standing nearly erect and roaring, Moonwatcher strikes a monstrous pose of defiance against anyone who would challenge his will.

Any story that spans great distances in time and space yet seeks to relate widely separated characters and events to one another must employ some kind of stylistic shorthand. "The Dawn of Man" depicts man's emergence as a technological being in a series of scenes portraying what he was before the change, how the change came about, and the consequences of it. Moonwatcher succumbs a second time to the thrill of his new power, after directing that power for the first time against one of his own kind. Beginning with a portrait of Moonwatcher framed against a vast and desolate landscape, the camera accompanies the *product* of his creative genius high into the sky where he hurls it. By metaphorical extension, we follow the man/machine relationship across the millennia to a future time. In both symbolic and physical terms, man breaks free of his terrestrial roots via his inventions, though it is interesting to note that the bone club has already begun to descend when the transition from prehistory to future occurs. In some respects, the disintegration of man's relationship to his technology has already commenced when we join it in the year 2001, despite first impressions to the contrary.

Moonwatcher's joyful roar of conquest fades into the past and is displaced by the sound of wind, similar to the winds of change at the beginning of "The Dawn of Man." Bypassing a long span of technological development, including the dubious achievements of *Dr. Strangelove, 2001* juxtaposes in glorious fashion the first human tool with the latest. In the blink of an eye, Moonwatcher's primitive bone club is displaced on screen by a similarly shaped, man-made spaceship orbiting the Earth. Had Kubrick executed this millennial jump cut before Moonwatcher killed his rival at the waterhole, the contrast between technology as something employed by man against man and technology as the apparently peaceful servant of man for man would have been less striking.

Reversing their order of appearance in "The Dawn of Man," machines appear before humans in the first scene from the year 2001. As it turns out, that reversal says much about who is a function of what in a human existence now totally dependant on technology. Originally a celebration of Nature on Earth, Johann Strauss's "The Blue Danube" Waltz is redeployed as an ode to humankind's liberation *from* terrestrial boundaries. Combining slow zooms and reverse zooms with tilts and pans (techniques which here lose some of their distinctions because of the absence of fixed reference points), Kubrick presents a lyrical impression of three-dimensional activity. Spaceships moving in relation to each other and to natural celestial bodies (often it is the *illusion* of movement created by camera position and motion, as in *Dr. Strangelove's* midair refueling scene) are refined examples of the same controlled order displayed by Moonwatcher wielding his bone club. But the harmony of space technology is, at first glance, free of the destructive violence evident in "The Dawn of Man" and *Dr. Strangelove*. Echoing humankind's visionary outreach, the camera moves repeatedly past and away from Earth, in one shot reaching out toward the Moon, where, we learn later, man has established a colonial foothold.

Various spacecraft and natural objects are rendered dance partners by their own graceful movements, by fluid camera movement, and by the presence of "The Blue Danube." But in spite of man's liberation from it, Earth remains at the center of this dance. Orbiting shuttles and satellites all adhere to the invisible security of its gravitational pull, while its visual presence within the black void of outer space provides emotional security. In contrast to its desolate and occasionally hostile face in "The Dawn of Man," Earth regarded from the perspective of men and women partially liberated from its boundaries appears as a beautiful abstraction, as sentimentally appealing as the glass paperweight that triggers warm memories (or fantasies) of childhood for the protagonist in *Citizen Kane.*

"The Blue Danube" continues as the camera cuts to the interior of a space shuttle. In the foreground, an ordinary ballpoint pen floats freely in the vehicle's weightless atmosphere, its shape and rotation recollecting Moonwatcher's airborne club and the spacecraft shown in the previous few shots. The direct cut from exterior to interior generates several ironic juxtapositions, and in its own way is as striking as the earlier transition from prehistory to 2001. The jump from bone club to spaceships implied a monumental leap in technological sophistication. The jump from spaceships to pen seems to reverse that impression. However, though a relatively simple tool in itself, the pen represents an invention (written language) no less complex or wondrous than space vehicles. Its power is more abstract but no less real.

More important than their physical appearances are the tools' contrasting relationships to their creators. The stately movement of spaceships is a controlled affair, making the waltz analogy appropriate. The pen, by contrast, floats at random, independently of human will, making the dance analogy ironic. Visible behind the pen are the listless arm and open hand of Dr. Heywood Floyd, the shuttle's sole passenger, asleep in his seat. He has lost his grip on the pen during a lapse of attention. And, through that otherwise trivial loss of control, Kubrick illustrates an important change in the relationship of man to his machines. Moonwatcher's technology was a simple, hands-on amplification of power. In Dr. Floyd's world, much of technology is a product of *collective* effort, operating beyond the hands and passions of individual man. The pen slips from Floyd's control, yet everything else about the space shuttle, on which he depends for both shelter and mobility in outer space, functions smoothly, either automated or under the direction of other people.

Though *2001* has been viewed so far only by audiences for whom space travel is not a routine experience, Kubrick postulates a future in which it has become so, at least for some people. From Heywood Floyd's vantage point, space travel is almost as routine as foraging for food was for apeman prior to the invention of the bone club. Several images convey to us the normalization and commercialization of space travel. A television screen on the back of the passenger seat in front of Dr. Floyd shows an automobile advertisement. Except for the fact that he is hundreds of miles above the Earth, Dr. Floyd could be napping in his easy chair back home. One of the most remarkable aspects of this and subsequent scenes is Kubrick's ability to create broad, passionately philosophical impressions out of otherwise mundane elements. Floyd's slumbering form, the television commercial, and the pen are all invested with aesthetic and moral definition far beyond what they derive from their immediate, trivial roles in the action. And that process of enhancement without distortion, of illuminating the extraordinary within the ordinary, continues as each new "trivial" element added contributes another layer of definition to the scene.

A flight attendant, dressed in a trim corporate uniform, enters the passenger cabin and retrieves Dr. Floyd's errant pen. She is an institutional figure cleaning up after a careless individual. But as an individual she is just as flawed as Dr. Floyd. Her movements are slow and awkward in the weightless environment. The graceful choreography of spaceships is not equaled by individual man or woman, whose feet graphically tell the tale in a beautiful close-up. Compared to earthbound apeman, her powers of mobility are incomparably greater, yet she appears pathetically uncoordinated in comparison with the vehicle in which she rides. Hers are a child's first steps, equivalent to Moonwatcher's clumsy first attempts to wield his bone club. Just as she is dependent on the shuttle to transport her through and shield her from outer space, the flight attendant relies on "grip shoes" to help her master the unfamiliar environment *within* that protective container. Her grip shoes bear a Pan American insignia — one of several recognizable corporate logos Kubrick uses to enhance our impression of space travel as a domesticated, institutional activity. Human existence in outer space is dominated by the vision of collective man, whose creative genius, organizational skills, and vast resources are vital to the survival of the individual. A "Caution" sign is visible in the doorway behind the flight attendant. It is the first of many guidelines provided by institutional man to the less diligent and more vulnerable individual.

When the camera cuts back to exterior shots, the shortcomings of individual man disappear. "The Blue Danube" plays again with no irony. As Dr. Floyd's shuttle approaches Hilton Space Station Five, a large structure in the shape of a double wheel, both objects appear on screen alongside the Earth. They are three separate but interrelated worlds, one natural and two artificial. The space station is dwarfed by and orbits around Earth. It is an artificial world unto itself but remains tethered to the Earth by gravitation and the need for resupply. The shuttle, in turn, is dwarfed by the space station. It adopts the larger vessel's rotation in order to dock with it. Like many human projects in Kubrick's films, the station is incomplete, with sections still under construction, just as individual man is still in the process of adjusting to conditions in outer space. The incompleteness of Hilton Space Station Five does not materially affect events to come, but it is symptomatic of ever-changing human existence and relates back to *Dr. Strangelove*, where the failure of Soviet officials to complete implementation of their Doomsday Machine by announcing its existence to the world rendered its deterrent capability null and void.

The landing approach of Heywood Floyd's shuttle to the space station is shown from a kaleidoscope of vantage points which, taken together, illustrate both man's navigational dependence on technology and the deceptiveness of any *single* vantage point. From the shuttle cockpit, with the camera in partly subjective alignment with the pilot, the space station appears to us through several visual frames, including a window and three computer screens. Each of these frames defines the space station in different terms and is roughly equivalent to *Dr. Strangelove*'s Big Board and, in a larger sense, to a movie screen. Numbers and equations fill one computer screen, a geometric navigational grid fills another, and graphs a third. The natural faculties of individual man are supplemented and sometimes replaced by highly refined, artificial perspectives generated by institutional man. Unlike Moonwatcher's handling of the bone club, maneuvering a spacecraft is too complicated a task for the individual to manage unaided. Therefore, he has fashioned for himself, through collective effort, an extra set of mechanical eyes, hands, lungs, skin, and brain. Within the space of a single widescreen image, Kubrick juxtaposes several distinct perceptual apertures, each supplying a different view of reality outside the shuttle. Coordination among these different views is echoed by the dance harmonies of Johann Strauss, which dominate the soundtrack to the exclusion of local sounds and thereby heighten our appreciation of the visual parallels being drawn.

The shuttle's cockpit window would seem to furnish a totally objective, natural view of the space station. But that is not quite true. Initially the station appears to rotate. But after the shuttle mimics that rotation in order to facilitate a docking maneuver, we get a second view through the same window. This time the station, though getting closer, appears fixed in space—

rock solid. In fact the station still rotates, but, because the shuttle and therefore the camera attached to it have changed orientation, our impression of the station is altered. A similar shift in perception occurs on board the space station. Initially, Kubrick gives us a boundless shot of outer space, with stars appearing to rotate around an invisible, fixed point. Visual containment occurs when the camera reverse zooms to incorporate an artificial frame around that initial impression. We are peering out into space through the open portal of the space station landing bay. The appearance of that artificial frame reduces the mild disorientation of our initial impression, which was like lying on the ground and looking up at the stars at night. It also implies, in the context of the previous shot from inside the shuttle cockpit, that the apparent rotation of stars around a fixed point is an illusion created by the camera's attachment to the space station. A subsequent, exterior shot breaks that illusion. Rotation formerly attributed to the stars returns to the station, which now appears tiny and fragile in the boundless and motionless (which, of course, is just another illusion rooted in another limited vantage point) void of outer space.

Lining all four sides of the landing bay are airtight compartments, each containing a group of men and women whose job it is to facilitate landings and take-offs. If the camera's perspective during the reverse-zoom shot is bound to and therefore limited by the space station and its rotation, it now overlaps and exceeds the separate vantage points of the various groups of landing bay personnel, each of which occupies a gravitational orientation different from the others and therefore has a somewhat different perspective of the view through the open portal. The aesthetic effect is rather like that of certain paintings by Caspar David Friedrich, in which we view Nature *with* his human figures but we also observe the *viewer* from a distance.

As Dr. Floyd's shuttle nears the space station, the camera glides forward between the station's double wheels and out toward deep space, as though eager to get on with the journey away from Earth. But there is an important stop to be made before that happens — a stop having to do with human adaptation and motivation.

"The Blue Danube" is displaced by the electric hum of sliding doors inside the space station. The doors are like theater curtains drawn aside to reveal a minidrama of the social order in outer space. The environment inside Hilton Space Station Five is a triumph of controlled yet informal routine. Official procedure is evident, but not oppressively so. Hilton employees in streamlined, modest uniforms assist visitors. Interaction is casually friendly but also very polite, unlike the frequent bickering that characterized apeman society. From his drab suit to the controlled manner and content of his speech, Dr. Floyd exemplifies the dominance of collective sensibilities. An unstated code of propriety governs individual behavior here, for the security and comfort of everyone concerned. Captain Mandrake and President Muffley would feel right at home. Generals Turgidson and Ripper and Dr. Strangelove would not.

Floyd is met by the head of station security — a title implying institutional regulation more strict than just a shared sense of decorum. But this official is unarmed, dressed as modestly as Dr. Floyd, and appears to intimidate no one. For all its emphasis on institutional control, *2001*'s depiction of society in outer space verges on the utopian. Its appeal is challenged less by the specter of totalitarian horrors (such as *Dr. Strangelove*'s elaborate plan for a postapocalyptic, underground society) than by subtler impressions of the negative effect a thoroughly mechanized environment might have on individual man.

Dr. Floyd's passage through a voice-print identification device indicates the extent to which institutional man regulates the movements of the individual in outer space. The mechanism for oppression certainly exists, but the spirit is largely absent. The many languages (including Russian) programmed into the device implies international access to the space station. *2001* is far removed from the Cold-War-fortress mentality of *Dr. Strangelove*. Public lost-and-found announcements play unobtrusively over the intercom. The space station operates and feels much like an airport terminal back on Earth. Among its pleasantly terrestrial features, not present on board Dr. Floyd's shuttle, is an artificially produced gravity.

Heywood Floyd's videophone call home is, like the first shuttle interior scene, another occasion where the film draws broadly significant impressions from what is for the character a mundane experience. Floyd calls his daughter, back on Earth, on the occasion of her birthday. A large videoscreen brings the shy, squirming, little girl into the phone booth with her father. Through a window behind him we see a spectacular, natural view of Earth, *un*naturally imbued with motion belonging to the space station to which Dr. Floyd and the camera are attached. The window and the videophone screen offer radically different perspectives of the same reality. Viewed from hundreds of miles away, the Earth reveals nothing of its tiny inhabitants. By contrast, the miracle of electronics brings one of those inhabitants into close proximity, while obliterating the much larger planet. Dr. Floyd is oblivious to the visual contradiction. But to viewers for whom space travel and videophones are not yet routine, the dichotomy is striking.

The miracle of videophone communication is not quite matched by the use to which Dr. Floyd puts it. His birthday greeting to his daughter is affectionate but uninspired. He says the conventional things, but not much more. In fact, his stale words seem more a buffer *against* strong emotional ties, which are stretched to the breaking point by the physical distances involved in space travel, than a means of conveying them. His love for his daughter is expressed *indirectly*, through the birthday gift he intends to get for her. By asking her to pick something more special than a telephone, her first choice, Floyd tries to elevate the occasion above the ordinary, which he is unable to do through words. The banality of some of the dialog in *2001*, not far removed from the frequent absurdity of dialog in *Dr. Strangelove*, betrays a smallness of vision counterpointed by Kubrick's expansive use of imagery and sound. But that banality is partly the result of the increasing isolation of individual man in the age of space travel, just as in *Strangelove* it is often a product of the freakish circumstances generated by nuclear deterrence. Floyd apologizes to his daughter for not being able to attend her birthday party, yet neither seems unduly upset about it. Separation has become a part of family routine.

Dr. Floyd's encounter with a group of Russian scientists aboard the space station follows the same collective protocols as his conversations with the head of station security and his daughter. The Russians are dressed just like the Americans, suggesting a blurring of national distinctions. Unlike General Turgidson and Ambassador de Sadesky, they share similar perspectives. They exchange news about family and friends. Elena, a scientist previously acquainted with Floyd, casually relates that her husband is working on an underwater project in the Baltic Sea and that as a result they do not see much of each other — much like the American and his daughter.

The first breech of decorum is committed unintentionally by Dr. Smyslov, who asks Floyd about a mysterious epidemic rumored to have broken out at the American lunar outpost Clavius. Though his demeanor scarcely changes, Floyd suddenly becomes defensive. He calmly yet firmly deflects the Russian's question with an appeal to a higher, institutional authority that both men respect: "I am not at liberty to discuss the matter." Under the strain of some traumatic occurrence on the Moon, a hint of Strangelovian Cold War political divisions returns to haunt an international, space-age utopia. But it is only a hint. Diplomacy conceals those divisions as Smyslov's concern about the consequences of a lunar epidemic for the Moon's other, international communities is suppressed by a unanimous desire to avoid confrontation. But, before dropping the matter, the Russian betrays his own hypocrisy by lowering his voice to a conspiratorial level so as not to be overheard by a passing space station employee. In other words, he would conceal from others (nonscientists) the state secret he would have Floyd reveal to him. Dr. Floyd, acting under orders from his government superiors, plants and then refuses to deny the rumor of an epidemic, thereby slyly encouraging the Russians to believe they have hit upon the truth. If they suspect an outbreak of disease at Clavius, the Russians are likely to stay away from the area, which is exactly what the Americans want.

The strategic isolation of Clavius (communication links are down and landing rights are being denied to foreign spacecraft) resembles that of Burpleson

Air Force Base, except that in *Dr. Strangelove* the instigator is a renegade individual (General Ripper), while in *2001* it is a collective ruling body. Everyone seated around the lounge table in this scene is aware that something of great significance has occurred at Clavius and that the United States has violated international protocols by concealing it. But their unanimous commitment to the *appearance* of international harmony overrides their curiosity and resentment. Tribal rivalries so evident in "The Dawn of Man" are muted in 2001, where peaceful cooperation is so important to survival and work in outer space. Embarrassed by his indiscretion, Dr. Smyslov silently appeals to Elena for a graceful way out of his confrontation with Dr. Floyd. She obliges by diverting the conversation back to pleasant small talk. Smyslov makes amends for his transgression by wishing the American the best of luck at Clavius, *whatever* his mission there may be. But, after Floyd departs, the scientists resume their conversation in their native Russian. Conflicts private and collective, though muted, have not disappeared from human existence in outer space.

Kubrick returns to a more abstract lyricism for Heywood Floyd's trip to the Moon onboard a second shuttle. "The Blue Danube" again displaces all local sound, or, in the case of exterior shots, the absence of sound. This shuttle is spherical, resembling both the Earth it leaves behind and the Moon to which it travels. And it functions as a world to its passengers. As during the previous shuttle scene, proportion is a function of relative position. As Floyd's vessel descends to the lunar surface, it is visually dwarfed by the new world, yet it in turn dwarfs the now-distant Earth. But from the vantage point of several space-suited individuals observing the landing from a distance, the shuttle and the Earth are equally dwarfed by the lunar landscape and the blackness of the cosmos.

The shuttle's occupants are indifferent to the visual splendor of outer space. Dr. Floyd has again fallen asleep in his chair. A flight attendant performs her duties in the same slow, cautious manner as her predecessor, while her colleague watches a televised martial arts contest. This trip to the Moon is at once passionately novel (for us, via the wide-ranging camera and the music) and casually routine (for the characters)— mind expanding and mind numbing. On one flight attendant's lap sits a food tray containing familiar vegetables to be ingested in an unfamiliar manner — through tubes. Institutional instructions for how to eat in a weightless environment are printed on the tray, another example of the individual's reliance on collective technology and guidelines when living in outer space.

A flight attendant enters the shuttle's automated galley to get a food tray dispensed by a corporate processor. With the aid of her grip shoes she executes a one hundred and eighty degree turn, then departs, upside down (from *our* unchanged perspective), into another weightless corridor. This simple, routine action on her part is elevated, thanks to the eloquence of Strauss and to Kubrick's economical camera work (shooting the scene in a single take and from a flat, frontal angle that emphasizes two-dimensional movement), into a dramatic example of how space travel scrambles old Earth perspectives. The effect is as exhilarating as it is disorienting. Up becomes down, and vice versa. Reinforcing that point, the camera retains its original orientation into the next shot, where the same attendant appears to enter the shuttle cockpit upside down. Then the camera revolves half circle to realign itself with her new vantage point.

Later, Dr. Floyd dines from a food tray. Another institutional "Caution" sign is visible in the background. And individual man once again proves his need of assistance. Floyd's attention is momentarily diverted, and the tray floats out of his lap. Like the errant pen from an earlier scene, this loss of control is at once trivial and symptomatic of individual man's weak grasp of his new environment (his expectations are still rooted in terrestrial experience) and of the technological tools he employs to overcome it. A more amusing example of that same maladaption occurs in the next scene. The graceful clarity of "The Blue Danube" counterpoints the clumsy bulk of printed instructions to a Zero Gravity Toilet, the very idea of which seems anachronistic. The humor is not in the instructions themselves, which are almost impossible to read, but in their inordinate length. The camera slowly reverse zooms to reveal Heywood Floyd studying those institutional guidelines with bemused concentration. If great achievements are made possible by technology in the year *2001*, once-simple activities are made complicated by new circumstances resulting from that progress. Revolutionary change is seldom smooth or coordinated in any field of human endeavor. This particular shot, as much as any other, exemplifies how 2001 brings the contradictions of human progress into illuminating alignment.

During exterior shots of the shuttle, its occupants are often visible as tiny figures in the windows. The vastness of outer space is juxtaposed with the extreme confinement of the people who have invented the means to traverse it. The shuttle's artificial interior light contrasts sharply with natural exterior light, visually reinforcing the discrepancy between those two environments. The shuttle is spaceman's version of apeman's cave, which afforded protection from the terrors of the primeval night. But apeman could leave his cave during the day. Man in space is strictly confined to his mechanical sanctuary, which is both a shield against Nature and an artificial environment that by its size and complexity mimics Nature. Technology has become the environmental challenge to man that Nature once was. Like the Moon and the Earth it resembles in shape, Dr. Floyd's shuttle is itself a new frontier for its passengers, not just a means of transportation *to* a new frontier. Machines loom so large in the life of man in outer space that they attain

Heywood Floyd's lunar shuttle displays a sphinx-like facial expression, with glowing eyes, foreshadowing the hostile emergence of HAL.

a kind of independent identity, at least in aesthetic terms. Kubrick gives Dr. Floyd's shuttle a "face" made up of various functional features on its hull. Windows become eyes. An airlock becomes a small, round mouth. This anthropomorphic impression is hinted at rather than hammered home in expressionistic fashion, as is the case with the worker-consuming "Moloch" machine in Fritz Lang's *Metropolis*. In *2001*, the relationship of individual man to collective technology is more ambivalent.

The shuttle's landing on the Moon is a crescendo of imagery and music, featuring elegant mechanical movement played out against the desolate lunar landscape. Rather than speeding up the action by editing out long stretches of the landing process, Kubrick lingers over and draws attention to it. The collective genius of man is evident in the graceful coordination of his machines, but man as a physical entity is no longer part of that harmony. Instead, he is captive to it. When Moonwatcher tossed his bone club into the sky, he also figuratively divorced man from the product of his creative will. Alexander Walker describes the price of technological power as follows: "For long sequences in the film the pace of people or objects on the move is perfectly controlled, calculated, predictable. Standardized movements are the conventional ones in space because they are the safe ones. Man has conquered the new environment, but the environment has controlled him, too, by compelling him to adopt other than his old, erratic, instinctive, human actions. Now he must program himself—become less of a human being, more of a machine"(Walker, 248–49).

Of course it could be argued that Moonwatcher's "erratic, instinctive" actions, like those of Alex in *A Clockwork Orange*, are no more a product of free will and not necessarily more admirable than the rigidity of movement imposed on him by conditions in outer space.

As with the previous shuttle's approach to Hilton Space Station Five, the lunar landing is executed by individual man employing multiple vantage points: natural sight supplemented by computer screen abstractions. Instead of landing directly on the lunar surface, the shuttle comes to rest on a landing pad inside a giant metal dome that opens to receive it. As its rounded shape suggests, the dome constitutes a *second* artificial environment separating Dr. Floyd from lethal Nature. Both it and the shuttle are inside-out variations on Earth. The dome opens with the same, precise, unvaried motion with which the shuttle approaches it.

As the mechanical landing pad completes the landing process by lowering the shuttle and its passengers into the protective embrace of Clavius, "The Blue Danube" concludes with an exquisitely slow rendition of its main theme, followed by a whirling flourish that punctuates the completion of Heywood Floyd's routine yet extraordinary journey from the Earth to the Moon. The shuttle descends into an enormous, red-lit chamber equivalent to the space station's landing bay, with tiny outcroppings of men and women visible in airtight chambers along either side. One artificial world descending into another, the shuttle again shows its "face," with eyes glowing brightly, like those of the leopard in "The Dawn of Man." But the shuttle's expression is ambiguous, sphinx-like rather than malevolent. After all, technology in 2001 greatly expands human capabilities and horizons. The price it exacts for that benefit is not immediately evident, and not fully realized until the advent of HAL. Visible behind the shuttle is the vague outline of a second, even larger "face" belonging to the Clavius landing bay. Meanwhile, the face of individual man is too small to be discerned among these mechanical giants.

Paralleling his conversation with Russian scientists, Heywood Floyd's conference with Clavius officials is a model of decorum, matched by the classical modesty and muted colors of their windowless meeting room. Contrast this set with the War Room in *Dr. Strangelove*. Both prominently feature conference tables. *Dr. Strangelove*'s is big and round, with government officials seated around it vying for power to control events. *2001*'s is small and rectangular, open at one end to accommodate a podium, which focuses collective attention and authority on *one* person. The walls are mostly covered by large lighting panels whose practical function is paralleled by a symbolic one. The panels are analogous to movie screens in general and to *Dr. Strangelove*'s Big Board in particular. Unlike the Big Board, however, they reflect nothing, which seems appropriate for a collective exercise in obfuscation so thorough that its most important topic (the discovery of an alien artifact on the Moon) is never directly mentioned.

Dr. Floyd and Clavius officials chat amiably before the meeting, while an official photographer takes official photographs for the official record of this important occasion. He performs his task with enthusiasm, capturing

Dr. Floyd's group from a variety of angles and distances. But his thoroughness is an illusion. He is recording a *staged* prelude to the main event, which does not begin until he departs. He is no investigative journalist. The limits of his mission are strictly determined by the authority of the people he photographs.

After obligatory social pleasantries, Dr. Floyd steps up to the podium and takes charge of the conference, on behalf of a higher political power known as The Council. Each person around the table has a notebook of some sort in front of him, yet no one uses it to challenge Dr. Floyd the way General Turgidson challenged President Muffley. Protest occurs, but it is even more discreet than what Dr. Smyslov offered aboard the space station. Only indirectly, through Dr. Floyd himself, do we learn that some of the Clavius staff object to the cover story about an epidemic. And each time he mentions such an objection, Floyd prefaces it with a mild chuckle that aesthetically diminishes its significance.

While standing at the podium, Dr. Floyd is flanked by two flags which collectively define him and his colleagues. One is the flag of the United States. The other denotes a larger, international solidarity that overlaps and is, under present circumstances, contradicted by the first.

Dr. Floyd's speech is almost as colorless as the lighting panels that illuminate him. He describes recent events on the Moon as "among the most significant in the history of the world," yet his flat tone of voice understates rather than conveys the emotional implications of those events. Unlike Moonwatcher, Floyd distances himself and his colleagues from the intense passions of revolutionary experience. And he is an apologist for The Council's effort to control the reactions of emotionally fragile individuals. He finds "personally embarrassing" the government secrecy and the distress it causes to family and friends of Clavius personnel, but he "accepts the need for it." In other words, as an individual he objects, but as a member of The Council he condones government deception. He endorses the cover story because he distrusts individual man: "The potential for cultural shock and social disorientation contained in the present situation, if the facts were prematurely and suddenly made public without adequate preparation and conditioning" reduces individual citizens to the status of children. "Adequate preparation and conditioning" is equivalent to the human reliability tests in *Dr. Strangelove* and, on a more extreme level, to the Ludovico Technique in *A Clockwork Orange*. Dr. Floyd and the Council would be horrified to know that the specter of private instability they fear lurks inside the very machine they will choose to lead an expedition in search of answers to the mystery they now conceal from their fellow citizens.

Dr. Floyd casually reminds his audience that formal oaths of secrecy must be obtained from all who have knowledge of the true facts behind the cover story. In *Dr. Strangelove* and especially in *A Clockwork Orange*, the individual's word of honor counts for nothing. His stability and obedience must be tested and conditioned before it can be trusted.

Heywood Floyd's third shuttle trip, from Clavius to site TMA-1, is a variation on the first two. "The Blue Danube," which previously highlighted the grace and beauty of the technology which makes space travel possible, is replaced here by Gyorgy Ligeti's "Lux Aeterna," or eternal light. Echoing the immensity and indifference of the bleak lunar landscape and the starlit universe beyond, "Lux Aeterna" is equivalent to the oppressive stillness of Nature in "The Dawn of Man." The Moon is to Dr. Floyd and his colleagues what the Earth was to apeman millennia ago. Vistas of ageless rock formations and vast, empty plains render man and his machines puny and tenuous by comparison. But closer shots of the shuttle give us glimpses of passengers moving around inside, shielded from Nature and largely oblivious to the gloom and wonder conveyed by the music.

From the pilot's perspective, inside the shuttle cockpit, the bleak lunar landscape appears as a physically and emotionally manageable phenomenon, neatly contained within the window frames and surrounded by artificial red light. Pulling back from the cockpit and entering the passenger cabin, the camera gives us a very different impression of man's latest suit of armor. As seen from the cabin, which is bathed in blue-white light, the red-lit features of the cockpit form yet another mechanical "face." But instead of peering outside at the natural world with individual man, this face seems to scrutinize the men inside, and with a vague disapproval.

One of Dr. Floyd's colleagues picks up a container and carries it through the cabin to his companions. Its elaborate label leads us to expect that it contains something vital to their mission. Contrary to expectation, that something is lunch. Institutional man leaves few things to chance, or private whim, in outer space. Even the simplest tasks are elaborately prepared.

Dr. Floyd and the other passengers wear spacesuits in preparation for a trip outside. Bulky with insulation, the suits will provide an essential layer of protection for individual man in a lethal environment. They are, in effect, miniature spaceships, supplying warmth and oxygen, though not mobility. Because they conform roughly to the contours of the human body, they have the aesthetic effect of transforming man's natural appearance. The thick silver fabric is not just an extension of man's will, as the bone club was of Moonwatcher's; it is a second skin to which he is physiologically bound. Increasingly in *2001* we must view man through the technological armor he creates for himself by collective effort. His artificial second skin, or mask, generates dramatic impressions that may either conform to or contradict impressions generated by his natural appearance. Like the elaborate costumes, hair styles, makeup, and formal poses in *Barry Lyndon*, technological surfaces in *2001* abstract our perception of the characters. But man in space is more profoundly dependent on his institutional trappings than he was in eighteenth-century Europe. And that increasing dependence on the product of his creative effort is linked in ironic counterpoint to his triumph over the forces of Nature to which he was originally subject.

Dr. Floyd and his companions casually discuss the state of food in outer space, remarking on the improvement in methods for making it taste more like Earth food. Terrestrial standards of reference are deeply rooted. Earth remains the spiritual if no longer exclusively the physical home of man, just as many immigrants who came to America clung for a time to the culture of the "old country." The topic of food also serves the men as a means of emotional containment when their conversation switches from the mundane to the momentous. One of the men congratulates Floyd on giving a fine speech to "beef up" morale at Clavius. Maintaining the same, casual demeanor they exhibited while talking about food processing, the three scientists turn their attention to the extraordinary discovery at TMA-1. They reduce a great mystery to a manageable commonplace, which may seem absurd and pathetic to those of us observing their behavior from the security of a theater seat or a living room sofa, but is perhaps more understandable to someone caught up in such an event. Film, like any art, can give us a taste of disturbing subjective experience while at the same time furnishing us with a broader, more detached, and critical perspective.

The scientists' conversation reveals that the unidentified object at TMA-1 was detected by one of man's mechanical eyes, which made visible to the human eye an otherwise invisible magnetic anomaly beneath the surface of the Moon. Like the computer screen images that help pilots navigate spacecraft, this is another technological enhancement which helps man see and master his environment. At the same time, however, those enhancements can diminish his emotional perceptions by removing him several times from the object he ponders. Floyd considers the implications of "deliberately buried" in the same dispassionate manner with which he expressed "complete sympathy" for the Clavius personnel who objected to the epidemic cover story. Meanwhile, a colleague offers him a cup of coffee, keeping the topic of TMA-1 incidental to lunch. Floyd sums up the evidence presented to him with characteristic understatement: "You guys have certainly come up with something." So unlike Moonwatcher, who reacted to the monolith and then to the invention of bone technology with emotional abandon, the three scientists practice emotional detachment like a religion. They permit themselves a few mild profanities in reference to TMA-1, but even these tepid outbursts are tempered by mild laughter.

TMA-1 is an excavated pit containing a half-buried monolith identical to the one in "The Dawn of Man." Illuminated by amber lights and walled in by metal panels, the pit is an oasis of artificial symmetry in an expanse of asymmetrical moonscape, starkly outlined by Earthlight. In "The Dawn of Man," the monolith appeared to apeman in a purely natural setting. This time, man has traveled far and dug deep to uncover it. The hole he has dug and reinforced forms, when viewed from a distance, a horizontal rectangle analogous to the vertical monolith. Both, whether created by human or alien intelligence, are breathtaking deviations from Nature, bold statements of will. The combination of amber light, gleaming metallic walls, and mysterious object give TMA-1 the look of a religious shrine, picking up the relationship between man and monolith approximately where it left off in "The Dawn of Man." But man himself has changed. He does not regard the mysterious object in quite the same way he once did.

A hand-held camera accompanies Dr. Floyd's group down into the pit. Ligeti's *Requiem* returns to the soundtrack, repeating its impression of vaguely religious passion from "The Dawn of Man." The passion of Dr. Floyd, however, is secular and scientific, rendering the music misleading and ironic. He and his companions approach the monolith cautiously, though not as furtively as apeman. Part of the reason for that caution is the bulkiness of their spacesuits and the unfamiliarity of lunar gravity. Their slow, deliberate movements give them the false appearance of reverence. Floyd circles the monolith, then approaches it, exhibiting none of Moonwatcher's hysterical agitation. In a beautiful close-up, he delicately touches the alien artifact. Like Moonwatcher's contact, it is an exquisitely tender moment of exploration. But there are important differences between the two encounters. Moonwatcher's hand was hairy and bestial. He was us, yet not us. Heywood Floyd is certainly one of us, but his hand is enclosed in an airtight glove that is part of his spacesuit. What we see making contact with and examining the monolith is the mechanical "face" of a man's hand. And because technology is vital to man's existence in outer space, it aesthetically intrudes on our perception of him and his activities.

TMA-1's religious aura dissipates when one of the scientists herds his companions together in front of the monolith for what amounts to a vacation snapshot. Apeman saw the monolith as an unfathomable mystery, arousing terror and fascination. To the scientists, the monolith's shape and the fact of its deliberate burial give it tantalizing definition. It is an astounding discovery, but not quite so overwhelming an intrusion into their lives as it was for apeman.

The scientists' relatively complacent attitude toward the monolith is shattered when it suddenly emits a piercing, high-pitched radio signal, taking them completely by surprise. They stagger back in confusion and pain, their photo session rudely disrupted. Emotionally and intellectually shielded from the shock of the Unknown, they are unexpectedly assaulted on a *physical* level, almost like the leopard attack on apeman. The scientists cannot even clasp their hands over their ears. For a moment their spacesuits become traps as well as sanctuaries, the monolith's powerful radio signal perhaps reaching them through the transceivers in their otherwise essential helmets.

Like the analogous discovery scene in "The Dawn of Man," this scene concludes with a subjective shot from the principal character's point of view. With Dr. Floyd, we see the Sun and Earth in linear alignment with the monolith's upper edge. The lesson he and his colleagues derive from the alien object will be different from Moonwatcher's. They pursue its electronic signal further out into space in order to acquire more knowledge. But for both Moonwatcher and Heywood Floyd, progressive change occurs only in the calm, reflective aftermath of their traumatic encounters with the Unknown.

Part Three of *2001*, "Jupiter Mission: 18 Months Later," pushes the human odyssey into space far beyond the comforting proximity of Earth. Isolation, dependence on technology, and a sense of uselessness become even more pronounced in the existence of individual man. The scene begins with a portrait of deep space from which the reassuring sights of Earth and even Moon are missing. Jupiter Mission spaceship *Discovery* then enters and fills the screen. It looks and moves like a world unto itself, obliterating our view of distant stars. Its forward section recalls the shape of Heywood Floyd's second shuttle. It serves its occupants in the same fashion, but to a much greater extent. The *Discovery* astronauts have no other worlds to which they can transfer. Situated halfway between Earth and Jupiter, *Discovery* is literally everything to its occupants, just as Earth was to apeman. Its slow, relentless, planet-like movement across the screen makes it seem more like a force of Nature than a product of human design, serving human will. In such a context, the melancholy lyricism of the Adagio from Aram Khachaturian's *Gayene Ballet* is less a celebration of technology, as was "The Blue Danube," than a disturbing echo of man's confinement within a wholly artificial environment.

Two subsequent shots modify our initial impression of *Discovery*. From a greater distance, the spaceship appears as a small, man-made outpost in the black void of outer space — a visual symbol of its creators' smallness and isolation. There can be no waltz here, because *Discovery* has no visible dance partners. Thus, in the opening three shots of this scene, the spaceship yields contradictory impressions rooted in different perspectives. It is both huge and tiny, imposing and fragile, natural-like and man-made. A side view reveals the vessel's elongated shape, its round head and bulky engines connected by a thin support structure. It vaguely resembles Moonwatcher's bone club, but with important differences. Moonwatcher imparted motion to his otherwise immobile tool. The astronauts aboard *Discovery* are propelled through space *by* their technology. Figuratively speaking, it holds them instead of the other way around.

Inside the spaceship, man at first appears to be reasonably well adapted to its artificial environment. Dressed as though working out at the local gym, Frank Poole jogs comfortably around the interior of *Discovery*'s sphere, where an artificially generated gravity lends him a familiar stability. Khachaturian's somber Adagio accompanies us inside the spaceship. Out of emotional sync with our first impression of Poole, it soon falls into harmony with subsequent images that reveal the loneliness and boredom of man on a deep space journey.

Expanding on a theme of visual disorientation begun with the flight attendant who switched galley corridors during Dr. Floyd's second shuttle trip, Kubrick films Poole from an angle ninety degrees off normal. The artificial environment of *Discovery* features a bewildering variety of gravitational planes with which the camera continually realigns itself. "Correcting" its perspective to match Poole's, it tracks him around the carousel. He casually shadowboxes as he jogs. But within this routine activity, the camera ferrets out a hint of emotional strain. Following from behind, we see the astronaut throw punches apparently aimed at three hibernation chambers, each of which contains an unconscious crew member, and at several empty crew chairs. Kubrick does not overplay an impression that his character probably does not share. Not all of Poole's punches are directed at targets implying the absence or insignificance of human beings. But those that are seem to be silent protests by one astronaut battling feelings of loneliness and worthlessness in an empty, automated environment from which he cannot escape. Aboard *Discovery*, technology's relationship to individual man is both supportive and destructive. Without the hibernation chambers, the spaceship's resources could not sustain three extra crew members during the long voyage to Jupiter. On the other hand, those same crew members are rendered all but dead by the machines which allow them to make the trip.

Mission Commander Dave Bowman's first appearance is as ambivalent as his partner's. He enters the sphere through a revolving, round corridor. But we see him as reflected off the round, red lens, or "eye," of the ship's main computer, designated HAL. This creates the optical illusion that Dave is trapped inside the computer, which in a sense is true for both astronauts, since they are physically confined to *Discovery* and its various extensions (pods and spacesuits). HAL is *Discovery*'s brain and central nervous system, coordinating and supervising all aspects of its operation. Our initial impression of Dave Bowman as a prisoner of the computer foreshadows later developments in their relationship. Yet Dave, like Frank, exhibits no conscious signs of discontent. He seems, at first glance, fully acclimated to his environment.

Bowman enters the carousel on a different gravitational plane than the one occupied by Poole. But their isolation from each other is more profound than that. They barely speak to each other, not out of hostility, but as a result of their separate routines and their emotional adjustment to a long period of isolation. The social amenities practiced so thoroughly by Heywood Floyd and his colleagues back home lose some of their potency way out here. Bowman, dressed in work clothes, has evidently come from attending to assigned duties. Poole, wearing a bathrobe, eating breakfast and watching television, seems to have just gotten out of bed. Sealed in one of the hibernation chambers is a third astronaut who is oblivious to the comings and goings of the other two. His routine is wholly removed from theirs, while their routines are largely removed from each other's. Dave fetches a food tray from the automatic dispenser and sits down beside Frank. Their meals, probably breakfast for one and supper for the other, appear identical. The food consists of unrecognizable substances of the same texture but different colors. Dr. Floyd's comment about the improvement of space cuisine apparently does not hold true this far out in the solar system, where man must make concessions to time, distance, and rate of consumption. But Bowman and Poole are adaptable. They consume their strange meal as if it were plain old ham and eggs.

To help the astronauts maintain an emotionally reassuring link to native Earth, television programming is broadcast to them via the giant communications dish facing backwards atop their forward-moving spaceship. The program's insipid theme music clashes with and then displaces the brooding, background Adagio. The former is almost an antidote to the latter, which conveyed to us an underlying discontent aboard the spaceship.

Within the safely contained television screen frame, a BBC newscaster, dressed in the same drab manner as Dr. Floyd earlier, employs a dispassionate tone of voice to verbally reduce the Jupiter Mission to comfortable dimensions. His interview of the spaceship's crew is superficial rather than probing, just like the program's theme music vis-à-vis the Adagio. Even in technical terms, the telecast presents a distorted, comfortable version of reality. The interviewer explains that a seven-minute delay between transmission of questions from Earth and reception of answers from *Discovery* has been edited out of the tape. The far-flung spaceship and its crew are thereby brought into alignment with Earth expectations, where instant communication is taken for granted by the average television audience. In other words, the telecast sidesteps most of the physical and emotional challenges posed by deep space travel. Kubrick, by contrast, lingers over them.

In his 1974 book *Supership*, Noel Mostert wrote about life aboard giant oil tankers plodding through the oceans of the world, operated by small crews living inside massive, largely automated structures. During a trek through the lower depths of one such vessel, Mostert began to appreciate why, as reported to him by one of the ship's officers, *2001* was so unpopular among tanker crews when it first came out. Many of the *Discovery* scenes must have cut close to the bone for men and women oppressed by feelings of isolation, boredom, and uselessness (Mostert, 95).

Bowman and Poole watch the Earth telecast dispassionately. Even more than Heywood Floyd during a videophone conversation with his daughter, the astronauts repress or filter their yearnings for home. The difference between Frank and Dave in the interview and Frank and Dave watching it on television is striking. When not performing for the folks back on Earth by putting a happy face on the Mission, they are stoically silent. Well trained and self-disciplined, they do not allow the conditions of life on board *Discovery* to interfere with their mission. But their emotional dormancy betrays the price of that accommodation.

Despite its false impression of life aboard *Discovery*, the television interview is a useful tool for explaining the design and purpose of the hibernation chambers. While in suspended animation their occupants do not dream, making their condition as much like death as sleep, until such time as institutional man chooses to revive them. Faces glimpsed through frost-encrusted windows look like those of corpses. The only visible traces of life are squiggly lines on a computer screen, denoting biological functions. Once again, individual man existing in outer space is perceived by us through a technological mask. We learn later in the film that the three hibernating astronauts were brought aboard *Discovery* already unconscious for a reason other than the conservation of resources. And that reason involves institutional man's distrust of the individual. Full knowledge of the mission might adversely affect the astronauts' emotional stability during the long, arduous journey to Jupiter. The hibernating crew members know about the alien monolith but are in no position to suffer from or disclose that knowledge. Bowman and Poole, meanwhile, are left conscious in order to help facilitate the journey, but they are not informed of the alien connection. "Emergency Awake Procedures" printed on the hibernation chambers suggest that institutional distrust of individual man does not override concern for his safety. Still, the line "Their efforts won't be utilized until we approach Jupiter," verbally reduces the hibernating astronauts to little more than pawns in a collective plan.

HAL is the technological bridge linking the fragmented perspectives of institutional and individual man, combining the scope and detachment of the former with the feelings and motivation of the latter. Both perspectives are evident during the interview. We see HAL as a single eye, or camera lens, surrounded by twelve computer screens, only one of which carries the telecast while the others monitor various aspects of the ship's operation. The astronauts, by contrast, attend to only one screen at a time. HAL's attention span is much broader than theirs. In another shot, we see the two astronauts from HAL's subjective point of view. They appear as small, nondescript parts of a larger whole that the computer is designed to oversee. We subsequently learn that HAL has "eyes" strategically placed all over the ship, making it easy for the astronauts to communicate with him but also giving him the potential, if not the inclination, to play Big Brother. The voice of HAL combines the vocal capacity of individual man with the mechanical rhythms of technology and the emotional detachment of collective man. It is a voice at once beautiful in its precision and disturbing for its lack of emotional range. The dispassionate sound of HAL's voice is sometimes undercut by the content of his answers during the interview. The interviewer detects self-awareness and pride in the computer when HAL describes his role in the Jupiter Mission and the spotless performance of his 9000 lineage. Unlike the five astronauts, especially the three in hibernation, HAL is put to the "fullest possible use" by the Jupiter Mission. Asked if he is "frustrated by your dependence on human beings to carry out actions," HAL replies, "Not in the slightest. I enjoy working with people." His dispassionate tone of voice suggests an immunity from emotional bias, yet the words "I enjoy" imply that emotion is indeed a factor in his perceptions. There is a disconcerting imbalance between his enormous responsibility within the Mission and his polite expression of respect for the astronauts whom he shelters, informs, feeds, and monitors. He speaks of them as equals, yet he is so obviously superior in many ways. Can a Napoleon relate as an equal to someone whose destiny he controls?

The nature of HAL's consciousness is a question central to any interpretation of *2001*. The interviewer notes that scientists disagree among themselves about whether HAL's reactions are a product of or merely mimic consciousness. Dave Bowman provides a clue to the mystery: "He acts like he has genuine emotions. Of course, he's programmed that way to make it easier for us to talk to him." So HAL's projection of emotion is a product of collective man's attempt to address individual man's need for companionship during prolonged space voyages. The most advanced piece of technology in *2001*, HAL is the culmination of all the "faces" vaguely detectable in less sophisticated machines seen earlier. He combines the breadth of vision and responsibility of collective man with the needs and motivations (or at least the appearance of them) of an individual. Even his name, HAL, is an odd mixture of the two, being both a common name for a person and an acronym of the computer's corporate origins.

One of the underlying ironies of this and later scenes is that HAL seems more human, in some respects, than either Bowman or Poole, and far more than the hibernating astronauts. But machines are not really more human than man in the year 2001; they have simply become more eloquent. The strain of life in outer space has forced the astronauts to become less emotional, more controlled. By an accidental overlapping of two unrelated design specifications, HAL unites aspects of perception that have become fragmented in man. As a machine with a great capacity to absorb and correlate information, the 9000 computer has, we discover later, been granted certain knowledge of the mission withheld from Dave and Frank because it might upset them and adversely affect their performance of duty. On the other hand, by virtue of his compatibility programming, HAL is possibly rendered vulnerable to the same emotional weakness of which the astronauts are suspected. Can the semblance of a personality cope with both the experience of a deep space journey and the full knowledge of its revolutionary goal?

Khachaturian's Adagio returns to the soundtrack in the next scene, which starts with another exterior shot of *Discovery* moving through outer space. But unlike exterior shots of Dr. Floyd's shuttle heading for the Moon, there is no sense of progress. The spaceship inches ever so slowly through a universe that appears unchanged, at least to the naked eye.

Frank Poole viewing a birthday greeting from his parents, via a telecast from Earth, is a more extreme variation on Heywood Floyd's videophone conversation with his daughter on a similar occasion. Poole shows no visible reaction to the message, which, because it is tape delayed, is an even more indirect form of communication than what the Floyds employed. He watches his parents' message the way most of us would a television program. It's not that he doesn't care about them; it's just that they are not in direct contact with him, plus he cannot afford the luxury of sentiment in his state of solitude. Superbly self-disciplined, he confines his reaction to a request of HAL to adjust his headrest as he lies on a tanning bed under a sunlamp (an artificial substitute for the real thing, as in General Turgidson's bedroom in *Dr. Strangelove*). He seems almost pampered. But the Adagio expresses his desolation for him. And HAL is not quite the humble servant he appears to be in this scene.

Mr. and Mrs. Poole's video message to their son is similar to Dr. Floyd's conversation with his daughter. Feelings of love and the pain of separation are muted and rendered manageable by expressing them in an oblique and trite manner. News about friends getting married, government payments getting straightened out, Frank's celebrity status with his mother's grade-school pupils, and obligatory regards to Dave Bowman may seem inadequate or even pathetic expressions of affection, but they are at least attempts to convey strong emotion under difficult circumstances. For a moment Frank's mother drops her guard and bestows a "God bless" on her son, in a hushed voice that betrays her deep concern for him. But she wants to cheer him up, not upset him. Toward that end, she and Frank's father conclude their message with a jolly rendition of "Happy Birthday," which counterpoints the Adagio that expresses the underlying sadness of all three characters. The scene concludes with HAL wishing Poole a happy birthday and Frank acknowledging it in the same perfunctory manner, almost the same breath, in which he asks the computer to return his headrest to its original position. The astronaut is not being rude; he is merely evading emotions which could aggravate his acute loneliness.

During Mr. and Mrs. Poole's taped message, Bowman is shown lying in his sleep chamber. Though not as extreme as that of the three hibernating astronauts, Dave's daily routine is isolated from Frank's as a concession to mission requirements. They work and rest in separate shifts. For the most part, companionship is provided by HAL.

One type of companionship HAL provides to the astronauts is a recreational challenge in an artificial environment swept clean of the natural hazards which threatened apeman. Frank Poole engages the computer in a game of chess — an abstract and safe form of competition rendered even more abstract by the substitution of computer-screen images for the traditional game board and gaming pieces. This is chess on HAL's terms. Man finds himself at an ever greater distance from his own creations. HAL's superior breadth of vision is obvious from the many other duties he attends to, illustrated on numerous computer screens, while competing with the astronaut. Poole, meanwhile, concentrates all of his attention on the game. Even so, HAL outmaneuvers and defeats him. But the terms of surrender are not harsh. HAL is apologetic in triumph. Frank is gracious in defeat. In a broader sense, however, Poole's "I resign" is a concession of power and authority by individual man to the technological embodiment of his collective genius and a hint of worse things to come.

Reversing the arrangement of the previous two scenes, Kubrick explores Dave Bowman's activities aboard *Discovery* while Frank Poole sleeps. HAL, of course, requires no rest periods. Though dressed in his uniform, Dave's services, like Frank's, are seldom essential to the operation of the spaceship. He passes his time drawing sketches of his hibernating crewmates. A backtracking camera accompanies him on a leisurely walk around the carousel, as it did Poole's shadowboxing jog earlier. Once again, Khachaturian's Adagio echoes an unspoken malaise. The music ends when HAL speaks, which dispels the astronaut's self-absorption. "Good evening, Dave" is the computer's concession to Dave's terrestrial orientation. In deep space "day" and "night" are quaint anachronisms. HAL seems equally patronizing when he notes an improvement in the quality of Bowman's sketches, which we see in a subjective shot from the computer's point of view. Dave has depicted his subjects in stark black and white, looking very confined and passive in their sarcophagal chambers. Like Poole, Bowman does not openly voice dissatisfaction with conditions aboard *Discovery* or perhaps even admit it to himself. But his drawings, along with Frank's figuratively targeted shadow punches, indirectly express it.

The first hint that HAL, too, is feeling the strain (or the semblance of strain) of a long and lonely space voyage occurs when, his voice becoming quiet and conspiratorial, he asks the astronaut a "personal" question. Their exchange is shown in alternative close-ups, suggesting that this is a more than

casual dialog. He tenta-
tively inquires if Dave has
had "second thoughts"
about the mission, then
confesses his own. It is the
first indication that HAL's
compatibility program-
ming might be interfering
with his mission responsibilities. By commenting
on "rumors about some-
thing being dug up on the
Moon" and the security
precaution of putting three
crew members aboard *Dis-
covery* already in hibernation, HAL is either seeking
a companion with whom
to share the emotional
burden of knowledge he
already possesses or is
probing for signs that
Dave is brooding about
the mission and is there-
fore a potential danger to
it. Bowman is suspicious.
"You're working up your
crew psychology report,"
he speculates. In other
words, he thinks HAL is
acting as Mission Control's
agent against him. The
"crew psychology report"
is *2001*'s equivalent of *Dr.
Strangelove*'s human reliability tests, the Ludovico
stage demonstration in *A
Clockwork Orange*, and
Stuart Ullman's field
report on prospective
employee Jack Torrance in
The Shining. All four are

On board shapeship Discovery, *astronauts Dave Bowman
(Keir Dullea, standing), Frank Poole (Gary Lockwood,
asleep), and their hibernating colleagues lead mostly solitary existences, their daily routines separate from each other.*

examples of institutional man checking up on the reliability of individual man. HAL's motivation for discussing Mission secrets with Bowman remains ambiguous. If he really intends to cultivate the astronaut as a friend and ally, Dave's knowledge of the computer's supervisory function on behalf of Mission Control blocks any real candor between them. HAL's sheepish apology would seem to confirm Bowman's suspicion.

HAL's sudden disclosure of the impending malfunction of *Discovery*'s AE-35 unit is either one institutional function (monitoring the spaceship's electronic network) overriding another (monitoring crew psychology) or a desperate attempt to divert attention from his rejected plea for conspiratorial alliance with Dave. If the latter is true, HAL's reputation for perfection works against him. Expected to predict mechanical failures aboard *Discovery* before they occur, and even to specify the manner of failure ("The unit will remain fully operational until it fails"), HAL is as inescapably locked into his prediction as the Soviets were into the programming of their Doomsday Machine in *Dr. Strangelove*.

The retrieval of the AE-35 unit produces a dazzling array of visual and aural impressions. An overhead shot of Poole at work reverse zooms to incorporate Bowman, also at work but standing apart and ninety degrees removed from the gravitational orientation of his partner. Each man appears to occupy a world of his own, yet for the first time we see both of them on duty at the same time, working as a team instead of alone or with HAL. At last they have a challenge to make them feel useful within the paternalistic confines of *Discovery*. Khachaturian's Adagio has faded from the soundtrack, its evocation of lethargy, arising in part from too much security, never to return. Many of the images of Bowman and Poole at work are subjective camera shots from HAL's various vantage points throughout the spaceship. From his perspective the renewed vigor of and alliance between the two men is a dangerous thing.

Moving slowly and cautiously, the astronauts transit the ship through a rotating shaft that takes them from one gravitational plane to another, like the flight attendant in the galley of Dr. Floyd's shuttle. Their caution extends into the next scene, in a different form, where they consult Mission Control before acting on the AE-35 problem. The voice of Mission Control is so formal and precise that it rivals HAL's as an expression of institutional dispassion. Even at a distance of millions of miles, collective man is still the voice of authority for the astronauts.

Dave Bowman's spacewalk outside *Discovery* is a dramatic demonstration of the extent to which individual man must conform to the pace, the shape, and the sound of machines that allow him to exist in a hostile environment. A tracking shot follows him through a corridor leading to the pod bay. The corridor constitutes one layer of artificial skin. Dave's spacesuit constitutes another. Shown from behind, the astronaut's face is not visible. We see man through the aesthetic filter of his suit of armor and hear him through the hissing of his pressurized air supply.

Inside the pod bay, extra spacesuits in assorted colors hang from a rack. They are artificial abstractions of the human form, clinically separated into their component parts. Helmets suspended above suits yield an impression of human fragmentation similar to the decorations on Alex's costume and some of the art objects in *A Clockwork Orange*. But *2001*'s spacesuits are practical, necessary devices. Only on a symbolic level do they make a moral statement. One of the helmets is missing its "body," currently being used by Frank Poole elsewhere in the ship. The visual suggestion of decapitation coincidentally foreshadows Dave Bowman's predicament several scenes later.

The spherical pods are smaller replicas of their larger parent, *Discovery*, which in turn resembles Earth in its relationship to individual man. But with their mechanical arms and mouth-like windows, the pods are also a cross between the planet-like spaceship and the more human-like spacesuits.

Dave Bowman's departure from *Discovery*, like Dr. Floyd's approach to Hilton Space Station Five, is shown from a wide variety of perspectives, each yielding a different dramatic impression. In extreme long shot, the tiny spaceship is visually overwhelmed by limitless outer space. In the foreground of that same shot, asteroids tumble swiftly and silently through the void, from and to nowhere in particular. Appearing for only a moment, they are tokens of a natural order indifferent to and unaffected by the activities and motivations of man. The utter silence of the asteroids sharply counterpoints the mechanized sound of Bowman's breathing. Sound and image briefly juxtapose disconnected realities passing by each other unnoticed in the cosmic night. Subsequent shots from Dave's vantage point inside the pod (sound and imagery now in sync) portray outer space as a starlit blackness neatly contained within the artificial frame of a window.

Frank Poole monitors the mission-within-a-Mission from inside *Discovery*. Clad in a spacesuit, minus the helmet, he is in a heightened though incomplete state of readiness in case he needs to rescue his partner from trouble. He watches Dave's progress through a window and on HAL's computer screens, while inside the pod Bowman employs a similar dual perspective.

Dave's pod rises over *Discovery*'s horizon like the Moon over the Earth's. Except for passing asteroids and distant stars, everything out here moves in conjunction with the spaceship. The communication dish rotates on an axis firmly rooted in *Discovery*. The pod maneuvers as though in orbit around the spaceship, and always with the larger vessel's original velocity as an implied part of its motion. Most dependent of all is the astronaut. An overhead shot from inside the pod depicts Dave as man re-created in mechanical form (the spacesuit), perceiving the outside world via computer-screen images, completely surrounded by his mechanized environment and artificially lit in red.

The image is as strangely beautiful as it is disturbing. Man becomes Machine while Machine becomes Man. Viewed from outside, the pod reveals its anthropomorphic "face," with mechanical arms and hands, an oval window for a mouth, and two small portals on either side of that window serving as eyes.

Viewed from above as he exits the pod, Dave's helmet looks like the head of an alien creature, with a blunt, beaked shape and two round markings that resemble hysterical eyes. Thus far in *2001*, technology has been created more and more in man's image, while individual man's growing dependence on that technology has to some degree reshaped him into its image. In the present shot, Dave looks like one machine emerging from another.

As Bowman cautiously maneuvers towards *Discovery*, we see his face in a close-up through the window of his helmet. The astronaut's humanity visibly returns. But with the touch of a button on his forearm, he switches off the artificial light in his helmet. The window goes black, the face disappears, and the once recognizable human becomes vaguely alien again. In and of itself, this action is trivial, but in aesthetic terms it dramatically illustrates the power of appearances in our assessment of what we see.

After Bowman returns to the spaceship, he and Poole examine the AE-35 unit with an electronic probe and HAL's computer screens, which make visible what would be invisible to the naked eye. In other words, the astronauts are to some extent dependent on HAL to evaluate HAL's original assessment of the unit as faulty. A computer scan of AE-35 indirectly alerts Bowman and Poole to a potentially more serious flaw in HAL. Institutional identification patches adorn the astronauts' uniforms. In the present scene, they act as Mission Control's watchdogs over HAL, which is a reversal of the crew psychology report he was assigned to do on them. Dave's use of a mild profanity to express frustration at being unable to locate the problem in AE-35 signals, in the context of the astronauts' rigorous emotional restraint, a serious concern about the inexplicable discrepancy between HAL's prediction and the results of the examination.

As relations between HAL and the astronauts deteriorate, the camera closes in on them, searching for clues to their emotions. Dave and Frank betray their feelings by mere flickers of facial expression. HAL's red "eye," meanwhile, remains inscrutable. But we get a hint of his feelings, or semblance of feelings, through subjective camera shots from his perspective. The first of these is a low-angle shot that depicts the astronauts as looming figures of menace; the second, from an "eye" attached to one of the pods across the room, shows the men as puny and insignificant — paranoia and disdain juxtaposed within the same personality, or pseudopersonality. HAL delays his moment of accountability by recommending that the AE-35 be put back in place and allowed to fail in order to pinpoint the as-yet-unidentified flaw. But this clever maneuver also paints him into a corner. If the AE-35 does not eventually malfunction, the flaw must be in *him*.

Bowman and Poole receive guidance from Mission Control, shown on only one of HAL's gallery of computer screens. The computer's omnipresent "eye" is part of that gallery. But because he is not officially credited with genuine emotion, including the instinct for self-preservation, his presence at the conference does not worry anyone else. In a flat, dispassionate voice, Mission Control relays to the astronauts its nevertheless startling conclusion that HAL's prediction, not the AE-35 unit, is faulty. Outwardly, at least, Poole and Bowman react with equal circumspection.

Mission Control's criteria for evaluating HAL's performance is itself perhaps flawed. By comparing his prediction with that of an identical 9000 computer back on Earth, officials conclude that one of the machines is in error. So nearly unthinkable is such an occurrence that man doubts his findings. "We are skeptical ourselves and are running cross-checking routines to check the reliability of this conclusion." So ingrained is man's faith in technology that he doubts one infallible computer's doubts about another infallible computer. Insulated in its pristine objectivity back on Earth, Mission Control cannot imagine that HAL's compatibility programming might have been affected by the burden of intense isolation combined with prior knowledge of the mission's real goal — a double burden from which the five astronauts were spared by isolating the informed but unconscious astronauts from their conscious but uninformed colleagues.

Put on hold by Mission Control, Dave and Frank attempt to pinpoint the problem by themselves. Their subsequent conversation with HAL is a verbal fencing match. The computer probes for signs of suspicion in the men, who in turn ask him to account for the discrepancy between predictions by the two 9000 computers. In the unemotional tone of voice from which he cannot deviate, HAL drops a passionate bombshell on the proceedings: "Well, I don't think there is any question about it. It can only be attributable to human error." A chilling remark, it strikes at the heart of man's faith in technology. It is equivalent to the first scrape of ice along the bow of the *Titanic*— an earlier mechanical marvel that failed its creator in spectacular fashion. In a reaction close-up, Dave Bowman blinks, like a boxer who takes a hard punch to the head and then tries to conceal the damage from his opponent. HAL expands on his hypothesis: "This sort of thing has cropped up before and it has always been attributable to human error." The pride that the BBC interviewer detected in HAL's responses earlier surfaces now as arrogance, aesthetically masked by a dispassionate voice. *Dr. Strangelove*'s triumphant institutional cry, "I have a plan!" culminates here in HAL, who *is* a plan, defending itself against its creators. As a machine programmed with at least the semblance of conscious identity, HAL is self-serving in his criticism of man, just as Strangelove was self-serving when he put forth his plan to preserve a nucleus of American society in the aftermath of nuclear war.

Frank Poole, in support of Bowman, challenges the performance record of the 9000 computer series. It is a poor tactic because he cannot fault the 9000 series based solely on its performance back on Earth, which takes into account neither HAL's compatibility programming nor the effects of long-distance space travel on that programming. HAL dismisses Frank's concern in the manner of a parent reassuring a child with a pat on the head. Dave Bowman bails himself and his partner out of a no-win situation by pretending to agree with HAL (patronization can work both ways), then changing the subject. Straining to seem casual, he stages a tactical retreat by asking Frank to help him check out a defective transmitter in one of the pods. Once the principal companion to both Bowman and Poole, HAL is now someone to be isolated and plotted against. He is regarded by the astronauts with the same distrust with which Mission Control regarded them when it concealed from them the truth about the mission.

The confrontation ends in ominous silence. The scene's final shot gives us an image within an image. The astronauts stand and depart, but we see them as reflected off of HAL's "eye" lens. Visually, the men appear trapped within the computer's field of vision, as did Dave during his first appearance in the film. But this time that symbolic impression is reinforced by the strategic situation. A camera shot of the astronauts entering the pod bay begins with the image of yet another of HAL's control panels, complete with computer screens and eye lens. It will be difficult to escape his scrutiny inside *Discovery*. In "The Dawn of Man" apeman found refuge from the leopard by retreating to a cave. Bowman and Poole try to evade HAL by retreating to the cramped interior of a pod — an artificial sanctuary within their larger artificial sanctuary.

The relationship of master to servant remains superficially intact as the men employ the computer's assistance to make the pod accessible to them. Once inside the pod, the astronauts are sealed off from HAL's sight, but not from his hearing. They are methodical about securing their privacy, but not thorough. Dave asks HAL to rotate the pod, thus confirming that the verbal link between them is still open. But this action results in the pod returning to its original position, with its window facing into the pod bay. After switching off the intercom, Dave repeats his command. No response. HAL cannot hear him or the conversation that follows. Unfortunately for the astronauts, Bowman's two precautionary commands cancel each other out. His first order to HAL, which was intended to be heard, renders him and Frank visually accessible to the computer's "eye." His second order, which was intended not to be heard or obeyed, fails to correct that strategic blunder.

In a broad shot of the pod bay, the conflict between man and a machine created in man's psychological and verbal image takes shape in metaphorical terms — a space-age variation on the legendary gunfight at the O.K. Corral.

Standing behind and aligned with HAL's console are three empty spacesuits. Hands at their sides seem poised to reach for invisible guns in invisible holsters. Standing or squatting opposite them are the three pods, the center one occupied by Bowman and Poole. Ironically, HAL's symbolic surrogates are more humanlike in appearance than are the astronauts'. But the surrogates are more than just symbols. They are also, or will shortly become, literal weapons in the struggle for survival between man and machine. And like the many weapons in *Dr. Strangelove*, they are fickle about whom they serve. No magic glue binds one weapon to one warrior, the way Excalibur served King Arthur. The spacesuit is at first an advantage to Poole against HAL, then to HAL against Poole, and finally to Dave against HAL. C pod, too, proves to be a benefit and a liability to both sides of the conflict.

A nearly subjective shot of C pod and its occupants from beside one of the hanging spacesuits gives us HAL's perspective of the enemy. The camera then reverses angle to provide what should be the astronauts' vantage point, from inside the pod, of their enemy. Through the pod window we see HAL's console, with its "eye," and one of the spacesuits behind it. But Bowman and Poole, in the foreground, face each other rather than the window, which they fail to recognize as a breech in their defenses. The pod window now serves as HAL's second "eye," peering in, instead of the astronauts' "eye," peering out. With that in mind, various lights on the pod control panel become HAL's symbolic, octopus-like "arms," reaching out to envelop the two men. Contributing to the astronauts' illusion of security are the absence of *Discovery's* background mechanical hum inside their insulated pod and the visible presence of routine maintenance activity on HAL's computer screen, which is deceptively positioned beside his secretly watchful "eye."

HAL is vital to Bowman and Poole's survival in outer space. Like parasites, they plot to destroy his sense of identity while preserving his automatic, regulatory functions. Their choice of descriptive language suggests that they regard the computer as a conscious entity with an instinct for self-preservation. Dave tries to imagine HAL's emotional reaction to the prospect of undergoing an electronic lobotomy. By ignoring the moral ramifications of such an act, his dialog with Poole seems chillingly inadequate: like Generals Broulard and Mireau coolly discussing the need to maintain discipline in the embattled French Army by making gruesome examples out of a few soldiers in *Paths of Glory*, or Dr. Brodsky casually noting the unintended and irrelevant (for him anyway) element of punishment in Alex's Ludovico conditioning in *A Clockwork Orange*. But are Bowman and Poole really plotting a murder in this scene? Does HAL deserve the rights of a human being? Or is he merely an electronic fiction whose convincing performance arouses undeserved sympathy in us?

Another reverse camera angle returns us to HAL's vantage point, from which we view the moving lips of the astronauts who unwittingly betray their plans to dismantle him. As in *Dr. Strangelove*, even the most elaborate precautions can be defeated by small details. HAL's ability to lip read is a comparatively modest skill, well within the capacity of individual man himself. Yet it gives him a big advantage in this scene.

When the astronauts enter C pod, we catch a glimpse of a message printed on the outside of its door. "Caution Explosive Bolts" is an example of institutional foresight, like so many others in Kubrick's films. The bolts are obviously intended to facilitate an emergency exit from the pod. That Kubrick would casually bring them to our attention well before his characters invest them with extra meaning is typical of his style. The unusual situation in which those bolts will eventually be used was probably not anticipated by Mission Control. Nor was there any way to predict for certain whose interests those bolts would favor.

Frank Poole's space walk outside *Discovery* begins as an abbreviated repetition of Bowman's, though with different goals. Dave retrieved the suspect AE-35 unit because HAL predicted its malfunction. Frank now puts it back for the secret purpose of testing the computer's reliability. Bowman monitors Poole's mission from inside *Discovery*, as Poole did Bowman's. In one extraordinary shot, the vision of man, as extended by technology, doubles back on itself. Bowman, through one of HAL's computer screens, looks over Poole's shoulder and out through the pod window at *Discovery*, from which Dave's vantage point originates. Subjective, subjective/objective and objective perspectives are all present in the same shot.

An exterior shot of Poole moving slowly toward *Discovery* is a replica of Bowman's approach in the earlier scene, until movement by the pod destroys the parallel. Rotating at the methodical pace that characterizes all of man's machines in outer space, the pod turns to "face" the astronaut. Formerly a tool of Frank and Dave acting against HAL, the pod is now appropriated by the rebellious computer. A subjective shot from what should be Frank's vantage point, were he not carelessly facing in the other direction, depicts the pod advancing menacingly on him/us, its metal arms outstretched. The camera cuts closer to the pod five times in rapid succession, creating an impression of aggressive intent and then associating that intent with HAL's tiny "eye" lens, visible below the pod window. It is suddenly clear, though only to us, that HAL is directing the pod's actions. It is his bone club, wielded against the creator who threatens his existence.

The actual murder of Frank Poole is conveyed to us via the soundtrack. The sound of pressurized air flow in his spacesuit stops abruptly. The cessation of a mechanical sound is the only voice Frank is allowed at the moment of his execution. Ordinarily that air flow is a rather unappealing sound. But present circumstances link it to Poole's survival and therefore give it an eloquence it would not otherwise have. When it ceases, Frank is consigned to the lethal silence of outer space.

From Dave's vantage point, through a computer screen aboard *Discovery*, we pick up the action after the crime has been committed. We see C pod tumble wildly out of control and out into space. Bowman is not in a position to connect HAL with Frank's predicament. Nor is he aware, in a much broader context, of the analogy between HAL dispatching the pod into the depths of space and Moonwatcher ecstatically hurling his bone club into the air after killing a rival with it. Does the human-like computer exhibit the same reckless joy in killing?

Frank Poole, shown from the same overhead angle that rendered him alien in appearance moments earlier, plays out his death scene through the mask of his spacesuit. The airless void robs him of his voice. He cannot scream in terror or cry for help. Jerking at his severed air hose, he is as pathetic and haunting an image of man reduced to abject helplessness as any Kubrick has ever projected. The power of this image stems partly from our aesthetic detachment from the character. Poole's mechanical outward appearance is starkly counterpointed by his futile, painfully human struggle to survive. Stripped of its air supply, the spacesuit becomes a death trap instead of a shield against Nature. In effect, it becomes an extension of Nature. Frank's movements gradually subside until he becomes nothing more than an inanimate, rotating object floating in space, like the passing asteroids shown earlier. He drifts away from *Discovery* and out into the starlit emptiness, subject entirely to the blind forces of Nature acting upon him rather than to his own will acting, via technology, upon them.

Dave Bowman's response to Frank's plight, shaped by both private concern and institutional training, is to mount a rescue mission. Unaware that HAL is responsible for Poole's mishap, Dave relies on the computer as a source of information about the incident. In a voice that cannot help being calm, the computer pleads ignorance and obediently follows the astronaut's instructions. In fact, without HAL, Bowman would be unable to execute his rescue mission. But in his concern for Frank, Dave forgets to put on his space helmet before leaving the spaceship in a pod. By this oversight, Bowman confines himself to the pod's artificially contained atmosphere.

The retrieval of Poole's body is an agonizingly slow process, in keeping with the constraints on human activity in outer space. The camera cuts back and forth between interior and exterior shots, while the soundtrack features counterpoint between various electronic sounds inside the pod and the absolute silence of outer space. Ironically, though it makes him more vulnerable strategically, Dave's lack of a helmet makes him more accessible emotionally. By forgetting to don his helmet Bowman in a sense restores to man the face that he and his fellow space travelers had largely conceded to their machines. Yet it is only a partial restoration. Dave's face, full of barely contained passion, is illuminated by reflected light from the pod's control panel.

Like the helmet, though to a lesser extent, that light redefines individual man in technological terms.

Alternating frontal shots of the pod moving rapidly through space and Bowman at the controls unite machine and man in a single effort. Inside the pod, sound and imagery reinforce that impression. The chirping of radar and the targeting grid visible on a computer screen represent the electronic means by which Bowman pinpoints his comrade. A view of empty space through the pod window, from the vantage point of Dave's unaided eye, illustrates the fact that he needs these technological tools to locate and transport him to his partner. The repetitive, mechanical sound of the tracking equipment becomes, on a metaphorical level, the cries of "Help me!" and "I'm coming!" between Frank and Dave, who on a literal level are rendered deaf, mute, and blind by conditions in outer space. Mechanical sound, therefore, acquires the expressive quality of a human voice, even though Kubrick preserves its purely mechanical flavor on a literal level.

Finally the small, lifeless body of Frank Poole becomes visible through the pod window. Bowman disengages the tracking equipment he no longer needs, yet he still requires technology to complete his grim task. Through hand grips, he gently manipulates the pod's arms and hands to grasp the armored form of his partner. This delicate, soundless maneuver generates an exquisitely tender image. The slow, mechanical pace of the pod's limbs expresses, by coincidental association with Dave's effort, the concern of one human being for another. Sometimes a mask can *heighten* rather than diminish a dramatic effect. Alexander Walker, in his analysis of *2001*, sees and hears

The emotions and condition of man are expressed through mechanical surrogates as Dave Bowman tenderly retrieves the body of his dead partner, Frank Poole (Gary Lockwood).

this episode differently. He describes Bowman's recovery of Poole's body as a display of "textbook efficiency and next to no emotion" (Walker, 254). It is true that Dave must control his emotions in order to perform his task. But he channels his emotions *into* that task and *through* the machines he uses to complete it. Kubrick portrays man at least in part through his creations and in the context of specific environments. Dave's face may be illuminated and abstracted by the lights from his instruments, but not so much so that we cannot see the grief, frustration, and then anger in his upturned eyes. He vaguely resembles Moonwatcher, whose primal struggle for survival he now shares. But Dave does not yet know the identity of *his* leopard.

The frontal close-up of Bowman's impassioned face is juxtaposed with a frontal close-up of HAL's inscrutable "eye" back on board *Discovery*. Whatever passions or pseudopassions occupy the computer's mind can only be guessed at from his actions, which he must execute through other machines. In a sense, HAL represents the mechanization of man pushed to the limit, beyond even what Bowman and Poole have endured. If HAL were not imbued with at least a semblance of human consciousness, his role in the film's epic tale of human awakening, creativity, and adaptation would be greatly diminished. He would be nothing more than a sophisticated, double-edged sword instead of man's metaphorical double. As it is, HAL's relationship to man is roughly analogous to the relationship between the Monster and Victor Frankenstein in Mary Shelley's 1818 novel about Promethean aspirations and unforeseen, disastrous consequences. A product of science, the Monster is both a mockery of and greater than his creator. He is capable of recognizing Victor's flaws while envying Victor's situation.

A shot of Dave's and Frank's empty command chairs, from HAL's perspective, confirms the absence of potential interference. Subsequent shots of the three unconscious astronauts in their hibernation chambers establishes all too clearly the vulnerability of any remaining human opposition. An opportunity presents itself for HAL to take control of his own fate. The nature of his capabilities and the situation of his foes render the crime that follows disturbingly abstract — a variation on his chess match with Frank Poole. Both assailant and victims speak and act through technological surrogates. This is a murder scene without dialog, without perceptible injury, and possibly without genuine consciousness on the part of anyone involved. Poole was at least able to act out his death struggle in pantomime.

HAL's usurpation of command is a masterful example of divide and conquer. Frank Poole was isolated from *Discovery* (his outermost layer of artificial, protective "skin"), then from C pod (layer two), and finally from the air supply in his spacesuit (layer three). Bowman's departure from the spaceship isolates the three remaining astronauts from any chance of rescue. HAL cuts them off from the sophisticated life support systems of their artificial cocoons. His attack manifests itself on computer screens only. There are no visible reactions from either HAL's "eye" or his victims.

A flashing red screen reads "Computer Malfunction," accompanied by piercing, repeated beeps which would ordinarily alert Bowman or Poole to the need for implementing the emergency reawaken procedures printed on the hibernation chambers. But Frank and Dave are not aboard, so the alarm goes unheeded. If HAL is truly a conscious entity, the institutional description "malfunction" does not quite fit the circumstances, which were not foreseen by Mission Control. If, on the other hand, HAL's action is the result of an electronic glitch, made to *look* like aggression by his compatibility programming, then the term is accurate.

One by one, the astronauts' internal functions, as recorded on a computer screen, are reduced to flat lines as their lives ebb. The white chambers which looked like coffins but in fact sustained human life now become what they appeared to be. "Life Functions Critical," accompanied by faster, higher-pitched, more urgent electronic beeps, signal a further deterioration in the astronauts' condition. The first designation to go critical is "Systems Integration," which measures the overall coordination of separate bodily functions. In other words, various physiological functions fall out of sync with each other before shutting down individually. It is the same strategy of divide and conquer that HAL pursued earlier against Frank and Dave — and that, in a sense, Mission Control pursued against all of the *Discovery* astronauts by putting some aboard fully briefed on the mission but already in hibernation and others conscious but not fully briefed.

"Life Functions Terminated" is a dispassionate, institutional description of the death of the hibernating astronauts, whose surrogate, electronic screams of protest have ceased. A long-shot overview of the three hibernation chambers duplicates a similar shot at the beginning of the scene. The background mechanical hum of *Discovery* returns to prominence. Outwardly, nothing has changed. But, beneath that deceptively placid surface, the relationship between individual man and technology has changed fundamentally. The scene ends the way it began, with a close-up of HAL's "eye" revealing no more of that change than it did earlier.

Returning to *Discovery* with Frank's body, Dave Bowman politely requests readmittance through the pod bay doors. At the same time, an interior shot of the pod bay conveys to us a strategic disadvantage of which Dave is not yet aware. On the rack behind HAL's console is the red helmet that Bowman, in his haste to retrieve Poole, forgot to put on. Mounted over HAL's "eye" and computer screen, the helmet looks like a hunting trophy. Dialog and imagery further counterpoint each other as man and machine sort out their new relationship. Bowman's repeated requests are met with silence. In an exterior side view, *Discovery* and the pod face off. They are motionless with respect to each other, but their movement in relation to the backdrop of stars creates the illusion that the larger vessel is stalking the retreating smaller one. *Discovery's* external features form the vague outline of a face. Its window-slit "eyes" project an impression of power and menace. The tiny pod, by contrast, holds out a human-like figure in supplication to its larger brother. Dave, Frank, and HAL all express themselves through technological masks here. Slow to comprehend his loss of authority, Dave repeats his command to HAL in a firmer tone of voice. Then, confused, his tone changes to one of meek inquiry. "Hello, HAL. Do you read me?" In medium close-up, his face is illuminated by lights from the pod control panel. One flashing segment of that light mimics the movement of Dave's mouth as he repeats his question — technology unconsciously mocking its creator. Meanwhile, inside *Discovery*, HAL devotes only one of his many computer screens to the confrontation with Bowman.

Dialog finally catches up with imagery as HAL deigns to answer Bowman while, in exterior long shot, pod and spaceship continue to face each other like David and Goliath. The computer's tone of voice is, as always, dispassionate. But what he says to Bowman, though sprinkled with tokens of politeness reminiscent of Dr. Floyd, transforms that lack of emotion into sarcastic understatement, delivered from a position of strategic superiority. Their verbal battle is complemented by alternating shots of the computer's impassive "eye" and Dave's increasingly passionate facial expressions.

Unlike Moonwatcher but very much like General Ripper, HAL needs to rationalize his aggression. His explanation for locking Bowman out of *Discovery* is a self-serving marriage of instinct for survival and institutional sense of duty. Claiming that he is essential to the success of the Jupiter Mission, HAL describes the astronauts' plan to disconnect his higher brain functions as worse than murder. It is an act of treasonous sabotage. From HAL's biased point of view, the deaths of the three hibernating astronauts are regrettable but necessary sacrifices to a higher, collective goal. The fact that they played no role in the conspiracy against him is conveniently ignored by his tortured logic. His justification for murder is equivalent to General Ripper passing off his sublimated sexual release as a moral imperative in the struggle between the free world and communism, or *Dr. Strangelove* portraying a hedonistic male fantasy as a patriotic sacrifice.

Bowman is badly outmaneuvered in his debate with HAL. His attempt to appease the computer with an expression of sympathy is undercut when HAL reveals knowledge of his and Frank's secret plan. Dave's denial of this revelation is in turn undercut when HAL reveals *how* he learned about the plan. Unable to pacify the computer, Bowman rashly declares his intention to force an entry into *Discovery* through an airlock, thereby circumventing the closed pod bay door. But as HAL points out, with compulsory understatement that translates aesthetically into contempt, Dave's lack of a space helmet would seem to block that alternate route. Backed into a corner, Bowman lashes out in desperation with an attempt to reassert his former authority by sheer force of will. It is a pathetic grasp for power based on a flimsy institutional fiction that was shattered when HAL committed murder, which even before that was weakened by internal contradiction when Mission Control assigned HAL to monitor the astronauts' mental health. Arbitrarily cutting off all debate, HAL exiles the astronaut to outer space and certain death.

Like an outraged Cain turned out of Paradise by a jealous God who refused to accept his offering (Bowman's pod holding out Poole's body to HAL's *Discovery*), Dave vents his impotent anger pointlessly by shouting out the name of his enemy, as though he could still command obedience. Looking fiercely satanic with his eyes upturned and his face brightly illuminated, Bowman struggles to master his anger and his terror. Long gone is our initial impression of man in space as a passionless cipher who has ceded his personality to machines. At the same time, however, it is essential for Dave to rein in his passions in order to save himself. In a heroic performance, he succeeds in doing so under tremendous pressure. HAL has transformed Dave's pod into a death trap the same way he did Frank's spacesuit and the hibernation chambers. Dave now cleverly transforms that death trap into a battering ram with which to force an entry into HAL's fortress.

Dave Bowman recapturing *Discovery* is roughly equivalent to Moonwatcher and his tribe retaking the waterhole from rivals. But the astronaut's evolved moral sensibilities complicate the task. In order to free the pod's mechanical hands for use against HAL, Dave reluctantly releases Frank Poole's body and grimly watches it disappear forever into the depths of space. Though Frank was beyond saving, giving up his corpse perhaps seems to Bowman like an act of betrayal — one more emotion to be overcome if Dave is to save himself. Turning away to jettison its human cargo, the pod is visually dwarfed by HAL's spaceship. But on returning to execute Bowman's assault on the airlock, that visual relationship is reversed. Viewed from inside the pod, and visually contained within the pod's window frame, *Discovery* seems far less imposing. If it wore HAL's expression of menace a short time ago, it reflects his worry now. Targeting a chink in HAL's armor, the pod now stalks the larger vessel instead of the other way around. Bowman's manipulation of its mechanical hands to open the spaceship's airlock is as ruthlessly efficient as HAL's earlier use of the same weapons to attack Poole. Meanwhile, exterior shots of the action, taken from a variety of angles, remind us of the overwhelming environmental context in which this local conflict is played out. The vast silence of the cosmos starkly counterpoints man's struggle for supremacy with the technology that helps him overcome it.

Bowman pauses for a moment before committing himself to an irreversible course of action. In frontal medium shot he looks powerful and menacing in his red spacesuit, his glaring eyes aggressively upturned. His appearance now anticipates our first impression of Alex in *A Clockwork Orange* and is far different from how we first saw Dave, oppressively contained within the circle of HAL's "eye."

Bowman's use of the pod's explosive bolts to blow open the pod door and propel himself, along with a jet of life-sustaining air, into *Discovery*'s open airlock is an innovative use of an institutional system for a private purpose, equivalent to HAL's transformation of a pod and hibernation chambers into lethal weapons. The bolts were originally designed to help astronauts escape *out* of a malfunctioning pod, not *into* a malfunctioning *Discovery*. The elaborate series of steps Dave must take in order to trigger the bolts is reminiscent of efforts by Major Kong and his crew to release their hydrogen bombs for use in *Dr. Strangelove*. In both instances, institutional man erects barriers between individual man and a potentially dangerous technology.

Dave turns around to face the rear of the pod. Without changing its position, the camera alters its focus to bring into sharp view a flashing computer screen that reads, "Caution — Explosive Bolts." Only then do we recognize his plan. Crouching down to prepare for his violent expulsion from the pod, Dave coincidentally appears to kneel in prayerful supplication before the flashing red screen. This impression proceeds entirely from the camera angle and is independent of the character's intention. Though his circumvention of HAL's lockout is ingenious, Bowman is still totally reliant on technology to achieve it. Moments before plunging himself into chaos, Bowman closes his eyes tightly — a reflexive act of withdrawal from imminent danger.

Viewed from inside the pod, Dave's bold maneuver is visually and aurally dynamic. His tension is echoed and reinforced by flashing lights and audio alarms. Viewed from inside the open airlock, which environmentally is an extension of outer space, the same maneuver looks and sounds very different. Without sound, violence seems more abstract, as in a silent film. But when Bowman closes the airlock and repressurizes it with air, he restores to himself the medium of sound that, in a sense, HAL took from him when he cut off verbal communication.

The screen dissolves from HAL's "eye," inscrutably observing Dave's invasion inside the airlock, to Dave Bowman's face, with its unequivocal expression of hostile determination. The astronaut stalks his prey through *Discovery*'s passageways, tracked by a hand-held camera attuned to his erratic breathing and to the content of HAL's verbal appeal for a truce, but in counterpoint to the steady, pressurized airflow in Dave's spacesuit and to the unchanging serenity of HAL's voice. Integrating parts of two separate systems (green helmet to red spacesuit), Bowman shields himself against *Discovery*'s internal environment, which HAL controls. Institutional identification badges sewn onto Dave's uniform lend an air of institutional authority to his personal crusade against HAL, who may embody the broad vision of collective man but whose selfish appropriation of the Jupiter Mission clearly violates the intention of Mission Control, even though that appropriation might have stemmed from HAL's assignment to spy on the astronauts.

Reduced to an arsenal of words only, HAL concocts a defense serving two separate but complementary needs: to fend off Bowman's attack and to evade his own sense of guilt. His speech, which Dave resolutely ignores, is full of absurdities. His neutral tone of voice and his inclination to euphemize are badly out of sync with his fear of death and with the severity of his crimes. "Just what do you think you're doing, Dave? I really think I'm entitled to an answer to that question." As duly appointed guardian over *Discovery*'s human crew, HAL might have a valid argument. But he lost that entitlement when, out of self-interest, he killed four of them. Referring to his homicidal actions as "very poor decisions" is equivalent to President Muffley describing General Ripper's nuclear attack to Premier Kissoff as "a silly thing." But Muffley employed such pale language to achieve the higher goal of forging an alliance with Kissoff in order to preserve world peace. HAL's motivation is less altruistic. Changing tactics, the computer recommends that Bowman "sit down, take a stress pill and think things over"—shades of S.A.C. issuing tranquilizer pills to bomber crews in *Dr. Strangelove*. But again the motivation is different. S.A.C.'s goal was to help soldiers survive after being shot down behind enemy lines. HAL seeks only to protect himself from Dave's anger.

Unable to deter Bowman by any other means, HAL makes a final, desperate plea for a return to the way things were. "I've still got the greatest enthusiasm and confidence in the Mission, and I want to help you." No longer equating himself with the Mission, or Dave with a threat to it, the computer attempts to regain his humble status as man's helpmate. But it is too late for such a compromise. The struggle between Dave and HAL is to the death.

HAL's brain is officially designated "Logic Memory Center," in neatly printed lettering as clean and dispassionate as the "Peace Is Our Profession" sign in Captain Mandrake's computer center in *Dr. Strangelove*. The interior of that brain is a visually beautiful evocation of institutional order, in keeping with the sound of HAL's voice, but at odds with his erratic behavior and the content of his speech. Unlike General Ripper's private office, HAL's inner sanctum does not reveal the idiosyncrasies of his personality. Furthermore, it appears to be designed to allow individual man access to it—an institutional precaution that, whether or not engineered with the present crisis in mind, proves advantageous to Bowman. Brilliantly illuminated in red, HAL's "brain" is outwardly a realm of perfect symmetry. It is modern man's most complex artificial reconstitution of natural elements. Its interior dimensions are analogous to the exterior dimensions of the monolith. If the monolith is, in one sense, *2001*'s generic symbol of man's creative vision, the Logic Memory Center is the most spectacular example of that vision. A pristine, magnificent representation of amplified and coordinated capabilities, it is also, however, a technological heart of darkness for Dave Bowman and for individual man in general.

In strictly visual terms, Dave enters HAL's "brain" as an alien intruder — a parasite. Viewed from overhead by a camera subjectively aligned with one of the computer's "eyes," Bowman seems less human visually than HAL does aurally. His helmet and gloves, appearing black in the red light, are bug-like. But each shift in camera perspective alters our impression. A side view of Dave disconnecting HAL's higher brain functions restores his facial expressions to us. Through the window in his helmet we see conflicting and fluctuating emotions: fear, aggression, confusion, and perhaps even remorse. He is not the relentless, unfeeling, reptilian predator his spacesuit sometimes makes him out to be.

HAL's dispassionate tone of voice counterpoints the desperation of his plea for mercy. But, in a peculiar way, that involuntary vocal restraint adds to the plaintiveness of his appeal and possibly to the discomfort Dave feels about destroying him. On some extremely detached level, HAL's plea is the protest against extinction of *all* individuals in an age of collective and technological supremacy. Once again, machines speak for man. "Dave, stop... My mind is going. I can feel it. [voice faltering] I'm afraid."

Unlike his earlier requests, HAL's plea is now simple and direct, stripping the conflict of its false institutional trappings, even though his tone of voice remains institutional. He addresses his assailant by name. And he no longer characterizes himself as the embodiment of the Jupiter Mission, but simply as "I." The consequences of Dave's assault are now personal ("*My* mind is going" and "*I'm* afraid") rather than collective. As with the Herculean efforts of Major Kong and his crew to complete their mission, we are aesthetically tempted to sympathize with the beleaguered computer. But the voice he employs so movingly now is the voice he denied to Frank Poole and the three hibernating astronauts in their defense against *his* attack. And it is a voice originally designed to *mimic* that of individual man. Its aesthetic appeal may therefore be built on an illusion.

As perceived subjectively by HAL, Dave enters the Logic Memory Center as an assassin whose shiny, black, reptilian head is given a grotesquely toothy "grin" by the reflection of a row of lights off the top of his helmet. This "tooth" effect derives from components of HAL's own "brain." Symbolically, this image reflects a transfer of power (teeth) from machine to man, or, in aesthetic terms, from man-like machine to machine-like man.

HAL's execution is painfully drawn out in the same inflexible, mechanical rhythms which govern other activities in outer space. Bowman employs a simple, manual device, a sort of key, to disengage a series of electronic circuits from the larger pattern of HAL's "brain." It is grimly ironic that the great 9000 computer is brought down by a weapon only slightly more advanced than Moonwatcher's bone club. Dave's magic key, by the way, is closely related to strategic phenomena in other Kubrick films: for example, to General Ripper's recall code and Major Kong's pliers in *Dr. Strangelove*; to the lock guarding Alex's bedroom door, his phony sob story which unlocks the Alexanders' front door and the combination of chemicals and conditioning that unlocks Alex's personality in *A Clockwork Orange*; to the key that opens Room 231 and the bolt that locks Jack Torrance in a food storage locker in *The Shining* etcetera. Each turn of Dave's key ejects a small, transparent component from HAL's circuitry. The slow, precise, unvaried pace of each ejection is the mechanical equivalent of bleeding to death. Because of their rectangular shape, each of the ejected components resembles the monolith. The word "Terminal" is printed above them. Institutionally defined as an electronic juncture linking separate components of the same system, the word acquires a second, contradictory meaning in the context of HAL's destruction. For the computer, "Terminal" now means "Fatal."

Dave is careful to disconnect only those portions of HAL's Logic Memory Center not vital to his own survival and to the Mission. His actions in this scene do not imply a total rejection of machines. Technology is merely being pared back so that it is no longer capable of independent action. Its uncanny vocal and psychological resemblance to individual man is removed as a threat to individual man, whom it has until now outperformed and upstaged.

HAL's demise is defined by the deteriorating quality of his speech. His appeals for mercy cease when, as a result of Dave's surgery, he loses awareness of the present. Regressing to recollections of the past, he becomes an earlier, more primitive version of the 9000 computer, performing pet-like tricks for his creator, Dr. Langley. His voice loses its superficial serenity, becoming labored and hesitant, like the awkward gait of flight attendants in the weightless environment of Dr. Floyd's space shuttles. The machine has lost the dance-like grace it once had. HAL's voice also lowers in pitch and becomes less human-like.

HAL's performance of "Daisy" is a final conscious or pseudoconscious act before he sinks back into a purely mechanical, inanimate state. The song is also, coincidentally, a touching metaphorical epitaph on the strained relationship between man and his technology. "Daisy" is a sentimental love song about a romantic mismatch which drives one of the partners "half crazy." The bicycle built for two is *Discovery*. The married couple that rides it are either

HAL and Dave or the unstable mix of collective and private perspectives programmed into the computer. In either case, the marriage ends violently. In one of Kubrick's passionate frontal shots, Dave appears uncomfortable in the role of HAL's assassin. Meanwhile, from HAL's degenerating perspective, the visual symmetry of the Logic Memory Center is reduced to chaos. His voice grinds down to a mechanical, inhuman halt while Dave's face lights up with emotions once sternly repressed.

Bowman's defeat of HAL restores to individual man some of the dignity stripped from him by collective man. The computer's demise accidentally activates a videotaped message from Heywood Floyd and Mission Control on one of the computer screens in the Logic Memory Center. Floyd reveals information about the Jupiter Mission not intended for Dave's ears until *Discovery* had safely attained orbit around the planet. Flickering because it is the by-product of an electronic malfunction, the message leaves Dave in emotional shock. He twists his head around uncomfortably to view it, like watching a movie on the ceiling. This physical disorientation echoes the psychological impact on Bowman, who appears wide eyed and open mouthed in a close-up. One assault follows on the heels of another.

Dr. Floyd reveals to Dave that the goal of the Jupiter Mission is to investigate the destination of a radio signal send by the monolith at the secret TMA-1 lunar site. Neither the origin nor the purpose of the alien artifact are known. Floyd also confirms our suspicion that HAL was given that information before the mission began. Mission Control invested far more faith in the computer than in its astronauts. But it failed to consider the effect of that burden of knowledge on HAL's compatibility programming. Dr. Floyd's message falsely presumes that *Discovery* is already in orbit around Jupiter and that the entire crew has been revived. Events have not followed that scenario. Dave Bowman learns of the alien connection immediately after suffering the loss of four comrades and battling HAL for his own life. Now completely alone in the double voids of deep space and *Discovery*'s cavernous interior, he is hit with the full emotional impact (the "cultural shock and social disorientation" Dr. Floyd referred to in his Clavius speech) of contemplating the existence of extraterrestrial intelligence.

Jupiter and "Beyond the Infinite" chronicles individual man's close encounter, sans much of his technological and institutional armor, with the unknown universe. "Infinite" is man's attempt to define that unknown. "Beyond" the infinite implies something *outside* human definition.

Linked to the monolith's two prior appearances in the film, Gyorgy Ligeti's *Requiem* returns to the soundtrack. This time the monolith appears floating, seemingly at random, near Jupiter. For the third time running, its role in man's life changes, befitting the fact that man himself has changed over the millennia. Originally a mysterious but inert shrine inspiring creative thought, it became a buried radio transmitter luring man further out into the solar system, and it is now something of an uprooted tour guide rotating through Jupiter space.

Jupiter and its moons restore to individual man a dynamic, three-dimensional sense of perspective. By contrast, the space between Earth and Jupiter was devoid of nearby objects and therefore generated an oppressive sense of emptiness and stasis. But if the giant planet and its satellites exist on a scale similar to that of the Earth and Moon, they are unfamiliar in other respects. Compounded by Dr. Floyd's taped message about an alien connection, they provide little reassurance. Even Dr. Floyd would not sleep through *this* journey.

The camera presents a series of impressions of Jupiter space, each of them introduced by the floating monolith. The inclusion of *Discovery* in the first of these shots establishes the camera's initial independence from Dave Bowman's point of view. Along with the monolith, we seem to drift haphazardly near the planet. Yet there is a purpose to Kubrick's visual selection and juxtaposition. Size and distance become relative in the context of the camera's shifting perspective. In shot number one, a distant Jupiter appears nearly equaled in size by one of its moons. Because it is slightly smaller, the moon appears to be further away but is in fact closer to us than is the planet it orbits. Shot number two reverses and exaggerates that visual relationship. A moon at foreground screen left dwarfs Jupiter at background screen right, which in turn dwarfs other moons at midscreen. Again, size disparity distorts our sense of distance. The tiny moons in the middle seem further away than the planet, which is clearly not the case when we envision all of the objects from an imaginary, detached vantage point. A third shot presents a mirror image of the second. In the fourth shot, a much closer Jupiter takes center stage and visually dominates *all* of its neighbors, including the moons and *Discovery*, even though they are much closer to the camera. Visible far in the distance, the sun seems tiny by comparison, though by objective measure it is much larger than Jupiter. The sun's changing position vis-à-vis the planet also produces a change in Jupiter's color, from striated to black. This entire sequence of shots vividly illustrates the ambivalence of perspective in Kubrick's work. Things are defined, sometimes wrongly, in relation to other things. For example, unreformed Nazi *Dr. Strangelove* is judged by American government officials differently during a nuclear crisis than he might be otherwise.

A fifth shot restores the monolith to the visual equation. The sixth is a comprehensive pan incorporating all the objects introduced thus far: Jupiter, its moons, the sun, spaceship *Discovery* with Dave Bowman's pod emerging from it, and the lingering monolith moving relatively up and away from the spaceship, as though enticing Dave away from his technological sanctuary and toward the unspecific promise of something greater. *Discovery*'s "eye" slits are no longer lit, as they were during Dave's confrontation with HAL. The 9000 computer is dead, and therefore the spaceship is once again just an inanimate tool of man. As for Dave, his departure from the security of *Discovery*, especially in the wake of recent events, is a testament to his durability and courage. Among all of Kubrick's individual characters, Dave Bowman most exceeds institutional man's pessimistic expectations. But because he is still dependent on technology to carry on with the Mission, we perceive Dave's virtues through the dramatic mask of the machine he occupies. A tiny, fragile-looking pod emerges from its cave, *Discovery*, to face the terrors of a mysterious cosmic night.

So far, the various objects in Jupiter space have appeared as a loose collection of separate phenomena. Then, suddenly, an impression of unifying order emerges out of that spectacular chaos. Jupiter's horizon occupies bottom center screen. Extending in linear alignment away from the planet are several of its moons. A reverse-angle shot shows Bowman's pod approaching the camera, in pursuit of the monolith. Another reverse angle, now subjective from Bowman's point of view, repeats the linear imagery from moments earlier, but with the monolith added. Whatever its origin and purpose, the monolith brings to Bowman (or is possibly just a symbolic token of the mysterious thought processes at work *within* Dave) an awareness of order and direction, reminiscent of the earlier experiences of Heywood Floyd and Moonwatcher.

The camera, still linked subjectively to Bowman, tilts up in the direction indicated by the alignment of Jupiter, its moons, and the monolith. This "finger" points out into deep space and is the equivalent of the monolith's radio transmission from the Moon to Jupiter. In Dave's mind, Jupiter space has acquired new meaning, just as a loose pile of tapir bones did for Moonwatcher. The "finger" symbolically stands for *any* discoveries about Jupiter which in turn might suggest new questions and give shape to new voyages of exploration further out into space.

Like earlier imagery in this scene, Dave's and our impression of linear alignment among various objects in Jupiter space is based on an illusion — the occasionally useful bias of a fixed point of view. The monolith appears to fit snugly between the second and third moons furthest from Jupiter, yet if considered objectively it is the *nearest* object to the camera. The moons in turn appear to direct our gaze *away* from the planet and out into deep space, but in fact-they extend outward from Jupiter and back toward the camera. Abstract patterns are not bound by literal reality, and therein lie their advantages and pitfalls. The monolith drifts away from the camera, maintaining its position relative to the second and third moons, and finally disappears into the blackness of space. Its role as visionary catalyst in the mind of Dave Bowman is over, for now.

Dave's journey "Beyond the Infinite" begins in a literal mode and then becomes more and more abstract. The starlight of deep space is overlapped and then displaced by images not meant to be exact representations of what awaits man outside the solar system. Kubrick seems less interested in speculating on specific details of the unknown than in subjecting his audience to a visceral experience of rapid, extreme, and baffling change conveyed through abstract images and sounds. Throughout this scene, the camera alternates between subjective shots from Dave's point of view and objective shots of his reactions to an overwhelming flood of incoming impressions.

As we begin our journey "Beyond the Infinite," the *Requiem* is gradually displaced by another Ligeti composition that seems to mimic the bewildering natural phenomena it accompanies. In a sense the opposite of Richard Strauss's joyously assertive *Thus Spoke Zarathustra*, "Atmospheres" reinforces our impression of Nature overwhelming Dave Bowman's capacity to comprehend or manage it. It is a musical depiction of chaos. Window frames, computers screens, and other forms of artificial containment have disappeared. They no longer shield man from his limitless new environment.

In the broadest terms, Bowman's journey "Beyond the Infinite" consists of breathless speed and ceaseless change. Vertical planes of light race by on either side of the screen, gradually shifting to horizontal. Colors careen from one end of the spectrum to the other. A new series of images appears: approximations of stars and nebulae and galaxies in perpetual metamorphosis. In this abstract mode, sound effects enhance the imagery. Volcanolike explosions accompany visual impressions of expansion on a vastly larger scale. Nothing appears stable or safely contained. The forces of Nature and of human imagination are stretched to their breaking points, echoed by music that rises to an almost unbearably high pitch.

A reddish form takes shape. Seeming more biological than astronomical, it hints at a dimension of *inner* space in what we till now assumed was exclusively a portrait of *outer* space. Two shots later, a white object resembling a sperm cell plows through the chaos. Possibly this is a metaphorical impression of Dave's pod, which carries the astronaut towards a kind of rebirth. Earlier in the film, the shape of *Discovery* yielded a similar impression.

Images become more realistic as the journey continues. Familiar mixes with unfamiliar. Starlight returns, overlapping unidentifiable patterns of light. Among the latter are a number of solid-looking objects directly ahead, each exhibiting an orderly pattern of light within itself and maintaining a constant distance from the camera, as though by intention. Are these the spaceships of alien beings? Or maybe the aliens themselves? Whatever they are, they remain tantalizingly just out of reach, as though beckoning Dave to follow. They encourage speculation yet confirm nothing.

A subsequent set of images takes us and Bowman into orbit around and then down to near ground level of some presumably far-flung planet in a remote solar system. It is an exhilarating yet disorienting mix of recognizable shapes and bizarre colors. Vistas of land, sea, and sky pass beneath and around us. Deserts, polar regions, mountains, and oceans are all familiar terrestrial formations, here rendered unfamiliar and forbidding by severe displacements of normal color. Kubrick employs distorted images of the Earth to suggest environments man might encounter on far distant worlds composed of different mixtures of elements, lit by different types of stars through different atmospheres. The familiar becomes bizarre, but only as defined by our terrestrial expectations, as in *A Clockwork Orange*, where Alex spends the second half of the film retracing ground he covered in the first half, but from a radically changed point of view.

Psychologically and physically, Dave Bowman withers under the assault of "Beyond the Infinite." Through the camera, we share in yet remain safely detached from (so we can also scrutinize) his experience. In reaction shots, Dave's head shakes with increasing violence inside a helmet that affords him little protection from this new environmental onslaught. By contrast, images of onrushing phenomena come to *us* through a *steady* camera which affords us greater protection.

A series of freeze-frame shots abstractly depict Bowman's state of shock. Mouth open in a silent scream, head and neck twisted awkwardly inside his helmet, Bowman tries in vain to avoid the assault on his senses and mind. The freeze-frame is a stylized device that in this case conveys the character's total, helpless absorption in a violent experience. Figuratively speaking, Dave is frozen in terror.

Freeze-frames give way to extreme close-ups of one of Bowman's eyes. Movement is restored to him, yet the "frozen" aspect of his vision persists in the hysterical expression of his eye and the involuntary reflex of his blinking. The color of his eye's iris is determined entirely by what it perceives, in much the same way the leopard's eyes reflected moonlight in "The Dawn of Man." The inherent color of Dave's eye is overwhelmed by his bizarre environment. Rather than absorbing and processing incoming impressions, Bowman is redefined *by* them.

As Bowman glides over the bizarre surface of an unfamiliar world, background music subsides into semicoherent murmurings that echo his blasted senses. Aside from Kubrick's use of reworked terrestrial images to convey an alien planet, a second interpretation of this part of the journey is possible. A prolonged reaction shot shows Dave's widely staring eye in extreme close-up. Each time that eye blinks, the color of its iris changes. Blinking becomes, at least in metaphorical terms, a defense mechanism, or a means of restoring normal visual function. Eventually, the harsh, alien colors are washed entirely out of his iris. Kubrick gives us no more subjective shots of the planet after this process occurs. Reality may not exist exclusively in the eye of the beholder, but the condition of that eye, and of the mind behind it, can certainly influence his *perception* of reality. It is even remotely possible that the planet Dave Bowman has been circling is Earth, and that damage done to his faculties by his exposure to phenomena "Beyond the Infinite" has rendered his home planet strange and terrifying.

The deceptive potential of any *single* perspective is especially evident in one particular shot from Dave's planetary tour. The traveling camera shows an area of whiteness through which dark specks seem to fly in all directions. Rumbling noise on the soundtrack combines with that imagery to suggest, briefly, that we are witnessing a volcanic eruption — the dark specks being ash or lava ejected from the cone. But as the camera continues on its way past this phenomena, we realize that the specks are fixed features on an ordinary, nonvolcanic mountainside. Color distortion, camera frame, camera movement, and soundtrack have combined to create a momentary illusion.

How Dave Bowman transports from "Beyond the Infinite" to a small apartment decorated in a familiar, terrestrial style is not precisely explained in the film, though clues are furnished both before and after the transition. The normalization of the color in Dave's iris, through blinking, reestablishes a measure of equilibrium in his world. Psychologically he either escapes to or is placed into a sort of recovery room. "Non Function" flashes on a computer screen inside his pod, perhaps symbolically informing us of his mental breakdown. A subjective shot from Dave's viewpoint through the pod window provides a visual frame of containment around his new environment — something he sorely lacked during his cataclysmic exposure to the Unknown. The oval window is a rather quaint pictorial enclosure around a tidy and motionless image, within which appears a *second* framed image — a painting in the graceful, neoclassical style of late eighteenth-century Europe. Unlike what he witnessed earlier, the painting's colors and shapes are familiar, unchanging, and soothing. A reaction shot of the astronaut reveals why he so desperately needs that stability. Inside the inadequate shield of his spacesuit, Dave trembles uncontrollably. His upturned eyes are those of a trapped, terrified animal. Never in 2001 has man seemed less empowered by his technology than in this shot.

Three subsequent shots take us outside the pod for a more comprehensive view of Dave's new sanctuary. A synthesis of modern clarity and genteel elegance, the apartment is a dreamlike creation probably drawn from Bowman's interest in art. Muted variations of tan, green, and white soothe the eye. Paintings depicting an idealized harmony between Man and Nature dot the walls — artistic visions from a period in history Kubrick will explore more fully in *Barry Lyndon*. The paintings are, in effect, small windows in the otherwise windowless apartment. Chairs, tables, a bed, and statuettes are neatly arranged around the room. How much more sympathetic is this example of man withdrawing profoundly into himself than General Turgidson's mirrored bedroom or the closed blinds of General Ripper's office in *Dr. Strangelove*.

Dave Bowman's escape from his journey "Beyond the Infinite" is an involuntary, defensive reflex. The mechanical hum of his pod subsides as though it had been switched off. Like the burned-out light bulb that signals an abrupt halt to Susan Alexander's involuntary operatic career in *Citizen Kane*, Dave's emotional and sensory circuits have tripped their breakers. But we view that breakdown in largely subjective terms, through *his* eyes and ears, even when we see him on screen. As a result of the damage done to him, his and therefore our sense of place and time is distorted, fragmented, uncoordinated. His escape and recovery from shock occurs in fitful, overlapping stages. Elements of one stage bleed over into the next before disappearing. The effect is surreal. Odd juxtapositions confuse both the astronaut, who is too traumatized to examine his own mental processes, and us, who partly share in his point of view.

Sound and sight are distorted and out of sync with each other. Random, unfamiliar, and disconnected noises arise from a soundtrack subjectively attuned to Dave. If, as Arthur C. Clarke's novel suggests, these strange sounds are the dialog of alien beings observing Bowman in a comfortable cage they have constructed for him, it is curious that they fade away and are replaced by sounds that make more sense as Dave slowly recovers. Eventually, as his meager powers of critical perception return, the logic of cause and effect reasserts itself.

In visual terms, Dave's recovery occurs in a series of time and space overlaps, or fitful stops and starts in which anachronistic elements coexist and large stretches of time are unaccounted for. The camera shifts back and forth between subjective and partly objective vantage points, but always within the larger subjectivity of Dave's self-manufactured sanctuary. Objectively impossible encounters are possible in this surrealistic realm, which is the creation of an injured mind.

A subjective shot from Dave's perspective inside the pod shows Dave, still wearing his red spacesuit, standing *outside* the pod and framed by its oval window. In effect, the astronaut sees himself a moment later in time. A closer shot of the "later" Dave, from the same camera angle but taken from outside the pod and therefore not from the vantage point of "earlier" Dave, depicts the astronaut looking back in confusion toward where he was a moment before. How did he get out here? The red spacesuit, a lingering remnant of his now abandoned journey "Beyond the Infinite," stands out in stark contrast to the muted, breathable, safe environment to which he has fled. A close-up reveals deep wrinkles around his eyes which were not evident in the close-up of him inside his pod only two shots earlier. His leap forward in time is greater than it first appeared to be. Dave's consciousness is sporadic — his memory almost nonexistent. The erratic sound of his breathing inside his helmet is a barometer of his agitation.

A nearly subjective shot from the vantage point of "later" Dave looks back to where the pod and "earlier" Dave were a moment before. It and he are gone. Unable to account for the pod's disappearance, Bowman shuffles forward slowly and unsteadily to explore the apartment. The camera accompanies him on this exquisitely tentative mission of discovery. The fact that he is now capable of *any* voluntary exploration is an indication of at least some healing since the freeze-frame images of him during his shattering encounter with the Unknown. But his painfully arthritic movements testify to the severe damage he sustained. A graceful painting on the wall behind him coincidentally mocks his awkward gait, just as "The Blue Danube" mocked the clumsiness of a flight attendant on board Heywood Floyd's first shuttle. Nonetheless, Bowman displays enormous willpower in the face of extreme adversity.

Dave enters the bathroom and confronts his own reflection in a mirror. He is stunned by his haggard appearance and perhaps at the passage of time it implies. Shattering experience has either scrambled his sense of time or speeded up the natural aging process. But at least his powers of critical reflection are beginning to return. Hitherto inexplicable noises are displaced by faint clicking sounds from a specific source off screen. Things are beginning to make more sense. Dave looks away from his present self, reflected in the mirror, and hesitantly pursues this new mystery. In a subjective traveling shot we peer with Bowman through the bathroom doorway and back into the room from which he came. The doorway is another frame of containment. Someone is seated at a table at the far end of the room, with his back to us. The clicking sounds we hear are made by his utensils as he eats. In view of Dr. Floyd's videotaped message, Dave's and our expectations are high. Is this stranger the alien who built the mysterious monolith?

The figure at the table senses something behind him, stops eating, turns around to look, and then gets out of his chair. He walks toward the camera, moving slowly and carefully. The scraping of chair legs on a bare floor is a major sensory event in this post-traumatic environment. The alien, however, turns out to be Dave Bowman himself, noticeably older than the younger Dave whose vantage point we still presumably share (the camera has not moved) from the bathroom doorway. Dave's vision has both doubled back and skipped to the future. White-haired, dressed in a green robe matching the decor of his cloistered sanctuary (the obsolescent, bright red spacesuit has disappeared into the past), Bowman has acclimated to his new world. He chews his food methodically and holds his arms stiffly at his sides, but he seems more at peace than he did earlier. The only disturbance of his present contentment is a vague, lingering *memory* of his former self. He walks to the doorway, towards what *was* the subjective camera aligned with his younger self. But that camera is now objective, at least within the larger confines of the character's fantasy. Dave Bowman, the spacesuited astronaut who dueled HAL and explored unknown regions of the universe, no longer exists in the conscious memory of an older Bowman still recovering from an experience he cannot bear to remember. Via the camera we discreetly flashed forward in time, eluding a moment of prescience for astronaut Dave Bowman and a moment of recollection for Bowman the old man. By overlapping two widely separated stages of Dave's recovery, the camera connects them in a way the character cannot. Or, to interpret this extraordinary shot in a broader context, man's exploration of the Unknown has led back to himself. Dave Bowman is hesitantly exploring the confusing universe of his own traumatized but slowly recovering mind.

With hindsight knowledge that it was Dave Bowman seated at the table with his back to us, the time-warp shot from younger Dave's perspective becomes a portrait of human vision in depth, though neither of the characters realizes it. Astronaut Bowman, to the best of his impaired ability, confronts his future self, who is framed and visually contained within the door frame. That older Dave, in turn, faces a framed painting on the wall — a work of art that soothes him with its familiarity and elegance. From present (younger Dave) to future (old Dave) to past (eighteenth-century painting), this linear arrangement is a depiction of man in *retreat*. With the disappearance of his pod, his red spacesuit, and his memories of a journey "Beyond the Infinite," old Dave has barricaded himself in his elegant, soothing cave.

The camera switches to a high-angle overview of old Bowman as he returns to his table. Redeploying his chair and napkin as though from years of habit, he resumes his meal. His monkish existence is even more a product of routine than it was aboard *Discovery*, under HAL's supervision. And his meal is a model of simplicity and familiarity. He eats *recognizable* food with *old-fashioned* utensils and from an *ordinary* plate resting on a lace tablecloth — a no-doubt welcome change from their revolutionary counterparts aboard *Discovery*. A *slow* sip of water is followed by the intake of a *modest* portion of food. Dave's movements are meticulous. And once again, what would ordinarily be trivial sounds, such as a glass being set down on a table, stand out sharply in an atmosphere of extreme restraint.

Then comes a startling disruption of this delicate routine. Reaching for something else, Bowman accidentally knocks over his water glass, which falls to the floor and shatters. In a side shot less emotionally detached than the previous two shots, Dave ponders the minor breakage that to his acute sensibilities is a major event. For the first time in a long time, he is able to withstand and even objectively contemplate something disturbing, modest though it is.

As in the previous time slip, sound jumps from present to future before imagery does, creating a surreal syncopation. We hear feeble breathing coming from off screen. Dave looks away from the broken glass and towards that new sound. He squints at what he sees, just as a younger Dave once squinted in self-defense when exposed to the phenomena from "Beyond the Infinite." A partly subjective shot from behind Dave's head shows him looking at someone lying on the large bed we saw unoccupied earlier. *Both* characters appear in the same transitional shot, suggesting that Dave is beginning to logically connect events widely separated in time, which he was unable to do earlier. The camera breaks free of Dave seated at the table and takes us closer to the person in the bed. Again it is Dave Bowman, now extremely old, bald, and obviously an invalid. He appears to be near death. He blinks, glances towards, and then reaches out painfully for something off screen. Figuratively speaking, he reaches *beyond* the familiar, soothing painting on the wall in the background — part of the decor he once employed against the shock of discovery. Alexander Walker interprets this as a gesture of greeting or gratitude toward some deity represented by the monolith (Walker, 265). I see it differently.

A partly subjective shot from over the bed's headboard shows elderly Dave reaching for the black monolith that stands out boldly against the neo-classical decor on either side of it. In symbolic terms, the monolith is an open door leading out of an apartment where earlier there was no visible exit. Promising nothing but hinting at anything and everything, the monolith becomes Dave's escape route from his own sanctuary, which became necessary to his survival because of what he experienced the last time he accepted the monolith's invitation.

A new camera angle reveals the absence of Bowman as he was when seated at the dinner table. 'It is ironic that only on his deathbed, at his lowest ebb of physical strength, does Bowman regain the emotional and intellectual vigor to once again explore the Unknown. A purely subjective frontal shot of the monolith from bedridden Dave's perspective is followed by a reverse-angle shot of Dave. The decrepit old man is reborn as a human fetus bathed in blue-white light. *Thus Spoke Zarathustra* once again heralds a great leap forward in the development of man. From the side, we see unborn Dave reach out for the off-screen monolith, the decor of his now unnecessary sanctuary visible through his amniotic sac. A subjective shot of the monolith from the fetus's point of view pictures the mysterious artifact getting closer. But it is the subjective camera, and therefore Dave (or Dave's imagination), that is in motion, not the monolith. We can make this assumption because background objects on either side of the monolith get closer to us at the same rate it does, which would not be the case if the monolith itself were in motion. The distinction is important because it implies that Dave rather than some anonymous deity or alien is the active agent in this scene. The camera subjectively follows the lead of fetus Dave's outreach. The black unknown of the monolith fills the screen, blotting out the finite and known features of the apartment.

The blackness of the monolith turns into the starlit blackness of outer space. We escape the claustrophobic security of Dave's sanctuary only to return to the starting point of Dave's original odyssey. But we return not to the Earth of Heywood Floyd, with its "Blue Danube" and graceful technology counterpointing the awkwardness of individual man. Beginning with a shot of the luminous Moon, the camera tilts down to show an even larger, luminous Earth, which is in turn outshone by the fetus that was Dave Bowman. Man, it seems, has finally outgrown both his terrestrial roots and his absolute dependence on technology. He inhabits the once-deadly environment of outer space as though born to it. He is at last a true child of the stars. It is an inspired yet purely metaphorical image. The individual known as Dave Bowman has not necessarily undergone this extraordinary transformation. But through his perseverance and courage, man as a *species* has transcended his limitations.

For all its impressive size and implied power, the Star Child is still just a child. Less than that, he is a fetus — a symbol of *potential*. In a final close-up, we see him as all wide-eyed wonder, with no specific record of achievement to evaluate. Kubrick apparently rejected Arthur C. Clarke's idea of showing the Star Child destroying a ring of nuclear bombs orbiting the Earth, which would have implied a wildly optimistic solution to the problems depicted in *Dr. Strangelove* and imbued Dave's rebirth with a godlike moral awakening. Aside from suggesting man's eventual adaptation to conditions in outer space and transcendence of technology, the Star Child is a tentative, embryonic symbol of human progress. Kubrick does not push the human odyssey beyond all frames of reference which he and we can grasp.

The screen fades to black as *Zarathustra* concludes. As the closing credits roll by, "The Blue Danube" figuratively returns us to *our* jumping-off point in the human space odyssey. Kubrick's next film, *A Clockwork Orange*, will drag us back to the terrestrial complications of a much nearer future, where we embark on a very different sort of odyssey in the company of a character far less exemplary than Dave Bowman, though more than a little reminiscent of Moonwatcher and HAL.

CHAPTER 3

A Clockwork Orange:
Crime in Punishment

A distinction must be made between the acts of a sovereign, who acts as a collective person, and those of a private individual, who has only his own feelings to consider. Politics allows and even commands the one to do what would be inexcusable in the other.
— Napoleon Bonaparte (Herold, 160)

I am apart from everybody. I accept no one's conditions.
— Napoleon Bonaparte (Herold, 56)

In Anthony Burgess's 1962 novel, *A Clockwork Orange*, a hedonistic young thug named Alex spews forth a biased narrative undercut by the speciousness of his language and by one spoken refrain clearly not originating with him. "What's it going to be then, eh?" has no meaning until midway through the book, when it is identified as a moral ultimatum issued by a prison chaplain to Alex and his fellow inmates (Burgess). By repeating that ultimatum throughout the novel, Burgess elevates it to the level of a *general* moral argument, independent of any particular character and implying choice in matters of good versus evil.

Stanley Kubrick's film of *A Clockwork Orange* grants Alex a large measure of influence over what we see and hear. The result is a volatile experiment in the aesthetics of good and evil. Impressions undercutting Alex's biased perspective result from Kubrick's sly tampering with images and sounds otherwise claimed by the protagonist. The splitting of Alex into two like-minded but separate characters, on-screen protagonist and off-screen narrator, generates another layer of ironic counterpoint. As for "What's it going to be then, eh?" Kubrick retains the line and its moral argument but keeps it shackled to the prison chaplain, whose methods of and motives for reforming criminals are portrayed as suspect.

A composer as well as a writer, Burgess more than once mingled the disciplines of literature and music. His protagonist in *Clockwork* frequently refers to music that inspires him to conquer the wicked world around him. Kubrick evinces a similar talent for synthesizing moving images with music and sound effects. One difference between the novel and the film is that Kubrick is able to employ music directly, rather than indirectly, to reinforce and counterpoint imagery. For an audience, the result is a potent, kinetic access to Alex's disturbingly joyful sadism.

Written fourteen years later, Burgess's novel is in some respects a variation on George Orwell's *1984*. *Clockwork* postulates a curious blend of creeping government totalitarianism and rampant juvenile delinquency. There are many hints of Soviet influence, including nadsat, the slang spoken by Alex and his peers. When Alex returns home from prison, he finds his position in the family usurped by an ugly laborer. However vile a character he may be, on some level Alex seems to be fighting Burgess's war against commonality, conformity, and perhaps even atheistic communism. Kubrick retains nadsat but tones down other Soviet elements, creating instead a more Western cultural milieu brimming with commercialized images of sex and violence, or private concerns flagrantly spilling over into public life.

Burgess depicts a cynical government rife with flagrant abuses of power. Prison inmates and Ludovico subjects are routinely beaten. Even Ludovico Project head Dr. Brodsky waxes eloquent about the value of his patients' ordeal. Kubrick, on the other hand, portrays a weak and desperate government sliding fitfully into corruption. Law enforcement abuse exists in the film, but it is for the most part concealed behind a crumbling facade of due process and professional detachment. Kubrick seems fascinated by the *juxtaposition* of dispassionate due process and passionate self-interest. The film's Chief Guard, a character much expanded from the novel, personifies the contradictions between private concerns and public duty. He sincerely tries to follow both the letter and the spirit of the rules he is charged with enforcing. But even *his* personal prejudices and desires occasionally creep into his performance of duty.

In the novel, prisoner Alex captures the attention of the Interior Minister, who is searching for a suitable candidate for rehabilitation, by killing a cellmate in order to showcase his brutality. In the film, Alex *downplays* his record of violence in the mistaken belief that the Interior Minister is looking for a penitent rather than an incorrigible inmate. He gets chosen anyway, thanks to the Chief Guard's equally misguided intervention. In a sense Alex *blunders* his way to power.

At the other end of the spectrum, Alex's insidious manipulation of events is sometimes more pronounced in the film than in the novel. Instead of reaching inside to unlock the door of the Alexander home, he slyly enlists his victims' compassion in order to gain admittance. And rather than turn his droogs loose once inside the house, Kubrick's protagonist uses them to execute his commands. The Alexanders, meanwhile, are gagged and silenced, later to perform only at Alex's behest. In the hospital, after his suicide attempt, Burgess's Alex intimidates his parents with threats of violence. In the film, he dominates them more subtly, through their grief and guilt. But appropriating what belongs to someone else for use against them works both ways. The novel has Alex bashing Catlady with a bust of his beloved Ludwig van Beethoven. The film puts that weapon in *her* hands, allowing her to steal some of his thunder.

Dr. Branom and Rubinstein, seconds in command of the Ludovico project and the political opposition to it, are men in the novel, women in the film. Acknowledging a decade of progress in the professional status of women, Kubrick contrasts that progress with the debasement of women in the commercial world, in the arts, and especially in the mind of Alex.

Burgess confronts Alex, just released from prison, with the new alliance of Dim and Billyboy, former enemies who now share a grievance against the protagonist. Alex cannot discern which one of them calls a halt to their subsequent attack on him. Kubrick sacrifices that irony to another, replacing Billyboy with Georgie, who was always Dim's ally. More self-disciplined than either Dim or Billyboy, Georgie is clearly the person who prevents Dim from killing Alex.

Kubrick juggles, eliminates, and adds to selections of music mentioned in the novel. Several compositions from which Burgess's protagonist derives inspiration for his violent exploits are condensed by Kubrick into Gioacchino Rossini's *The Thieving Magpie*. Alex is, after all, a master thief who steals from anyone, including the great classical composers, in order to further his own pleasure. Rossini's *William Tell* Overture, which in the novel emanates from Alex's bedroom stereo during his tryst with two teenage girls, is frenzied *background* music in the film, satirizing that tryst as a ludicrously mechanical affair. The song "Singin' in the Rain" is added to the film as a kind of second personal anthem for Alex, along with Beethoven's "Ode to Joy" from the *Ninth Symphony*. Like the "Ode," it proves to be a double-edged sword. And two of Edward Elgar's "Pomp and Circumstance" marches are added by Kubrick as ironic expressions of institutional due process.

Burgess delays the answer to his rhetorical question, "What's it going to be then, eh?" until *Clockwork's* final chapter, which against his wishes was deleted by the publisher of the first American edition. Moral redemption comes to Alex as the ordinary consequence of growing up. A maturing Alex yearns for a quieter, traditional, middle-class contentment. Encountering Pete, his reformed droog, and Pete's wife, Georgina, Alex contemplates the pleasures of marriage and fatherhood. It would be silly to fault Burgess for the bourgeois nature of Alex's reformation. Who among us would rather encounter Alex the sadist than Alex the stodgy family man? But for Burgess to dismiss the protagonist's crimes as products of passing youthful exuberance, and to overlook the psychological damage done to him by his enemies, seems like wishful thinking.

In his introduction to the new American edition of *Clockwork*, Burgess defends his restored portrait of Alex's moral transformation against critics who saw it as a sellout. "The twenty-first chapter gives the novel the quality of genuine fiction, an art founded on the principle that human beings change" (Burgess, viii). He goes on to equate Kubrick's film with the edited version of the novel, condemning both as being rooted in the notion of unalterable human character. And he describes this artistic disagreement in odd terms. "The American or Kubrickian *Orange* is a fable; the British or world one is a novel" (Burgess, viii). Is this America versus the World, or perhaps the British Empire? After beginning his introduction by distancing himself from what he came to regard as an immature novel, Burgess suddenly reverses direction and passionately reclaims it from what he evidently regarded as the oppressive legacy of Kubrick's film. And yet he dedicated his 1974 novel, *Napoleon Symphony*, to the director.

Contrary to Burgess's interpretation, I see in Kubrick's *Clockwork* an extraordinary moment of moral redemption far more convincing than what occurs in the novel's restored chapter, and all the more compelling for the unfavorable circumstances that doom it to failure. That moment occurs during an incident not found in the novel. After being turned out of house and home by his parents and their new lodger, Alex wanders the streets in a suicidal funk. There he encounters the Tramp he once beat nearly to death. Before mutual recognition rekindles bad feelings between them, Alex displays unprecedented compassion and generosity by giving the beggar his last few coins. Maybe the experience of being powerless to prevent someone else (Joe, the lodger) from depriving him of what he took for granted (home and family) has made Alex more sympathetic to the suffering of others. But no moral awakening occurs in a vacuum. Every personal odyssey intersects with others which may not complement it. The Tramp is in no mood to credit Alex's reformation.

* * *

Over the course of a story in which his fortunes rise and fall and rise again, Alex embodies the opposite extremes of ruthless exploitation and abject victimization. We experience with him the forbidden thrill of brutal manipulation and the degradation of being manipulated by others. His victims' terror, suffering, and vengeful joy are reflected in him. We gain an understanding of their experiences through his. In an *actual* world of violent events such as

Clockwork depicts, no one directly involved could cultivate all of the conflicting perspectives brought to bear in the film. More than likely, a participant would get caught up in a single point of view, while a detached observer might not appreciate the emotional forces involved. *A Clockwork Orange* attempts to generate a breadth and depth of perspective nearly impossible outside a work of art.

2001 ends with a close-up of the Star Child, who is the optimistic rebirth of astronaut Dave Bowman after he regains his appetite for exploration. *A Clockwork Orange* opens with a close-up of Alex, a preverse, adolescent variation on the Star Child, with an insatiable appetite for conquest. Roughly analogous to *2001's* "Beyond the Infinite," *Clockwork* begins with an assault of bright colors during the brief opening credits. Then Alex's face fills the screen in full frontal close-up. He is introduced to us as one more visual shock in a film that thrives on them.

Dr. Strangelove opened with a juxtaposition of private and institutional elements. *Clockwork* begins in a similar manner. The close-up of Alex is accompanied by an excerpt from Henry Purcell's "Music for the Funeral of Queen Mary." Performed on synthesizer and juiced up with sound effects approximating physical punches, Purcell is subjectively filtered through Alex's drug-fueled mind. On a more detached level, however, the music is a formal lament for the death of an institutional authority figure. And in view of the pathetic state of collective authority as depicted in the film, it is a fitting prelude to the story that follows. "Queen Mary" both echoes what the character feels and, by its title, comments on the dubious morality of those feelings.

Whatever else he lacks, Alex possesses a knack for embellishing and twisting things to achieve a specific effect. His bowler hat is a veritable symbol of British reserve that here conveys a very different impression. Slung low over Alex's forehead, it accentuates his cold stare. Adding to the effect are spidery fake lashes adorning one eye, creating an unbalanced look. Alex's aggressive, upturned glare is reminiscent of expressions we saw on General Turgidson and Dave Bowman. But they were reacting to specific challenges (President Muffley and HAL). Alex's aggression seems directed at the world in general, perhaps even at us.

In a visual sense, *Clockwork* begins where *Psycho* ends. At the conclusion of Alfred Hitchcock's 1960 film, the camera dollies forward into a tight shot of Norman Bates, on its way passing by the neutral, institutional decor of a police holding room. Norman looks directly into the lens and at us, grinning a chilling invitation to emotional intimacy with his madness. Kubrick reverses that sequence, beginning with a frighteningly intimate close-up of his grinning protagonist and then pulling the camera back, presumably to place him in a public setting independent of his monumental ego. Instead, that setting seems more like an *extension* of Alex. We see the Korova Milkbar and its patrons as he would have us see them. As though inviting us into his world, he tips his drinking glass to us as we retreat. One of Kubrick's most striking uses of the camera, this reverse dolly opens up the film frame, adding layer upon layer of definition to its central image.

Alex drinks, of all things, milk — hardly the customary beverage of hardened criminals. But our impression of that milk is subsequently modified. White lettering on the wall behind Alex advertises three variations of the Korova drink, while narration explains the meaning of those words. "Milkplus" is milk laced with drugs which produce an energy boost, which Alex in turn employs as a tool to enhance his experience of ultraviolence. White is also the dominant color of Alex's attire, and that of his droogs, where again its traditional symbolic value is overturned. White shirts and trousers are modified by the addition of white codpieces around which the boys arrange their hands and drinking glasses in deliberately sexual poses. The white of their costumes is offset by black hats and jackboots. Alex sports fake, bloodspattered eyeballs on the cuffs of his shirt. Representations of human anatomy are dissected and reassembled, or employed as fragments, by his creative vision. He does to Purcell's music what he does to the human eye. Like Dr. Strangelove, he destroys the integrity of his raw materials before adapting them to his own needs.

The Korova Milkbar seems tailor-made for Alex even though he has not actively shaped it the way he has his own appearance. White plastic figures of nude women in sexually servile postures function as tables and beverage dispensers. Decorated with unnaturally colored hair (hair-plus), they are, like Alex's fake eyeballs, preverse idealizations of the real thing. Propping his feet on one of them, Alex seems in perfect harmony with his surroundings. The Korova could be his fantasy world. Instead it is a *public* setting in which private visions of sadomasochism are given free rein, on a decorative level. Purcell's funeral music is in part a lament for this lapse of public propriety.

Alex's gang members, Georgie, Dim, and Pete, are dressed like their leader. Pete, especially, imitates Alex in attire and posture, perhaps because he relies more heavily on Alex to give direction to his life. But all three droogs are subordinate to Alex, playing Goering, Goebbels, and Himmler to his Hitler. As the camera retreats from this quartet, patrons, bouncers, and plastic fixtures fall into place as submissive subjects, palace guards, and handmaidens. Alexander Walker equates the camera in this scene with a frightened courtier withdrawing cautiously from a fearsome monarch (Walker, 270). Even Alex's narration begins with a godlike "There was me ... that is, Alex," and extends outward from there. All of his perceptions are emotionally chained to that point of origin. And we, the audience, participate vicariously in his rampant egotism.

Clockwork's second scene begins in the same visual style as the first, but with an ironic reversal of content. An initial close-up shows us a bottle of booze clasped by someone's hand. Alex's Purcell lingers just long enough to overlap and counterpoint an inebriated voice singing "Sweet Molly Malone." A slow reverse zoom reveals that singer to be an old Tramp, sprawled out against a concrete underpass. The direct cut between scenes juxtaposes two radically different relationships between individual man and institutional environment. Everything in the Korova Milkbar complements Alex's desires. But the Tramp, also wearing a bowler hat but to a very different effect, is trapped in a less amenable world. One notable contrast between the two scenes is their initial subjects. Both characters alter their perception with drugs. But Alex's milk-plus appears only *after* he does. It serves him, sharpening his perceptions of the outside world. The Tramp's world revolves around liquor, the *first* thing we see in his scene. It *dominates* him, dulling his sense of self and his painful awareness of the ugly, inhospitable world around him. Unlike Alex's music, which completely fills the soundtrack in the first scene, the Tramp's song rings hollow and is interrupted by fits of belching. He sings a sentimental tune about a bygone age. As the camera pulls back from him, he seems to shrink inside the indifferent world of the present.

Alex and his droogs enter the Tramp's world as two distinct sets of figures. His arms slung over a walking stick perched across his shoulders, and lit from behind by a street lamp, Alex approaches the Tramp as a preverse Christ figure, bringing light and vitality but certainly not deliverance to a world of gloom. But the same street lamp throws the shadows of Alex and his droogs across the concrete and over the prostrate old man. Anything *but* godlike, these shadows depict the boys as prehistoric beasts — massive torsos on stumpy legs advancing toward their helpless prey.

This is the first of several scenes in which Emperor Alex takes stock of his realm and his subjects. His antagonism towards the Tramp runs deeper than mere sadism. As the narrator explains, Alex objects to the Tramp on aesthetic, philosophical and, bizarre as it sounds, moral grounds. He hates the man for being old, which implies the inevitable mortality of all men; for his unkempt appearance, which betrays a lack of self-discipline; for his sentimental retreat to the past, which betrays defeatism in the present; and for his useless whining, which makes his other faults seem worse. Alex's use of such words as "filthy," "old," "rotten," and "stinking" to describe his victim suggests a rather prudish intolerance. He despises weakness as much as he bristles at any defiance of his own will. Seldom an artist to idealize weakness, Kubrick presents the Tramp much as Alex describes him. His protests *are* annoying, if understandable from a more detached perspective. But the Tramp's use of "stinking" to describe the modern world which Alex represents is an effective turnabout of the narrator's insult. And his social critique contains a veiled reference to *2001* and the vast resources devoted to space exploration while Earth civilization disintegrates.

Alex's assault on the Tramp is an exercise in sadistic embellishment. He enhances his sense of dominance by toying with his victim. Alex applauds the Tramp's singing, which the old man misinterprets as sympathy, then rams his walking stick into the Tramp's stomach. He cruelly draws out the confrontation by encouraging his victim's complaints before beating him senseless. Georgie, Dim, and Pete are Alex's enthralled audience as well as cohorts, aping him and feeding off the fruits of his diabolical viciousness, yet obviously not sharing fully in his malevolent vision. They could just as well be sitting in a theater watching *Clockwork* on screen. Through the droogs, Kubrick anticipates the inevitable, superficial, sadistic reaction of part of his film's audience. It is useless to defend *Clockwork* or any other cinematic depiction of violence and cruelty by refusing to admit that some viewers will, in effect, censor it by taking from it only what gives them a quick, vicarious thrill. But then, Alex and other characters in the film illustrate that *anything*, including some of society's most revered articles of faith, can be perversely misused.

Anticipating the beating to come, the Tramp averts his eyes and retreats to the nostalgia of a patriotic song that, ironically, *celebrates* violence ("I *fought* for thee"), though it is violence sanctioned by society. His song is drowned out by the gleeful yells of his attackers, who batter him in an almost choreographed assault. The camera cuts to a long shot, allowing us to feel their terrible enthusiasm undisturbed by gruesome close-ups of its consequences.

After conquering the specter of old age, Alex next tackles the challenge of his peers. For the third scene in a row, Kubrick opens with a close-up followed by a reverse zoom or dolly that modifies our initial impression. We hear Gioacchino Rossini's Overture to *The Thieving Magpie*. A close-up of a large fresco takes us back visually to an artistic style roughly contemporaneous with Rossini's opera — a style reminiscent of paintings in Dave Bowman's sanctuary in *2001* and looking forward to *Barry Lyndon*. Counterpointing this combination of sound and image are a girl's screams of distress from off screen, which abruptly displace the joyful yells of Alex's gang from the previous scene. The two vocal expressions are as oddly similar in outward appearance as they are opposite in the emotions from which they spring. Perversely, the girl's screams furnish a singing voice for operatic music that has been separated from its original text.

As it pulls back, the camera reveals the figurehead of a crowned monarch decorating the proscenium arch over a stage. But he is a powerless king. The entire theater is in a state of disrepair and disuse, as is the once multifunctional casino of which it is a part. The deserted stage has been appropriated by Billyboy and his gang, who enact a sordid, real-life drama at a location originally intended for *feigned* displays of human passion and conflict. Huge masks at the back of the stage wear frozen expressions of shock, as though outraged at the violation of their pretend world by crude reality. Billyboy's gang and their victim are visible both directly and as shadows thrown up on the back wall, two different impressions of the same action. Kubrick films the rape from a flat angle commensurate with a theater audience's point of view. At the conclusion of the reverse zoom we see the ungainly crime on stage in ironic counterpoint with the graceful painting above it. Rossini's background music substitutes for the abandoned piano at the foot of the stage. It, too, seems out of sync with the clumsiness of Billyboy and his droogs.

Like Alex's gang, Billyboy's combines historically anachronistic elements in their costumes to create a new effect. But the aesthetic similarity ends there. The rape is a clumsy affair. By contrast, Alex's assault on the Tramp was viciously efficient, and therefore more insidiously appealing.

The camera reverses angle to reveal Alex and his droogs standing in shadow at the back of the casino, watching the show. We have been observing Billyboy's exploits from Alex's vantage point. *The Thieving Magpie* now falls more comfortably into sync with the protagonist's point of view. By making his presence known to Billyboy, he appropriates his rival's stage and expands it to include the entire casino. Billyboy's one-act play becomes Act One, Scene Three of Alex's grander production. Director and star, Alex makes his entrance by kicking a bottle noisily across the floor. The strategic element of surprise is sacrificed to the cause of theatrical effect, which enhances Alex's sense of control. Kicking the bottle and calling out "Ho, ho, ho" is Alex's way of throwing down the gauntlet. The casino, like *2001*'s waterhole, is an object of territorial dispute.

Freely mixing alliteration, archaic second person, metaphorical allusion, and sexual taunt, Alex lands the first blow of the contest — a verbal punch which his overmatched rival scarcely acknowledges. Grinning broadly, Billyboy spits to show contempt for his foe's choice of weapon, then returns fire in *his* preferred manner — actions counterpunching words.

Alex enters this scene the same way he entered the previous one, as a preverse Christ figure. The Tramp, cast as a figure of evil by Alex because of his weaknesses, was exorcised rather than saved. The girl being raped fares better. Entirely by coincidence, Alex becomes her savior by diverting Billyboy's attention. Suddenly inconsequential, she escapes unnoticed. Yet narrator Alex's unflattering description of her makes it clear that compassion has nothing to do with her salvation. In Alex's eyes, she is no damsel in distress. Distress, in fact, is not a condition likely to touch his heart. Chivalry here is a blind function of circumstance.

The ignoble spectacle of four young men beating up one defenseless old man is counterpointed by that of Alex and his droogs taking on a numerically superior force, the accidental result of which is the liberation of a woman originally outnumbered five to one. The link between evil and cowardice, so often a morally convenient cliché in films, is not a consistent measure of Alex's character, any more than Major Kong's ignorance cancels out his courage in *Dr. Strangelove.*

Imaginatively inspired by Rossini, Alex completes his theft of Billyboy's production. And again he combines disparate elements into a new scenario. Nineteenth-century opera blends with a fight montage straight out of a Hollywood-western saloon brawl. All is rhythm and excitement in a battle subjectively presented through Alex's feelings, though not literally through his eyes. We are meant to enjoy, even wallow in, his ultraviolence — for the time being.

Classic Hollywood westerns typically relish the thrill of a fight, but just as typically impose a righteous outcome in order to satisfy our collective moral sensibilities. Alex and his droogs violate that formula. They do not fight to save the girl, long fled, and their vicious attack on Billyboy's gang outlasts any moral or strategic justification. Violence lingers for the sheer pleasure of it. Alex administers the coup de grâce to his rival with howling, wild-eyed ecstasy.

But Alex's triumph is suddenly challenged. A distant police siren signals the arrival of institutional authority. Society is about to reclaim the derelict casino from Alex, just as Alex took it from Billyboy. Alex's preverse genius for battle is evident from the fact that he not only savors it more intensely than do his companions, he is also more capable of dispassionate strategic thought during that enjoyment. Tearing himself away from Billyboy, he whistles his gang to attention and orders a tactical retreat. Dim, a slave to his own emotions and therefore the General Turgidson of *A Clockwork Orange,* is the slowest to respond. The boys trumpet their exit from the theater with shouts of victory. But by leaving before they originally intended, they yield to authority represented by the siren. The symphony of overlapping sounds which Kubrick constructs in this scene illustrates the shifting relationships among the characters: from the screams of a girl being raped, to the happy yells of Billyboy's gang joining battle with their rivals, to Alex's howls of triumph over a prostrate Billyboy, to the symbolic police siren that puts the victors to flight, to the parting, reluctantly deferential yells of Alex and his droogs — all overlaid to various effect by Rossini's Overture.

Speed replaces ultraviolence as Alex's avenue to power as he and his droogs race down a rural road in a stolen sports car. The Durango-95 is a mechanical extension of Alex in the same way a B-52 was of Major Kong, an entire bomber wing was of General Ripper, and a space pod was of HAL and then Dave Bowman. The letters DAV on its license plate might be a discreet reference to the astronaut from *2001.* Alex's drive through the countryside is a scaled-down version of Bowman's journey "Beyond the Infinite." Alex sees it as a close encounter with and triumph over Nature. Skeletal trees, momentarily illuminated by the car's headlights, hurtle by on either side. From a subjective vantage point inside the vehicle, we see oncoming traffic veer off the road, intimidated by Alex's challenge. Alex describes his sensation of power as "real horrorshow," which is something of a contradiction in terms. "Horrorshow" is derived from horror films, which are notable for arousing strong emotions within a safe framework of play-acting. A country road is a relatively safe route. Dave Bowman, on the other hand, was overwhelmed by a far less controlled encounter with Nature. "Real horrorshow" became *real horror*. Only when Alex returns to the countryside later in the film, under less favorable conditions, does his experience of Nature approximate Dave's.

Georgie, Pete, and Dim, gathered on the passenger side of the automobile, are simply along for the ride, howling with delight at an experience supplied to them by Alex. Dim holds onto his hat in the blast of wind and screams "Bastards!" at the anonymous drivers scattering before him. Georgie flies through the night looking like the Wicked Witch of the West in *The Wizard of Oz* (1939). Together with Pete, scrunched down nearest Alex in the front seat, they form a trio distinctly apart from their leader, whose joy is more fiercely concentrated and jealously private than theirs. Darting occasional glances in their direction, Alex settles into a trance-like, straight-ahead glare. He is the conductor, the Durango-95 his orchestra, and the droogs merely members of his adoring audience.

After seeking out and facing down the challenges of old age, rival youth, and Nature, Alex sets out to conquer the sanctity of "Home." The right to privacy for anyone *else* constitutes, for Alex, a diminution of his own freedom. Switching off the mechanical "eyes" of his extended self, he and his droogs creep up on a rural house which presents a "face" of its own in the arrangement of two exterior lights (eyes) and a sign (mouth) that reads "Home." But like the "face" of Heywood Floyd's shuttle in *2001*, that of "Home" wears an ambiguous expression, vaguely foreshadowing the potential aggression of Alex's next victim the way the shuttle "face" foreshadowed HAL's.

Alex's battle music carries over from the previous two scenes until the camera cuts to inside the house, where for the moment the concerns of its owners still hold sway. Mr. Alexander is a middle-aged writer, dressed in a comfortable robe, seated at his desk, typing. Behind him is a well-stocked bookcase. He is an intellectual accustomed to seeing the world through the abstraction of written words. Like Dave Bowman in his sanctuary, Mr. Alexander's existence is sheltered and tranquil. His home shares the aesthetic severity though not the sadomasochistic flair of the Korova Milkbar. Its sparse and neatly arranged furnishings perhaps reflect its owner's dispassionate and orderly view of the world. Mrs. Alexander, considerably younger than her husband, sits reading in a chair vaguely reminiscent of the hibernation chambers aboard *Discovery*.

The doorbell chimes a miniature, muted rendition of the fate theme from Ludwig van Beethoven's *Fifth Symphony*, first movement. It is a thin, quaint approximation of the original, indicative of the Alexanders' insulation from the world outside their door. Only on a symbolic level do the chimes convey the shattering fate that approaches them. The entryway from which Mrs. Alexander confronts their caller is transformed into a giant chess board by black and white floor tiles which are doubled and trebled by mirrors on the walls. As she opens the door to Alex, we see three images of Mrs. Alexander and only one of him. The door remains chain-locked. The strategic advantage is still hers, until Alex shrewdly turns *her* compassion to *his* advantage. He fabricates the story of an injured friend in need of medical attention. Mrs. Alexander accepts his lie at face value, and, as a result, her caution battles with her sympathy. Mirrors place her image on both sides of the door, figuratively in opposition to and allied with Alex. But she disarms his plea for help with a lie of her own, telling him there is no phone in the house. Then her husband's untimely intervention tips the balance back in Alex's favor. Mr. Alexander's expression of concern for the allegedly injured party is tepid, which is understandable considering his state of comfortable insulation. But it is sufficient to persuade his wife to unlock the door through which Alex and his droogs pour in. Mrs. Alexander is overwhelmed by figures multiplied in the entryway mirrors.

Invasion from outside reduces the Alexanders' domestic routine to chaos, which Alex then reconfigures to suit his own whims. His droogs, wearing masks as a concession to the threat of identification by the police, consolidate his control. Juxtaposed close-ups of Dim and Mr. Alexander depict an ironic visual similarity between assailant and victim. Dim gapes through his clown mask and gropes Mrs. Alexander with his left hand. Mr. Alexander, *his* gaping mouth contorted by pain and shock, tries to ward off Georgie's attack with *his* left hand.

As the new master of the house, Alex imposes himself on his hosts and their property. Whistling for attention and waving his walking stick like a conductor's baton, he begins his symphony of sadism. His droogs are no less his instruments than are the Alexanders, but they are willing members of the band, allowed to share in his fun. Replacing the Rossini Overture as Alex's battle music is his a cappella rendition of "Singin' in the Rain," a lighthearted declaration of joy in the face of an indifferent and sometimes hostile world. The song conjures up images of Gene Kelly transforming puddles of rain into effervescent assertions of himself. Alex, too, choreographs his happiness. Employing a walking stick and jackboots instead of an umbrella and tap shoes, he does the old soft shoe into Mr. Alexander's ribs and across Mrs. Alexander's face. "Ready for love" translates into "Ready for rape." Alex's coincidental role as a rescuer of women two scenes earlier is rudely overturned here, as is our impression of his courage in the face of superior numbers.

The Alexanders are forced to provide choral back-up in Alex's production. Their cries of pain punctuate the song's lyrics at precise moments of his choosing. Meanwhile, Dim mindlessly apes Alex's performance. The tenuous nature of his alliance with Alex is brought home when Alex tucks his stick carefully between Dim's legs. Dim giggles in mock alarm, forming a brief trio with the Alexanders' *genuine* cries of pain. For the present he basks in the sunlight of Alex's approval. Later in the film, Alex's stick will visit the same part of Dim's anatomy in a less congenial manner.

Completing his deconstruction of Mr. Alexander's world, Alex hops up on the writer's desk, dances a manuscript into disarray, overturns the desk, and then collapses the bookcase onto it. The outrage continues as he robs the Alexanders of their powers of speech, which only moments earlier he had appropriated to enhance his own pleasure. He gags their mouths with rubber balls dropped from his codpiece, adding a symbolic sexual element to their humiliation. The Tramp at least was allowed to voice a protest before being beaten.

The rape of Mrs. Alexander is a dramatic crossroads in *Clockwork*. It is the first time in which our empathy with Alex is stretched beyond the breaking point. Unlike Billyboy's gang and the Tramp, the Alexanders are shown in gruesome close-up as Alex has his way with them. Savoring his power, he makes an elaborate production out of stripping Mrs. Alexander in front of her anguished husband. She is both a target of violence and an instrument of emotional torture employed against Mr. Alexander. Alex cuts holes in her outfit, exposing first only those areas of sexual interest to him. She is recostumed to suit the new role he assigns her and, in the process, is reduced to mere fragments of anatomy, like the fake eyeballs on Alex's shirtsleeves and the plastic figures at the Korova. Dim, meanwhile, plants slobbering kisses on her thighs and buttocks. He is cruder, yet, if any distinctions can be made at this level of depravity, somehow less cruel than Alex. Unaware of Mr. Alexander's distress, it is enough for Dim to humiliate his wife.

Pulling down his pants and preparing for action, Alex taunts Mr. Alexander and, by way of a subjective camera, *us* as well, "Viddy well, little brother. Viddy well." For the first time in *Clockwork*, we share the vantage point of the victim instead of the aggressor. Alex's is a *double* taunt: aimed at Mr. Alexander on behalf of Alex, but also aimed at the film audience on behalf of Kubrick, who would have us ponder our previous emotional identification with Alex. Both Alex and his narrator persona have referred to us as "brothers." But in Alex's lexicon, where there is no room for such concepts as kinship and equality, the term signifies contempt and subservience. The clown mask which had been a defense against identification by the police now becomes an offensive weapon of sexual taunt as he pokes his phallic nose in Mr. Alexander's (and our) face.

The scene concludes with a close-up of Mr. Alexander, his face upturned in a grimace of horror as he helplessly watches the rape of his wife. The horror overwhelms him and, subjectively through him, the soundtrack as well. Purcell's grim "Funeral" music returns, blotting out the recent memory of Alex's lighthearted song. Its implied lament for the death of institutional authority is now linked to the erosion of self-restraint and collective faith in Mr. Alexander. His agony is juxtaposed with that of his wife, while Dim's upturned clown smile mocks them both.

A weary Alex returns with his gang to the Korova Milkbar, which no longer seems an extension of his will. Purcell lingers on the soundtrack, but now as a hangover from Mr. Alexander's ordeal rather than fuel for Alex's sadistic inclinations. Milkbar employees, no longer appearing as royal attendants, barely acknowledge his arrival.

After the cruelty of the previous three scenes, this one features two bizarre examples of chivalry. Pouring himself a moloko-plus, Dim apologizes to the plastic milk dispenser for putting his hand between her legs. He even addresses her by name. No such courtesy was extended to Mrs. Alexander. Of course, Dim's good manners here are undercut by his facetious delivery.

Alex, on the other hand, displays *real* chivalry towards a *real* woman, but for selfish reasons. The object of his respect distinguishes herself by her carefree attitude and her singing ability. Dressed in conventional attire at odds with the Milkbar's decor, she and her companions seem untroubled, even amused, by their alien environment. Quite by coincidence she dispels the blue funk into which Alex sinks after his orgy of ultraviolence. Her impromptu solo rendition of the "Ode to Joy" from Beethoven's *Ninth Symphony* does the trick. She becomes for Alex "some great bird ... flown into the Milkbar," her gaudy silver-and-gold eye makeup like a pair of soaring wings. Alex regains the alertness he had earlier. From his perspective, the camera zooms in on the singer, obliterating the rest of the Milkbar, now part of the wicked world he seeks to escape. Of course, under any other circumstances she would rate the same low regard as did Mrs. Alexander.

Obviously not a Beethoven fan, Dim blows the singer a raspberry. Alex, without even glancing in the direction of the offense, silences it with a painful rap of his stick across Dim's legs. The gang is a miniature society within the larger social order, and it is no democracy. The nature of Dim's relationship to Alex, whom he served faithfully in previous scenes, is suddenly made clear. He is of value only to the degree that he promotes Alex's selfish pleasure. Alex justifies his punishment by accusing Dim of violating public decorum. In truth, Dim's crime is that he displeased Alex.

Surprised and hurt by Alex's betrayal of solidarity, Dim allows his anger to run away with his better judgment. Step by step, their confrontation escalates. Alex turns up the verbal heat. Dim trumps that maneuver by

Alex (Malcolm McDowell, right) tips his glass to a woman after punishing Dim (Warren Clarke, left) for insulting her. Intimidated, Pete (Michael Tarn) and Georgie (James Marcus) meekly observe the action. In the previous scene, all four boys cooperated to rape a different woman.

challenging Alex to physical combat, which Alex in turn tops by accepting the challenge with a cold smile. Again he steals his opponent's fire. Dim wisely backs down. Georgie and Pete, silent spectators, share in Dim's humiliation. They rebelled and failed vicariously through him. Scrutinizing Alex for signs of weakness, they found none. Dim acknowledges restoration of the old order by suggesting that everyone go home. "Righty, right?" he asks meekly. "Righty, right," Pete and Georgie echo contritely. Alex brings this litany of submission to a formal close with a cheerful rendition of the same. But this scene has exposed cracks in the foundation of his empire, cracks which will later split wide open.

The revival of Purcell on the soundtrack echoes the revival of Alex's dominance at the end of the second Milkbar scene. A direct cut, however, places him in a different situation that challenges him in a new way. Without skipping a beat, Alex picks up the music where it left off at the Korova, but to a radically different effect. He literally whistles in the dark as he walks home alone in the predawn gloom, the camera tracking with him through a

littered wasteland with the anonymous institutional name of Flatblock 18a
Linear North. This setting is as ugly and depressing as the old Tramp's. But
Alex defies it by kicking a piece of garbage out of his path.

As Alex enters the Flatblock lobby, Purcell's music returns to the background. Transformed into a Beethovenesque elegy removed from Alex's subjective grasp, it comments on the hostile relationship between the protagonist
and his surroundings. Alex kicks an empty bottle across the garbage-strewn
floor, as he did earlier to signal his challenge to Billyboy. But this time the
enemy is more difficult to pinpoint and overcome. He kicks half-heartedly
at a broken elevator door. Its tinny reply speaks volumes about the decrepit
state of collective facilities, and it is not as satisfying to Alex as the cries of
pain he elicited from the Alexanders. He plods listlessly up the stairs.

Broken furniture and a bra hanging on the stairway railing are tokens
of private rebellion. But the most striking evidence of battle between individual and institutional perspectives in the lobby is a large mural featuring
rigid, two-dimensional figures of seminude men performing various coordinated, socially redeeming tasks. A fusion of Greco-Roman and modern indus-
trial styles, the mural harkens back to a scene in Kubrick's *Spartacus* where
patrician Crassus complains about the degrading submission the nation
demands of even its most exalted citizens. One is also reminded of the so-
called "social realism" artistic style once mandated in some communist countries. All the faces in the mural wear the same blank expression, contrasting
with the egocentrism of Alex's face in *Clockwork's* first shot. The England
depicted in Kubrick's film is headed in different directions at the same time:
one leading to the ideal of absolute State control and the other to the ideal
of complete freedom for the individual. The mural has been vandalized by a
rebel hand. Printed dialog and chalked genitals give its anonymous characters a crude semblance of personality. Someone, possibly Alex, reintroduces
self-interest into a fantasy of uncomplicated solidarity.

Unlike the flatblock lobby and grounds, Alex's bedroom is tidy. No longer
playing to an audience, he removes his fake eyelashes. Still playing to himself, however, he jumps onto his bed with acrobatic precision. The spoils of
his recent conquests are tossed unceremoniously into a drawer under his bed.
They are materially useful to him but otherwise offer little emotional payoff.
Alex is less interested in loot than in power. Out of another drawer he retrieves
his pet boa constrictor, Basil — a metaphorical expression of that power.

As the evening winds down, Alex turns to a new source of inspiration.
And he is eclectic in his resources. In his stereo an audiotape of Beethoven's
Ninth Symphony replaces one by a contemporary pop musician with a pseudo-
Russian name. Music reaches Alex's ears through a wall of speakers that
must surely produce sound-plus. Beethoven's slashing scherzo propels him,
and us, into a subjective fantasy composed of various objects around the

room plus other ingredients originating in Alex's mind. Music, religion, capital punishment, an explosion, and vampirism are all linked together in a diverse but morally chaotic impression of power.

Shots of Beethoven's stern face imprinted on a window shade convey the composer's defiant mastery of his art in the face of many hardships. The poster image of a woman experiencing sexual pleasure becomes sadomasochistic only when the camera, subjectively tied to Alex, tilts down to include Basil in the picture. The snake plays Alex's surrogate and less-than-loving penis coiled between the woman's outstretched legs. She is treated the same as the plastic Korova girls.

The camera continues its downward tilt to reveal four white statuettes of Christ (Christ-plus), linked arm in arm. The statuettes are subsequently broken up into fragments by rapid editing. These piecemeal images, each with its own meaning, are figuratively made to dance with one another (interposed close-ups of Christ's "dancing" feet) by Alex, who participates vicariously in the roles of both crucifier and crucified. He savors inflicting the torment evident on Christ's face, bloodied by a crown of thorns, while simultaneously participating in the defiance of Christ's fists, upraised against a wicked world of injustice and pain. Heads bent in submission and arms raised in protest are multiplied images of defeat and triumph. Alex, ever the opportunist, feeds off the contradictory powers associated with each and is oblivious to the irony of doing so. A reaction shot shows him with eyes aggressively upturned and mouth curled in orgasmic pleasure.

The narrator's description of Alex's rapture, "Gorgeousness and gorgeosity made flesh," affirms its nearly tangible potency. "Like a bird of rarest spun heaven metal" takes us back to the singer at the Korova and to Major Kong's gleaming B-52 in *Dr. Strangelove*. "Like silvery wine flowing in a spaceship, gravity all nonsense now" conjures up impressions of spaceships waltzing gracefully through outer space in *2001*. However differently, all of these images convey empowerment.

Alex's fantasy is undercut when the camera cuts directly to the following morning while Beethoven's mighty scherzo continues uninterrupted on the soundtrack. Local music that echoed and fueled Alex's sense of power suddenly becomes background music satirizing his inability to sustain that feeling. Alex lies asleep in bed, with Basil curled up at his feet. A splendid evening of ultraviolence, literal and imagined, has left him with a hangover. Yet Beethoven's defiant spirit perseveres, in the music and on the window shade portrait. A second poster, hanging in the shadows above Alex's weary head, depicts the composer on his deathbed. Though his music lives on, Beethoven dies. Likewise, Alex cannot possibly sustain the level of inspiration and energy he displayed the night before. Exhausted, he begs off school when awakened by his mother.

Alex's parents, Em and Pee, are an unimpressive pair. Em, a middle-aged woman trying to recapture her youth in a plastic miniskirt and purple wig, makes only a token effort at persuading her son to go to school. Her concern for him is soothed away by sleeping pills. Like the drunken Tramp, she avoids rather than confronts the challenges in her life. Pee, conservatively dressed and balding, at least wonders aloud about Alex's recurring sickness and the late night "odd jobs" that precede it. But he is too timid to act. Pee and Em are neither uncaring nor cruel parents. They are merely ineffectual and silly, like the plastic flower with the smiley face sitting on the kitchen table between them as they discuss their wayward son.

Beethoven carries over into a later hour of the morning as Alex slowly recovers from his lethargy. A beautiful close-up of the combination lock on the outside of his bedroom door confirms the sanctity of his privacy within the family's collective domain. But as Alex exits his bedroom, his yawning, bleary face is juxtaposed with the ever-piercing gaze of the windowshade Beethoven. His slouching, butt-scratching stroll down the hallway and into the living room is out of sync with the music. We see the master manipulator in an off moment — Napoleon picking his nose. Like "The Blue Danube" in *2001*, Beethoven's music dances in and out of alignment with the imagery it overlays.

The first challenge of Alex's new day comes in the repulsive form of his Post Corrective Advisor, Mr. Deltoid, who waits for him in his parents' bedroom. It is an unpleasant surprise visit, like Alex's intrusion on the Alexanders. That, plus the collective authority invested in him, gives Deltoid a strategic advantage. He is a State-appointed surrogate for the faded authority of Pee and Em, and both he and Alex are aware of that fact. Deltoid sits on the edge of the bed with his hands passively folded, but with a leering, confident grin. Three times Alex refers to him as "brother," meaning inferior. And three times he retracts it, substituting the more respectful "sir." Standing coyly in the doorway, Alex faces his adversary stripped of his usual weapons, save deceit and wit.

Mr. Deltoid summons Alex to the bed to administer an official scolding, then lays hands on the young malchick for selfish reasons. The very name Deltoid refers to a shoulder muscle, reducing the character, at least in Alex's retelling of the story, to the equivalent of the plastic eyeballs on Alex's battle uniform. Waxing sanctimonious about being the "one man in this sore and sick community who wants to save you from yourself," Deltoid grabs the boy's crotch. "Save you *for myself*" is closer to the truth.

Correctly surmising Alex's involvement in the assault on Billyboy's gang the previous night, Deltoid employs two very different arguments to change the young man's behavior: one, the threat of prison, is institutional; the other, respect for Deltoid's efforts on his behalf, is personal. "Me, who's sweated over you," takes on an unpleasant double meaning in light of his sexual interest in Alex, who, leaving the bed in pain after Deltoid's slap, appears unconvinced by either argument.

Suppressing his sexual urge, Mr. Deltoid strikes a more professional pose while commenting on society's inability to curb juvenile crime. Noting Alex's good home, loving parents, and intelligence, he puzzles, "Is it some devil that crawls inside you?" Deltoid's frustration is symptomatic of institutional authority figures in *Clockwork* and amounts to a crisis of faith in the individual's ability to consciously restrain himself. A scientifically trained expert in human behavior, he momentarily reverts to a simpler, superstitious explanation of evil. Like the Doomsday proponents in *Dr. Strangelove*, frustrated government authorities in *Clockwork* will seek out revolutionary solutions to a chronic problem. Of course, Deltoid is blissfully unaware that his own behavior contributes to the erosion of a system whose failure he claims to lament.

Mr. Deltoid's institutional status prevents Alex from retaliating directly for his ill treatment. But he gets an *in*direct measure of revenge when Deltoid takes a drink of water from Em's denture glass. Noticing the offensive object inside, Deltoid recoils in disgust. The dentures' big grin becomes Alex's grin of triumph, and ours through him.

Alex's visit to the Music Bootick, accompanied by a synthesized rendition of the march from Beethoven's *Ninth Symphony*, is the equivalent of a royal promenade through the palace. Dressed like a resplendent figure out of Europe's aristocratic past, or Kubrick's own *Barry Lyndon*, Alex nudges his walking stick up and down over his shoulder, like a violinist bowing his instrument. A wide-angle lens creates a glittering showcase for Alex's stroll and exaggerates our impression of his pace, as he casually peruses merchandise and nods condescendingly to clerks.

But we are *not* back to Scene One. The store's customers and employees pay no special attention to their self-appointed liege. By contrast, their counterparts in the first Korova Milkbar scene seemed to arrange themselves in frozen majesty around him. In order to command attention at the service counter, Alex must rap his stick four times on the floor—a variation on Beethoven's fate motif which the night before announced his more auspicious arrival at the Alexander home.

Standing at the service counter are two teenage girls sucking on phallic ice sticks. They are not very impressed when Alex approaches them. But, perhaps because the encounter is in public and he wears no disguise, he plays the gentleman with them, extending a friendly invitation to *mutual* pleasure. Glancing at one of their drooping ice sticks, he commiserates, "Bit cold and pointless, isn't it, my lovely?" He does not have to read sexual meaning into the ice stick, because it already exists by design. But what Alex has in mind for his "little sisters" is, in its own way, equally cold and pointless. The girls succumb to Alex's tickling alliteration and leering innuendo, which contains a hint of incest intended to spice up the invitation.

Alex's sexual romp with the teenage girls back in his bedroom is a frenzied affair shown in a single take by a fixed camera shooting in fast motion and accompanied by an accelerated, synthesized version of Rossini's *William Tell* Overture. This is background, not local, music. Along with unusual lighting that renders the characters anonymous, these visual and aural effects distance us from what we see. Alex is being satirized, not romanticized. He and his partners make sex look mechanical, like a slapstick chase from a silent movie. Predictably, Alex's sexual appetite exceeds that of his companions, whom he repeatedly undresses and brings back to bed, as if it were an endurance contest. Nevertheless, the orgy is as close to a democratic experience of pleasure as Alex allows. The girls even take turns trying on Alex's bowler hat, which the night before had been an untouchable symbol of his imperial rule.

William Tell carries over into the next scene, where its frenzy counterpoints and then adjusts to a very different situation confronting Alex. Sexual conquest is displaced by a formidable challenge to Alex's contentment as he descends into the Flatblock lobby where his three droogs unexpectedly await his arrival. Dim amuses himself by playing race car driver, using an overturned baby carriage as a car seat and its dislodged wheel as a steering wheel. Like Alex, if less sophisticated, Dim reassembles broken fragments into new configurations for his own pleasure.

Bolder than Georgie and Pete, perhaps because he does not appreciate the risk, Dim mocks the royal status Alex forcefully reasserted for himself the previous night. Alex's carefree descent down the stairs changes abruptly to a ballet of caution. "To what do I owe the extreme pleasure of this surprising visit?" is a lie. Surprises are seldom pleasant to a tyrant. Alex thrives on his ability to surprise *others*. The droogs' unexpected visit is no more welcome than was Deltoid's.

Rebellion takes shape in body language as well as words. Georgie leans against the back of Dim's overturned carriage, as though steering Dim's infantile bulk. If the carriage and the wheel are Dim's playthings, Dim is Georgie's weapon against Alex. Pete, meanwhile, sits on the floor off to one side, nervous and noncommittal.

Alex extends a phony hand of conciliation by offering "Appy polly loggies," a fragmentation and elaboration of "apologies." He finds inspiration for counterattack in a happy confluence of visual elements. Georgie casts a shadow on the mural in the background. The head of his shadow is positioned suggestively close to an erect penis drawn, originally in protest against a very different enemy, on one of the human figures. In symbolic terms, Georgie obeys the command scribbled above his head. Meanwhile, Dim's shadow appears beneath the authoritative foot of the same mural figure. Taking his cue from that abstract impression of domination and subservience, Alex straddles poor Dim, placing his codpiece directly in front of the big droog's mouth while fixing Georgie with a hard stare. The mural/shadow image (two abstractions combining to form a third) serves Alex as a model for action. He merely reverses the arrangement. Instead of telling Georgie to "kiss it," he inflicts that humiliation on Dim. The more intelligent Georgie will get the message. Alex expands on the metaphor by plopping down in Dim's lap and prodding the droog's mouth with his walking stick, which is no less phallic than his codpiece.

"Let's get things nice and sparkling clear" is Alex's demand for a restoration of the old order. But instead of backing down, as occurred the night before, Georgie demands a "new way," which is crudely echoed by Dim, who used to ape Alex. No more discipline for Dim plus a revised crime agenda are two stipulations of that new way. Georgie is more a common thief than a sadistic control freak. He dreams of wealth, while Alex dreams of domination and destruction.

Outnumbered two or maybe two and a half to one, Alex is smart enough to see the need for a strategic retreat. He heaps false praise on the initiative he claims to have taught his droogs. But what he really wants from them is abject obedience. Dim and Georgie naively accept Alex's praise at face value. A stop at the Korova to get Alex sharpened up on moloko-plus before embarking on a "mansize" robbery is Georgie's first general order.

Like the orgy scene, Alex's counterrevolution is shown in abstract form. Fast-motion cinematography gave us a detached, satirical view of the orgy. Slow-motion cinematography gives us an equally distorted yet subjective view of Alex's attack on the droogs. We see the event partly through the protagonist's keen faculty for objectively calculating the strategic dynamics of a situation. The narrator credits music emanating by chance from a nearby open window for inspiring Alex's offensive. What we hear, however, is Alex's standard battle music, *The Thieving Magpie*, originating in his mind. It is the same music he called upon the previous night, when his droogs performed *with* rather than *against* him.

It all seems so clear in slow motion and from the right camera angle. Walking along a marina, the four boys make up a revealing strategic arrangement. Alex grips his walking stick in both hands, ready for action. Surrounding him are his former droogs and would-be partners. Pete, bringing up the rear, walks in step with his former leader, probably out of long habit. Georgie and Dim flank Alex, walking in step with each other and noticeably *out* of step with Alex. But their casual expressions reveal no awareness of their vulnerability. They carry their weapons loosely. Envisioning the overall situation, including himself, from the detached vantage point which the camera supplies to us, Alex perceives that vulnerability. It is the right moment to attack. And despite its dubious tactics and purpose, his attack is strangely beautiful in its efficiency.

Georgie, the quicker adversary, is put out of action first. Pete, in prime position to retaliate from behind, timidly backs away, as Alex anticipated he would. Dim, strong but slow, counterattacks but is easily sidestepped and then dumped into the marina along with Georgie. Alex has anticipated both the nature and the direction of resistance. He crouches down at the water's edge, pulling a knife out of the top of his walking stick. This action parallels General Ripper pulling a machine gun out of his golf bag in *Dr. Strangelove*, except that Alex's walking stick has already been defined as a weapon, whereas Ripper's gun emerged from something deceptively benign.

While unsheathing the knife behind his back, Alex extends a helping hand towards Dim in front. A subjective camera places us in Dim's position, but with foreknowledge of Alex's harmful intent. Despite Alex's narrative chumminess, the camera occasionally reminds us of the position we would likely occupy in the protagonist's empire. Alex, in a carefully controlled act of discipline, cuts the back of Dim's hand, creating a visible reminder of the price of disobedience. Georgie painfully observes from nearby. Alex keeps his left hand extended in mock conciliation while Dim flings himself in the opposite direction. That cruel sarcasm will not be forgotten by his victims.

Alex consolidates his victory over the "new way" by altering Georgie's plan to stop at the Korova, directing his humbled droogs instead to a pub called the Duke of New York. New York suggests an American influence, just as Korova suggests a Russian. British society has to some extent broken up and recombined with elements once foreign to it. The Duke of New York has warm wood furnishings and a relaxed atmosphere. And although the waitress wears a plastic miniskirt and a colored wig, she is a considerable improvement over the Korova's plastic nudes. Alex drinks straight liquor, not the moloko-plus intended for him by Georgie and Dim. All three droogs sit with their eyes downcast in defeat while Alex, hunched over like a bird of prey, glares holes through them. The situation appears to be back where it was the previous night, at the doleful conclusion of Dim's brief, solo rebellion. Narration informs us of Alex's attitude, which is cynical in its blend of contempt tempered by a sense of "when like to give and show generous to his unders." The word *like* betrays Alex's lack of understanding. He reduces generosity, which is alien to his outlook, to a strategic ploy. Even at that, his heavy dose of sarcasm undercuts its effectiveness.

Alex demands and gets a formal surrender from his droogs. "Well, now we're back to where we were, yes? Just like before and all forgotten? Right, right, right?" But it is not in Alex's power to eradicate bitter memories of humiliation. Rubbing salt in their wounds, he compels Georgie to reveal the details of his "mansize" robbery, which Alex then appropriates for his own.

The camera cuts to the next scene, inside the home of the gang's intended victim, while Georgie's description of what *was* his plan overlaps on the soundtrack. Alex's battle music continues; only his target has changed. Initially we see Catlady as Alex, drawing on Georgie's description, imagines her — an abstract extension of her surroundings. Doubled over upside down, with her legs spread apart, she resembles the female figures in paintings on the wall behind her — portraits of sexual submission similar to the poster woman in Alex's bedroom and the plastic figures at the Korova. Catlady's bad taste in art may be trendy, but, when she unwinds from her exercise position to answer a knock at the door, she breaks free of Alex's distorted perspective. Complaining about the disruption of her workout, she does not *sound* like a mute, helpless victim.

Living alone in the country, Catlady appears to be an ideal victim. Sometimes, however, isolation is not a disadvantage. When Alex tries to enlist her help for his allegedly injured friend, she refuses to open the door. Unlike Mrs. Alexander, Catlady has no spouse to reinforce the compassion Alex tries to exploit. In a different sense, Catlady is not as isolated as Georgie described her. Familiar with Alex's modus operandi from newspaper accounts of the Alexander attack, she is doubly suspicious of his sob story. While he searches for an alternate invasion route into her house, she telephones the police. Of course, a free press can bestow strategic advantage on *anyone*, moral or immoral. For example, Alex's return to power at the end of *Clockwork* is fostered by the same institution that now contributes to his downfall.

Outside Catlady's house, Alex improvises a new plan which, however, divides *his* forces rather than hers. Against the Tramp, Billyboy, and the Alexanders, Alex and his droogs formed a united front. After using Dim as a stepladder to reach an open second-story window, Alex leaves his troops idle and unsupervised — a perfect opportunity for them to improvise a plan against *him*.

Alex's confrontation with Catlady is a battle between unyielding wills. Though startled by his sudden appearance inside her private sanctuary, she does not panic. Alex's sarcastic efforts to terrorize her and thereby increase his own pleasure fail miserably. Standing at opposite ends of the room, both characters are juxtaposed with art objects that comment on them by way of similarity and contrast. Alex is astonished to see a large, plastic, oddly inverted sculpture of male genitalia sitting on a table next to the door. In a society permeated by sexual representations of women, this reverse variation on the Korova figures comes as a shock to Alex, who hypocritically questions its owner's morals. The sculpture dwarfs Alex's phallic mask, with which he tormented the Alexanders. For once, Alex is upstaged on his own terms.

Catlady, meanwhile, strikes a defiant pose that superficially resembles a painting on the wall behind her. But in that painting the woman's breast is exposed and she has a gag over her mouth, making her situation more like that of Mrs. Alexander. Catlady, by contrast, orders the "little bastard" out of her house.

Ever resourceful, Alex turns a liability into an advantage by toying with the sculpture his foe values so highly. One shot shows her far in the background, dwarfed by Alex's arm in the foreground, his fingers touching her precious possession. Alex finally gains the upper hand through his victim's emotional attachment to an object. Ownership rather than conscience is her Achilles heel. The plastic genitals are an extension of Catlady's sense of self, which Alex violates. It may seem absurd that a woman could feel violated by a stranger fondling an oversized, plastic penis, but people can form emotional attachments to almost anything.

After softening up Catlady by handling her property, Alex returns to a verbal attack, mocking the nature of their brief acquaintance by casting himself in the role of student magazine peddler opposite Catlady's prospective customer. In other words, he plays supplicant to her, which is a cruel reversal of how he really perceives their relationship. Again, however, she refuses to perform according to his script. So he returns to a physical, if indirect, mode of attack, threatening to damage her sculpture, just as he wounded Mr. Alexander by raping his wife.

By sheer coincidence, Catlady counterattacks with a statuette of Beethoven — the nearest blunt object. Unwittingly she appropriates a representation of Alex's favorite composer for use against him. Aesthetic content has no allegiance. During Alex's bedroom fantasy, Beethoven's music was forced into alliance with a symbol of male sexual power (Basil) and against the poster woman who was the victim of that power. Now an effigy of the same composer is forced to do battle *against* a symbol of male sexuality and on behalf of a woman who is Alex's intended victim.

Catlady's battle with Alex is filmed with a handheld camera that moves in and out between the circling combatants, alternating points of view as she swings the Beethoven bust at him while he fends her off with the plastic genitalia. With Catlady's frenzied participation, Alex transforms their scrap into a comic ballet set to the music of Rossini. Then the unexpected happens. Alex gets knocked down by a blow to the head. Lying on the floor, he loses grip on his own weapon, which for a moment looks more like an undignified human backside than giant testicles. In fact, it looks like one of Catlady's paintings of submissive women. For the first time, Alex is forced to play the victim in one of his own productions. But not for long.

No longer able to afford toying with Catlady, he trips her up. She drops her weapon. He regains possession of his and brings the affair to a brutal conclusion. Two alternating subjective shots depict aggressor and victim from each others' perspectives. Catlady lies on the floor with her mouth and arms wide open in terror. Looming over her is Alex, holding the sculpture, his mouth and eyes wide open also, but in triumph. From Catlady's vantage point, Alex is a grotesque, overwhelming specter of phallic aggression. Mask, sculpture, and codpiece appear in linear alignment, adding up to phallus-*plus*. From Alex's perspective, Catlady's death resembles the portraits of submissive women on her walls. She is reduced to anatomical fragments no more deserving of mercy (in *his* mind) than the plastic eyeballs on his shirtsleeves. On the soundtrack, her dying yell is transformed into the yowl of her pet cats. How chillingly easy it is for Alex to bash her when she is nothing more to him than a hideous caricature.

The sound of a distant police siren disrupts Alex's unexpectedly difficult victory. Kubrick's handheld camera lingers for a moment, echoing the protagonist's confusion. Unlike his performance at the derelict casino, Alex is slow to regain composure. His strategic retreat is clumsy rather than choreographed. He stumbles to the door, fumbles with the doorknob, and lurches out into the entryway past a group of cats as indifferent to his plight as they are to their dead owner's.

A close-up of a milk bottle held by a bandaged hand. Another hand taps the bottle in pleasurable anticipation. A quick reverse zoom reveals a whole new challenge facing Alex. Dim stands holding a milk bottle and facing the front door of Catlady's house. On either side of the door are Pete and Georgie. Alex steps out through the door and, too disoriented by his recent struggle to appreciate his vulnerability, appears surrounded by a new enemy. He has removed his phallic mask, in effect signaling that the game is over. But the droogs retain theirs. *Their* game is just beginning. Dim's milk bottle is borrowed from several sitting on the front steps. Catlady clouted Alex with a bust of his musical hero. Alex bashed Catlady with her own sculpture. Now Dim employs Catlady's morning consignment of milk to overthrow Alex, who is finally forced to take the dose of milk-plus intended for him by his droogs until he overthrew their plans back at the marina.

Alex is caught by surprise when struck on the side of the head with the milk bottle, in delicious slow motion recollecting his triumph at the marina. In previous scenes, we parted company with Alex's victims at their lowest point of degradation. This time we remain with the victim. Georgie, Dim, and Pete dance away from the scene, laughing joyfully and leaving Alex writhing in pain on the ground. Visually bracketing him are two stone statues of lions with the heads of women. Symbolic guardians of Catlady's home, they represent an ironic revenge for their dead owner.

Police captivity brings an unexpected upswing in Alex's power. From an impression of total defeat on Catlady's doorstep, Kubrick wisely skips over the process of arrest and cuts directly to the scene of Alex being interrogated by the police inside a whitewashed, windowless, institutional room. Despite his captivity and injuries, he seems to enjoy a strategic advantage over his captors, who sit looking up at him in apparently impotent silence. "I know the law," he gloats, refusing to answer their questions. Due process restrains as well as empowers the police. A clean bandage over Alex's injured nose attests to that restraint, even mandated compassion, as applied to the handling of alleged criminals. But law enforcement is made up of *individuals* who, like certain members of S.A.C. in *Dr. Strangelove*, sometimes skirt the law in order to fulfill a personal agenda. Isolation works against Alex now the way it worked *for* him during encounters with his victims. The presiding authority in this scene is a passive, middle-aged, uniformed Inspector who outwardly personifies due process. But he employs a younger, aggressive subordinate to circumvent that frustrating barrier and force Alex's cooperation while he watches from a distance. He rebuts Alex's battle cry by pointing out that "knowing the law isn't everything." Yet he is uncomfortable with his illegal method of interrogation, smoking a cigarette to distract himself.

Tom is the police goon who torments Alex, whom he resembles in demeanor. Alignment with the State is all that distinguishes Tom's cruelty from that of his victim. When Alex foolishly challenges Tom by belching in his face, Tom retaliates by jamming his thumb into the prisoner's wounded nose, negating the repair it received at the hands of institutional man and making clever use of Dim's violence to mask his own. He taunts Alex the way Alex taunted the Tramp. Yet he cloaks his brutality with moral outrage over Catlady's plight. Retribution can never be totally isolated from the sadistic impulse. The prisoner's clever counterattack, launched from a submissive position, catches Tom off guard and forces the Inspector to join in a battle from which he had preferred to remain aloof, like a movie audience.

The calm, civilized atmosphere of the reception area outside Interrogation Room B masks the illegal violence occurring inside. A desk sergeant calmly sips tea and eats supper. A bulletin board behind him features a recruiting poster that asks rhetorically, "Have you got what it takes to be a policeman?" while depicting a friendly bobby guiding a young boy. Like S.A.C.'s "Peace Is Our Profession" motto in *Dr. Strangelove*, the poster presents an idealized view of police work contradicted by what we see elsewhere. Mr. Deltoid arrives and chats amiably with the Inspector, who exits Interrogation Room B and asks the desk sergeant for paper towels, as though someone in the other room had spilled a spot of tea and wanted to tidy up. He shifts easily between brutality and politeness, just as Heywood Floyd effortlessly juggled courtesy and deception during his conversation with Russian scientists in *2001*.

Alex sprawls in a corner of the Interrogation Room, his blood staining the white wall and his white clothing. Little remains of his self-styled battle uniform. He is in the preliminary stages of being reduced to basic elements, later to be recostumed by institutional forces beyond his control. A reverse angle-shot, from his perspective, depicts a coalition of his enemies. Mr. Deltoid and the Inspector stand with their hands in their pockets, hypocritical figures of institutional restraint sandwiched between the two police goons who did most of the dirty work, their shirt sleeves rolled up. Sanctimoniously declaring "Violence makes violence," the Inspector excuses police brutality by transferring all blame to Alex and ignoring the fact that Tom *enjoyed* beating up on the prisoner. He tosses Alex an appropriately white paper towel to wipe away the incriminating yet satisfying evidence of police power. Alex imitates the Inspector by transferring responsibility for his own crime to his former droogs, even though he was clearly their leader at the time. Mr. Deltoid follows suit, masking his private grudge against Alex behind a facade of moral outrage over the assault on Catlady.

News of Catlady's death becomes Deltoid's instrument of revenge against the young man who sullied his professional reputation and rejected his sexual advance. Laughing in a revolting manner, he derives greater pleasure from Catlady's death than Alex derived from killing her. But he wastes his advantage as quickly as he gains it. His hope that Catlady's death will torture Alex's conscience presumes that Alex *has* a conscience, and there is little evidence of that. Passing up a chance to hit the prisoner, Deltoid opts instead to spit in Alex's face. Paper towels were less than adequate to clean up the bloody mess caused by the police, but they prove very satisfactory in dealing with Mr. Deltoid's largely symbolic assault. Wiping the spit off his face, Alex flashes his Post Corrective Advisor an arrogant smile in the scene's final shot. Meanwhile, from the reception area comes the sound of a typewriter tapping out a no-doubt sanitized official account of Alex's interrogation.

Part Two of Alex's odyssey through a wicked world begins with a radical reversal of the beginning of Part One. The film's first image was a close-up of Alex that expanded to incorporate the entire Korova Milkbar into his sphere of influence. Now, in several aerial long shots, we see an institutional order so large that individuals are reduced to anonymous specks within it. Alex is sentenced to prison after being convicted of Catlady's murder. The narrator explains: "This is the real weepy and like tragic part of the story beginning, my brothers and only friends." The word "like" again betrays his lack of appreciation for what he talks about. Recollecting past events in his life, the narrator speaks from a narrow perspective after being "cured" of the State's Ludovico "cure" for his violent behavior. A remorseless sociopath, he cannot sympathize with anyone who is powerless, including himself. Instead he solicits *our* sympathy for his beleaguered alter ego because it is useful to him. In the context of this blatant attempt at emotional manipulation, the melancholy slow section of Rossini's *William Tell* Overture generates as much bathos as pathos. Alex's fall from power contains an element of tragedy, but it is tragedy embedded in irony.

If *Clockwork*'s early scenes were Alex's private productions, in which other characters played roles he assigned to them, check-in at Staja 84F is clearly the Chief Guard's production, with Alex as a reluctant performer. Instead of *The Thieving Magpie*, we hear the Chief Guard's barking, staccato voice. His meticulous movements and strict control over the movements of others is reminiscent of Alex's inspired choreography. But the Chief Guard exercises power *through* rather than in defiance of the prevailing social order. And, contrary to Alex's knack for improvisation, the Chief Guard is rigid to the point of absurdity in his performance of duty. He is almost a Gilbert and Sullivan caricature of Victorian discipline. Unlike Mr. Deltoid and the Inspector, the Chief Guard possesses a quaint, unshakable faith in a social order that no longer resembles his idealization of it. Old-fashioned and silly, the Chief Guard is nevertheless a curiously noble character because of his strict adherence, sometimes against his personal wishes, to the rule of law.

Check-in at Staja 84F is an exercise in the power and the banality of due process. The admission room is spartan and impersonal. White walls are rendered even more antiseptic by the glare of naked light bulbs. Much of the wall space is devoted to neat stacks of boxes containing the personal property of inmates, who are figuratively reduced to manageable blocks fitted into prefabricated slots recollecting the immaculate symmetry of HAL's Logic Memory Center in *2001*. Uniformed prison warders, too, appear less as individuals than as abstract extensions of the State.

Alex's admission to prison is an identity-stripping process, yet nothing as severe as what Alex did to *his* victims. He enters Staja 84F dressed in a suit and tie, thus already deprived of his preferred attire. The moment his handcuffs are removed, restoring to him a small measure of mobility, he is stripped of his name and reduced to inmate number 655321. And he must literally toe a line on the floor while surrendering his possessions to the State. Contributing a sour note to the Chief Guard's symphony of due process by casually tossing a candy bar onto the desk, 655321 is ordered to repeat that action *properly*. He complies, but with a hint of exaggeration and a trace of smile that mocks the Chief Guard's furious commitment to even the most trivial rules. Acting through a subordinate, the Chief Guard records the prisoner's surrendered property. Everything, except as noted, will be returned to Alex when he is released, because that is the law. And for the Chief Guard, the law is sacred. But even the Chief Guard cannot completely mask his private opinions in the performance of a public duty. He notes derisively that Alex's address book is made of *imitation* red leather. And he bristles at Alex's flippant reference to the Church of England as the C of E.

Despite his intentional and unintentional gaffes, Alex quickly adapts to his keeper's way of doing things. While being relieved of the last of his clothing, he participates enthusiastically in a bureaucratic trio. Alex and the Chief Guard sing out an exchange of questions and answers, probing into matters that would be considered very private in the outside world, while a warder supplies syncopation with an inventory of Alex's surrendered clothing. The Chief Guard punctuates this lyrical piece by dropping his clipboard onto the table before proceeding to the next movement. The clipboard is both a talisman and a tool of collective due process, containing official paperwork defining his world and his prominent place in it. It is to the Chief Guard what "World Targets in Megadeaths" and the Big Board are to General Turgidson in *Dr. Strangelove*.

The final stage of admission to prison is for Alex the most degrading. Now naked, he is subjected to a rectal examination by the Chief Guard. In a figurative sense Alex is "raped" by the State, acting through the Chief Guard. Of course, such an assault cannot be compared to Alex's literal rape of Mrs. Alexander. There is nothing overtly self-serving about the Chief Guard's performance of duty, as there surely would have been if Mr. Deltoid were in his position. At the end of the scene, Alex is sent off for a bath to wash away the remaining stink of individuality about him. He has no control over his fate, yet his predictable and restrained treatment at the hands of the Chief Guard is an improvement over his situation at police headquarters.

The Chief Guard is less interested in rehabilitating prisoners than in subjecting their deviant behavior to a strict set of rules. By contrast, the prison Chaplain seeks to reform inmates from the *inside* out. Sunday chapel service is his production no less than admissions is the Chief Guard's. A frontal close-up of him in clerical regalia, sermonizing from a pulpit, invites comparison with the film's first close-up of Alex. But subsequent enlargement of the camera frame depicts a less congenial relationship between the central character and his environment.

A big, full-faced man, the Chaplain preaches fire and brimstone in a lilting Irish brogue. His sermon provides its own music as well as message, and he obviously merges his private identity and passions with institutional Christianity. His and the Church's message takes the form of a threat to unrepentant criminals. Crimes committed in this life will earn everlasting punishment in the next. The Chaplain's instruments of persuasion are rhetorical and therefore heavily reliant on hyperbole. Hell's darkness is "darker than any prison" (dark-*plus*). Fire is "hotter than any flame of human fire" (fire-*plus*). The enthusiasm with which he describes each torture suggests that he vicariously participates in the divine power which allegedly inflicts it.

Cutting away from the Chaplain to members of his flock, the camera shows us the limits of his influence. We see the Chief Guard framed within a high arched window behind him. The window resembles one that might be found in a church. But it is a largely secularized image, with no stained glass panels and plenty of steel bars to physically reinforce the Chaplain's purely rhetorical shackles. The Chief Guard, still wearing his State uniform, has removed his cap in deference to the Chaplain's home ground. They are institutional allies in society's war against crime. But the Chief Guard looks bored. He does not share the Chaplain's vision, even though he respects religion as a traditional force in society. Many of the prisoners gathered, however, do not. Though respectfully dressed in suits and ties, they largely ignore the sermon. Two are asleep. One watches the Chaplain, but with a smirk on his face. Another takes advantage of the service to blow kisses at Alex, who appears less than pleased by the attention.

The thin veneer of reverence is shattered when one of the prisoners belches loudly. Incensed, the Chaplain has no other recourse but to turn up his rhetorical heat. Same weapon, more force. It doesn't work. Another prisoner blows him a raspberry, prompting the Chief Guard to intervene and restore order. Giving up his frontal attack, the Chaplain calls on the inmates to sing Hymn 258 from the Prisoners' Hymnal. The Chief Guard, standing between the shepherd and his sheep, commands, "A little reverence, you bastards!" Church and State operate hand in hand in this scene, though with little success, judging by the prisoners' reactions.

Hymn 258 is a crude synthesis of sacred and secular messages. Each line begins with an "I" followed by a ritualistic repentance of wanderlust. "Sheep" and "child" refer to individual man. "Fold," "shepherd," and "Father" represent institutional man. "Love" translates into submission.

Alex's position in this struggle between the State/Church alliance and wayward prisoners is ambivalent. He sits at the Chaplain's right hand, apart from and above his fellow inmates. Though hardly the potentate he appeared to be in the film's first shot, he is at least a minor courtier in the Chaplain's royal court. His red armband is a badge of rank, distinguishing him from the other prisoners. As an instrument of the Chaplain's crusade, Alex finds a congenial home within Staja 84F. He fakes a show of allegiance by singing Hymn 258 with false enthusiasm. But the Chaplain is no fountain of power from which Alex can rejuvenate himself, the way Alex's droogs once fed off *his* joyous productions of ultraviolence. The overhead projector screen over which Alex presides elicits only derision from the other prisoners.

The narrator sums up his alter ego's situation. "It had not been edifying, indeed not," refers not to moral edification but to an amoral feeling of mastery over the conditions of one's life. His grim description of Alex's two years in prison contains verifiable facts but also dubious claims of abuse intended to arouse our sympathy for him. We see direct evidence of "leering criminals" but not of "being kicked and tolchocked by brutal warders," which is not the Chief Guard's style.

Escape from prison blues comes to Alex through his imagination. Denied any meaningful exercise of power through his alliance with the Chaplain, he appropriates a more abstract resource of the Christian faith. In the tranquil environment of the prison library, Alex pursues "edification" by reading Bible stories under the approving smile of his new institutional father. The world of books he once contemptuously trampled at the Alexander home is now, because of his confinement, a source of comfort to him. Though contemptuous of the Chaplain, Alex curries favor with him by showing interest in the "big book" and an apparent eagerness to be reformed. But there is a huge difference in their interpretation of scripture, evident in the contrast between their Bibles. The Chaplain carries a small copy. Alex reads from an oversized edition (Bible-plus).

We first see Alex in this scene as the Chaplain sees him — a pious cherub clutching the Good Book and lost in reverential wonder. Then we see the Chaplain's revered Gospels through Alex's eyes — a highly selective re-creation that liberates him, at least in the realm of fantasy, from Staja 84F. Paper stubs mark the "best" parts of the Bible, as they might flag the most titillating passages of an erotic novel. The imagined sound of wind arises on the soundtrack, wafting Alex and us from the dreary present to an exciting, satisfying past, just as it took us from humankind's savage past to his promising future in *2001*. A shot of Christ being hounded to his crucifixion includes Alex as a wild-eyed, fashionably attired Roman soldier, whipping his victim forward. This impression corresponds to shots of Christ's bloody, bowed head in Alex's bedroom fantasy many scenes ago. Witnessing this event is a crowd of passive spectators reminiscent of most of the government officials in *Dr. Strangelove*'s War Room.

A second Bible-inspired fantasy shows Alex carving up the opposition in battle. A third portrays him enjoying the fruits of that victory, lounging in a sensual paradise, nibbling grapes. A reverse zoom surrounds him with attentive, half-nude handmaidens. Alex, the center of this hedonistic fantasy, rolls his eyes and marvels at the sheer opulence of his good fortune. But a snake lurks in his paradise. Unlike her two companions, the woman on Alex's right (screen left) lies passively on the cushions, a vague expression of discontent on her face. If Alex fantasizes his way out of prison, what form of escape from *his* domination does *she* fantasize? Kubrick has inserted an ironic counterpoint to Alex's fantasy *within* that very fantasy.

As always, Alex fuses disparate elements to create a satisfying new whole. Rimsky-Korsakov's *Scheherazade* has little or no connection with the Bible or even Christianity, but in this instance it is both effective and curiously appropriate. Based on exotic adventure stories told by a sultana as desperate to

Daydreaming about Bible stories in the prison library, Alex (Malcolm McDowell) fancies himself surrounded by the submissive handmaidens of his conquered enemies. But one of his sex slaves appears to be fantasizing her own escape from the role Alex assigned to her.

escape death by their telling as Alex is to escape confinement, *Scheherazade* amplifies the grandeur of Alex's persecution of Christ and the luxuriousness of Alex's dalliance with handmaidens.

Alex's reverie ends when the Chaplain touches his shoulder. *Scheherazade* fades away, replaced by the Chaplain's voice quoting one of *his* favorite Bible passages: "Seek not to be like evil men, neither desire to be with them, because their minds studieth robberies and their lips speak deceit." While saying this, he casts an accusatory glance at other prisoners in the library. Alex, who moments earlier imagined himself as just such an evil man, encourages the Chaplain's misperception of him by playing the penitent. And he does so for a strategic purpose.

Referring to Alex alternately as son and as 655321, the Chaplain unwittingly reveals his dual allegiance to the overlapping but not always complementary perspectives of Church and State. And it is through that duality that Alex pursues a sacred avenue to secular salvation. He steers the Chaplain into one of the library aisles (once again, books prove useful to Alex) in order to conceal their conversation from other prisoners who might covet what he wants. The Chaplain places a reassuring arm around Alex's shoulders, while Alex keeps *his* hands piously folded. But in spite of his fawning behavior, Alex does not get what he wants. The Chaplain reads his own frustrations into

Alex's. Referring indirectly to his vow of celibacy, the Chaplain assumes Alex yearns for sex. But like his assumption about the nature of Alex's interest in the Bible, this is not quite accurate.

Armed with fragments of information gathered through prison gossip, just as Catlady was armed with foreknowledge of Alex's modus operandi when he called on her, Alex mentions a new treatment which can lead to early release from prison. The Chaplain withdraws his reassuring arm. *He* perceives the new treatment as a threat to his institutional power base. The remainder of their conversation is somewhat at cross-purposes. Alex cares nothing about the name, the nature, or the moral ramifications of the mysterious treatment. He just wants out of prison. The Chaplain, adopting a broader view, has ethical doubts. So Alex adjusts his plea for freedom to one for redemption: "I want for the rest of my life to be one act of goodness." But the Chaplain does not see the new treatment as a tool for producing goodness. Sympathetic but unconvinced, he returns his arm to Alex's shoulders and defers the entire matter to divine guidance. Alex outwardly submits to that unpromising course, but adds a subtle bribe directed perhaps at the needs of his more *earthly* father: "Instruct thy son and he shall refresh thee and give delight to thy soul."

We next see Alex in the prison exercise yard: a drab, concrete enclosure with no view of the outside world except a patch of gray sky. Identically dressed prisoners shuffle along a painted white circle. Alex walks and talks with the fellow inmate who made unwelcome sexual overtures to him at chapel service. Ever flexible in adapting to new conditions, perhaps the protagonist has compromised in order to satisfy frustrated sexual urges of which the chaplain spoke earlier.

Meanwhile, inside Alex's empty cell block, a procession of institutional authority figures occurs that will alter the course of Alex's personal odyssey. The white corridor is transformed into a cathedral of secular faith by the combination of camera angle, wide-angle lens, vaulted ceiling, and musical accompaniment. The Chaplain, the Chief Guard, the prison Governor, and several warders make up a loose alliance of Staja 84F's official perspectives and powers. Their attire is uniformly dark and austere. Accompanying them is the Interior Minister from the national government, looking casual and optimistic in his gray suit. This scene is obviously *his* production. Edward Elgar's "Pomp and Circumstance" March No. 1 plays as background music. A traditional anthem for commencement rituals, it heralds a graduation from weakness to strength for the Interior Minister and Alex. The Chief Guard's barking voice, representing a conflicting faith, counterpoints that music.

The Interior Minister pauses to examine one of the cells. Among the contents which identify it as Alex's are two effigies of Beethoven. A large crucifix plus photographs of nude women also stand out in the clutter of possessions. The Minister notes the anachronistic presence of Beethoven, but he departs with no indication that he has found what he is looking for. There is also no evidence that the Chaplain has put in a good word with him on Alex's behalf.

We return to the exercise yard as it was earlier, but with the addition of Elgar's music. From near Alex's vantage point in a line-up, we see the Interior Minister enter the gray yard from a golden corridor, as a potential savior who could deliver him from bondage. But like Alex's own Christ-like arrival in the equally drab world of the Tramp, the Minister will prove an ironic Messiah.

Along with Alex we hear the Minister debate the Governor on the subject of crime control. They agree on the problem of prison overcrowding, but disagree on a solution. The Governor advocates more prison space. The Interior Minister proposes a radical departure from traditional policy. More prisons means a greater tax burden on the resentful public and dwindling support for the Minister's political party. Instead there is to be an assault on the *roots* of crime, which presumably reside in the individual criminal. "Kill the criminal reflex, that's all," is a simple and comparatively inexpensive solution to a complex problem, as was the Doomsday Device in *Dr. Strangelove*. But the Interior Minister hints at a *second* motive behind the reform. "Soon we may be needing all our prison space for political offenders" points *Clockwork* in the direction of *1984* and a police state.

Alex, prisoner 655321 (Malcolm McDowell) plays the Interior Minister (Anthony Sharp) off the prison's Governor (Michael Glover) and Chief Guard (Michael Bates) in order to liberate himself.

Padding his argument for change by discrediting present policy, the Interior Minister makes a ridiculous doublethink assertion that prisoners "enjoy their so-called punishment." An opportunistic Alex boldly joins in the debate. "You're absolutely right, sir," he shouts. Nothing he has said, done, or fantasized thus far suggests that he enjoys confinement. He claims so now simply to get the attention of and curry favor with an influential public official.

Assuming the Interior Minister is looking for a deserving candidate for a conventional rehabilitation program, Alex downplays the brutality of his criminal record. The Chief Guard, despising the arrogant and deceitful young inmate, tries to shut him up. Failing that, he *emphasizes* the brutality of Alex's crime, assuming that this will make him an unacceptable candidate. To the surprise of both, Alex's record of violence is perfectly suited to the Interior Minister's needs. Listening to the Minister expound on Alex's brutal qualifications is like listening to Mr. Deltoid exult over Catlady's death because it serves as ammunition for his personal revenge against the protagonist. Prisoner 655321 fits the publicity profile of the government's plan to improve its image. The jaded public would not be impressed by the rehabilitation of a *minor* criminal. For the moment, high administrator and lowly inmate share the joyful promise of "Pomp and Circumstance." The Chief Guard scowls impotently at his grinning foe as the scene concludes.

Opposing the Interior Minister's new program, Staja 84F's Governor has apparently been studying the beliefs of his enemy. Lying in a wire basket on his desk is a dog-eared copy of B. F. Skinner's *Walden Two*, a vision of social utopia that postulates "a special behavioral science which can take the place of wisdom and common sense and with happier results" (Skinner, viii). When Alex is brought into his office to sign papers giving himself over to the Ludovico Project, the Governor openly criticizes what we in retrospect recognize to be, like Skinner's proposals, a piece of behavioral engineering designed to bypass the old maxim "Know thyself" on the way to social harmony. The Governor advocates instead the traditional solution of an eye for an eye, failing to recognize that the State is made up of diverse individuals who are not always public-spirited about doling out punishment. Dim and Georgie's later stint as policemen illustrate the flaw in his logic.

Whatever the strengths and weakness of his argument, the Governor has already lost the debate. Shouted at, forbidden to speak in his own defense, and forced again to literally toe the line in this scene, Alex quietly outflanks his enemies by signing the consent forms that remove him from their custody. The Chief Guard vents his frustration by shouting, "Don't read it! Sign it!" The Governor, to his credit, is more thorough in his devotion to due process, even when he opposes its results. He explains in general terms to Alex the meaning of the consent form. But that explanation leaves out details about the treatment itself. With the same mighty stroke of a pen by which he surrendered his personal possessions, Alex liberates himself from Staja 84F. He flashes his blue-eyed victory grin. But as is so often the case in a Kubrick film, things are not what they first appear to be.

Elgar's "Pomp and Circumstance" March No. 4, another formal ode to institutional advancement, belongs entirely to Alex as he is transferred from Staja 84F to the Ludovico Medical Facility. Despite being handcuffed and led by the Chief Guard at a typically martial pace, Alex has the upper hand. The music celebrates his graduation from prison to expected liberation in a matter of weeks rather than years. Alex punctuates his triumph by broadly parodying his jailer's military gait when they reach their destination.

Staja 84F and the Ludovico Centre are aesthetically very different. The Chief Guard, all starch and vinegar in his uniform, stops abruptly in front of the Enquiries Desk, as though there were a white line on the floor for *him* to toe. The Centre scientists, by contrast, look relaxed and informal in their white lab coats, surrounded by undemonstrative decor. Captain Mandrake, President Muffley, and Heywood Floyd would feel right at home here. The one exception to the neutral decor is a large, red-orange sign that provides directions to the maze of departments within the facility. A variation on *Dr. Strangelove*'s Big Board, the sign is a guide to the collective faith of the people gathered beneath it. It signifies their gospel no less than the clipboard does the Chief Guard's and the Bible does the Chaplain's.

A uniformed Centre guard named Charlie takes charge of the prisoner, but he is little more than a token representative of old-style law enforcement. He does not even bother to handcuff Alex, to the consternation of the Chief Guard, who warns the scientists of Alex's brutality and deceitfulness. Dr. Alcott, presiding Centre authority in this scene, calmly replies, "Oh, I think we can manage things." This seems like a victory for Alex over the rigid discipline of Staja 84F. But Alcott's serenity is a measure of his confidence in the Centre's ability to deal with deviant behavior. Contrary to the Chief Guard's assumptions, the Ludovico scientists harbor no sentimental illusions about Alex, whose smug pleasure at being escorted to a room instead of a cell is misplaced.

The elaborate paper transfer of Alex's custody, performed on the Chief Guard's clipboard, is an institutional march to the music of Elgar. The polite signing and distribution of numerous official forms lends a ritualistic air of legitimacy and civility to what is essentially a hostile exchange of power between two different government agencies. The Chief Guard's fastidious handling of the paperwork, in spite of his opposition to the Centre, illustrates his passionate fidelity to due process.

Life at the Centre appears to be a big improvement over life at Staja 84F. Charlie stands a very relaxed guard duty outside Alex's unlocked door. Inside, Alex lies in bed, dressed in pajamas, eating breakfast and reading a magazine.

The room is light, airy, clean, and uncrowded. On the other hand, it contains nothing of his personality, not even the Beethoven effigies he was allowed to display in his prison cell. Though in some respects a model of humane treatment, Alex's room at the Centre is as sterile as his inner vision soon will be.

Among the few possessions restored to Alex at the Centre are his name and the privilege of addressing his superiors by their names rather than "sir." Dr. Branom is the Centre's equivalent of Staja 84F's Chief Guard, serving as Dr. Brodsky's assistant in the same way the Chief Guard serves the Governor. Her white smock and identification badge are equivalent to the Chief Guard's uniform and crown insignia. Out with the old, in with the new symbols of institutional power. Dr. Branom is more courteous but no less firm in exercising control over Alex's life. Her arrival signals an abrupt end to his leisurely breakfast. "We're going to be friends then, aren't we, Alex," sounds, more like a statement than a question. Dr. Branom establishes her authority over Alex in a less theatrical but more convincing fashion than did the Chief Guard.

While Branom converses with Alex, the camera zooms in to a close-up of the *true* arbiter of future relations between individual and institutional man. Experimental Serum 114 is as transparent as its official purpose. Alexander Walker notes the numerical analogy to the CRM 114 circuits on board Major Kong's B-52 (Walker, 292). Both are technological tools that lock human beings into a narrow path of perception and behavior. Branom's assistant holds a silver bowl containing the serum as though it were the healing power of holy communion, which is precisely how its advocates view the new drug.

Not surprisingly for a behavioralist who regards her patient as something akin to a laboratory rat, Dr. Branom gives evasive answers to Alex's questions about the treatment awaiting him. But when he naively compares the Ludovico films he will be viewing to an ordinary trip to the movies, she momentarily drops her veil of professional detachment and, like a sadistic mad scientist in a horror movie, *relishes* her power over an unsuspecting victim. Her piercing eyes, the tilt of her head, and the sardonic edge in her voice betray her forbidden pleasure. The specter of Dr. Strangelove lurks in all of us. But on another level of interpretation, Dr. Branom plays righteous avenger for Alex's many female victims. And he has much to atone for in that regard.

An audiovisual theater is the stage for overlapping private and public dramas. Trussed up in a white straitjacket, his head and eyelids clamped into an inescapably receptive position, Alex is reduced to a captive audience at someone else's horrorshow, just as Mr. Alexander was forced, for Alex's edification, to watch the rape of his wife. And, like his victims, Alex is unattractive in his abject helplessness. He is an almost comic figure, occupying a front row seat but stripped of the traditional option of a horror-film audience to look away from the screen when the experience becomes unpleasant. Thomas Nelson notes that Alex's Ludovico headgear resembles a crown of thorns (Nelson, 155). Alex suffers a Christ-like martyrdom to the behavioralist faith of a new Roman Empire, yet he did not hesitate to sacrifice *his* victims to the cause of his own pleasure.

The chair into which Alex is strapped resembles a device of torture, and from his vantage point it functions that way. But, from the scientists' point of view, it was not designed as such. A medical technician, wearing a white uniform that sanctions all he does, secures Alex into the chair but also administers soothing eye drops to prevent discomfort and injury. He is yet not a torturer.

Seated far behind Alex, at the back of the theater, are a group of Ludovico scientists, including project head Dr. Brodsky. All of them wear white lab coats. To them, Alex is a small, abstract player in an epic scientific drama. Brodsky's relationship to the patient is impersonal but not passionless. After all, his professional reputation is linked to Alex's performance. Banks of monitoring equipment, attached by wires to Alex's head, are visible behind the scientists. Dr. Brodsky perceives and relates to Alex largely through the abstract impressions supplied by those machines — impressions that simplify the subject, just as various paintings and cat yowls simplified Catlady for Alex at the moment he killed her.

The first of Alex's viddy sessions features a beating and a rape, highlights of ultraviolence with the dull parts edited out, like Alex's hatchet job on the Bible back in the prison library. A wide-eyed child, Alex happily takes it all in. Anything presented in a vivid, exciting manner is deemed by him to be both "good" and "realistic," when in fact the violence on screen consists of fake punches, fake blood, and exaggerated sound effects. The film clips present a stylized violence infused with a lyricism that renders it in some respects more appealing and memorable than the real thing. Alex acknowledges as much when he remarks, "It was beautiful. It's funny how the colors of the real world only seem really real when you viddy them on the screen." Film, like other art forms, provides a magical combination of passionate involvement, safe detachment, and order.

Alex's enjoyment of the film clips is gradually displaced by a feeling of sickness induced by the serum injected into him earlier. He is robbed not only of his ability to choose what he sees, but also of his physiological reactions to what he sees. Elements of his own body are recruited by the State in its assault on his criminal tendencies. Instead of appealing to Alex's deficient conscience, Ludovico taps directly into his sadistic impulses. Various facets of Alex's perception are deconstructed, then reconstructed to promote a different pattern of behavior. Divide and conquer. Overexposed to an experience he can no longer tolerate, Alex's eyes resemble the plastic eyeballs that once decorated his shirtsleeves. He even refers to them as "glazzballs," as though they were things separate from the rest of him. Initially pleasant movie images are now an assault on his artificially heightened senses. He employs battlefield terminology when speaking of their "line of fire." Ludovico Hell is acute physical and emotional distress that cannot be resolved. Unlike Dave Bowman's escape from chaos in *2001*, there is no sanctuary for Alex. In fact, his predicament comes close to realizing the Chaplain's vision of divine punishment. Belching uncontrollably in an effort to relieve his acute nausea, he is unable to perform the one act which would normally do so.

Near the back of the theater, Dr. Brodsky, his head crowned by a bright crescent of projector light as though imbued with some divine spirit, calmly describes to his colleagues what is happening to the patient. Alex's off-screen cries of distress, muted by the distance between front and back rows, form a dramatic counterpoint to Brodsky's dispassionate discussion of "death-like paralysis" and "deep feelings of terror and helplessness." Brodsky does not enjoy Alex's suffering in the way Alex enjoyed the suffering of *his* victims, yet the doctor's utilitarianism yields the same result as his patient's sadism. For Brodsky, "deep feelings of terror and helplessness" are but a necessary evil along the road to a greater good.

The "rewarding associations" Alex is expected to make during this session are rewarding primarily for Brodsky and the Interior Minister. Observing Alex's reactions to the screened violence that flickers in reflection across the scientist's glasses, Dr. Brodsky clearly does not make the same "rewarding associations" he expects of Alex. Dr. Branom, however, appears uncomfortable about her patient's agony, even though in the previous scene she briefly enjoyed the anticipation of it. On both ends of the emotional spectrum, from cruelty to compassion, she demonstrates a greater capacity than does her boss. But if she has moral doubts about the treatment, they are insufficient to override her fidelity to the project and to Brodsky.

"Timesteps," a synthesized composition by Walter Carlos, reflects Alex's terrifying descent into Ludovico Hell, where he is master of nothing. Crazy twangs and bangs echo blows delivered on the Ludovico movie screen. But they do not yield an impression of *controlled* violence, as did similar sound effects during *Clockwork*'s opening scene.

Alex discusses his first Ludovico session with Dr. Branom back in his bedroom. Lying in bed, a cup of coffee in hand, he ponders his ordeal with philosophical detachment that he once dismissed as "for the gloopy ones," meaning pointless. He does so now only because he cannot act to change it. He is being transformed from the clockwork mechanism he was (whether by environmental influence or genetic propensity) into a clockwork mechanism the State prefers him to be.

Dr. Branom passionately articulates the gospel of behavioral science, just as the Chaplain did the gospel of Christianity. But Branom's gospel is newer, fresher, less rhetorically rootbound, and in practical terms more potent than the Chaplain's. Three low-angle close-ups of Branom convey the strength of her conviction. Perhaps she requires passion in order to overcome her moral qualms about the suffering caused by Ludovico. "Dr. Brodsky is pleased with you" is her equivalent of a papal blessing. The behavioralist creed may pretend to be strictly objective, but there is an evangelical edge to Branom's sermon. "Violence is a horrible thing," she declares. In despair of individual man's capacity to comprehend that horror, her faith bypasses the conscious mind and targets the body. Ludovico reduces the learning process to a set of conditioned reflexes. Previous institutional crises of faith in Kubrick films produced Plan R, the Doomsday Machine, and HAL.

Her mouth quivering with passion, Dr. Branom unwittingly betrays the hypocrisy of her faith. She equates a healthy state of mind with a revulsion against *all* violence, which is the attitude being programmed into Alex. And yet she can barely contain her own joy at the violence done to Alex, ostensibly for his own good and the good of society. Passion of *any* kind is a form of violence, including Dr. Branom's sense of righteousness. Depicted in a low-angle close-up which concludes this scene, Branom's passionate sense of purpose is juxtaposed by direct cut with a notorious example of an equally passionate but discredited faith, which Alex is then conditioned to reject.

Session two of the Ludovico treatment features an institutional variation on the more personal violence of session one. Documentary film footage, including clips from Leni Riefenstahl's *Triumph of the Will*, shows Adolf Hitler at one of the colossal Nazi Party rallies in 1930s Germany. Flanked by two droogs who mimic his movements at a respectful distance, and surrounded by massive formations of his political pawns, all adorned in Nazi regalia, Hitler strides triumphantly across a concrete plain. Visually he is dwarfed by his surroundings, yet as far as the eye can see the world has arranged itself around him, according to his wishes. The concrete is partitioned into large squares. If the chessboard analogy from Alex's assault on the Alexanders is brought to bear on this scene, all of the chess pieces are controlled by one man.

A synthesized rendition of Beethoven's Ode to Joy march accompanies these images, infusing them with a seductive lyricism. The same music accompanied Alex's regal promenade through the Music Bootick. The parallel is obvious. Only scale and historical context differentiate the two characters. On a more troubling note, the ambitions of Alex and of Hitler cannot be wholly divorced, in either aesthetic or moral terms, from those of Branom and Brodsky, who have appropriated the art of Reifenstahl and Beethoven for use in their own plan. Even Kubrick, by assembling *Clockwork* partly from preexisting works of art, evinces that ambition. We all do.

Expanding beyond the prewar confines of *Triumph of the Will*, the Ludovico movie adds documentary footage depicting Hitler's lust for power, as institutionalized in the Third Reich, pushing across German borders and incorporating neighboring countries by military force. One of the last images features a statue depicting happy children dancing around a crocodile, while behind them a city burns — joy in the midst of danger and destruction, individual man blissfully ignoring, even defying, the wicked world around him. Think of Alex whistling gaily to himself while strolling home through an ugly, garbage-strewn neighborhood. Undoubtedly such a parallel was not intended by the Ludovico scientists. But it probably was by Kubrick.

Gradually Alex recognizes the musical accompaniment to this historical antipageant. The composer who once allegedly tore up a dedication of his *Third Symphony* to Napoleon, upon learning that the Revolutionary General had rechristened himself Emperor of France, would not likely be thrilled to have his work associated with Nazi aggression. Alex, however, might have dreamed up such a combination on his own. But in the context of Ludovico conditioning, that combination is a threat to his very capacity for creative association. And so he objects to it.

The ensuing debate is an exercise in frustration for the protagonist. Each side misunderstands the other and pursues the matter at its own pace and in its own style. Brodsky and Branom, puzzled by the cry of "It's a sin!" from someone they assumed lacked any moral sensibility, methodically try to ferret out an explanation. Alex, growing ever more impatient and desperate, fails to tailor his plea to his particular audience and therefore fails to persuade them.

Alex insists it is wrong, "using Beethoven like that! He did no harm to anyone. Beethoven just wrote music!" This is a shallow interpretation of the composer's relationship to his art and of that art to the world at large. And it is a hypocritical position for Alex to take. More than anyone else in the film, Alex arbitrarily appropriates music for his own use. It is his personal loss of Beethoven as a source of inspiration that he objects to, not any injustice done to the composer's memory. And as for Beethoven, no composer ever "just wrote music." Music is an extension of the composer's will. It is an instrument of power, however abstract.

Dr. Branom looks concerned about Alex's torment but again does nothing to stop it. Dr. Brodsky, for whom Alex's suffering is an accident irrelevant to the goal of the Ludovico Program, remains stubbornly indifferent to Alex's protests, because he believes only what Alex's *body* tells him. When pressed to defend his position, he falls back on the heavenly grace of due process. "The choice has been all yours," he says, referring to the consent forms Alex signed. In strictly legal terms, that is true. But he fails to take into account Alex's ignorance of the treatment when he consented to undergo it. Finally, there is a third perspective of Alex's Ludovico ordeal. Dr. Brodsky offhandedly remarks that Staja 84F's Governor, an opponent of Ludovico reform, should be pleased at the suffering Alex now endures.

Desperate, Alex gropes for a strategy to retain custody of his beloved Ludwig van. Sensing an evangelical edge to Brodsky's argument, he claims to have had a moral awakening. "You've proved to me that all this ultraviolence and killing is wrong, wrong and terribly wrong. I've learned my lesson, sir. I see now what I've never seen before. I'm cured, praise God!" But Alex pitches this argument to the wrong audience. It might have worked with the Chaplain, but not with a disciple of behavioralism. Unmoved, Brodsky replies sternly, "You're not cured yet, boy." In Brodsky's scientific view, *everyone* is a child, except perhaps his own caste (the elitist flaw in his faith).

Frustrated, Alex switches to a more secular approach. "It's wrong because it's like against society." Betrayed again by his use of the qualifier "like," Alex merely regurgitates words and phrases he has heard before, in hopes they will get him out of a tight spot. And even if his moral awakening were genuine, Brodsky would not believe it. If Alex's hypocrisy and deceitfulness are being satirized in this scene, so are the inflexible perceptions of the Ludovico scientists. Brodsky arbitrarily ends the debate, promising that Alex will be a free man in less than a fortnight. By legal definition that is true. But Brodsky's definition of freedom is nontraditional, to say the least.

Throughout this scene, Beethoven's march throbs on the soundtrack, performing two overlapping dramatic functions. As background score to the Nazi documentary footage, it serves the Ludovico scientists in their effort to recondition Alex. But when the camera cuts away from the Ludovico theater screen and enters into the debate between Alex and his doctors, the music echoes the passions of two irreconcilable perspectives.

Alex's final exam is staged in the Ludovico Auditorium and consists of questions directed at and answers supplied by his involuntary physiological reflexes. The occasion also furnishes Ludovico advocates with a public showcase for their controversial program. Alex is one among several featured performers in a two-act morality play. The Interior Minister serves as Greek Chorus. The assembled audience, formally dressed and seated respectfully, with official programs on their laps, consists of journalists and various members of the government, including such Ludovico opponents as Staja 84F's Governor, Chief Guard, and Chaplain. The larger drama in this scene, within which the Ludovico demonstration is embedded, features the audience's reactions to what they see.

Alex stands alone on stage, shielding his eyes from the spotlight glare of collective scrutiny. He is well groomed and dressed in a proper suit and tie, which the State intends to demonstrate reflects his *inner* self. Producer, financial backer, and narrator of this piece of theater, the Interior Minister assures his audience that Alex has not been altered by temporary measures, such as hypnosis, in order to make the State's case more convincing. Padding his argument, he contrasts Ludovico rehabilitation with prison incarceration, which taught Alex "the false smile, the rubbed hand of hypocrisy, the fawning, greased, obsequious leer," and so forth. His point is valid but conveniently self-serving. Before the Ludovico option, the Interior Minister would undoubtedly have *defended* the existing penal system against such criticism. The hypocrisy of his argument can be read in his *own* hands, which unwittingly become the "rubbed hand[s] of hypocrisy" he condemns in others.

Speaking as though from revolutionary faith, he announces the impending end of all violent crime. But being a cynical politician, he speaks out of both sides of his mouth. Sitting down to enjoy the show, he smiles a "false smile" of solidarity at Dr. Brodsky, on his left, then confidentially confesses to a party hack, on his right, that his faith in Brodsky is a result of his party's desperate position in the popularity polls. Like the overburdened Soviets and the frightened Americans in *Dr. Strangelove*, the Interior Minister lashes his wagon to the nearest live horse.

The Chaplain offered only rhetoric in support of his vision of rehabilitation. The Interior Minister offers a more convincing *demonstration*. "But enough of words. Actions speak louder than. Action now. Observe all." Because that *demonstration* is merely one part of a larger drama, we observe much more than the Minister intends. The three officials from Staja 84F applaud politely, but without enthusiasm. The Chief Guard, in particular, cannot hide his disapproval.

The first Ludovico morality play is accompanied by Terry Tucker's "Overture to the Sun," a metronomic mix of fatalism and joy, or the joy *of* fatalism. The play is a celebration of human constraint rather than wisdom. Its hero is the Ludovico-conditioned reflex. Alex's costar is a sarcastic man with an irritating voice. Without provocation, he heaps verbal and physical abuse on Alex, who is eventually roused to retaliate, as most of us would be. But his punch is stopped in midair by the disabling sickness of Ludovico. Unable to defend himself, Alex is pushed to the stage floor and forced to lick the sole of his tormentor's shoe. The camera observes this action from a variety of perspectives: a low-angle close-up from the victim's vantage point; a side view that conveys the Chief Guard's keen personal interest in the action; and a long shot of the two performers which depicts them as silhouetted abstractions of good and evil, as defined by the State.

Smirking at Alex's ordeal, the Chief Guard derives pleasure from the Ludovico demonstration, of which he expressed disapproval only moments earlier. Also enjoying the show, but for different reasons, are Dr. Brodsky and the Interior Minister. Seated with their hands passively clasped in their laps, they are indifferent to Alex's suffering. Validation of the Ludovico Program by Alex's degrading performance is what pleases them. But though they exchange a look of mutual satisfaction, their perspectives are not identical. They represent a marriage of convenience between science and government. Each serves the interests of the other, for the time being.

The Interior Minister rings down the curtain on Alex's ordeal before it embarrasses members of the audience who, unlike the Chief Guard, wish to remain emotionally detached from it. On cue from his director, Alex's tormentor stops his performance and, tracked by the spotlight, moves with thespian flair to center stage to accept the audience's applause. As indifferent to Alex's plight as are Brodsky and the Interior Minister, he merely *feigned* cruelty. Alex, momentarily left in the dark, writhes in *real* pain. Which is more despicable: the straightforward sadism of the Chief Guard or the cool indifference of Ludovico advocates who reduce violence and suffering to passionless abstractions within a higher pattern of logic?

Act Two features the sexual complement to the violence of Act One. Stepping out onto the stage is a shapely, bare breasted young woman. Her hair an artificial silvery white and her face expressionless, she is the living embodiment of her plastic Korova sisters. Purcell's "Funeral" music, another ghost from the Milkbar, echoes Alex's passionate interest in her. A subjective camera gives us an idea of the narrow focus of his interest. The closer she gets, the more she is reduced to her exposed breasts, as were Mrs. Alexander and, in a sense, the Bible. But Alex is not the only man present to feel lust. The Chief Guard gapes at the nude woman. Even the Chaplain reacts. Inspired, Alex imaginatively appropriates the spotlights, which have thus far scrutinized *him* so pitilessly, for his own purpose. They become the "light of heavenly grace" illuminating his prey.

Looking up from the floor at his ideal sex slave, Alex sees two mountainous breasts he wants to scale and conquer. Between them is a face that seems to challenge him to do so. From the woman's perspective, Alex is an unimposing figure, incapable of possessing her. In profile, we see Alex reach greedily for her breasts, then fail miserably as the Ludovico sickness strikes again. He sinks to the floor and appears to kowtow to her. The power of Purcell's music seems to belong to the woman. In fact, it belongs to her sponsors: the Interior Minister and Dr. Brodsky. Like her male predecessor, the actress detaches herself effortlessly from her feigned relationship with Alex, then finds *genuine* gratification in the audience's boisterous applause. The fact that much of that approval is a product of the same lust that has been suppressed in Alex occurs neither to the actress nor to her admirers. The Chief Guard, who moments earlier perceived Alex through the eyes of his male tormentor, now sees the actress through Alex's eyes. The Interior Minister, satisfied that his point has been made, again calls a discreet halt to the proceedings.

Act Three of the Ludovico demonstration begins as the State intends, with the Interior Minister and his star performer sharing the collective spotlight. For selfish reasons, Alex accommodates himself to his ally's scenario, claiming to have suffered no ill effects from it. But, "Feel really great, sir," is contradicted by the belch his *body* produces. In this instance, however, institutional man ignores physiological truth in favor of verbal illusion. Alex shamelessly ingratiates himself by inquiring, "Did I do well, sir?" But the "I" that performed well on the Ludovico stage was Alex's body, not his mind. The problem of criminal rehabilitation has been reduced to a simple equation in which A, the impulse to commit violence, equals B, nonviolent behavior.

The Chaplain's disruption of the Interior Minister's sermon is not on the official program and therefore replaces the State's Act Three with an unscheduled Act Four, performed under the same harsh light of institutional scrutiny. "Choice!" is the clergyman's cry of protest against the demonstration. "Self-interest, the fear of physical pain, drove him [Alex] to that grotesque act of self-abasement. Its insincerity was clearly to be seen. He ceases to be a wrongdoer. He ceases also to be a creature capable of moral choice." Accurate, but also hypocritical. "Fear of physical pain" and "self-interest" were the same appeals the Chaplain made to prison inmates when he warned of the tortures of Hell awaiting unrepentant sinners. The Interior Minister addresses his challenger as "Padre," rendering him vaguely foreign to the English audience. He dismisses the Chaplain's argument as obscure, then borrows the clergyman's evangelical rhetoric in order to defend Ludovico. Appealing to both old and new faiths, he describes the reconstructed Alex as "your true Christian, ready to turn the other cheek, ready to be crucified rather than crucify," then concludes on a more scientific, pragmatic note. "The point is that it *works!*"

Alex finds himself in the clutches of opposing institutional forces, each claiming to defend his best interests. He sides with the Interior Minister simply because it will get him released from State custody. In the scene's final shot, Alex smiles at the auditorium audience, who clap their approval of the government's demonstration. But neither he nor the Interior Minister can anticipate the consequences of their collaboration when it is exposed to the chaotic world outside the Ludovico Centre.

Part Three of Alex's odyssey, in which he plays the victim to several of his former victims, is a reversal of Part One. Carrying his bundle of belongings (the Chief Guard kept his promise), Alex returns home smiling and confident. His key still unlocks the front door. But, little by little, his loss of status becomes apparent. A thin, innocuous, popular song from an off-screen radio replaces his thunderous Beethoven. The combination lock that stood guard over his bedroom is gone. Inside the room, his prized possessions have been replaced by sports posters and a pair of dumbbells. As he stands in the doorway, Alex's frown is counterpointed by the mildly erotic facial expression of a woman in a painting on the wall behind him. As is often the case in *Clockwork*, coincidental aesthetic similarities (the postures of Alex and the woman are alike) mask very different emotional realities.

In the living room, Alex's parents and a stranger casually read newspapers trumpeting his release from prison with sensational approval. The free press has done its job exactly as the Interior Minister anticipated. "Murderer Freed: Science Has Cure" says nothing about the Ludovico Revolution's new definitions of "freedom" and "cure." To Pee and Em, sipping tea as they read, Alex is an almost anonymous character in a far-off drama, as were the Alexanders to Catlady. They are surprised to see him walk into the room. Where did they *think* he would go?

Adjustment to change proves difficult for everyone concerned. Alex expects to take charge of the family right where he left off two years earlier. "Hi, hi, hi there, my Pee and Em" sounds just like "Hi, hi, hi there, my little droogies." A fake punch to his father's chin elicits the expected flinch of fear. "Well, still the same old place then, eh?" naively ignores the stranger seated next to his mother on the couch.

Alex's confrontation with Joe, Pee, and Em's new lodger, is unflattering to both. First, Alex's claim to be "completely reformed" is bogus. When Joe declares his right to retain Alex's former place in the family, Alex tries to punch him. Ludovico conditioning, not a reformed conscience, stops him from doing so. As for the lodger, he rightly chastises Alex for the pain caused to Pee and Em. But he acts out of self-interest, not genuine moral outrage. And his boast that he will defend Pee and Em's tranquility with his very life proves empty. Intimidated by Alex's aborted punch, Joe retreats to Em's comforting arms. If not for the Ludovico treatment, he would be beaten up and bounced from the apartment in short order. And though stopping Alex's violent attacks was its intention, the State did *not* foresee its action serving the selfish interests of someone else.

Alex's sickness is, as Joe observes, repulsive. He may be a swine for saying it, but aesthetically he is correct. The lack of power is seldom attractive. But power can exist in many forms. When Alex discovers he cannot physically dislodge Joe, he tries a less direct tactic. After learning that his personal property was confiscated by the police, in order to compensate his victims, and that Basil was destroyed, Alex clutches his few remaining possessions to his chest and cleverly uses his sad plight to make Pee and Em feel guilty about turning him out. But Pee avoids that trap by appealing to a higher, institutional code of ethics. Joe cannot be evicted from Alex's room because he has already paid next month's rent. Wringing his hands in hypocritical dismay, Pee avoids admitting to Alex and to himself that he and Em *prefer* Joe to be their son. Joe then builds on Pee's defense, riding to the rescue of his adopted parents, and not coincidentally serving his own cause, by declaring it his *duty* to protect them from "this young monster, who's been like no real son at all." Like Pee, Joe too rubs his hands together while defying Alex, though to a more deliberate purpose. Between *his* hands he cradles one of Em's, soliciting her maternal affection.

Stymied, Alex starts to cry. For the first time, he shows pity for someone powerless, even if it is himself. Ironically, his capacity for pity has been encouraged by the Ludovico constraints on his capacity for violence. Joe, meanwhile, justifiably dismisses the protagonist's tears as a phony ploy for sympathy. Think of the sob stories Alex fed the Alexanders, Catlady, and the police. But once again, legitimate criticism is entirely self-serving.

Unable to force Joe out or to persuade Pee and Em to take him back, Alex stakes a weepy claim to martyrdom. "I've suffered and I've suffered and I've suffered, and everyone wants me to go on suffering." Not quite. Staja 84F's Governor and Chief Guard want him to suffer, as will his former victims. But for many characters Alex's suffering is incidental to other priorities.

Closing in for the kill, because he knows Alex cannot physically retaliate, Joe presses his advantage too far. His harsh accusations upset Em. She and Pee are largely pawns in a power struggle between the young men. Joe returns to Em's side to comfort her, reprimanding Alex for making her cry. Certainly Alex bears primary responsibility for causing pain to his parents. But it is Joe who rekindles memories of that pain in order to drive a wedge between parents and son.

Wiping away his useless tears before departing, Alex vindictively heaps upon his parents the blame for all his woes, present and future. The soundtrack becomes a symphony of conflicting emotions, featuring Alex's parting curse, Em's remorseful wailing, Joe's self-serving reassurance of her, and Pee's futile attempt to mollify everyone's hurt feelings. Music from Rossini's *William Tell* Overture echoes and parodies every one of those voices. Alex storms out of the room while Pee and Em retreat to the comfort of a family hug with his victorious rival.

William Tell carries over from Alex's debacle at home to his lonely walk along the Thames River. But this time it is a straightforward rather than an ironic echo of his plight. Tracking with him, the camera zooms in to an intimate close-up of his face as he gazes out over the river, then follows the direction of his suicidal thoughts to the tranquil water beneath a bridge. White gulls wheel gracefully over the river's smooth surface, creating an enticing impression of oblivion diametrically opposed to feelings associated with the great bird of prey Alex envisioned at the Korova. Instead of conquering the wicked world, Alex dreams of escaping from it, like the alcoholic Tramp.

"Can you spare me some cutter, me brother?" breaks Alex's suicidal reverie. That same old Tramp sidles up to Alex and begs for money. And for the first time in his selfish life, Alex shows genuine compassion for another human being. With no ulterior motive and very little money to spare, he gives the old man several coins from his pocket. Kubrick wisely presents it as a brief and unselfconscious rather than a full-blown moral awakening. And it is ironic that Alex's change of heart comes about through the suffering he endured as an indirect result of Ludovico conditioning, which was never intended to awaken his conscience. For a moment, Alex demonstrates a capacity to "learn the error of his way" (Joe's parting taunt) that Ludovico advocates had forsaken. But his reformation is ill timed. For what he was and for what he did to the Tramp earlier in the film, Alex richly deserves what he is about to get. But for what he shows signs of becoming, he does not.

Mutual recognition renders Alex sick at the mere recollection of past violence and inspires the Tramp to seek violent revenge. The camera reverse zooms to place this private encounter within a larger conflict between generations. The Tramp calls upon other transient old men to join in a crusade against *his* enemy. They form a rather loose alliance. Among the words employed by the Tramp to rally his companions to his cause, "young" probably carries more emotional weight than "swine," "murderous," and "pig." The elder warriors do not rise to the Tramp's defense so much as they individually strike back, through young Alex, at a world that has escaped their feeble grasp. The first of them to reach Alex, after the Tramp trips him up, grabs the young man's bundle of belongings and runs away, less interested in avenging an old wrong done to a friend than in stealing a few items of clothing to perhaps barter for food and drink.

The geriatric assault on Alex lacks the brutal lyricism of Alex's assault on the Tramp. Low-angle close-ups from Alex's perspective portray his attackers as grotesque and ineffectual, all quivering jowls and feeble rookers. And the tramps undermine their own cause in yet another way. One of them refers derisively to Alex as a "vagabond," a term of contempt equally applicable to the assailants. *Self-*contempt accounts for at least some of their rage against the protagonist.

Alex is rescued from the ancient mob by an institutional force which earlier failed to protect the Tramp from *him*. He is helped off the pavement by two uniformed policemen whose hands grasp his shoulders in support, recollecting an earlier image, in the Ludovico Auditorium, of the Chaplain and the Interior Minister resting their hands benevolently on Alex's shoulders. Though the clergyman and the politician both claimed to be acting in Alex's best interest, they opposed each other. The two policemen act as a team, but, as it turns out, *not* in Alex's best interest. Seen from behind, and therefore as anonymous institutional figures, the policemen fulfill their duty as protectors of public order, a service particularly vital to someone as defenseless as Alex. But when viewed from the front, they acquire private identities and motivations which contradict their official duties. Alex looks up in horror to see

Dim and Georgie in police uniform. The ineffectual assault on Alex by the old derelicts is displaced by the chillingly potent image of Dim, in low-angle medium shot, looking surprised and delighted at this unexpected opportunity. Purcell's "Funeral" music returns to the soundtrack, this time echoing Dim's rather than Alex's power. But its extrinsic meaning, as a lament for the death of collective authority, is particularly relevant to this scene. The same crown insignia that appeared on the Chief Guard's cap now appears on Dim's. But in spite of his uniform, Dim is still Dim, from his long hair to his bitter memories and taste for violence.

Georgie is shown from the same low angle as Dim, but from an oblique rather than a frontal prospect, rendering him less menacing than his partner. For Kubrick, Dim was the better choice for conveying a threat because he is more impulsive in his desire for revenge. Georgie, more sophisticated, coolly points out the delicious irony of the encounter. He and Dim, whose allegiance to Alex was never more than a matter of convenience, have found a new and safer path to power in the camp of their old enemy. And they give new meaning to the slogan, "Have you got what it takes to be a policeman?" on the recruiting poster at the police station. The State has apparently lowered its standards in a desperate attempt to stem the tide of crime.

Like Alex's assault on Catlady and his subsequent beating by the police, Georgie and Dim conceal their dirty work from public view. Their trip into the country parodies an earlier adventure. The sleek Durango-95 is replaced by a blocky, white police van that in a sense is no less stolen from the State than the sports car was from its owner. An electric sign on the van's roof reads, "Stop ... Divert," while an arrow points to one side — probably a routine signal to traffic offenders. Georgie and Dim, however, divert Alex in the *opposite* direction, for a highly unofficial purpose.

A handheld camera tracks all three characters from behind, conveying the power of Alex's enemies and his helplessness to resist it. Shrubbery along the path rushes by in the same horrorshow fashion as trees along the country road during the Durango-95 adventure, but no longer for Alex's edification. Perhaps this is not Dim and Georgie's first such trip into the country. How many other personal enemies have been "diverted" here?

Incapable of physical resistance, Alex tries diversionary tactics. He appeals first to the policemen's sense of institutional justice. But his claim to have been punished for his crimes and cured of his violent tendencies falls on deaf ears. Dim, in typical fashion, apes the words "punished" and "cured," which to him are meaningless legal abstractions. Avenging Catlady's murder is the furthest thing from his mind. Pursuing a different argument, Alex calls upon shared memories of a time when all three characters were allied against the forces Dim and Georgie now represent. But he fails to see the past through *their* eyes. "I don't remember them days too horrorshow. Don't call me Dim no more, either. Officer, call me." Demanding to be addressed by his institutional title, Dim rejects the past and embraces the present, in which he holds a strategic advantage over Alex. But at the same time he mocks the very government that invests him with power, taunting Alex, "This is to make sure you *stay* cured."

Using a tool of his new profession to avenge an old grievance, Georgie bashes Alex in the stomach with a blackjack. That and subsequent blows are accompanied by synthesized clangs and bangs which in *Clockwork*'s first scene seemed to be a function of Alex's will. But no longer. His head forced into a trough of water and held there by Dim, Alex's ordeal seems to go on forever. Dr. Brodsky's blandly delivered description of Ludovico Hell as a "sense of drowning" acquires literal meaning here. But the scientist did not enjoy Alex's suffering for its own sake. Dim and Georgie do. For Alex, the result is pretty much the same.

Georgie finally signals Dim to stop. Less a slave to his emotions, he recognizes the problem a dead Alex might create. Like Alex, who once signaled a strategic retreat in the midst of a satisfying triumph over Billyboy's gang, Georgie has the makings of a leader. Dim reluctantly releases Alex, but with a promise of more payback to come. He naively assumes that his current advantage over Alex will hold true for all future encounters. Georgie's otherwise prudent restraint may have unwittingly undercut that assumption. These three characters never meet again during the course of the film. But after Alex's restoration to full sadistic power, one can imagine the likely consequences for his former, rebellious droogs.

Dim and Georgie leave Alex at his lowest ebb of power thus far in the film. Bloodied and half drowned, unable to stand, he cries out in agony and protest. The Nature he once fancied himself conquering in the Durango-95 now, from his vantage point of pain and despair, turns on him. Thunder, lightning, and rain descend on him like the wrath of God, in concert with Purcell's music, which concludes with a variation on the "Dies Irae." And as Alex lurches into the familiar setting of one of his early triumphs, the music harkens back ominously to the ordeal of one of his victims.

Seeking the warmth and security of home, after being rejected by his parents, Alex unwittingly returns to a "Home" he once destroyed. From outside, the Alexander residence looks very different than the way it once did. The electric sign in the driveway once yielded an ambiguous facial expression. Now it burns with vaporous rage. Previously Alex and his droogs crept up on the house stealthily, as thieves, with a *phony* plea for help. Now, from the same camera angle, Alex stumbles and crawls towards the house as a true suppliant. Illuminated by high-contrast lighting from the house, Alex's environment is a nightmare vision of Hell. And he is no less a figure of blighted existence than the stunted, twisted, leafless tree along his path.

By contrast, the situation inside the house appears nearly the same as it was two years earlier. Mr. Alexander sits typing at his desk. The bookcase, its contents restored to order, stands behind him. The doorbell chimes the same fate theme. And Mr. Alexander again inquires blandly, "Who on earth could that be?" The only notable differences between this introductory image and its predecessor are the shawl over his shoulders, hinting at a fragile state of health, and newspapers headlining Alex's release from prison next to his typewriter, implying his professional interest in that event.

The camera, as it did long ago, pans to Mr. Alexander's right, following his gaze. We expect to see Mrs. Alexander. Instead we see a bodybuilder named Julian, working out with dumbbells. By a curious coincidence, dumbbells (Joe's and Julian's) figure in the changed circumstances affecting both Alex and Mr. Alexander. Obviously the relationship between husband and wife has been superceded by something very different, something echoing Mr. Alexander's new, hostile relationship to the outside world.

The metaphorical chess match between Alex and Mrs. Alexander this time shapes up entirely in favor of her replacement. In the entryway, Alex is a triple image of dependency rather than dominance. To peals of thunder, he collapses into Julian's arms and is gently carried inside, very differently than Mrs. Alexander was carried by Alex's droogs.

Typical of Kubrick's penchant for staggered revelations, we discover that Mr. Alexander is confined to a wheelchair, presumably due to Alex's handiwork, only after he leaves his desk. Though he is physically more vulnerable than before, altered circumstances give him a strategic advantage. Alex's inability to commit violence, Julian's imposing presence, and the absence of Alex's droogs more than compensate for Mr. Alexander's infirmity, or would if he recognized his old assailant. The fact that he does not is a source of great joy to Alex, who along with his droogs wore a disguise during his previous visit.

Taking advantage of his anonymity, Alex blames his pathetic condition on the police, tossing in a respectful "sir" to sweeten his appeal. Mr. Alexander's passionate reply, "I know you!" accompanied by an aggressive, Kubrickian glare, is a moment of crisis for Alex. But it turns out that his host recognizes him only as a celebrity, a "poor victim of this horrible technique," and not as his old assailant. Alex is delighted to confirm that identity but unwittingly seals his doom by doing so. He does not understand the nature of Mr. Alexander's interest in him as a public commodity. Regardless of any subsequent revelation about their personal relationship, Alex is from this moment fated to undergo a terrible ordeal.

Unlike the lukewarm compassion which led Mr. Alexander to admit Alex to his home two years earlier, his compassion now is a coincidental byproduct of his fanatical hatred for the government. The antagonism Mr. Alexander felt towards the old Alex has been channeled into a holy crusade against State tyranny — a crusade in which the new Alex has an important role to play. Crippled emotionally as well as physically, Mr. Alexander relishes Alex's tale of police abuse because it feeds his own hunger, just as Cat-lady's death fed Mr. Deltoid's. His concern for the protagonist is a grotesque mockery of kindness. Words of pity are contradicted by his twitching, blinking, thumb-biting anticipation of a political bonanza. He vigorously condemns the State's crimes against Alex, exaggerating them in order to justify his own cause, but takes little notice of Alex's injuries until he realizes that his guest's well-being is, for the moment, crucial to his cause.

Soaking in Mr. Alexander's bathtub, Alex finds relief from his cares. Nature's chaos is replaced by the pleasant dripping of water from a faucet. A washcloth lies across Alex's eyes. Literally and figuratively blinded to any concern beyond his luxuriating physical senses, he fails to notice a familiar robe hanging on the bathroom door — a ghostly reminder of a night of violence two years earlier. Nor is he aware that the song he slowly works his way into, "Singin' in the Rain," is another haunting relic from a past he shares with Mr. Alexander. He makes the same mistake he did with Dim and Georgie two scenes ago. Remembrance of things past is never quite the same for two people. For Alex, the song conjures up carefree days of unimpeded freedom. For a man who associates it with the rape of his wife, the memories are very different.

Just outside the bathroom, Mr. Alexander plots Alex's role in an upcoming political scenario. Until he recognizes the music seeping under the door, he is passionately absorbed in a telephone conversation with his institutional superior, to whom he describes Alex as a powerful weapon against creeping State tyranny. Mr. Alexander aligns himself with "great traditions of liberty," yet his insistence that the common people "must be led, sir. Driven. Pushed!" betrays a crisis of faith in man's ability to reason no less than did the Interior Minister's embrace of Ludovico. Mr. Alexander pretends to be a defender of Alex's civil rights, yet he reduces the young man to a pawn within a broader defense of freedom. After hanging up the phone, he seems lost in the anticipation of a political coup, his hands folded as though in prayerful gratitude for Alex's arrival. Only gradually is he lured out of that reverie by a recognition of Alex's serenade to himself, which ironically grows louder and more confident. An extreme low-angle shot of Mr. Alexander hunched over in his wheelchair, listening intently, subjectively distorts the imagery with his passion. His face is a grotesque mask, with upturned eyes, mouth open in a constricted scream, hands gripping paralyzed legs and his entire body trembling uncontrollably. The contents of his bookcase, the intellectual source of his political ideals, appear far above him, now irrelevant. We hear Alex's song through *his* ears, its melody degenerating into a series of sharp reverberations that echo Mr. Alexander's recollection of a terrible encounter two years earlier.

The stage has literally been set by Mr. Alexander when Alex sits down alone at a table in the living room and eats food laid out for him. A bottle of wine sits at his right hand. The back of the room has been darkened to focus attention downstage. Alex unwittingly contributes to the scenario by donning his host's old robe, reversing their previous roles. Three unoccupied chairs surround his, anticipating the arrival of additional players in Mr. Alexander's production. Alex enjoys his meal but vaguely senses the hidden forces at work against him.

Mr. Alexander's entrance onto this stage is strangely dramatic. Descending from the shadowy background, he appears as a composite of crippled body, mechanical wheelchair, and Julian's strong legs. But despite his fragility, he possesses a strategic advantage over Alex. Not yet realizing that his disguise has been breached, Alex continues to play the fawning beneficiary of his host's kindness. Seated at the table, he is bracketed by the increasingly hostile glare of Mr. Alexander and the passive but imposing presence of Julian. The content of their ensuing conversation is friendly, but its tone is hostile. Mr. Alexander's suppressed rage produces bizarre behavior, like Dr. Strangelove struggling to control his misanthropic glee in front of other government officials. At times, the scene resembles a classic horror film, with Alex's host impersonating Boris Karloff in such otherwise nonthreatening lines as "Of course" and "I phoned some friends while you were having your bath ... They want to help you." His anger is barely contained and masked by a higher, institutional need that promises eventually to satisfy it. In the meantime, he toys with his victim, employing sound effects as surrogate tolchocks. His sudden, piercing intrusion of, "Food alright???" and the exaggerated smack of a wine bottle on the glass table are blows directed at Alex's tranquility. The wine, too, is a weapon. As Frank pours a glass for his guest, the camera shows his arm looming over Alex, the same way Alex's once loomed over Catlady as he toyed with her precious sculpture. Suddenly suspicious of the offering, Alex asks Frank to join him in a drink. But Mr. Alexander turns his physical infirmity into an asset by declining on account of ill health.

Surviving the drink he feared might poison him, Alex brims over with misplaced confidence. But Mr. Alexander's command to have a second glass, spoken with bared teeth and another loud crack of wine bottle against tabletop, evaporates that security. Alex obeys, then sets his glass down *quietly* so as not to further aggravate his host. Mr. Alexander shatters that veneer of calm by introducing the subject of his wife — the link in their pasts. Alex tries to avoid it by casually feigning ignorance: "Is she away?" But Frank, trembling with barely suppressed rage, rubs his nose in it. "No, she's dead!"

Embittered by the State's possibly legitimate explanation of his wife's death as due to pneumonia, Mr. Alexander elevates his private rage into a cynical view of society as a whole, just as General Ripper translated his sexual paranoia into America's crusade against communism. Frank's political philosophy equates his wife with Alex, who raped her, as mutual victims of society. But as he wheels closer to Alex and talks of helping him, the sinister edge returns to his voice, undercutting his benevolent words.

Alex wants to flee but is prevented from doing so by the forbidding presence of Julian. A ringing doorbell perhaps signals an even worse fate for him. When offered a third glass of wine, Alex is this time happy to accept it, as a brace against what he fears is to come. But Dolin and Rubinstein, Frank's political cronies, seem harmless at first. A pudgy, balding, middle-aged man dressed in a brown sport coat with elbow patches, Dolin does not *look* like a revolutionary. Rubinstein, played by the same actress (Margaret Tyzack) who played Elena, the soul of discretion in *2001*, appears equally friendly. With polite greetings, apologies for the late hour of their visit, and vague offers of help, the two visitors dispel Alex's anxiety and bring to Mr. Alexander's private theater of vengeance an air of collective disinterestedness, even compassion.

With everyone seated at the table, Alex appears surrounded by "allies." Officially, Dolin is in charge of the proceedings. Frank, Julian, and Rubinstein are his droogs. Rubinstein, skillfully concealing her true intent behind a pleasant voice, probes for information about Alex's Ludovico conditioning, seeking to transform the government's weapon against crime into a weapon against the government. As her focus of inquiry narrows, Beethoven's *Ninth Symphony* again becomes a source of power for anyone in a position to exploit it.

Answering Rubinstein's questions openly, Alex naively assumes that her political agenda harmonizes with his personal wishes. He pads his tale of woe, drawing out for dramatic effect his description of the suicidal urge Ludovico encourages in him. His revelations will indeed serve the Dolin camp by highlighting the government's cruelty, but in a manner Alex will not like.

Throughout the interview, Mr. Alexander glares at Alex like a coiled snake ready to strike, his visible passion out of tune with the dispassionate demeanor of his colleagues. Now that he knows Alex is his former assailant, Dolin, Rubinstein, and Julian become tools serving *his* personal agenda, just as Dr. Strangelove drew everyone in the War Room into *his* personal orbit.

The feeling of impending doom Alex describes in order to solicit sympathy turns out, thanks to Mr. Alexander's behind-the-scenes manipulation, to be unwittingly prophetic. The drugged wine takes effect and Alex falls face forward into his plate of spaghetti. Rubinstein quietly completes her notes and closes her notepad. She and Dolin are perhaps a little uneasy about their deception of the young man they claim to be defending. But that discomfort, like Dr. Branom's during Alex's Ludovico viddy sessions, is insufficient to alter their actions. Dolin breaks an awkward silence with quiet congratulations and instructions. Mr. Alexander, by contrast, is beyond embarrassment, pulling Alex's head up by the hair and glaring daggers at its tomato-smeared face.

The process of Alex's reawakening from a drug-induced sleep is duplicated by the camera, which begins with a close-up of him lying face down on a bed and then slowly reverse zooms to reveal his surroundings. The scherzo from Beethoven's *Ninth Symphony* permeates the room from an unseen source below. The depth of Ludovico's hold on Alex is evident from the fact that he experiences sickness even before regaining full consciousness. Narration characterizes the enemy as "pain and sickness all over me like an animal," an animal of terrifying intimacy because it is derived from Alex himself. Beethoven's once "glorious" *Ninth* is now the "dreaded" *Ninth*.

Dressed no longer in Frank's old robe but in the suit of clothes with which he left State custody, Alex is given back the *public* identity he had in the newspaper photographs of his release. Intervention in his life by Dolin's organization is concealed because it is his public identity that Dolin seeks to exploit. Figuratively concealed beneath that suit and that identity is Frank's old robe, from Mr. Alexander's private drama of revenge, of which neither the public nor Dolin are aware. The bedroom in which Alex finds himself trapped betrays no secrets either. Its modest decor is a refreshing change from the starkness of many of *Clockwork*'s locales. Yet circumstances make of it a torture chamber from which Alex cannot escape. He must face the music he so arbitrarily misused earlier in the film.

In the room below Alex's, another combination of close-up and reverse zoom draws an ironic analogy between the relationships of Alex and Mr. Alexander to their environments. Resembling the portrait of Beethoven on Alex's bedroom windowshade, Mr. Alexander gazes up in furious ecstasy at the ceiling, through which Alex's cries of pain rain down on him. He could be Beethoven raging against and triumphing over deafness. Turning the tables on his wife's rapist, he forces Alex to provide reluctant choral accompaniment, just as *he* was once forced to accompany Alex's sadistic production of "Singin' in the Rain." But like the diabolical Dr. Strangelove before him, Mr. Alexander is a contradictory portrait of power and weakness. His whole face twitches with spastic passions. As the camera pulls back, we see his instruments of torture: an audiotape player with two speakers pointing upward, arranged with classical symmetry on either side of Frank's crippled form, investing him with technological power in the midst of physical weakness. He is no less a king on his throne than Alex was in the film's opening shot.

Retaining Mr. Alexander as its focal point, the camera broadens its scope to add his companions' reactions to Alex's ordeal. Standing behind Frank, Rubinstein and Julian look up in the direction of Alex's desperate pleas, noting them, perhaps even a little distressed over them, but passively accepting the political logic that makes them a necessary evil. The last character brought into the film frame is Dolin, on whose billiard table Frank's instrument of torture rests and within whose political crusade Frank's private vengeance plays out. Like Dr. Brodsky, Dolin remains emotionally aloof from the grubby particulars of his plan to bring about a just social order. His attention is focused on the billiard table and the balls he methodically rolls across it, reducing Alex to an abstraction in a game of power in which he, theoretically, champions the rights of individual man.

Alex escapes his agony along the only route open to him — a route conveniently *left* open by the folks downstairs. Not only is he a victim of their violence, he is compelled to inflict it on himself. From Alex's point of view, the bedroom window is a beacon of heavenly light similar to the light shining on Mr. Alexander's face downstairs. He lurches to that window, opens it, and jumps out, seeking an oblivion far more extreme than the old Tramp's booze or Em's sleeping pills. Alex's leap to freedom is split into objective and subjective shots, the first observing from the ground below as he exits the window, the second careening towards the sidewalk from his perspective. His scream is our scream, and our camera blacks out with him.

Narration invokes the convention of a disembodied character who usually stands apart from the fortunes and perceptions of characters depicted on-screen. An amused, off-screen Alex mocks the idea of such sublime detachment by reminding us, while the camera surveys his broken body lying in a hospital bed, that his existence is tied to that of his on-screen self. His appearance is visually transformed by the cast that literally holds him together. For the time being, he is as dependent on medical technology as *2001*'s astronauts were on space technology.

An extreme long shot places Alex in the institutional setting of a hospital room. He groans weakly, in pain. From somewhere unseen comes a corresponding moan. This duet is repeated. Then, suddenly, the curtain around an adjoining bed thrusts open and out rush a bare-breasted nurse followed by a doctor pulling up his pants. They rush to the aid of their patient. This is a little joke about aesthetic illusion. The nurse's moan of pleasure, when visually isolated from its source, blended convincingly with Alex's groan of pain. They are similar sounds proceeding from opposite experiences. And as for the behavior of the nurse and the doctor, they are two people momentarily satisfying their personal desires in the midst of their professional duties. *Their* example is trivial. The examples of Mr. Deltoid, Tom, and Mr. Alexander are not.

Back when Alex sauntered into the lobby of his apartment building, Purcell's "Funeral" music conveyed to us his diminished power vis-à-vis the world around him. The same music is now heard over a series of newspaper clippings condemning the Interior Minister's government for its cruel treatment of Alex. Photographs depict him as an unsmiling man under siege. The same free press that he manipulated to such advantage upon Alex's release from State custody now turns against him. But, in a larger sense, the music is a lament for the clockwork shallowness of the press, which failed to question the morality and practicality of the Ludovico Technique at the moment of its apparent triumph, and which now fails to question the circumstances of the Program's disgrace.

One tidbit gleaned from the articles adds to our impression of events. Alex is described as "one of the first" Ludovico subjects, implying the existence of earlier subjects whose fortunes or misfortunes we know nothing about. The fate of the Ludovico Program is inextricably linked to the public's perception of it through *Alex*'s case, in part due to Dolin's intervention.

Alex's slow resurrection to power begins at the expense of his parents and occurs while he is still bedridden. Purcell's somber music, carried over from the previous scene, echoes Alex's battered condition but counterpoints the surprising advantage he derives from that infirmity. Because the newspapers now portray Alex as a victim of cruelty, Pee and Em feel guilty for rejecting him. His face discolored by bruises, his body encased in plaster, and his head held rigidly in place by a metal contraption (similar to the Ludovico head clamp, but used to a very different purpose), Alex transforms his pitiable condition into a weapon of intimidation. In that context, the plaster cast on his head looks more like a warrior's helmet than a token of weakness. Even his difficulty speaking contributes to his parents' guilt and therefore to his gratification. From Alex's point of view, the fruit basket they have brought as a peace offering contains a wrapper that reads "Eat me." This, figuratively speaking, becomes Alex's reply to his parents' belated concern for him.

Em, true to character, cries at the unpleasantness of the encounter. Pee, also true to character, soothes her and himself by explaining away Alex's harsh words, attributing them to Alex's pain rather than to Alex himself. Pee's subsequent attempt at appeasement is rendered especially unappealing by its internal rhyme. "Your home's your home when all's said and done, son."

The same backtracking camera that lent regal authority to Alex's stroll through the Music Bootick and transfer to the Ludovico Centre now imbues the hospital psychiatrist, Dr. Taylor, with an aura of authority as she pushes her cart of instruments through hospital corridors towards Alex's room. Dressed in the uniform of science, she does not even break stride as she greets the uniformed police guard at the door. The guard, like Charlie at the Centre, is more a token than an active player. The lab coats have taken over all the important duties. Purcell's "Funeral" music, shifting its dramatic role for the third time in as many scenes, counterpoints the power of Dr. Taylor's confidence but also laments the state of corruption to which her profession will sink in this scene.

Though Alex appears to be recovering nicely, he is not yet master of his surroundings. Like Dr. Branom before her, Dr. Taylor takes firm charge of events, removing Alex's magazine so that he can participate in *her* production. Unlike Branom, however, her relentlessly cheerful disposition and singsong voice betray nothing of any private feelings behind her professional mask.

Dr. Taylor characterizes her visit as "just part of hospital routine." In fact, like Heywood Floyd's trip to the Moon in *2001*, it has little to do with routine. Alex jokingly asks if they will discuss his sex life — a layman's stereotypical view of psychiatric inquiry, and as naive as his comparison of the Ludovico viddy sessions with a trip to the movies. The slide show Taylor presents is the equivalent of those sessions, except that Alex's relationship to the State has changed and therefore so has the nature of his treatment. He dimly senses the change in that relationship but cannot yet define it or work it to his advantage. So he probes for information, asking questions of Dr. Taylor that garner no more information than did his initial questions to Dr. Branom regarding Ludovico. Even *we* cannot tell from her performance to what extent Dr. Taylor is a knowing agent of the government's face-saving efforts. Whatever her complicity, her sunny disposition lends a ghoulish edge to the spectacle of her profession, usually considered an independent institution (like the free press), acting as a tool of partisan politics by reversing its usual criteria for assessing mental health.

Another variation on the film/audience relationship, Dr. Taylor's slide show reduces life to simplified, cartoon outlines. Unlike the Ludovico scientists, her purpose is not to saturate Alex with sadistic sensations but to probe for them. Both the Ludovico films and the slide show are designed to expose Alex's brutality, but to opposite ends.

The slide show begins with an emotionally neutral drawing of a peacock, two men, and an innocuous question. Alex, once he catches on that Dr. Taylor wants spontaneous rather than thoughtful reactions from him, blurts out a nonsensical reply. Taylor praises him and he laughs gleefully, like a child rewarded. The second, third, and fourth slides depict conflicts and a sexual encounter, to which Alex responds increasingly like his old self. By slide number five, he "progresses" to the point of *imposing* a violent interpretation on a drawing as emotionally neutral as the first. But his revived taste for violence exceeds the capacity of his damaged flesh. Raising his broken arm to strike a blow, he is stopped from doing so by a stab of pain. Nevertheless, his body is slowly being nursed back to health by order of the same government that turned it against him.

Dr. Taylor, taking notes on a clipboard as much a tool and symbol of institutional due process as was the Chief Guard's, is evasive about the test results. Alex wants to know how many answers he got right. She insists, "It's not that kind of a test, but you seem well on the way to making a complete recovery," which is something of a contradiction in terms. By linking Alex's recovery to the revival of his capacity for violent thought and action, Dr. Taylor signals approval of what the State previously deemed evil and unacceptable. Alex *did* provide the right answers and is quick to detect the State's change in attitude towards him. He fixes the psychiatrist with a glare and asks point-blank when he can leave the hospital. But her unflappable equivocation cannot be breached. So Alex wisely bides his time, waiting for a better opportunity to make his bid for power.

Alex begins the final scene of *Clockwork* still bedridden and dependent on institutional care. He must be fork fed his meal by a nurse's aide. But this impression of weakness is counterpointed by a reverse-angle portrait, from Alex's perspective, of the visiting Interior Minister, a nurse, and a doctor, gathering at his feet and dwarfed by his immobile legs. Tokens of physical infirmity are transformed into tokens of political strength. "Hi, hi, hi there, my little droogies," he greets his visitors, as though they were Georgie, Pete, and Dim from the old days.

The Interior Minister, like many other characters in the film, seeks to improve his strategic situation by means of isolation. Guard, doctor, nurse, and nurse's aide are all sent out of the room as a prelude to his delicate negotiations with Alex. The ensuing conversation is a debate between darkness and light. The Interior Minister wears a shirt with snake-skin designs on it, allegorically defining his role in this scene as that of Satan, tempting the white-draped, physically vulnerable but hardly innocent Alex with an apple, in the shape of a political bargain.

The Interior Minister opens negotiations by remarking on the privacy of Alex's hospital room, stressing the consideration extended to the patient by his government sponsors. Alex quickly undercuts that advantage by redefining pampered privacy as loneliness and pain. The latter he well knows was inflicted by Dolin's organization but is perceived by the public to be the government's fault. The Minister's weak pawn thus becomes Alex's more potent knight. The loser in this initial skirmish registers the blow by uncharacteristically fumbling his next words. But he recovers quickly and changes tactics, attempting to establish a friendlier and more personal rapport with Alex. That offensive, too, is blunted when Alex plays on their new intimacy to emphasize the Minister's *personal* responsibility for Alex suffering "the tortures of the damned." The casual manner in which Alex speaks of his ordeal indicates the extent to which he reduces it and the Interior Minister's guilt to abstract pawns in a game of political power. Alex is not morally outraged by the State's mistreatment of him. He regards it simply as a bargaining chip.

Despite his increasing confidence, Alex still cannot negotiate food into his mouth. The Interior Minister, seizing an opportunity to ingratiate himself, becomes Alex's surrogate nurse's aide. His feeding of Alex continues to the end of their conversation and is gradually transformed by Alex into a symbolic act of subservience. Smacking his lips and nodding broadly, he opens his mouth to *demand* satisfaction, rather than passively receive it as he did from the nurse's aide.

With great reluctance, the Interior Minister acknowledges the newspapers' account of events as the interpretation which, whether true or false, must be dealt with. He tries to absolve himself and his government of responsibility for Alex's situation by blaming the Ludovico Program on others. "An inquiry will place the responsibility where it belongs" is a euphemism for "where it will do me the least harm," and is no different than Alex blaming Catlady's death on his droogs. Prudently, the Interior Minister names no names. But Dr. Brodsky's position in the matter is no doubt precarious. The marriage of convenience between government and behavioral science has ended.

Accusations directed at Dolin's organization and at Mr. Alexander are accurate, yet hypocritical. Dolin exploited Alex for political ends, but so did the Interior Minister. Mr. Alexander's personal grudge against Alex is discredited by the Minister, for whom it is a political liability. "He found out that you had done him wrong" becomes "At least he *believed* you had done him wrong." The brutality that once rendered Alex a favorable subject for the State's Ludovico Program is now downplayed in order to make their new partnership seem less unsavory. Equally vague is the fate of the troublesome Mr. Alexander: "We put him away for his own protection ... and also yours." And, of course, the government's. Not even Alex, with his new political clout, can discover more about Frank's fate.

The bribe offered to Alex in exchange for his cooperation consists of a secure future with a good job and a good salary. Alex demands details, but his benefactor outmaneuvers him by keeping the terms of the deal fuzzy. An even more impressive demonstration of the Minister's negotiating skills is his subtle way of casting doubt on the State's moral debt to Alex. He preserves deniability by describing Alex's rewards as compensation "for what you *believe* you have suffered." By qualifying Alex's grievance with "believe," the Minister puts him on the same shaky footing as Mr. Alexander, who "believed" Alex had done him wrong. The press's view of events, too, is called into question when the Interior Minister characterizes it as arbitrary: "The press has *chosen* to take a very unfavorable view of what we tried to do." A master politician, he concedes as little as possible on every front. And he gets as much as he can by the same means. "As well as for services yet to be rendered" places an open-ended obligation on Alex's half of the bargain. But Alex's exaggerated nod of the head suggests that he is a *knowing* participant in this unholy alliance.

After all of his oblique signals, the Interior Minister finally asks the payoff question: "Do you understand, Alex? Do I make myself clear?" With characteristic hyperbole, Alex acknowledges. And he does so with the same phrase he once used to acknowledge the *warning* of another authority figure, Mr. Deltoid. But with Deltoid, Alex maintained a formal appearance of deference by calling him "Sir." The Interior Minister, by contrast, is reduced to "Fred." Advantage to Alex.

Again exhibiting the "rubbed hand of hypocrisy" he once condemned in prison officials opposed to the Ludovico Program, the Interior Minister announces a surprise gift for his new partner. Alex is delighted. The Minister smiles in snake-like triumph. He has directed this scene almost flawlessly to the conclusion he desired.

The simultaneous arrival of a huge new audio system, playing the climax of Beethoven's "Ode to Joy," and a contingent from the press signals a double resurrection. The power of Alex's favorite music is restored to his emotional palette by the government that stole it from him. In a shot from his vantage point, we see a flock of admirers gather at his feet, presenting him with floral bouquets such as an opera star might receive after a captivating performance. Reverse-angle shots show the Interior Minister sharing in the spotlight, embracing Alex's bandaged shoulders. Giving the thumbs-up signal for victory, they bask in the heavenly light of favorable publicity. Individual and institutional man attain unholy alliance, just as at the end of *Dr. Strangelove*.

But *Dr. Strangelove* has several main characters. *A Clockwork Orange* is fundamentally the story of *one* character's fall from and restoration to power, and it is to his jealously private point of view we divert in the film's last shot. Withdrawing into his own imagination, Alex transforms his triumph over the wicked world into a symbolic, slow-motion fantasy in which he lies naked on a field of snow, screwing (certainly not making *love* with) a young woman. She is on top, in the dominant position institutional man usually occupies over the individual. But Alex obviously controls the action from below. A group of spectators in Victorian costume applaud his brazen display of passion. This fantasy reverses an earlier scene, in the Ludovico Auditorium, in which government officials applauded Alex's *in*ability to have sex. By fortuitous accident, Alex has reformed the State instead of the other way around. In this context, the "Ode to Joy" satirizes the same synthesis of private and collective vision that "We'll Meet Again" did in *Dr. Strangelove*. Alex's final words, "I was cured all right," signals a cathartic but chillingly ironic release for those of us who have accompanied him on his roller-coaster ride from power to helplessness and back again.

"Singin' in the Rain" returns to the soundtrack as the final credits roll. Alex's alternate personal anthem, it echoes his triumph over an indifferent and sometimes hostile world. This is the famous Gene Kelly version, from the 1952 MGM musical of the same name, putting a formal, institutional stamp of approval on Alex's evil resurrection.

A Clockwork Orange is a nightmare odyssey into the fickle relationship between aesthetics and ethics, with Alex as our satanic guide and Kubrick providing ironic counterpoint. No other Kubrick character is given such free rein to manipulate our perceptions. Alex *bloodies* us with both the illicit thrill of aggressive power and the terror of falling victim to it. Kubrick's next film, *Barry Lyndon*, is an aesthetic antidote to *Clockwork*, portraying a world of comparative elegance and restraint, but at heart no less permeated by a bewildering array of conflicts and alliances.

CHAPTER 4

Barry Lyndon:
Paradise Hollow

Now dark, now glittering, now reflecting gloom, Now lending splendor...

— Percy Shelley ("Mont Blanc")

After the garishness of *A Clockwork Orange*, Kubrick turned to the comparatively restrained world of *Barry Lyndon*, featuring a protagonist as generous by inclination as Alex is selfish. William Makepeace Thackeray's novel, like Anthony Burgess's *Clockwork*, is told from the less-than-credible point of view of its protagonist. Reminiscing about his youthful adventures from a nostalgic perspective of old age, the title character is an incorrigible braggart, spouting huge inconsistencies, his selfish emotions coloring every description. Kubrick retains narration, but in the form of an anonymous voice divorced from the emotions of the characters on screen. Dispassionate, precise, and possessed of an understated wit, the narrator furnishes an elegant framework around events visually depicted. But his insights are matched by his oversights, and his point of view is occasionally undercut by imagery or music. "He offers us a comfortable and ironic detachment from Barry's rise and fall, while he fails to see Barry's emotional complexity or moral growth" (Nelson, 170–71).

Like its narration, the film's visual account of events is largely unaffected by the protagonist's personal biases. Imagery is fashioned after eighteenth-century European painting. Architecture, costumes, the characters' poses, and even Nature adhere strictly to neoclassical concepts of balance and restraint, rooted in the notion of an unshakable order invested in man, man's creations and Nature by an omnipotent deity. But just as he subtly undercuts the narrator, Kubrick maneuvers his camera *through* these seductive still-life portraits to make us aware of relationships that contradict the aesthetic ideal evoked. If *Clockwork* explored the pitfalls of intimacy with a single character, *Barry Lyndon* exposes the deceptive charms of a broader, collective outlook.

By filtering events through the memory of his protagonist, Thackeray constructs a tale of high adventure featuring a cast of famous characters participating in historically momentous events. Extravagant coincidences, complicated intrigues, and improbable reappearances have the effect of consolidating the world, connecting the protagonist on a continuing basis to everyone and everything in it. The film, in contrast, sends Redmond Barry out into a big, often lonely, and overwhelming world where chance encounters with strangers continually change the course of his life. His baptism of fire as a soldier in the British Army, unlike that of his literary counterpart, occurs at an historically insignificant skirmish that is nevertheless significant enough for *him*.

In the novel, members of the Brady family pop up again in Redmond's life long after they jilt, deceive, and dispense with him. The film has Redmond ranging far and wide across Europe, adapting himself to new situations and new characters while carrying the emotional baggage he accumulated in previous relationships. That baggage, rather than the reappearance of old faces, is the glue which links together separate settings, situations, and characters. Eighteenth-century Europe is for the individual a vast universe, where distances are great, travel slow, and communication limited. In this respect, Barry's situation resembles that of Dave Bowman in *2001*. In *A Clockwork Orange*, by contrast, action occurred within a relatively localized area, in which Alex's repeat encounters with other characters was not only a useful dramatic device but also seemed plausible.

Redmond's frequent recourse to violence in the novel is one measure of his disregard for public decorum. He physically punishes Nora Brady for being unfaithful. In the film, he cannot *properly* revenge himself on Nora, so instead he attacks his rival for her affections. And even that act of violence is confined to the traditional form of a duel. Working his way up the social ladder, Thackeray's protagonist bullies Lady Lyndon into marrying him, disrupts a church service, makes tasteless alterations to Castle Hackton, physically attacks Lord Crabs for failing to secure him a peerage, and is neither embarrassed nor repentant over his public thrashing of Lord Bullingdon. His victims, in turn, are less than discreet in their retaliation.

The film stresses the dominant role of propriety in the lives of its characters, who often exercise power *through* rather than in defiance of institutional devices. And for all its exposure of hypocrisy, the film embraces its characters more fully than does the novel. For example, Redmond's long-term romantic relationship with Lady Lyndon consists of both genuine affection and cynical calculations of social advancement. Their passions alternately ennoble and mock the rigid conventions of style through which they feel compelled to express themselves, just as in *2001* the characters do through technology.

Thackeray's protagonist is a cynical rogue totally committed to worldly definitions of success and power, yet contemptuous of the social rules governing individual man's behavior in pursuit of those treasures. Kubrick's protagonist is, by inclination, generous. And, as he makes his way through an often corrupt world, his compassion proves alternately a strategic advantage (rescuing Captain Potzdorf) and a disadvantage (sparing Lord Bullingdon's life in a duel) in events not even depicted in the novel.

* * *

George Friedrich Handel's "Sarabande" is both passionate music and music in strict baroque form. Played over the opening credits, it illustrates the synthesis of private passion and collective order that will dominate the protagonist's life. Its dirge-like fatalism critiques the rigidity of genteel society.

Part One of Redmond Barry's odyssey through genteel Europe is subtitled, "By what means Redmond Barry acquired the style and title of Barry Lyndon." Concise and dispassionate, this summary of events to come, like the film's narration, reduces the protagonist's life to a manageable, dry outline of facts. Its almost smug sense of detachment and superiority aesthetically matches the form but is challenged by the passion of Handel's music.

Establishing a pattern for everything that follows, *Barry Lyndon's* first scene consists of a single, passionate act and the multiple filters through which we perceive it. Almost a still-life portrait, it offers the first of many painterly images reminiscent of period art. Nature in *Barry Lyndon* is visually prominent yet thoroughly domesticated, selectively chosen and idealized by a genteel perspective. We hear a *light* breeze and the *soft* chirping of birds. Human invention, too, detaches us from the first event we witness. A stone fence winds across the screen's lower half, separating us from a pistol duel between two men in the top half. The fence is equivalent to the white lines in *Clockwork's* Staja 84F, except that this time the barrier is applied to *us*. In addition, the duel itself is a ritualized containment of human passion. Finally, a canopy of green foliage completes the aesthetic encirclement of a contest of wills which would otherwise be as blatantly violent as the hostile encounters in *Clockwork*. The duel is a struggle to the death, painted in pastels and observed from a discreet distance which diminishes the shock of it and renders it elegant. We see none of the "red, red vino on tap" that so thrilled Alex.

Narration contributes another emotional barrier to this scene. A Mozartian voice, scrupulously modulated and rich in subtle inflection, reveals that one of the combatants, Redmond Barry's father, "had been bred, like many other sons of a genteel family, to the profession of the law." "Bred" indicates the degree to which the life of individual man is shaped by the customs of his social class. With nothing more than a modest narrative pause and two muted gunshots to mark the passing, a life of some prominence is snuffed out. The elegance of the scene remains undisturbed by what is, for one of the combatants, a catastrophe. In addition, Mr. Barry's death is rendered slightly absurd by the disclosure that it resulted from a dispute over the purchase of horses — a fairly innocuous transaction which, in this hypersensitive age, becomes a matter of the highest personal honor. So, collective perceptions not only aesthetically diminish the impact of a man's violent death, they encourage his participation in the duel in the first place.

Mr. Barry's widow grieves in the dignified, restrained fashion of the day. Modestly dressed, carrying a bouquet of flowers, her face betraying little emotion, she strolls demurely near her rural cottage. A reverse zoom surrounds her with a pretty landscape but also complicates her situation with a suitor. Impeccably dressed for the occasion and keeping his hands clasped behind his back, he expresses his passion with great restraint.

The third scene begins with a close-up of a statuette depicting a child. An idealization, the statuette invests childhood with a physical grace beyond its years. The camera slowly reverse zooms from this object, symbolic of the dominance of collective order (contrasting with *Clockwork's* first reverse zoom, which illustrated the dominance of Alex's fiercely private ego), to include young Redmond Barry and his cousin, Nora Brady, in the frame. Like the statuette, their individuality is masked by their highly formal attire and demeanor. Through windows behind them, we see and hear a thunderstorm — not a raging tempest, but instead a *modest* exhibition of Nature's fury, neatly contained by the decorative window frame and the muted soundtrack.

Through the social constraints that bind them, we detect something of the characters' true emotions. Redmond gazes at his cousin with sentimental adoration, gently mocked by the narrator but softly echoed by Sean O'Riada's "Women of Ireland." Nora Brady returns Redmond's gaze with one that is hard and shrewd. Her behavior is no less elegant but is less spontaneous and more calculating. She is Redmond's first encounter with the cynical undercurrent of the Age of Gentility.

Nora and Redmond have just concluded a game of cards as the scene begins. She dictates the terms of settlement, incorporating the game into her larger strategy for conquering Redmond's heart. By hiding a piece of ribbon between her breasts and challenging him to claim it, she gives the game a sexual component it did not originally have. A side view of them forms an ironic parallel to a similar shot of Alex and the Ludovico stage temptress in *Clockwork*. Despite differences of fashion, both women issue sexual challenges. And for different reasons (conditioned reflexes in Alex, modesty and inexperience in Redmond), neither man can rise to that challenge. Gallantly restricting his gaze to Nora's face and hands, bypassing the promise in between (a promise on which Alex *fixated*), Redmond hesitates. Nora flagrantly encourages him by placing his hand on her breast. He locates the ribbon, trembling with a poignant mixture of delight and embarrassment. The film contains many such moments where symphonic passions are channeled into chamber music forms.

Nora calls Redmond a liar when he claims that his pleasure derives solely from finding the ribbon rather than from his search for it. She cannot see herself through Redmond's reverential eyes and therefore assumes that his motivations are as selfish as her own. Relishing her power over him, she cuts through the pretense of games playing and, taking his helpless head into her hands, kisses him. It is an elegant kiss, but motivated less by love than, as we learn later, by Nora's desperate need to find a husband — a need instilled in her by tradition. She may control Redmond in this scene, but her own perceptions are shaped by forces outside herself.

From romantic maneuvers one-on-one to pomp and circumstance on a public scale, the scene shifts to an outdoor parade drill performed by a British Army regiment. Individual identities are submerged in a collective ritual. Colorful uniforms march in precise formation beneath enormous national banners, to the traditional fife and drum of "The British Grenadiers." The camera reverse zooms to place this military extravaganza within a complementary green landscape, then adds a crowd of civilian spectators whose drab attire and loose arrangement are less eye-catching than the regimental spectacle.

Captain John Quin is the regiment's ranking officer. He is a peacock bawling out commands, brandishing his ceremonial sword and executing stiff-necked maneuvers to perfection. For him, the drill is a source of great *personal* pride, rather like *Clockwork's* Chief Guard supervising prison routine. Captivated by conventional measures of a man's worth, Nora is impressed with Quin. Captivated by Nora, Redmond is jealous of him. The crowd, meanwhile, is dutifully impressed by a State-sponsored event intended to raise civilian donations to meet the challenge of an ever-anticipated French invasion. Evidently a "regiment gap" existed long before a "missile gap," or *Dr. Strangelove's* ultimate exercise in military paranoia, the "Doomsday Gap."

At a picnic after the parade drill, Captain Quin and Nora Brady transform an Irish jig into an elaborate courtship ritual. Nora is dressed symbolically in white. Though not a virgin, she nevertheless *looks* the part in the conventional terms so important to these characters. Redmond observes them silently from nearby, not yet willing to challenge his rival. Like Nora, he too is overly impressed with Quin's rank, bearing, and uniform.

Walking alone after the picnic, Redmond and Nora quarrel over Quin. The camera first observes them in extreme long shot, visually rendering them as insignificant details in a natural setting. But as their argument intensifies, they stroll nearer the camera and become more visually prominent, counterpointing the picturesque serenity surrounding them.

Nora's power over Redmond, so evident in their first scene, dissipates in the light of new developments. Another sentimental Irish folk tune accompanies them on the soundtrack, but this time it is out of sync with the protagonist's sentiments.

Taking Redmond by the hands, Nora tries to pull him into her view of the situation, just as she pulled him into their first kiss earlier. Unable to convince him that Captain Quin means nothing to her (evidence at the picnic suggested otherwise), she switches tactics and appeals to their shared collective sensibilities. By traditional criteria, Quin is far superior to Redmond as a matrimonial catch. Redmond, ignoring such logic for the dictates of his heart, threatens to challenge the Englishman. Nora then tries to intimidate him by pointing out that Quin, by virtue of his military rank, must be a valiant soldier, skilled in combat. But Redmond's jealousy overrides that judgment as well. In contrast to their first encounter, they part company as antagonists rather than affectionate allies.

Redmond vents his frustration through physical labor at his mother's farm. A reverse zoom surrounds him with a serene landscape at odds with his turbulent emotions. A subsequent reverse zoom juxtaposes the elegant courtship of Nora and Captain Quin with the complementary beauty of a shimmering river valley. Mild counterpoint is provided by the characters' *dialog*. Arriving in midconversation, we hear Quin claim that Nora is the only woman he has ever loved, "except four others." So perfect are the setting, the costumes, his soft tone of voice, and the lilting background music that Quin's little qualification barely registers a false note. Nora turns his confession to her own advantage by countering it with a conventional cliché about women, which, in her case, happens to be false. "Your passion is not equal to ours. We bear but one flower and then we die." Quin swallows the bait, flattered that he should be the first and only love of her life. *We* already know that he is not and soon discover that neither was Redmond.

A reverse-angle camera shot adds characters we did not previously know were present. Nora's brothers, Mick and Ulick, act as chaperones to the romantic couple. But their presence reflects more than a concern for propriety. As reported by the narrator, they have a private, financial interest in the outcome of the affair. If Quin is Nora's pawn in a bid for social prominence and economic security, both of them are, in turn, pawns for Mick and Ulick.

Redmond's inopportune arrival endangers the various interests of the other characters by destroying the tender spell Nora has woven around Quin — a spell dependent on its isolation from her other romantic activities. Pulling Nora aside (*his* hands now control events, as *hers* did in their first scene), Redmond sabotages her relationship with Quin, employing the ribbons she once used to manipulate *him*. "I must have forgotten them somewhere" is Nora's attempt to trivialize the ribbons. But Redmond's bitter reply, "Yes, you did,

Nora," gives her words a meaning the opposite of her intent, redefining forgetfulness as betrayal.

Captain Quin is outraged at having been fooled by Nora's declaration of love. Like Alex attempting to deceive Catlady with the injured-friend ploy he had already used against the Alexanders, Nora plays the ribbon game once too often, and it backfires. Quin pulls out his own set of her ribbons (what variation of hide and seek did *they* play?) and angrily tosses them to the ground at her feet. She is exposed as a liar by two lovers whom separately she had been able to manipulate.

The other interested parties enter the fray at this point. Ulick confronts Redmond, while Mick tries to mollify the Englishman. With his hat removed and his hair wafting in the breeze, Quin now seems less a creature of propriety than of passion. He lashes out at those who have humiliated him. But his attack is rooted in yet another collective sensibility. Cultural superiority presumably gives him a strategic advantage over his enemies. "I've had enough of Miss Brady here, and your Irish ways!" That same national distinction contributed to Nora's preference for the Captain in the first place. Mick appears to be more than a physical match for Quin, but his financial need of the Englishman causes him to beg for forgiveness rather than avenge the insult. Quin rejects Mick's plea and resolutely departs, pursued by Nora. Mick vents his frustration on Redmond, but only in words. Decorum, plus perhaps Redmond's imposing physique, dissuade him from physical violence. By asking what business Redmond has interfering in the relationship between Nora and Quin, Mick demonstrates his ignorance of Redmond's romantic stake in the matter. Literally surrounded by hostile Brady forces, Redmond is equally oblivious to *their* concerns. This scene is a symphony of intermingling private interests and conventional, collective forms of behavior.

Like many interior locales in *Barry Lyndon*, the dining room at Brady Castle visually dwarfs its occupants and is a measure of institutional man's dominance over the individual. An establishing shot pictures genteel order restored since Redmond's disruption of it. Nora and Captain Quin sit beside each other at the dinner table. The rest of the Brady clan is gathered around them. Conversation is congenial and subdued. No details are discernable. The harmonious *tone* of conversation tells the story. Individual characters contribute their indistinguishable parts to a harmonious whole.

Redmond's entry causes barely a ripple of change, but a series of close-ups reveal the romantic conflict embedded within the harmonious whole. "Women of Ireland" returns to the soundtrack as a subjective echo of Redmond's undaunted love for Nora. He gives her a look of devotion and accusation. Her reaction betrays a trace of shame, mixed with uneasiness at Redmond's unpredictable presence at so carefully scripted an event. She is divided between lingering affection for Redmond and a desire to improve her social condition, as well as her family's, by marrying Quin. A brief pause as she spoons her soup conveys to us her moment of indecision. Then the moment passes, along with the last vestige of her romantic attachment to Redmond.

Captain Quin daubs his chin with a napkin, as though tidying up the small mess created by his rival's presence. The gestures and expressions of the three characters involved in this surreptitious triangle are given dramatic potency by Kubrick's camera placement and choice of music, while dialog plays counterpoint by adhering to the general impression of conviviality. Nora's father, unaware of the undercurrent of romantic tension, invites Redmond to join the celebratory gathering. Redmond accepts, but his heart is clearly not in it.

Smugly confident, Quin takes the offensive by maneuvering Nora's father into making a formal announcement of his engagement to Nora. Mr. Brady has no idea he serves as Quin's pawn in the Captain's silent duel with Redmond. Quin, on the other hand, does not have full control of that pawn. Brady calls on Quin to kiss Nora, which he does with a stylish swagger that must surely gall Redmond. But then Brady presses Quin's advantage beyond what the Captain intends, calling on his guests, including Redmond, to toast the engaged couple. A toast is a formal gesture of approval, not just passive acceptance.

Quin's hand is overplayed, just as Nora overplayed her ribbons. Redmond's refusal to drink to the engagement violates the etiquette of the occasion. The agreeable hum of conversation ceases. The initially isolated trio of Redmond, Nora, and Quin now intrudes on the entire gathering. Raising the stakes of their confrontation, Redmond answers Quin's symbolic slap in the face by tossing his unemptied glass into the Englishman's face. Quin, who moments earlier behaved so diffidently towards his Irish hosts, reverts back to national bigotry, refusing all Irish aid for the rather small cut on his forehead. Former allies of convenience are now convenient targets of anger, lumped together with the offending Redmond. All alliances are in flux.

Quin demands that Redmond be punished for his transgression. Redmond, in turn, pounces on that demand by offering Quin a chance to administer the punishment himself. Disrupter of decorum in this and the previous scene, Redmond nevertheless proves himself a man of his era, like his father before him, by pursuing power through traditional means. However opposed their private interests may be, the two rivals play by the same set of institutional rules. Quin must either publically suffer the dishonor of Redmond's insult or agree to a duel.

Redmond's walk home in the company of Captain Grogan, Quin's brother officer, is a reverse variation on his earlier walk with Nora. Both scenes begin with a disagreement, but one ends in a parting of the ways while the other produces a new alliance. Attempting to dissuade Redmond from the duel, Grogan lays out the logical reasons against it, including Nora's faithlessness and Redmond's debt of gratitude towards Mr. Brady for generosity extended since the death of Redmond's father. But the younger man remains true to his feelings, insisting that he will pursue his cause even in defiance of the Church, whose bells ring in the distance. Captain Grogan, in defiance of the military uniform he shares with Captain Quin but in harmony with his Irish heritage, suddenly changes his tune. His challenge was a test of Redmond's resolve. Satisfied with the results, he gives Redmond an affectionate hug and calls him a man "after my own soul." Quin has won the devotion of Redmond's cousin, but Redmond has apparently captured the loyalty of Quin's junior officer.

In a setting as calm and beautiful as that of his father's duel, Redmond confronts Quin in the same ritual. The scene begins with a close-up of pistols being loaded. The flow of a river in the background mirrors the relentless flow of the ritual, as does Handel's "Sarabande," which here performs much as "When Johnny Comes Marching Home Again" does in *Dr. Strangelove*. A reverse zoom reveals layer upon layer of detachment separating the combatants. Two seconds serve as dispassionate points of contact between Redmond and Quin, presumably guaranteeing fair play. Far overhead, tree branches form a canopy over the event. Violence is aesthetically contained within a pretty frame. Social forces operate in a similar manner, yet there is something oppressive as well as attractive about the latter. Custom may soften the violent urges of individual man, but it can also encourage them with exaggerated notions of honor.

Without the prestige of his institutional uniform and identity to shield him, John Quin looks nervous and vulnerable. He wears instead a white, ruffled shirt — the "uniform" of genteel membership he shares with his rival. A muffled drum is added to the music. Cadence remains the same throughout the scene, but changes in instrumentation reflect dramatic shifts in the action. The first of these shifts occurs when the combatants choose their weapons.

Redmond hesitates in accepting a pistol from Ulick, temporarily disrupting the proceedings. The uninterrupted music plays counterpoint to that pause. Grogan, who empathizes with Redmond's devotion to a romantic cause but also recognizes its folly, seizes an opportunity to repeat his argument against the duel. In effect, he offers Redmond an escape from fate. The protagonist need only acknowledge his inferior status as boy rather than man in relation to his opponent. Quin, almost too frightened to speak, accepts Grogan's proposal, then dooms it to failure by unwisely amending it with a stipulation that Redmond apologize in order for their dispute to be honorably settled. His pride overruling his fear, Redmond refuses to compromise.

The duel resumes, falling back into sync with the music and running its course to an institutionally defined resolution. Or maybe not. In such a strictly regulated affair, any deviation from form stands out. Redmond notices that the pistol handed to him by Ulick is not his own. Ulick has an excuse, and Redmond accepts it. By trusting implicitly in the power of tradition to guarantee fairness, Redmond commits a strategic blunder. Only later will he learn the cost of it.

The seconds step aside to give the quarreling gentlemen a more direct access to each other. The Englishman, his hair again wafting in the breeze, is terrified. His trembling pistol arm conceals one of his eyes. The other eye, open wide in panic, gains in expressive power as a result of its singularity, much as Alex's decorated eye gained from apposition to its unadorned partner in *Clockwork*. But in Alex's case the effect was designed by the character and yielded an impression of power. Quin's eye involuntarily betrays fear. Viewed from a similar camera angle, Redmond is a portrait of confidence, *both* of his eyes contributing to a symmetrical expression of determination. Not surprisingly, he gets off the first and truest shot. Quin, discreetly viewed in extreme long shot, cries out and collapses to the ground.

The duel's aftermath is accompanied by a more contemplative version of the "Sarabande," on harpsichord. Institutional form remains unchanged, yet private emotions speaking through that form have changed considerably. Redmond appears more stunned than elated by his victory. Grogan, Mick, and Ulick remove their hats out of obligatory respect for the dead Englishman. Mick rebukes Redmond for depriving the Brady family of financial security. In retrospect, however, this seems less a spontaneous reaction than a calculated maneuver to get Redmond away from Quin's body as quickly as possible.

The carry-over of a single beat from the "Sarabande" juxtaposes the duel's rigidity with the informality of Redmond's reception back home by his relieved mother. He seeks refuge in the same place he tried to forget about Nora. The genteel device by which he stripped, exposed, and killed Captain Quin is not recognized as legal by the State. The narrator tells us it is Redmond's "destiny" to be a wanderer. In the sense that various collective forces have pushed him into a duel and then branded him a murderer for winning it, that statement is accurate.

A quiet meal inside the Barry house provides a leisurely, appealing portrait of rustic charm and maternal love, with no trace of cloying sentiment or sniggering caricature. By shooting most of this brief scene in a single, static shot, Kubrick achieves a painterly quality of essential characteristics distilled into what is nearly a still life. Steam rising from cups and a pot of tea adds a warm touch of animation to this idyllic image. Prudent editing renders subsequent close-ups more potent than they would otherwise be.

Ulick's argument in favor of Redmond's immediate departure for Dublin is sound, though in retrospect suspiciously motivated. Mrs. Barry's counter-argument is motivated by loving concern but is not sound. Remaining silent, Redmond allows Ulick to be his instrument of persuasion. Eventually, however, Redmond himself must destroy his mother's naive illusion that he will be safe at home. Only then does the camera cut to a poignant exchange of close-ups between them as they painfully face the necessity of parting.

Riding away from home, Redmond faces a bleak, empty landscape that seems to promise nothing but loneliness and hardship. Ulick comforts Mrs. Barry with an arm around her waist as they bid her son farewell. Hindsight will undercut that impression. He is *happy* to see his cousin leave.

Music forms a bridge from one scene to the next, projecting the sorrow of Redmond, Mrs. Barry, and Ulick onto a portrait of Nature that, as if in sympathetic response, amplifies our sense of Redmond's solitude. In extreme long shot, he rides slowly towards us, dwarfed by the surrounding landscape. A crow caws in the distance. Dark, wind-blown clouds shroud a massive hill in the background. Redmond seems a lonely and fragile figure in the expansive gloom. Then narration undercuts this impression, revealing that Redmond is secretly delighted to be liberated from home and family and sees his future as an adventure. The maternal concern depicted in the previous scene can be, from the point of view of its object, as oppressive as it is comforting. Redmond is, for the first time, master of his own life. Or so it seems. The satisfaction he expected from killing Quin never materialized, yet an unanticipated satisfaction comes to him as an indirect consequence of their duel.

As if to catch up with Redmond's secret contentment, the skies begin to clear and the sun shines pleasantly during the next stage of his journey. In extreme long shot, he approaches a picturesque country inn. Contributing to the attractive setting are anonymous figures of two gentlemen relaxing at an outdoor table. They are nothing more than tiny details in a harmonious whole, until the camera cuts closer as Redmond approaches them. Perhaps distracted by the joy of his new-found freedom, he pays them little regard. But the camera is more discerning. Without changing their deceptively casual postures, the men display a keen interest in Redmond. Captain Feeney, the older of the two, discreetly probes for information about and tries to delay the departure of the young traveler. There is a trace of Alex in Feeney's predatory smile, offset by a pair of grandfatherly spectacles.

The camera returns to its original overview as Redmond rides away from the inn. Outwardly, nothing has changed. But our initial impression of a congenial world has been undercut by intimations of danger. The tender sentiment of "The Sea Maiden" is displaced by the disturbing drum rolls of Sean O'Riada's "Tin Whistles," which carries over into the next scene, where a dense green thicket of gnarled tree branches and the caw of a crow coincidentally highlight

Redmond's new vulnerability, of which he is not yet aware. From the sadness of leaving home to the pleasure of independence to the hazards of isolation, it has been a quick trip. Concealment in the forest aids Redmond's flight from the law, but it also makes him vulnerable to other outlaws. Just as Dim and Georgie revenged themselves on Alex in an isolated rural setting, Feeney and Shamus have left the inn to confront Redmond in a more remote location.

Redmond is lured into a trap by the sight of a man standing in the middle of the road, facing in the other direction. Curiosity blunts wariness, and the trap is sprung. Captain Feeney, highway robber, suddenly wheels around and points two pistols at Redmond. Shamus, also armed, rides up quickly from behind. Encirclement complete.

The robbery of Redmond is in some ways peculiar to its age. Like Redmond's duel with Quin, it is executed in an orderly, almost courteous manner. Gentility, however preverse a shape it takes, extends deeply into the perceptions of individual man. "I'm Captain Feeney, at your service," is a mockery of courtesy. Redmond is very much at Feeney's service. The highwayman concedes nothing to Redmond's appeal for honor among thieves. Nor does an appeal to sentiment keep him from stealing the money given to Redmond by his mother. And self-preservation dictates that Redmond be deprived of his horse as well. Nevertheless, Feeney spares Redmond's life, does him no bodily harm, and allows him to keep his fine pair of boots. Though his polite words may be hypocritical, the Captain's *actions* in some respects conform to genteel propriety.

Redmond next appears in a variation on an earlier one-shot scene, when he began his journey. An extreme long shot juxtaposes him with a gloomy, shrouded hill looming in the background. But, this time, the visual impression of desolation harmonizes rather than clashes with his state of mind. Redmond is as he was when he first left home, minus his horse, twenty guineas, his joyful sense of freedom, and his taste for adventure.

Outside a pub in a small Irish village, a uniformed British Army recruiter makes his pitch to the local men. Perched on a stool, speaking perhaps to a partly inebriated crowd, and reading from a prepared script, he takes full advantage of circumstances in the same unscrupulous way Captain Feeney did in the forest, but in the service of the State and therefore legally. Playing off his audience's provincial naiveté, he promises glory, social advancement, and financial reward, while downplaying the less pleasant aspects of military service. He concludes with an obligatory pledge of loyalty to King and country, but *personal* incentives rather than patriotism will inspire his targets to sign up, as they did government officials to rally around Dr. Strangelove's bizarre, immodest proposal in *Dr. Strangelove*. After escaping the confines of home and family, and paying a heavy price for it, Redmond now *welcomes* the embrace of an even larger institutional sanctuary, trading one set of apron strings for another.

In a Kubrick film, no far-reaching plan ever works out exactly as intended, and no journey ever reaches its destination as originally envisioned. Redmond's diversion from Dublin to an army encampment is only the first of many interruptions and digressions in his life. Some of them are chosen by him while others are forced upon him. Like an infant learning to walk, or *2001's* shuttle flight attendant adjusting to weightlessness, Redmond is trained to march in step with other soldiers. He is back in school again, to his good fortune, as the narrator wryly points out. Just as Alex knowingly uses the Interior Minister to free himself from prison, Redmond benefits from the Army's desperate need of new recruits to avoid police arrest for the murder of Captain Quin.

But there are snakes in Redmond's new sanctuary. Relaxing at dinner, the soldiers of Redmond's regiment wear identical uniforms, matching the British flag flying high above them. In visual terms, individuality has been submerged in a single group identity. But personal pride and aggression continue to operate within that deceptive unanimity. Individual soldiers can either manipulate or fall victim to their shared perceptions. Redmond unwittingly violates an unwritten code of toughness by complaining about the grease in his cup. For his indiscretion, he receives a roar of derisive laughter from his comrades. Out of that *general* expression of contempt arises a *private* challenge from a burly, Irish veteran named Toole, who distinguishes his challenge from the regiment's as a whole by standing up. Directly above and behind him flies the British flag, symbolizing a collective order that now serves his personal sadism. It is indicative of the film's pre-Revolution sensibilities that one Irishman employs his English identity to browbeat a fellow Irishman.

Toole mocks Redmond's fussy, civilian palate, swilling from the same filthy mug Redmond rejected. It's a nice bit of theater by which he transforms the rest of the regiment into his supportive audience. But, unexpectedly, from out of that audience arises a foe. For whatever private reason, whether a past grudge against Toole, an unlikely compassion for Redmond, or a sadistic whim, the new player allies himself surreptitiously with Redmond, challenging Toole by proxy. Redmond becomes his weapon, while he in turn supplies ammunition for Redmond's until-now empty gun. And he executes this maneuver while remaining anonymous and therefore relatively safe from Toole's retaliation. The theater of contempt Toole set in motion suddenly turns against its creator. Redmond, with the help of his prompter, reverses roles with Toole by suggesting that the big veteran lives in fear of his own wife — a much deeper insult than the charge of finicky eating habits. Redmond even improves on the insult supplied by his secret ally, doubling back on a taunt of which he was the victim moments earlier. Reviving the towel Toole implied the protagonist needed, Redmond asks, "Mr. Toole, is it a towel of your wife's washing? I hear she wipes your face with one." He transforms the enemy's weapon into a weapon against his enemy, even as he himself is being used as a weapon by a third party. Meanwhile, the regimental audience Toole forged into an ally now betrays him, laughing derisively *with* Redmond and Redmond's ally.

Humiliation and anger push Toole beyond the rules of regimental behavior, which he initially played to such good advantage. He threatens to bash Redmond with a wooden stool. Redmond replies by brandishing a knife. We are almost back to the waterhole confrontation in *2001*. But the hand of institutional authority intervenes to restrain the savagery of individual man. Viewed in medium shot, Toole's forward thrusting head dwarfs the British flag in the background and, by implication, the social order it symbolizes. But what that flag represents demonstrates its power in the form of an officious stick wielded by an army officer whose authority is sufficient to separate the antagonists. As it turns out, the officer has no intention of suppressing their private squabble. He merely channels it into a sanctioned, manageable form. "Gentlemen! Gentlemen!" he reprimands, and so they prove themselves to be by obeying his commands.

The battle between Redmond and Toole is artificially confined to a red, white, and blue square made up of other members of the regiment. The combatants fight barechested, or stripped of their military identity. Unlike Captain Quin, Toole appears more than a match for Redmond. The presiding officer sanctifies the proceedings by ordering the combatants to shake hands and by setting forth the limits of combat. "No biting, kicking, or scratching. The last man to remain standing is the winner." Not exactly the rules for chess, but still a far cry from Alex's free-for-all with Billyboy in *Clockwork*. Genteel boundaries, though stretched, remain intact.

Other members of the regiment are comfortably positioned to identify with and yell encouragement to whoever lands a punch and to sadistically enjoy the pain and humiliation of whoever takes one. Surprisingly, the smaller but leaner Redmond proves a better boxer, repeatedly knocking down the wild-swinging Toole. The crowd, wishing to prolong its entertainment, repeatedly yells for Toole to get off the ground and return to the fight, until he can no longer do so. Knowing the proper time to stop attacking his foe, Redmond is hoisted aloft as champion by his peers, who share as generously in his triumph now as they did earlier in Toole's humiliation of him. He tentatively raises his arm in acknowledgement of his victory over Toole and, more broadly, over the world at large.

Redmond's regiment musters with others in an impressive, colorful display of military coordination. "Lilliburlero" reinforces a visual spectacle in which individual soldiers are reduced to anonymous parts of a larger and grander whole. Narration expands our perspective of this gathering by placing it in the larger context of England's participation in the Seven Years' War.

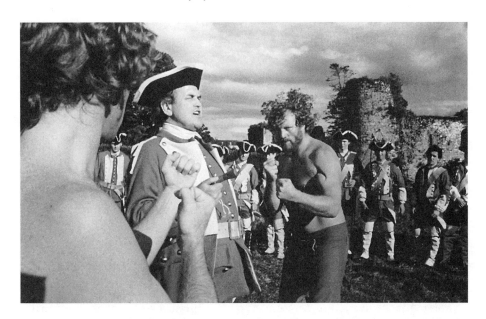

Private passions play out within a rigid, collective framework. Redmond Barry (Ryan O'Neal, back to camera at left) battles Toole (Pat Roach) inside a formal square made up of their regimental mates, who selfishly cheer the winner and jeer the loser. An army officer (Norman Mitchell) sanctions but also sets limits to the violent contest.

Standing at attention, Redmond observes Captain Grogan ride by on horseback. Grogan winks at him in fond recognition, but neither deviates from his assigned role in the collective flow. The camera returns to an overview in which the two characters are lost within the military proceedings, which, as with Captain Quin's parade drill earlier, is observed by a fascinated group of civilian spectators. Only later, in the privacy of a tent, can they get reacquainted. Though still in uniform, Redmond and Grogan have removed their caps and converse as equals rather than as soldiers of unequal rank. Grogan gently reprimands Redmond for not writing home to alleviate Mrs. Barry's worry. Redmond's excuse, inspired by his institutional sense of duty towards his parents, is that he was too ashamed of losing the money his mother gave him and the pistols he inherited from his father. Grogan dismisses that excuse as insignificant compared to the private, emotional bond between a mother and a son.

Grogan dispels Redmond's lingering romantic delusions about Nora by revealing her marriage to Captain Quin and the conspiracy to fake Quin's death in the duel. The time-honored tradition by which Redmond trapped the honor-bound Englishman into combat was thus transformed by the Brady brothers into a device for getting rid of Redmond. Grogan admits to getting money for participating in the deception, which implies that, however much he admired Redmond's stubborn devotion to love, he did not completely empathize with it. His promise to provide for Redmond's needs out of that money sounds like a guilt offering.

Kubrick lights this night scene entirely with candles. Technical innovation contributes to an aesthetic effect. Candlelight is not merely decorative in *Barry Lyndon*; it surrounds and acquaints us with the look of an era in many ways different from our own. In this scene, it accentuates the warm affection between Grogan and Redmond even when their dialog adds a note of cynical counterpoint. Candlelight does for *Barry Lyndon* what the natural-like lighting and profound silence of outer space did for *2001*. For viewers who prefer that more familiar aesthetics be imposed on unfamiliar settings and situations, the results are perhaps more annoying than intriguing. But in order to fully appreciate the perceptions and actions of Kubrick's characters, it is important to get a feel for the worlds in which they operate.

Backed by "The British Grenadiers," a ship carrying Redmond's regiment plows across the English Channel towards the Continent. This is the Ship of State in an idealized form, as much a product and symbol of national will as Major Kong's B-52 was *supposed* to be in *Dr. Strangelove*. But narration challenges our visual impression of a clear and unanimous collective purpose by suggesting that there were many and various causes of the Seven Years' War. No one participant, individual or collective, embodies them all. Even its military alliances are ephemeral, for the moment consisting of England and Prussia against France, Sweden, Russia, and Austria.

Without skipping a beat, "The British Grenadiers" shifts from background music reinforcing the nautical image of collective will to live music accompanying a land battle. A traveling side shot depicts Redmond and his regiment advancing as a unit, in sync with the fife and drum music. A reverse zoom expands this impression of mass military precision. Redmond is lost in a sea of red, white, and blue. Figuratively speaking, the narrator continues the reverse zoom by further enlarging our view. "Barry's first taste of battle was only a skirmish, against a small rear guard of Frenchmen, who occupied an orchard, beside a road, down which a few hours later the English main force would wish to pass." Each qualifying phrase reduces Redmond's baptism of fire within the larger pattern of the Seven Years' War. Yet this marginal skirmish is "memorable enough" for the protagonist. It is, in fact, a major turning point in his life.

A volley of French gunfire collapses row upon row of British soldiers, like toys flattened by a child's hand. Trained to ignore their fallen comrades and their own fear, fresh troops move up to replenish thinned forward ranks, falling into step with the unbroken collective stride. This maintenance of rigid formation distinguishes genteel warfare from the evasive, zigzag movements of soldiers in *Dr. Strangelove* and *Full Metal Jacket*.

Another French volley knocks Captain Grogan to the ground, mortally wounded. The camera subjectively halts with Redmond as he breaks rank in order to help his friend. Red-trousered legs march past them without interruption. Only moments earlier, we and the protagonist were participants in that mass movement, passing by other wounded and dead. Redmond discards his rifle and embraces Grogan. A brief, subjective French view of oncoming British soldiers being decimated by yet another volley is now entirely out of sync with the minidrama of Redmond and Grogan. The camera returns to the principal characters while the soundtrack continues to register the noise of battle, generating counterpoint. Redmond carries Grogan off the battlefield to a nearby grove of trees that provides them with privacy. Mud soils their uniforms, further obscuring their institutional identities.

Before dying, Grogan makes a confession. Of the two hundred guineas he got out of Mr. Brady for participating in the rigged duel, only one hundred are left for Redmond, to whose welfare Grogan earlier pledged the entire amount. Gambling, or self-interest, depleted the rest. Yet under present, dire circumstances this revelation endears Grogan to Redmond more rather than less. For the kiss of friendship Grogan requests, Redmond removes his army cap, paying formal respect to his dying comrade. But Grogan's death during that kiss triggers in Redmond a spontaneous reaction that overrides *all* formality. Collapsing on Grogan's chest, he sobs out his grief. This is Redmond emotionally unfiltered, as we will see him again on very few occasions in the film.

Redmond's disillusionment with army life grows in the next three scenes. Pictured standing alone among his sleeping comrades gathered around a campfire, he broods over his situation. The camera slowly zooms in on his unhappy face, isolating him from the other men. "The Sea Maiden" returns to the soundtrack, echoing his nostalgic yearning for the home he was once happy to leave. Hardship frees him from the army recruiter's deceitful grasp, just as hardship placed him in it. The narrator discreetly reinforces our appreciation of the difference between war as an abstract idea and war as an experience. Among the grubby underpinnings of military glory in which Redmond is compelled to participate is the theft and destruction of the property of hapless farmers. The stolen lamb Redmond carries away with him is somewhat symbolic of his own loss of innocence. Then there is the drudgery of army camp routine. A close-up of water buckets reverse zooms to identify Redmond as their carrier, just as a similar reverse zoom in *Clockwork* revealed the old Tramp to be a slave to booze.

Redmond's desertion from the Army is prompted by an accidental confluence of desire and opportunity. While fetching water outside camp, he stumbles upon a conversation between two British officers bathing in a river. Their problem becomes the solution to his problem. Music reflecting his nostalgia for home is displaced by a conversation which promises to fulfill that yearning. The bathers take advantage of their isolation to express illicit romantic feelings for each other. Along with their uniforms, they have shed their collective identities. Standing behind a tree, Redmond is concealed from the bathers, just as they are concealed from the regiment. One of the officers complains about a courier assignment that will separate him from his lover. Redmond, on the other hand, can shed *his* unwanted assignment by taking upon himself the unwanted assignment of someone else. Like *2001*'s HAL, Redmond acquires power by observing without being detected (HAL reading the lips of Poole and Bowman as they plot against him) and acting without being observed (HAL attacking the hibernating astronauts).

The Prussian and English Armies are allied but separate and therefore not completely harmonious organizations. Redmond plays one off the other by posing as a British officer traveling behind Prussian lines, enjoying both freedom of movement and minimal accountability. The "Hohenfriedberger March," composed by Prussia's King Frederick, becomes Redmond's private, ironic ode to victory over *all* institutional domination. His triumphant procession through a corridor of Prussian soldiers is equivalent to Alex's transfer from Staja 84F to the Ludovico Centre. Both victories, however, prove temporary. Redmond, like Alex, has moved into a new, unfamiliar, and therefore hazardous social arena.

Riding away from the war zone, Redmond intends, according to the narrator, to return home by way of neutral Holland. But the best-laid plans often go astray in a Kubrick film. Redmond's desire to return to Ireland yields to a very different desire when he encounters an attractive young German woman named Lischen. The language barrier between them hinders yet somehow simplifies their communication in this age of verbal elaboration. A bargain for food serves also as a romantic overture.

Beginning with a medium shot of Redmond, Lischen, and Lischen's baby seated at the supper table in Lischen's farmhouse, the camera cuts closer to the characters only when their subtle exchange of feelings warrants it. Soft candlelight illuminates the scene. Distant thunder heightens our impression of the trio's snug, safe isolation from the world at large. This is the dream-like flip side of what in *The Shining* will become a nightmare of isolation for the Torrance family. Redmond enjoys with Lischen a romantic idyll he never achieved with Nora Brady. But this time he is not quite so naive. His dialog with Lischen blends romantic passion with tactical maneuvering that barely disturbs the outward appearance of propriety. "It must be hard for you to be alone" encourages Lischen to reveal her feelings so that he might exploit them to a mutually satisfying end. Distracted by his appeal to her loneliness, Lischen stops feeding her baby and encourages Redmond to confess his own hardship. He briefly resists ("I'm an officer and I must do my duty," which happens to be a lie), then gives in. Mild protest from the neglected child, who wants only to be fed, offers gentle counterpoint to the growing intimacy between the two adults.

The sentimental "Women of Ireland" returns to the soundtrack for the first time since Redmond's card game with Nora. He and Lischen take each other's hands. But Redmond is not the gullible young man he was with Nora. He identifies himself as Jonathan Fakenham, the officer whose identity he stole earlier. The genuine tenderness of this interlude is tempered by our recognition of Redmond's deception. Their gentle first kiss is far removed from the bizarre and violent sexuality of *Dr. Strangelove* and *A Clockwork Orange*. One of *Barry Lyndon's* most lyrically intricate scenes, the alliance between Redmond and Lischen is delicately balanced between passion, restraint, and manipulation.

Later we see Redmond driving cattle home from pasture, having exchanged his officer's uniform, which he stole, for a farmer's livery, which he borrows. Neither role was originally his, but at different times each of them suits his wishes. Too soon he is back in uniform, bidding farewell to Lischen. Their fragile, private idyll is threatened by the expected return of Lischen's husband and the continuing possibility of military pursuit.

A close-up of the two lovers, their heads touching in mutual affection, tells only part of the story that has passed between them. Their farewells are spoken in German, suggesting a strategic tilt in Lischen's favor. More importantly, Lischen addresses her departing lover by his true name, which means that Redmond has told her the truth about himself, placing his welfare in her hands. Narration further modifies our impression of their relationship by revealing, in counterpoint to the romantic imagery and music, that Redmond is only one in a series of surrogate husbands Lischen has employed to ease her loneliness. She is not quite Nora Brady, who ruthlessly manipulated Redmond for her own gain. But her initial appearance of guilelessness, which made her seem to be what Redmond used to be, was misleading. Like any chance meeting between two people, Redmond and Lischen encounter each other at particular points in their separate journeys. And those journeys help shape the role each will play in the other's life.

Romantic diversion ended, Redmond resumes his journey where it left off. The "Hohenfriedberger" returns, displacing the "Women of Ireland" that earlier displaced *it*. His next encounter features a juxtaposition of opposites. And again, narration contributes essential information to that impression. A group of civilian men, guarded by Prussian soldiers, trudges past Redmond going in the opposite direction. They are conscripted recruits for the Prussian Army. In an adjacent pasture, a dog herds sheep for *his* master. Redmond and the recruits relate to the martial joy of the "Hohenfriedberger" in different ways. He is individual man employing a false institutional identity to escape his institutional shackles. They are individuals forcibly given new institutional identities in order to serve the King's political ambitions. For a moment the King's music celebrates two contradictory yet simultaneous victories.

A third encounter for Redmond is neither as pleasant as the first nor as inconsequential as the second. He meets up with a Prussian military column led by Captain Potzdorf. Both sides halt, as does the music, awaiting the outcome of this meeting. The hollow sound of wind and a treeless landscape heighten our impression of Redmond's sudden vulnerability.

Spoken in masterful English, Potzdorf's questions are as incisive as they are superficially courteous. Redmond's calm demeanor and military papers pass inspection, but his sense of direction does not. He is headed away from his official destination. Potzdorf takes sly advantage of his adversary's mistake. In exchange for food, shelter, and better maps, he begs the "honor" of Redmond's company along the correct route to Bremen. Like Captain Feeney, Potzdorf puts an elegant face on his exercise of power. Outmaneuvered and outnumbered, Redmond has no choice but to accept the invitation. Circumstances compel him to join what he ignored in the previous scene. The "Hohenfriedberger" resumes, but this time on a note of triumph for institutional rather than individual man.

Inside Prussian headquarters a leisurely reverse zoom places Redmond at the center of a congenial group of Prussian officers, superficially recollecting an image of Alex comfortably situated in the Korova Milkbar. Narration, however, sketches in details which contradict the analogy. Captain Potzdorf, seeking to draw his opponent out into the open, asks many questions about England. Redmond conjures up phony stories to cover his ignorance. The "Hohenfriedberger," now sung by officers at a nearby table, seems again to favor the protagonist.

Potzdorf primes and then exposes Redmond's fanciful fiction. "You will have to pardon me. I know so little about your country of England. Except that you are the bravest nation in the world and that we are really fortunate to have such allies." "You are," in place of "Yours is," generously equates Redmond with the "brave" institution he fraudulently hides behind. Redmond swallows the flattering bait and grows careless. Caught off guard dealing in outdated information, he is arrested.

A new camera angle reflects a new strategic situation. Stag racks are now visually aligned with Potzdorf and his sergeant. The "Hohenfriedberger" that seemed friendly to Redmond a few moments earlier fades away. He tries to stand and protest but is restrained by the collective power implied in the mere touch of a Prussian soldier's hand on his shoulder, the same way Alex was restrained by Mr. Alexander's touch, which carried the implied power of Julian's strength. Captain Potzdorf levels State charges of "impostor" and "deserter" against Redmond.

Potzdorf's terms for surrender are both harsh and hypocritical. Redmond must either volunteer to join the Prussian Army or hang for deserting from the British Army. The Captain's previous enthusiasm for the alliance between Prussia and England now seems disingenuous. Prussia's need for fresh recruits is, for him, more pressing than the cause of British military justice. And yet, conforming to the Prussian Army's internal notion of fair play, Potzdorf offers Redmond the customary bounty if he will enlist. The facade of Prussian due process is preserved in what is essentially a dishonorable transaction that violates the due process of an ally. Alex benefited from a similar schism between Staja 84F officials and Ludovico advocates in *Clockwork*.

Lost again in the collective order of an army, this time outfitted in blue rather than red, Redmond seems worse off than before, because the Prussian Army has even less respect for individual rights than did the British. Narration reinforces the point by describing the Prussian Army, "so renowned for its disciplined valor," as a sham composed of "men from the lowest levels of humanity, hired or stolen from almost every nation in Europe."

Redmond's resurrection to power occurs as the accidental consequence of a battle in which he is a reluctant participant. Our first impression of that battle is one of emotional detachment. From inside Prussian field headquarters, we look out subjectively through a gun portal at the distant enemy, like a movie-screen image of war. Our gun fires. We cannot tell if an enemy soldier is hit as a result. The gun is withdrawn back into the relative safety of Prussian headquarters.

Approaching the building from outside, Captain Potzdorf seems equally indifferent to the suffering of his men and the danger to himself. Once inside, he coolly surveys the performance of his troops and peers through a gun portal, as we did moments earlier. But, this time, the illusion of detachment is shattered by a cannon shell that reduces the Prussian stronghold to a chaos of smoke, fire, and debris. Potzdorf is trapped under a portion of collapsed ceiling. He calls out for help, but his soldiers' instinct for self-preservation overrides his authority. They are as indifferent to his fate as he was to theirs outside — except for Redmond. Reacting spontaneously from compassion, he rescues Potzdorf from death, risking his own life in the process. Corruption previously attributed to him by the narrator has not yet consumed him entirely.

Like his victory over Toole in the British Army, Redmond's advancement in Prussian service is celebrated within a formation of his peers. A Colonel Bulow conveys the official gratitude of King Frederick, who in reality is probably unaware of Redmond's existence. Ceremony creates the illusion of solidarity between the greatest and the humblest members of society. Within that ceremony, layers of detachment lend emotional gravity to the occasion. Redmond's monetary reward is kept in a special box, resting on a decorative pillow, held by one of Bulow's subordinates. All this embellishment for two lousy coins.

Summoned forward to receive his reward, Redmond meets with a contradictory reception. Bulow's personal *criticism* of his corrupt ways is expressed within the impersonal confines of collective *praise* for his bravery under fire. But Redmond, becoming more and more like *Clockwork's* Alex, transforms an insult into a tool. Respectfully denying Bulow's accusations, he turns them into a device for ingratiating himself further with Captain Potzdorf, who stands next to the Colonel. And his appeal is calculated to flatter Poztdorf both as a personal ally and a regimental leader. By playing the sycophant, Redmond manipulates the Captain the same way Potzdorf manipulated *him* several scenes earlier. And as he executes this role reversal, a new piece of music quietly rises on the soundtrack. Wolfgang Amadeus Mozart's genteel march from *Idomeneo* replaces the "Hohenfriedberger" that he had lost to Potzdorf. Mozart is Redmond's new ode to joy as the camera returns to its initial overview of a ceremony that outwardly appears unchanged. But within its rigid framework, Redmond has employed the tactic of divide and conquer to improve his situation in a hostile world not of his choosing.

The Seven Years' War ends. *Idomeneo* transports Redmond's resurgent power into a new, civilian setting. An extreme long shot of a broad Berlin boulevard depicts the splendor of a genteel social order that transcends national borders. Anonymous, fashionably dressed individuals and stylish carriages pass leisurely between rows of perfectly trimmed trees bracketed by elegant buildings, all beneath a pastel blue sky. Inside one of those buildings individual man is dwarfed by high doorways and ceilings, ornate furniture, and an enormous mirror. Elaborate attire, makeup, formal gestures, and formal language continually reinforce our impression of individual man reconstituted to suit a collective ideal. Redmond enters in his Prussian Army uniform. He walks past towering pillars, which are often a symbolic measure of collective force in Kubrick's films. On the far wall sit white marble busts — the purest expression of individual man recast as an abstraction. Redmond halts precisely in front of a large desk that conveys the social prominence and power of the government official who sits behind it.

As Minister of Police and therefore the highest-ranking person in this scene, Herr von Potzdorf remains seated and does not speak directly to Redmond. His nephew, Captain Potzdorf, serves as intermediary between the two in a rather unsavory piece of business. The Captain addresses Redmond by his common name. Redmond respectfully addresses his superiors by their titles. Captain Potzdorf's proposition to Redmond targets the young Irishman's self-interest rather than his sense of duty. He offers Redmond an honorable discharge from the Army, a secure position in civilian society, and a chance to move in high social circles. Yet in choosing Redmond to be his secret agent, Potzdorf yields to a sentimental streak in his own largely cynical out-look. "Redmond, your loyalty to me and your service to the regiment has pleased me very well." Note that "loyalty to me" comes before "service to the regiment." The fact that Redmond saved his life in combat has allayed the suspicion with which he initially regarded the phony Lieutenant Fakenham. Yet he fails to consider the influence that sentiment could have on *Redmond* when he assigns the young man the task of spying on a fellow Irishman, who is allegedly spying on Prussia for Redmond's homeland (has the Prussian/English alliance fallen apart?).

In their eagerness to close the deal, the Potzdorfs reduce the distance between themselves and Redmond. The camera, reflecting this increased intimacy, closes in as well. Captain Potzdorf approaches his protégé, while Herr Minister finally deigns to speak directly to Redmond, who, to the revived strains of *Idomeneo*, achieves a tactical victory from an inferior position by telling his masters what they want to hear: "I'm interested in anything that can be of service to yourself and to Captain Potzdorf." Unspoken, but in the thoughts of all three men, is "and myself."

The Captain's scheme to use Redmond as a spy involves the same tactic Redmond employed to desert from the British Army. A false identity is manufactured out of official documents. But Redmond's deception served a private cause and therefore was condemned by the Captain. Potzdorf's lie serves a higher, institutional cause and is therefore, presumably, morally justified. Fashionably dressed and occupying a large, richly decorated hotel suite, the Chevalier de Balibari appears to be a man in perfect harmony with his environment. A huge chandelier overhead is almost as overwhelming a symbol of collective grace as was the fluorescent halo in *Dr. Strangelove's* War Room. Redmond enters this paradise accompanied by his victorious *Idomeneo*. But the music stops as his determination to spy on Balibari yields to other feelings. He sees in the Chevalier a man who has attained a privileged existence. Add to that the sentimental appeal of Balibari's Irish heritage, and the combination is too much for the homesick protagonist to resist. Without lifting a finger, the unsuspecting Chevalier conquers the agent of his enemies. Prussian defeat is snatched from the jaws of victory, since Balibari had already accepted Redmond's credentials as legitimate before Redmond confesses to deception. The initial image of Redmond in this scene, from the Chevalier's point of view, as a small figure neatly framed and contained by doorway, pillars, and chandelier has proven surprisingly accurate.

Redmond drops his official pretense in an extraordinarily *un*genteel display of emotion, which the narrator softens by describing it in dispassionate terms. In one respect, Redmond's passions betray him by working against the Prussian promise of reward for services rendered. In another, however, they *liberate* him from a growing cynicism in which all emotions are feigned for the purpose of strategic gain. Luckily for him, the Chevalier is equally sentimental beneath his formal exterior. Touched by the same nostalgia for home that possessed Redmond, Balibari comforts his compatriot with a hug. The two enemies have become allies.

Redmond again stands at attention before his Prussian masters, but this time as the Chevalier's agent against the Potzdorfs instead of the other way around. His report on Balibari's activities consists of accurate yet useless information. His credibility as a spy is maintained, but at no substantial cost to the Chevalier or himself. Captain Potzdorf circles behind Redmond, pondering what he hears. The camera, meanwhile, circles behind Herr Minister, acting as a stand-in for Redmond's secret ally.

Inside his hotel suite, the Chevalier hosts a card game for the esteemed Prussian Prince of Tobingham. In long shot, everything and everyone appears to be a faithful extension of genteel custom and aesthetics. This is competition cushioned by multiple layers of detachment. Giovanni Paisiello's "Cavatina," from *Il Barbiere di Siviglia*, celebrates the elegance of the occasion. And though that elegance will be undercut by personal conflict, its seductive power is acknowledged by Kubrick. The "Cavatina" is *love* music.

At first we perceive the card game on two different levels, one visual and the other revealed to us by narration. Redmond appears to be nothing more than Balibari's servant, catering to the wants of his superiors, until narration informs us that he and the Chevalier surreptitiously employ that role to cheat the Prince. Redmond's keen eyesight more than compensates for the reduced sight of the Chevalier, who wears a patch over one eye.

The camera cuts closer to the action to pick out signs of self-interest in the otherwise smooth flow of decorum. After the Chevalier *casually* plays a card, we see his one good eye riveted on his opponent — the same aggressive expression displayed in *Clockwork's* first shot by Alex's equally asymmetrical glare. Serving as scorekeeper, an acquaintance of the Prince glances from one player to the other, amused by their contest yet risking nothing himself.

Narration places an historical frame around this scene by noting that gambling was, at the time, a passion among gentlemen throughout Europe. It is a controlled, legal form of competition by which one man can assert power over another. The game ends in Balibari's favor. The scorekeeper smirks discreetly as he tallies up the Prince's losses. Possibly he derives some private satisfaction from Tobingham's defeat, as did Redmond's secret ally from the humiliation of Toole.

Tobingham stands and accuses his host of cheating, assuming the same theatrical, arrogant posture Captain Quin did while kissing Nora Brady in front of Redmond. His *real* anger, however, can be read in his eyes. Balibari, meanwhile, conceals his own fierce determination beneath such polite words as "Your grace" and "I beg you." Without shouting or throwing a punch, the antagonists commit themselves to a duel which could easily kill one of them.

Back at Herr Minister's office, Redmond stands facing his masters, who bracket him. From their vantage point, he is neatly framed by the doorway behind him, just as he is presumably contained (by the promise of reward) within their plot. Regarding the dispute between Tobingham and the Chevalier, Redmond tells them that the Chevalier's tactics were fair and that Balibari intends to press for a duel to satisfy his claim on the Prince. The fact that Redmond's opinions are trusted puts pressure on the Potzdorfs and Tobingham to settle up rather than call the enemy's bluff. In fact, however, he serves as a propagandist for the Chevalier, who, in view of his age and diminished eyesight, probably prefers to avoid a duel. The Potzdorfs consult with each other out of Redmond's earshot. Obviously he is not an *equal* partner in their schemes.

But Redmond is *nearly* an equal partner with the Chevalier. In private, they drop the facade of master and servant (which was in itself a scam promulgated by the Prussians) and plot strategy against their enemies. The Chevalier's connection to the Austrian government provides him with leverage in his personal challenge to the Prince of Tobingham, just as a connection to the Interior Minister helped Alex against Staja 84F's officials in *Clockwork*.

In view of Balibari's link to the Austrian state, the only way for the Prussians to discreetly blunt his challenge to Tobingham is to quietly remove him from Prussia without harming him. Toward that end, they rely on Redmond's intimate knowledge of the Chevalier's daily routine, the regularity of which is in keeping with genteel habits.

Nothing appears out of order the following morning when, promptly at ten o'clock, the Chevalier walks in evenly measured steps into the elegant hotel lobby, through a large door opened for him by a uniformed servant (another layer of detachment), and to his waiting coach. But the man atop that coach is not the Chevalier's usual driver (Redmond, posing as Laszlo), and several Prussian soldiers are on hand to forcibly alter the Chevalier's daily excursion. Unfortunately for them, the Chevalier they confront is Redmond in disguise. As instruments of the Potzdorfs, Tobingham, and King Frederick, the soldiers are familiar only with their orders, not with the Chevalier's physical appearance. Likewise in *Dr. Strangelove*, Colonel "Bat" Guano, operating under orders from President Muffley by way of General Faceman, encounters a situation at Burpleson Air Force Base out of sync with his mission. The Prussian soldiers, acting on behalf of higher authority, revise the Chevalier's morning routine. Redmond, conspiring with and posing as the Chevalier, revises the cast of the Prussian production, making it his own. By inquiring as to the whereabouts of his usual driver, Laszlo, Redmond strikes a deliciously ironic note, since Laszlo is the weapon he earlier consented to become on behalf of the Prussians.

Like Captain Feeney's robbery of Redmond, the kidnapping in this scene is softened by courtesy and restraint. It is almost a *negotiated* settlement, with violence only an implied threat. Balibari's mild show of resistance compels the officer in charge to be slightly more direct about that threat, which he then softens with the offer of a bribe on behalf of the Prince of Tobingham, whose initial refusal to pay any part of his debt to Balibari is thus compromised.

Redmond enters the coach without the Prussians, whom he has betrayed, laying a hand on him. *Idomeneo* returns as his personal victory march. Narration completes our impression of his triumph. "And so, without papers or passport, and under the eyes of two Prussian officers, Barry was escorted across the frontier, into Saxony and freedom. The Chevalier himself had uneventfully crossed the frontier the night before." Papers, passports, and soldiers are all means by which the State regulates the movements of individuals within its borders. Redmond eludes the first two and transforms the third into a formal escort to freedom.

The aristocratic society to which Redmond is subsequently introduced is a magnification of everything "noble" he saw in the Chevalier. An immense castle jutting up into the clear sky at dusk is a visible token of feudal priviledged. If the Chevalier's card game with Tobingham was a fine example of genteel elegance, the scene inside Lord Ludd's castle pictures that elegance at its apex. The table is larger, the game more elaborate, the participants more numerous and lavishly costumed, the candlelight richer, and the chandelier overhead a more prominent symbol of the collective spirit that shapes the scene. Paisiello's "Cavatina" returns, this time with vocal accompaniment that makes it an even more passionate echo of the visual splendor.

On the host's side of the gaming table, Lord Ludd occupies the center of an elaborate collective arrangement. Two attractive women sit on either side of him, as emblems of his privileged status and as fanciful good-luck charms. Like the candelabra with which they are visually aligned, they embellish Ludd's experience of the game. Other spectators crowd around this trio. Along with the women, they participate vicariously in the fortunes of their host, even as they add to his pleasure.

The game is conducted in French, as a concession to Lord Ludd. The two competitors differ in their approaches to the game. Ludd enjoys gambling as a diversion. He trusts his expendable fortune to Lady Luck, nibbling in mild anxiety at the fingertips of his female companions. But, for the Chevalier, gambling is a livelihood. He struggles to repress his emotions, which reveal themselves in his clenched fist and intense stare. After his first triumph over Ludd, Balibari employs a decorative board to rake in his opponent's captured chips, avoiding any overt impression of avarice by not directly touching the prize, which in turn is only a symbolic representation of money, which is again once removed from the things it can buy. Meanwhile, Lord Ludd releases the fingers of his luckless ladies and accepts his loss with a sour little expression of displeasure.

As a suppliant, Ludd speaks in English to solicit credit from the Chevalier. Redmond serves Balibari as an intermediary, like the board Balibari used to gather in his chips. This being a contest between gentlemen, the credit is extended. Ludd kisses the woman on his left as though rewarding her for his good luck. Like remoras to a shark, the women are keenly attuned to their host, who is their source of entertainment and material well-being. The Chevalier silently watches the transfer of credit with keen interest. Though honor bound to extend the loan, he cannot afford to lose it. And so he overrides luck by cheating. Meanwhile, Lord Ludd takes the hands of both his good luck charms, as though to double his chances for victory. A palmed card guarantees otherwise.

Feigning indifference to his loss with an unconvincing smile, Lord Ludd reverts to his native language to declare its insignificance. Defiantly reclasping the female hands that proved such inadequate guardians of his fortune, he tries to achieve an aesthetic victory in the face of financial defeat. But Redmond discreetly calls attention to his unpaid loan. Ludd concedes his signature on a promissory note. Yet even in this act of surrender, he tries to salvage a little dignity by assuming the arrogant, hand-on-hip pose employed by Captain Quin and the Prince of Tobingham before him.

Like Tobingham, Lord Ludd refuses to pay his debt. But for all his effete mannerisms, he is willing to fight to back up his refusal. And he would probably be more than a match for Balibari, except for the older man's ace in the hole. Redmond's dueling skills "maintained the reputation of the firm, so to speak." Which is to say that Redmond is still a frontline soldier in someone else's army, even though that someone is a friend.

The duel restricts aggression to choreographed thrust and parry. It is a minuet version of Alex and Catlady's wildly improvisational dance of death in *Clockwork*. The contest is closely matched until Redmond ends it with a deft and surprising maneuver. With the tip of Redmond's sword pressed against his chest, Lord Ludd drops his own weapon and announces that he will pay his debt promptly. Redmond, abiding by the rules of the game, steps back and bows to the loser. But the fierce look on his face betrays aggression only barely contained by his genteel sensibilities.

Despite their victory, the "firm" of Balibari and Barry is a fragile enterprise. Their aristocratic victims have too many strategic advantages. With Ludd's castle looming in the background, a coach carrying the two professional gamblers beats a hasty retreat. The narrator expands our picture by pointing out that such flight is a way of life for them.

A luxurious spa in Belgium is another stop on their precarious tour of European high society. But Paisielli's celebratory "Cavatina" is here displaced by Franz Schubert's more somber *Piano Trio in E-flat*, echoing the growing discontent felt by Redmond. His yearning, outwardly concealed, is explained to us by the narrator as a cynical desire to acquire financial security through marriage to a woman of wealth. After many bitter experiences of the world, the sincerity of Redmond's love for Nora Brady yielded to the mixture of affection and deception in his relationship with Lischen, and now to cold manipulation in his initial dealings with a third woman. "As so many gentlemen had done before him" places Redmond within an unofficial genteel tradition that contradicts his original inclinations and the official myth of gentility.

The spa's enclosed courtyard is a model of order and containment. Its rectangular pool is surrounded by evenly spaced statues and walkways, which are in turn shielded from the outside world by a manicured wall of shrubbery and trees. Within this cloistered paradise, fashionably dressed men and women walk in measured steps along appointed avenues. If not for the vast difference in circumstances, their situation would be comparable to inmates walking along a painted circle in *Clockwork's* prison exercise yard. The pace of the *Piano Trio* matches their movement, while its somber tone echoes Redmond's discontent. Meanwhile, the camera both mimics and cuts across the grain of their movement, simultaneously reflecting and criticizing their devotion to custom.

Both Redmond and the Chevalier observe the people strolling in the courtyard below. But only Redmond, preoccupied by thoughts of social advancement, focuses in on one group among them. The new characters on Redmond's stage are the Lyndon family. They reveal nothing about themselves through dialog, but their demeanor, articulated by the narrator, betrays a "firm" emotionally divided against itself.

Sir Charles Lyndon, a functionary at the English royal court, is the head of his family yet is enfeebled by disease. Confined to a wheelchair, he steers this way and that while being pushed by a servant. His entourage, including a wife and son, dutifully follow his wavering course. Schubert's music now echoes Lady Lyndon's unhappiness as well as Redmond's. The Reverend Samuel Runt, Lady Lyndon's personal chaplain, appears less unhappy with his situation, since he materially benefits from her discontent. Lord Bullingdon, Sir Charles's son, looks as unhappy as his mother, to whom he is excessively attached.

A gambling session at the spa provides the film's third variation on a theme. Lady Lyndon and Reverend Runt place bets at the gaming table. Redmond and the Chevalier are seated opposite. Technically the two pairs are adversaries. But this time there is a game *within* the game, making allies of adversaries and adversaries of allies. A different form of cheating occurs, with Schubert's Piano Trio highlighting a discreet series of adulterous dance steps — a dance for three, it turns out.

Lady Lyndon glances briefly at Redmond, then looks down and fingers her pile of gambling chips. Her attraction to the handsome stranger duels with her sense of propriety. She repeats the action, then peeks at Runt to see if her impropriety has been noticed by the official guardian of her Christian conscience. The chaplain smiles back at her, suspecting nothing. Redmond, meanwhile, stares with blatant affection at Her Ladyship, until he, too, is overcome by embarrassment and looks away. The romantic current between them, generated by the combination of his desire for security and her desire to escape an empty life with Sir Charles, is momentarily broken.

While an anonymous gambler (we cannot see his face) standing behind Lady Lyndon crosses his fingers for good luck (a useless strategy against the dishonest Chevalier), the game *within* the game continues. Incorporating that larger game into their surreptitious courtship, Redmond hands chips to Lady Lyndon for making a winning bet. A gambling *loss* for the firm of Balibari and Redmond becomes a romantic *investment* for Redmond. Reverend Runt, glancing from Redmond to Lady Lyndon, finally recognizes what is going on between them and becomes a third player in what started out as a duet. His discreet disapproval modifies the scene, briefly suppressing what had been Lady Lyndon's increasingly open display of passion.

The chaplain fingers his chips in disapproval, then watches Lady Lyndon finger *her* chips to a different purpose while staring at Redmond. Runt shifts his gaze to her face. Reacting to his critical scrutiny, she looks away from Redmond and furtively toward the Reverend. Redmond's adoring gaze, too, is disrupted by the clergyman's intrusion. But the tide of passion is too strong to be resisted for long. Earning her first close-up of the scene, Lady Lyndon gazes directly at Redmond, ignoring Runt's disapproval. Then, violating rules of marital fidelity but remaining faithful to genteel form, she liberates her illicit liaison from Runt's dour scrutiny by departing for a breath of air. Runt, respecting decorum and Her Ladyship's superior status, does not challenge what he knows to be her deception. As an instrument of the Church, his moral objection is understandable. But any threat to the marriage of Lady and Sir Charles Lyndon is also a *personal* threat to his comfortable situation within that family. An anonymous gambler occupies Lady Lyndon's vacated chair. The lyrical interplay of emotions among Redmond, Lady Lyndon, and Reverend Runt dissipates with the replacement of one member of their trio.

Lady Lyndon's stroll out onto the veranda is tracked by a camera that matches her deceptively calm pace. Appearing alabaster white in the moonlight, she is a living version of the statues visible behind her. Part flesh-and-blood woman and part abstract ideal, she is a glowing, strangely beautiful variation on the distinctly *in*elegant, plastic figures in *Clockwork's* Korova Milkbar. She is as much a captive of genteel sensibilities as the Korova girls were of a more sadomasochistic perspective. The only visible sign of her feelings is her relatively deep breathing.

Redmond, after a discreet delay, pursues Lady Lyndon. He, too, looks like a living statue. His hands are folded behind his back in a posture of restraint reminiscent of his mother's suitor back in the film's second scene. Lady Lyndon keeps her back to Redmond in a phony display of indifference, but she breathes ever more deeply as he approaches. She *half* turns towards him. Releasing his hands to active duty at last, he completes her turn. Slowly they move into a kiss so circumspect that their bodies make no other contact. Their illicit affair begins so delicately that the two sculpted lovers behind them seem more passionate than the *real* lovers, just as *2001*'s HAL outwardly seemed more emotional than his astronaut companions. Schubert's music, echoing the fulfillment of mutual desire, resolves itself into a more cheerful, major key. But, as always in Kubrick, this is a *temporary* harmony, splendidly isolated from the interests of other characters and from contrary feelings within the lovers themselves.

The illicit affair between Redmond and Lady Lyndon continues in the most discreet, even conventional, manner. Boating on a river along with numerous other couples, they hold hands but scarcely look at each other. Redmond is even detached from the *labor* of courtship, leaving the task of rowing the boat to a hired man. And narration questions the depth of Her Ladyship's romantic passion. "To make a long story short, six hours after they met, Her Ladyship was in love." Lady Lyndon's marital situation is apparently such that *any* man of sufficient youth, vigor, and charm could have satisfied her, as was also the case with Lischen. Yet events later in the film suggest that her love for Redmond is, or at least becomes, genuine.

The lovers stroll through a park, which is a genteel reconstruction of Nature consisting of a rectangular pond and meticulously pruned foliage. Beyond its boundaries is a landscape less altered by man. And though this comparative wilderness does not quite escape the grasp of genteel aesthetics, its counterpoint to the park is a subtle reminder of the more extreme conflict between man and Nature in *2001*.

After conquering Lady Lyndon's heart, Redmond must duel with her lord and master. The spa lounge is a magnificent institutional setting for their confrontation and would appear to favor Sir Charles, whose legal claim to Her Ladyship is irrefutable. Bathed in a sea of candlelight, the lounge is occupied by gentlemen of means enjoying congenial companionship. Schubert's Piano Trio, by now linked to the romance between Redmond and Lady Lyndon, concludes with Redmond's arrival at the table of his rival.

Mindful of his inferior social rank and legal position, Redmond keeps his hands passively clasped behind his back throughout this scene. He politely greets Sir Charles's companions, who reply in kind. Sir Charles, on the other hand, can afford to be more aggressive, and he openly accuses the young man of cheating with Lady Lyndon.

By feigning ignorance of any wrongdoing, Redmond converts Lyndon's verbal trap into one of his own. He suggests that Sir Charles's accusations proceed from drunkenness, which elicits a burst of incredulous laughter but no effective retort. Redmond's subsequent claim to have sought out Lady Lyndon for spiritual advice is so outrageous that it triggers the intended reaction. In a long shot that places him in the context of his tranquil surroundings, Sir Charles breaks out into loud and uncontrolled laughter that, due to his ill health, becomes a choking fit. His companions and the other lounge patrons seem embarrassed by the disturbance.

Sir Charles's bitter reference to Lady Lyndon's alleged preparations for his death creates yet another opportunity for Redmond to bait him. "I hope you're not thinking of leaving us soon," encourages that very prospect by further upsetting the feeble old man. Sir Charles tries again to portray Redmond as a wife stealer, then concludes his attack with a statement of defiance, "I'll live to see you hang yet," and he then sits back smugly to await the reply. It comes in due time and in a soft voice. "Let those laugh that win" for the first time implicitly acknowledges a rivalry between the two men. It also implies that the contest will be decided at a later time. And time is clearly on the side of the younger man.

In the wake of Redmond's quiet departure, a thoroughly frustrated Sir Charles is victimized by his own passions, which Redmond deliberately agitated. He falls into progressively worse fits of coughing. Losing the power of speech, he is suddenly seized by a sharp pain in the chest. A bottle of heart pills are his only chance for survival. But a second, more excruciating, spasm robs him of basic motor control. The pills fly out of his hands. Sir Charles is reduced to a grotesque squeal of pain, a shockingly ungenteel impression in keeping with other Kubrick portraits of characters stripped of all control over their lives. Lyndon's companions awkwardly rally around him. One of them, no doubt relieved to escape an unpleasant situation, leaves to fetch a doctor.

As we watch Sir Charles battle for his life, the soundtrack jumps forward in time to intrude a gloomy counterpoint. In a funereal tone of voice, the narrator quotes from Sir Charles's official obituary — the traditional and often sanitized benediction to an individual's life. The old boy is dispatched with full honors that discreetly exclude information about his agony, the sad state of his family relationships at the time of his death, and the critical role Redmond Barry played in that death. The overlapping of imagery and narration punctuates the enormous disparity between death as experienced by the individual and death as abstractly envisioned by institutional man. The image of Sir Charles's suffering is snuffed out when the camera cuts to a black screen. The obituary fades out more gradually, overlapped and displaced by the first, somber notes of Franz Schubert's "Impromptu No. 1 in C Minor," which both mourns the death of one man and laments the shallowness and dishonesty of institutional man's chronicle of that death. In a broader context, it also foreshadows the downfall of Redmond Barry, Sir Charles's conqueror, and therefore anticipates the fatalistic prologue to Part Two of the film: "Containing an account of the misfortunes and disasters which befell Barry Lyndon." What follows on screen contradicts that gloomy prophecy. Redmond's marriage to Lady Lyndon secures for him a more privileged and stable existence than he enjoyed as either a professional gambler or a soldier. Still, it is a victory achieved according to a genteel timetable. A full year has passed since they met.

Dressed in clerical regalia and surrounded by the trappings of organized religion, Reverend Samuel Runt solemnly delivers the wedding sermon. The ceremony is a device by which society consecrates and controls relations between men and women. Each member of the wedding party is in his or her appointed place. Redmond and Lady Lyndon stand before and humbly below the chaplain. The Chevalier, Mrs. Barry, and Lord Bullingdon stand on either side of the betrothed couple, representing a variety of perspectives. Balibari is now an incidental character in Redmond's life, perhaps even a liability. After the wedding, he disappears.

Just as *Clockwork's* Chief Guard derived power and pleasure from enforcing prison rules, Reverend Runt relishes his prominent role in the ceremony. He cannot stop a marriage he opposes, but he can use his sermon to indirectly criticize Redmond. Glancing at the protagonist, he lists the *wrong* reasons for getting married. Then, shifting his gaze to the bride and softening his tone of voice, he speaks of the *proper* reasons for marriage. Runt's criticism of Redmond is probably valid, but it is also the product of Runt's selfish desire to maintain his profitable influence over Lady Lyndon. Redmond, lost in a private contemplation of his good fortune, seems oblivious to Runt's disapproval.

Lord Bullingdon is added to the dramatic equation when Runt addresses an aspect of marriage that affects his personal interests. The prospect of Redmond and Lady Lyndon having children of their own jeopardizes Bullingdon's inheritance and, more importantly, his place in his mother's affections. Even without a rival sibling, Bullingdon's emotional hold on Lady Lyndon is challenged by her love for Redmond. Yet he remains outwardly respectful of the ceremony.

Members of the wedding party travel home to Castle Hackton in two carriages. Antonio Vivaldi's *Cello Concerto in E Minor*, third movement, accompanies on the soundtrack. A dirge-like piece, it counterpoints the sunlit landscape, Redmond's happy situation as husband to a beautiful countess, Lady Lyndon's happy situation as wife to a young, vigorous, and affectionate young man, and the narrator's disclosure that Redmond, with the approval of the British crown, has joined his name to that of his wife and is now officially Barry Lyndon. Once more, the protagonist benefits from a change in institutional identity, as he did three times before. The carriages pass by a peasant and his dog, who represent a humble lifestyle Redmond has, through luck and skill, avoided.

Inside the two carriages, four characters react differently to the marriage of Redmond and Lady Lyndon. Two frontal medium shots, the first of Barry and Her Ladyship and the second of Lord Bullingdon and Reverend Runt, convey the dissonances and harmonies of the viewpoints involved. The newlyweds sit in silence. Each provided the other with an avenue of escape from prior discontent. Yet their alliance has no common purpose once their separate goals have been achieved. The music echoes this sense of mutual isolation even before the characters act it out.

Bothered by smoke from her husband's pipe, Lady Lyndon makes several discreet gestures to communicate her annoyance before reluctantly asking him to extinguish it. Barry responds by blowing smoke in her face. Then he smiles, kisses her, and continues smoking. In these few gestures, he shatters their romance and spells out the harsh new terms of their relationship. Finally in a position to enjoy privilege and security, Redmond takes cruel advantage of it. For Lady Lyndon, the unhappy fate of being shackled to a

Honeymoon's end. Officially united by marriage but emotionally divided by private interests, Barry (Ryan O'Neal) and Lady Lyndon (Marisa Berenson) occupy the same carriage but gaze out at the world through very different windows. The luxury of their surroundings puts an elegant facade on the disintegration of their relationship; a facade matched by their facial expressions.

bitter, impotent old man has been exchanged for the equally unhappy fate of being shackled to a vital but selfish young man. Vivaldi's music falls into alignment with her sad awakening, while remaining a portent of Redmond's future downfall. The two characters are as far apart emotionally as were Charles Foster Kane and Emily Norton at the conclusion of their breakfast montage in *Citizen Kane*. They turn away from each other. The honeymoon ends almost before it begins. Husband and wife occupy the same carriage but gaze out at the world through separate windows.

Reverend Runt and Lord Bullingdon, riding in the second coach, play out the same scene in reverse. The family's two emotionally disenfranchised members cautiously move toward an alliance. Lord Bullingdon, arms defiantly crossed, frowning, shows his displeasure. Runt's demeanor is more neutral, in keeping with his professional standing. Sensing the boy's anger, he probes for and then slyly encourages Bullingdon's resentment of Barry. Bullingdon casts his objections in institutional terms, disguising his private motivation, which is fear of losing his mother's love. Curiously, his resentment is directed more at his mother, whom he loves, than at Barry, whom he hates. Reverend Runt's prompting redirects that resentment towards Barry.

The chaplain wisely keeps his own opinions to himself. The boy serves Runt's interests better as a lone malcontent than if they conspired to separate Lady Lyndon from Redmond. At the conclusion of this one-shot episode, Runt and Bullingdon sit silently gazing out at the world through their separate windows, as did Barry and Lady Lyndon before them. Yet their thoughts and wishes harmonize instead of clash.

The alignments and realignments among the Lyndons of Castle Hackton transpire in a series of family portraits separated by wide gaps in time but so tightly linked in their collective movement towards dissolution that they makeup an intensely lyrical montage. Vivaldi again sets the tone, sometimes clashing with and sometimes reinforcing what we see on screen.

A close-up of a sleeping baby slowly reverse zooms into a genteel snapshot of the ideal family. The baby, named Bryan, clutches one of his father's fingers while being cradled by his mother, Lady Lyndon, who is in turn cradled by Barry, who gazes fondly at his new son. The shot begins with a close-up of Bryan, because he is the emotional glue that binds this trio together. In this dramatic context, Vivaldi's music strikes a note more poignant than sad. Narration provides a formal birth announcement to accompany this portrait. To say that Lady Lyndon "presented" Barry with a son echoes a conventional eighteenth-century European view of the family structure, in which the woman is regarded as the junior partner. For the moment, however, Barry's patriarchal dominance appears benevolent. Husband and wife are reconciled by the birth of their son. But this first Lyndon family portrait is equally notable for who it does *not* contain: Lord Bullingdon and Reverend Runt.

The next portrait destroys the impression left by the first. Redmond embraces two bare-breasted women rather than his wife and son. A reverse zoom adds several of Barry's old army cronies, carousing and drunk like their host. Vivaldi is temporarily displaced by an a cappella rendition of "The British Grenadiers," sung by some of the revelers. This second "family" portrait is a male fantasy reminiscent of Alex's harem daydream in *Clockwork*, except that Barry's fantasy has come true. Narration typically softens the discrepancy between this scene and the preceding one. "Her Ladyship and Barry lived, after awhile, pretty separately" puts a genteel face on infidelity.

A third family portrait follows as a consequence of the second. It begins with a close-up of Lady Lyndon and Lord Bullingdon, their heads touching in mutual affection. Her loss is his gain. Barry's infidelity allows the boy to recapture his mother's primary affections. Both mother and son, however, look unhappy, as they did during their listless stroll with Sir Charles at the spa. Though restored to each other, they are once again isolated from patriarchal power. Sir Charles could not supply it, and Barry cruelly withholds it. The camera reverse zooms to complete the portrait by adding little Bryan. Lady Lyndon's hands lie protectively on or near both of her sons. But she suffers more from Barry's desertion than they do. Narration makes the point with delicate sarcasm. "She preferred quiet. Or to say the truth, he [Barry] preferred it for her, being a great friend to modest and tranquil behavior in women." In other words, Barry morally aligns himself with society's traditional constraint on women because it conveniently isolates Lady Lyndon from his worldly affairs, even as he brazenly violates society's rules of marital fidelity.

Music by Johann Sebastian Bach accompanies the third family portrait, echoing the characters' discontent. In the next scene, it becomes their immediate means of expressing that discontent. Lady Lyndon, Lord Bullingdon, and Reverend Runt makeup an instrumental trio, entertaining themselves in Barry's absence. The overall elegance of the scene is tempered by a close-up of Lady Lyndon's sad face. Lord Bullingdon, restored to his mother's affections, seems less troubled. And Reverend Runt appears the least disturbed of all. Alienation between Barry and Lady Lyndon has restored her emotional dependence on him. Thus, the musical trio in this scene is not unanimous in feeling. Only Lady Lyndon merits a close-up because she most deviates from the overall harmony.

In the first of a series of periodic establishing shots, Castle Hackton is shown from a distance, framed by a glass-smooth lake, emerald landscape, blue sky, and puffy white clouds. But the harmony of this image is shattered when the camera cuts to a fifth family portrait. Lady Lyndon strolls the manicured lawns, with Runt and Bullingdon providing chivalrous escort, allowing her to determine the group's route and pace. For the first time since the wedding, all the family members are brought together in the same scene, and in a way that violates any illusion of solidarity. The camera, interrupting its tracking of the first trio, zooms in through a gap in the trees, penetrating the veil of propriety, to spy Barry embracing a maidservant, with Bryan's baby carriage nearby. Though elegantly posed and framed, this second trio mocks the first one. Also grouped with Barry and his lover is the statue of a woman, symbolically standing in for Lady Lyndon, whom Barry has reduced to an attractive prop in his social life, equivalent to the plastic Korova girls in *Clockwork*.

A close-up of Lady Lyndon's left hand shows a gold wedding band shining with hollow symbolism on her fourth finger. Lord Bullingdon, motivated by both compassion and self-interest, takes that hand in his. It is a poignant clash of institutional (the ring) and private (the handclasp) realities. Vivaldi's *Cello Concerto* returns, conveying to us the hurt Lady Lyndon discreetly refrains from expressing. She departs without a word of protest. The music critiques not only Barry's cruelty and the narrator's rather unsympathetic description of Lady Lyndon's "melancholy and morbid temperament," but also the fashionable passivity with which Her Ladyship accepts her fate.

Runt and Bullingdon make poor substitutes for an estranged husband. The next portrait, featuring another trio, shows Lady Lyndon and two female friends passing an evening at cards. Her Ladyship plays without enthusiasm, her thoughts hopelessly invested elsewhere, in her faithless husband. The largeness of the room accentuates the emptiness of her existence. Meanwhile, Reverend Runt sits at her side, content to be her emotional crutch in bad times.

The camera slowly zooms in on Lady Lyndon to capture subtle gestures and expressions that modify our initial, remote impression of elegance. She issues what amounts to an official yawn, indirectly signaling her friends that the game is about to end. She asks Runt for the time, then stares vacantly, wondering about her missing husband. Finally, she calls a halt to a game that has been an unsuccessful diversion from her real concern.

Lady Lyndon's depression is even more profound in the next scene, which begins with a close-up of her sad face. A reverse zoom modifies that impression, placing her in an elaborately decorated bathtub. Loneliness and luxury mix in the same image. Though her face conveys numbing sorrow, she maintains a graceful pose as though from habit. Compare this ironic impression of well-being to the equivalent shot of Alex relaxing in Mr. Alexander's bathtub in *Clockwork*. Lady Lyndon is a virtual still-life portrait, her white skin sculpturesque, as it was on the veranda at the Belgian spa. The mirror-smooth water in the bathtub adds to that effect. She is at once Barry's frozen ideal of a subservient wife and a portrait of emotional distress. She is like *2001*'s Frank Poole, lying under a sunlamp and indifferently watching videotaped birthday greetings from his parents. Both characters are profoundly isolated from loved ones: Poole by sheer distance and Her Ladyship by neglect. Shades pulled down over a window behind Lady Lyndon reflect her emotional withdrawal. They are equivalent to General Ripper's closed window blinds and Dave Bowman's windowless sanctuary.

Lady Lyndon listens indifferently to a servant reading from a French love poem. Perhaps she fantasizes about what love *could* be for her, in the way Alex fantasized his way out of prison by way of Bible stories. But Lady Lyndon's dream comes true. Barry enters the room and asks the servants to leave. Caught between the wishes of two different masters, they hesitate awkwardly until Lady Lyndon nods agreement. Visually aligned with an *un*shaded window in the background, Barry attempts to rescue his wife from the emotional dormancy to which he drove her. And he seems motivated to do so by genuine love and compassion rather than by selfishness.

On the wall behind the two characters is a painting that depicts a genteel idealization of love. A man gallantly kneels in front of his lady. Barry and Lady Lyndon slowly work their way into and beyond that pose. In the picture, the woman appears higher than the man and is strategically dominant. By contrast, Barry stands above his wife. Lady Lyndon looks up at him with resignation rather than recrimination or an appeal for deliverance. Then, in a surprisingly direct and unadorned expression of feeling, Barry tells her, "I'm sorry." However inadequate as compensation for the suffering he has caused her, the sheer simplicity of his apology, especially in an age of elaboration and obfuscation, makes it convincing.

Redmond's apology is the first step toward realizing the vision of love pictured on the wall behind them. Lady Lyndon takes the next step. With a trace of revived hope in her eyes, she overcomes her torpor and extends her hand to Barry, who kneels beside her and takes it in his own. In close-up, Barry and Lady Lyndon move into a kiss as passionate as it is gentle. Barry's eyes close. Lady Lyndon's eyes close only partly. She is understandably hesitant to recommit herself to a love that betrayed her the first time around. Finally, ecstatically, she surrenders to the moment and closes her eyes completely. But this romantic portrait is possible only because of the absence of other family members. And that splendid isolation will not last.

Barry is next shown surrounded by servants helping him dress and by tailors trying to sell him their garments: two sides of the same gold coin. Barry commands attendants who cater *to* his needs and is simultaneously courted by another class of people who seek financial gain *from* him. His social position creates new, expensive appetites which will later cost him dearly.

Lady Lyndon arrives, carrying Bryan, with Lord Bullingdon and Reverend Runt submissively in tow. She is now confident enough to interrupt her husband's business affairs with a warm greeting. She announces her intention to take the children for a ride into town. Obviously her period of confinement to Castle Hackton is over. They kiss affectionately.

Lord Bullingdon spoils this otherwise harmonious family portrait. When called upon to give his stepfather a "proper" kiss, he refuses. Barry is less concerned with the boy's true feelings for him than with Bullingdon's formal and public *appearance* of respect, which affects Barry's stature in the eyes of others. Lady Lyndon enters their contest of wills on the side of her husband. Long forgotten is the episode in which Bullingdon took her hand to shield her from Barry's cruel infidelity. "Is that the way to behave to your father?" implies full recognition of Barry's paternal authority.

Bullingdon broadens his attack to include his mother, using the sacred memory of his biological father to do so. Never particularly devoted to Sir Charles when the old man was alive, Bullingdon now conveniently canonizes him in order to retaliate against his unfaithful mother, whom he has *always* loved. Officially, he charges Lady Lyndon with infidelity to Sir Charles. In truth, she is charged with emotional desertion of her son. And she reflexively acknowledges the power of that insult by slapping him, which she justifies by claiming that it was in defense of Barry rather than of herself. Little Bryan, meanwhile, protests against the disturbance of *his* private world by crying, just as Lischen's baby reacted to his mother's neglect in an earlier scene.

Typical of Kubrick characters, Barry deals with his enemy in isolation, administering punishment away from prying eyes and ears. As in a duel, Bullingdon's coat is removed, eliminating one buffer between himself and his adversary. Dressed casually in his robe, Barry administers the whipping in a spirit of casual confidence rather than fierce desperation — six lashings only, dealt out with moderate force. Bullingdon, unable to challenge Barry directly, tries hard not to give his stepfather the satisfaction of hearing him cry out in pain.

Barry dictates terms of surrender to his stepson. He is not inclined to be sadistic, as were Alex and Dr. Strangelove, but warns Bullingdon that if provoked he could become so. The boy wisely refrains from forcing the issue. He departs only after receiving permission to do so, and he closes the door *softly* behind him so as not to further antagonize his stepfather. Barry walks off screen in the opposite direction. All in all, it has been a relatively restrained confrontation.

The proof of Barry's victory over Bullingdon is in the time lapse between the whipping incident and the next scene, which begins with a frontal close-up of the son of Sir Charles, now grown to a young man. Perhaps a decade has passed, with no appreciable change in the strategic situation. But the expression of discontent on Bullingdon's face implies that his resentment of Barry continues to burn, and it counterpoints the sounds of merriment from off screen. A "German Dance" by Franz Schubert echoes that merriment.

Bullingdon is holding on to a woman's hand. A lover's? The camera slowly reverse zooms to complete the picture. The hand belongs to his mother, at whose feet he sits. His love/hate relationship with her has swung back in favor of love. Several overlapping alliances stand out in the expanding family portrait. With Bullingdon at the center, Barry and Mrs. Barry are seated at screen left, while Lady Lyndon and Reverend Runt occupy screen right. Whether by accident or subconscious design, demarcation occurs along old lines of loyalty. But from a different perspective, the four adults occupy the same level, while Lord Bullingdon, sitting on the ground, is the odd man out, his only link to the group through his mother. The Barrys, Lady Lyndon, Runt, and a crowd of invited guests are all contentedly focused on some entertaining diversion off screen, whereas Bullingdon is preoccupied with his private thoughts. Narration articulates his unspoken discontent. "His hatred for Barry assumed an intensity equaled only by his increased devotion to his mother" suggests a direct relationship between the two emotions.

Bryan's eighth birthday party is the reason for this gathering. And how different his situation is from Bullingdon's. Playing assistant to a hired magician, he shares in the applause for successfully executed tricks. He is both pampered audience and featured attraction in this production. Counterpointing the reverse zoom that placed Lord Bullingdon in a world opposed to his will, a medium shot of Bryan opens up to reveal an extravagantly arranged world of which he is the monarch. Squeaking with delight, he rides in a miniature coach pulled by two colorfully adorned sheep. Other children makeup his entourage, while Barry and Lady Lyndon provide adult supervision.

A twilight silhouette of the Lyndon estate leads us into an even more magical scene of indulgence. Having entered the ranks of privileged society after being a renegade, Barry now finds it convenient to reinterpret his past for the edification and education of his son. Reinforced by Schubert's music and by the warm glow of candlelight, Barry transforms his grim period of military service into a bedtime story of grand adventure. In Barry's reinvention of the past, the hyperbole of the army recruiter's false promises is realized and improved upon. Instead of being a bit player in a terrifying and degrading slaughter, Barry takes center stage in a rousing battle against his country's enemy. Chaos, fear, abuse, grief, and dishonor are banished. History is revised so that Barry may shape his son's perception along more orthodox lines.

Bryan, clutching a toy animal, is captivated by his father's storybook rendition of war. Like every armchair warrior and many film audiences, he gets his vicarious thrills at little cost. The darkness of his bedroom frightens him more than Barry's fairy-tale slaughter. And it is another measure of Barry's fatherly love and indulgence that he allows Bryan to keep a candle lit. Mrs.

Barry, emotionally more detached than her son, appeals to Bryan to overcome his fear.

The serenity of the bedroom scene carries over into the next. A boat containing four passengers glides leisurely on a river meandering through the Lyndon estate. Lady Lyndon and Bryan, by virtue of gender and age, ride up front. Lord Bullingdon and Reverend Runt row from the seat behind. This is a miniature, family-sized version of the ship of state that carried Barry's regiment to war. King George was the implied master of the latter. From the smaller boat, Lady Lyndon and Bryan wave a greeting to *its* off-screen master — Barry. Bullingdon glares with subdued hostility in the same direction. He and Runt gently steer the boat away from Barry. The fact that Bullingdon is able to alter the boat's course metaphorically reflects his latent legal power over the estate.

A reverse zoom places the boat and its occupants within a visual frame formed by a bridge spanning the river. Barry and his mother stand on that bridge. Only now does it become clear that they were the objects of Lady Lyndon and Bryan's greeting and Lord Bullingdon's veiled snub. As patriarchal head of the estate, Barry's power envelops the four people in the boat, symbolically suggested by the framing effect of the bridge. But Mrs. Barry sees beyond the symbolism.

After demonstrating more objectivity regarding Bryan than did Barry in the previous scene, she now reveals her capacity for ruthless strategic thought. She recognizes her son's precarious legal position vis-à-vis Lord Bullingdon and maneuvers to correct it.

Mrs. Barry's manipulation of her son is brilliant. Beginning with a celebration of his success in life, she slyly inserts a reminder of her own sacrifices on his behalf, cultivating in him an emotional debt which encourages his cooperation in her plans for his future. With a mother's bias, she declares Lady Lyndon very fortunate to have landed so fine a husband, though this was not so obvious during their first year of marriage. Barry's natural qualities are contrasted favorably with the artificial virtues bestowed on other men by the accident of birthright. But Mrs. Barry is a realist and a conformist. Entitlement is how society measures quality and bestows power. Any further improvement in Barry's situation must occur through traditional channels, though not necessarily by honest means. Like the rigged duel Barry fought with Captain Quin and the Chevalier's cheating at cards, Mrs. Barry would maintain the appearance of propriety while circumventing its spirit. But her conviction that money "well-timed and properly applied, can accomplish anything" proves not wholly true. Bolstering her argument by reminding Barry that he is responsible for securing Bryan's future as well as his own, Mrs. Barry maneuvers her son into a quest for a peerage, which would represent a full rather than an honorary membership in aristocratic society.

Driven by an implanted need to better his social position, Barry ventures outside his personal monarchy at Castle Hackton and into a larger world where he must play suppliant to people with greater power. Playing cribbage with Lord Harlan, Barry employs the game as an indirect means of currying favor with an influential acquaintance. Harlan, in turn, is merely a sponsor to an even higher level of institutional power, embodied by the Thirteenth Earl of Wendover, who in turn is useful to Barry because of his influence with the King. Barry is urged to "fix upon" the Earl as a means to advancement — a phrase conjuring up images of Moonwatcher fixing upon tapir bones in order to attain greater control over *his* fate. Anthony Sharp, who plays Lord Harlan, portrayed the Interior Minister in *Clockwork*. Both characters advance the private interests of their film's protagonists.

The supreme confidence of the Earl of Wendover, whose long noble lineage implies stability, is conveyed in both visual and verbal terms during Barry's audience. A slow reverse zoom surrounds the Earl with the rich appointments of his residence. He is, it seems, too secure to be smug about it. His tone of voice is serene rather than arrogant. And so is his lecture to Barry. "When I take up a person, Mr. Lyndon, he or she is safe. There is no question about them anymore." Thanks to his heritage and his friendship with the King, Wendover has weeded out most of the social uncertainty in his own life, and he has the power to do so for others. So secure is his position within the firmament of English society that he can even afford to acknowledge the arbitrariness of its value system. "My friends are the best people. Oh, I don't mean that they're the most virtuous, or indeed the least virtuous, or the cleverest or the stupidest or the richest or the best born. But the best. In a word, people about whom there is no question." In other words, his power is transcendent. "Best" becomes a nebulous value judgment, applicable to people for no other reason than that Wendover is their sponsor. Or so he would like to believe.

A shot of a fountain depicts one man carrying a large vessel made heavier by numerous streams of water pouring into it. In the context of Barry's quest for a peerage, the fountain is a metaphor for the heavy burden poured into his mind by his mother, soon to be joined by others related to it. Barry is once again a soldier in someone else's crusade.

The quest begins with an elaborate picnic for influential acquaintances. Wendover, Lady Lyndon, Barry, and Lord Harlan sit together on the lawn. The Earl, because of his superior title and his importance to Barry's cause, merits the undivided attention of the other three as he tells a tale of "astonishment" and "anger" in a most dispassionate tone of voice. A slow reverse zoom places this intimate quartet within the larger gathering of important people. This larger group, though linked to the central quartet by Barry's invitation and quest, is oblivious to the Earl's little story, which fades out of hearing as the camera widens its scope. The smaller and larger groups are separate but interlocked layers of Barry's life. Gathered near the central quartet are the trio of Mrs. Barry, Bryan, and Reverend Runt. For the moment, they are incidental players in Barry's production, though Mrs. Barry is the prime instigator of and Bryan a major reason for it. Reverend Runt is merely along for the ride, while Lord Bullingdon stands to lose power if it succeeds. Narration, meanwhile, contradicts this almost unanimous impression of harmony by forecasting the eventual failure of Barry's quest.

The quest moves indoors to a formal dinner hosted by the Lyndons. Beginning with a shot of Barry seated at the head of the table, the camera travels slowly down the table's length, supplying a visual feast of abundance and reserved conviviality. As it was at Brady Castle many scenes ago, conversation is reduced to a pleasant, collective hum to which individual details are subordinated. Schubert, in effect Barry's battle music, continues uninterrupted from the previous scene.

The only false notes at this sumptuous banquet come from Lord Bullingdon and the narrator. Barely noticeable as the camera passes him, Bullingdon is the only person not conversing with his neighbors. His silence is a passive protest against his stepfather's scheme. Narration, meanwhile, contradicts the harmony from without, revealing that Barry's quest for a title involves secret bribes, discreetly described as "loans," to an unnamed nobleman close to the King.

To become a member of the aristocracy, Barry must *look* the part in terms of possessions as well as demeanor. In pursuit of that image, he assembles a collection of paintings with which to impress the elite. Accompanied by his sponsors, Wendover and Harlan, Barry makes a solemn show of scrutinizing various works of art for sale, as though he really cared about their aesthetic qualities. The painting that catches his eye was, according to its owner, done by an artist named Ludovico Corday. Coincidentally, or maybe not, Ludovico is also the name of the psychochemical treatment by which Alex tries to advance *his* cause in *Clockwork*. Both tools will exact a cost.

The subject of the Ludovico Corday painting admired by Barry is eminently traditional and safe. The Adoration of the Magi was a *proper* theme into which an eighteenth-century European painter could pour his inspiration. Barry need not be concerned that the painting might offend his influential acquaintances. And this again strengthens its parallel to the Ludovico Technique. Defending his revolutionary program against criticism by the prison chaplain, the Interior Minister describes it in persuasively orthodox, Christian terms acceptable to officials who will pass judgment on it.

Realizing Barry's interest in purchasing one of his paintings, the owner avoids appearing crass *and* jacks up the potential price by being evasive. "Well, this is one of my best pictures. But, if you really like it, I'm sure we can come to some arrangement." "Best" no doubt holds the same flexible meaning for him as it does for Wendover. The music of Schubert shifts into a particularly triumphant dance rhythm between "if you really like it" and "I'm sure we can come to some arrangement." The separate interests of Barry and the owner attain harmony. The music momentarily belongs to both. But we have already been alerted by the narrator to Barry's financial extravagance in his quest for a title, and so the owner's manipulation of the purchase price is, in a sense, a triumph at Barry's long-term expense.

The pinnacle of Barry's quest is his presence at a mass audience with the King of England. Standing in a long line of dignitaries waiting to receive royal recognition, he is little more than a bit player in a State production. Yet, through his show of subservience, he improves his status. Form is everything. There is no room here for genuine intimacy, even between friends. Wendover and the King limit their conversation to polite small talk about conventional matters. The King employs his collective identity, "We," as though speaking for the entire nation when expressing concern over the health of Wendover's wife. The Earl, meanwhile, paints a righteous, self-serving portrait of his two sons, who, as soldier and clergyman, pursue very different careers, equally revered by society yet not always in moral harmony.

Wendover introduces the King to Barry, but it is the action of an anonymous attendant (is *this* the person who received Barry's bribe?) that results in the King pausing to spend extra time with him. The attendant further ingratiates loyal subject with monarch by revealing that Barry has raised a regiment of soldiers to fight rebellion in America. For an Irishman, an outlaw, a victim of deceptive British Army recruiting tactics, and a deserter to claim credit for such an orthodox act of patriotism illustrates one of the film's central ironies. Barry is very much a prerevolutionary protagonist in a prerevolutionary world. He does not sympathize with others who have defied the established order. He wishes to elevate his station *within* that order, not overthrow it. The King's reaction to Barry's efforts, though favorable, does not quite harmonize with Barry's ambition. He urges the protagonist to raise another regiment and accompany them into battle. Barry, of course, has no intention of reenlisting in the army. Still, his royal audience has been beneficial, in the manner of Alex's first encounter with the Interior Minister in *Clockwork*. Circumstances, however, are a bit different. Barry's presence in the lineup is by itself sufficient to advance his cause. And he is aided by two allies who help him get special attention from the King. Alex, by contrast, must violate prison rules and defy the Chief Guard in order to get that attention.

Barry's success on a public stage is counterpointed by the price he pays behind the scenes. The camera zooms in to an extreme close-up of a bank draft being signed. Like the CRM 114 radio and the S.A.C. code book, both subjects of similar zooms in *Dr. Strangelove*, the draft is an essential tool in a specific plan. But a subsequent long shot highlights Barry's dependence on others to make use of that tool. He sorts out the bank drafts, but it is Lady Lyndon's signature that legitimizes them. Barry occupies center screen, but is not the center of power. Seated to his left is the family solicitor, Graham, who is his instrument only by way of Her Ladyship. Narration expands on Barry's situation by pointing out that skills in one field of endeavor do not guarantee, and sometimes even work against, success in another. After all, Major Kong's courage, determination, and resourcefulness work *against* his country's survival in *Dr. Strangelove*.

Lord Bullingdon and Bryan, who had slipped from our view in recent scenes, reappear in what begins as an isolated drama of their own but ends up having a major impact on Barry's quest. Supervised by their tutor, Reverend Runt, the boys are on their best behavior. But as soon as he leaves the room, Bryan strays from Runt's parting instructions to continue with their schoolwork. The limits of institutional power are further illustrated by a large map of Africa in the room. The map depicts coastal regions in some detail, while the continent's interior is left blank. Europeans had not yet comprehensively explored and charted the geography, much less the cultures, of Africa.

In Runt's absence, Lord Bullingdon continues dutifully with his studies, like the steady ticking of the clock. But his bored half-brother sloughs off his school assignment and creates a new production of his own. He slumps in his chair and asks pointless questions of Bullingdon, who displays admirable patience. There is no indication in this scene that the older boy sees the younger as an extension of Barry and therefore a sworn enemy.

Bryan finally destroys all semblance of classroom discipline by trying to steal Bullingdon's pen. Both boys claim ownership, making their contest a dangerous but apparently unwitting parallel to their latent competition for the Lyndon inheritance. Clearly Bryan is the aggressor here, escalating the confrontation by slapping his rival across the face. Provoked, Bullingdon spanks him.

After a series of medium shots takes us into this private dispute between two brothers, a long shot pulls us back to a position of relative detachment. Barry, drawn by the ruckus, enters the room through the same doorway Runt exited and sees Bullingdon paddling Bryan. Adult supervision is restored, but, because of his private bias, Barry assesses the situation differently than would have Runt. He misinterprets a commonplace sibling argument as a battle for survival between his own son and the son of Sir Charles, inflating a trivial incident into a family crisis.

Barry's subsequent whipping of Lord Bullingdon turns back the clock many years to a similar scene, after the boy defied his stepfather in public.

Punishment remains the same (six lashings), but two key circumstances are different. First, Barry's reason for punishing his stepson this time is based on a false assumption, which was not the case earlier. Second, Lord Bullingdon now has a young man's pride. After receiving his whipping, he verbally challenges Barry's authority rather than meekly retreating. He declares boldly, if nervously, "I will kill you if you lay hands on me ever again." But by raising the stakes of their confrontation, Bullingdon increases the danger to himself. Barry's anger is visibly greater than when he faced a mere child. His whispered command for Bullingdon to leave is as much an effort to restrain himself as it is to control his adversary.

If the whipping is a variation on a prior scene, so is the music recital that follows. Years earlier Lady Lyndon, Lord Bullingdon, and Reverend Runt formed a trio in response to Barry's neglect. Her Ladyship and Runt are back at their instruments, but Bullingdon is absent. In his place sits a chamber orchestra, hired to entertain an audience who will have something to say about Barry getting a peerage. Lady Lyndon and the chaplain are now participants in, rather than outcasts from, Barry's quest for security. By implication, *he* is the third member of their trio.

Into this carefully staged production steps the exiled Lord Bullingdon, bent on destroying it. He pushes open the door to the room with immodest force, which is then carefully muted by a servant. Additionally, Bullingdon arrives with potent weapons to take command of the occasion. He leads Bryan by the hand, using the boy as a living symbol against his father and mother. Bryan, as blissfully unaware of his appointed role in this little drama as he was of his role in escalating the conflict between Bullingdon and Barry two scenes earlier, clomps forward noisily in a pair of his half-brother's shoes. He is Bullingdon's soloist; the shoes are Bullingdon's musical instrument.

Two conflicting patterns of order duel in the course of one shot. Backtracking with the boys, the camera reveals more and more of Barry's carefully arranged world. One by one, Barry's audience turns away from the recital and toward the source of disruption. Runt's flute and then Lady Lyndon's harpsichord drop out of the music. The orchestra continues to play for awhile without them, but as an absurd remnant of a dead campaign, like HAL singing "Daisy" in *2001.*

After deconstructing Barry's scenario, Lord Bullingdon builds one of his own. Genteel style remains but serves a different master now. Bowing in mock respect to his mother, Bullingdon confronts her with two sons who have rival claims to the Lyndon inheritance and to her affections. Sir Charles once bitterly complained about Barry, "He wants to step into my shoes!" His son now makes that metaphor literal and employs it much more effectively against the same enemy. Lady Lyndon is initially paralyzed by the audacity of her elder son's attack. Dropping to one knee in a formal gesture of submission, Bullingdon turns next to Bryan, who remains ignorant of the prank's underlying purpose. "Dear child, what a pity it is I am not dead for your sake," lays bare Lyndon family politics for the assembled guests. Then, shifting to a more aggressive, sarcastic mode of attack, Bullingdon targets Barry. By addressing his stepfather as "Mr. Redmond Barry," he strips him of the exalted name bestowed by the State after Barry married Lady Lyndon.

Strategic advantage shifts to Lady Lyndon, always more confident when allied with Barry, as she challenges her son. Moving into a medium shot of the boys, she physically reclaims Bryan from Bullingdon's selfish grasp. She transforms her eldest son's kneeling position of mock submission into a *genuinely* inferior posture by declaring her reasons for favoring his younger brother. But when she moves to quit the field of battle, with Bryan (her prize) in tow, Bullingdon stands up and visually reverses strategic roles with his now smaller mother. He maintains a formal appearance of respect for her yet employs that formality to sarcastic effect. His voice is louder and harsher than before. The battle has intensified, yet the weapons remain rhetorical. The charges he hurls against her and at Barry are institutional in nature. He even makes Lady Lyndon bear the shame of Barry's infidelity, of which she was the *victim!* Wilting under his attack, she breaks down in tears and, taking Bryan with her, flees the room in defeat.

Our impression of Bullingdon's victory over Lady Lyndon is undercut by a close-up of Barry, looking furious. The genteel restraint which, though strained, has thus far governed the combatants is suddenly and violently shattered when Barry physically attacks Bullingdon. *This* is the price Bullingdon pays for insisting that Barry treat him as a man rather than a boy. Barry becomes as nakedly homicidal as Moonwatcher. A handheld camera jerkily follows the action as he flails away at the young man. Lady Lyndon reenters the room with Bryan; then, horrified, she withdraws again. Bryan, on the other hand, is fascinated, even delighted, by the spectacle he briefly witnesses. For him it is grand horror show, like his father's war stories. Yet, only moments earlier, he just as naively enjoyed playing *Bullingdon's* weapon against Barry, not realizing that his half-brother's success will result in his own future disinheritance. He is a pint-sized General Turgidson.

The shocked reactions of Barry's guests illustrate the extent of his calamity. Wendover "gallantly" shields a young woman (probably not his wife) from the disturbance. Mrs. Barry tries in vain to stem her son's imprudent outburst. The influence she wielded over his pursuit of a peerage evaporates in the heat of his rage. Lord Harlan, looking disgusted, reflexively straightens his coat, restoring order to his person. *Dr. Strangelove's* Captain Mandrake does the same when he first realizes that General Ripper has violated the military chain of command. Lord Bullingdon's white-stocking legs, visible beneath Barry's larger figure, look terribly fragile. Order is restored slowly and painfully. Several men from what *was* Barry's audience gang up and subdue him. But they go about it with the same reluctance and awkwardness as Sir Charles's companions when they rallied to help him during his heart seizure.

Power and weakness play off each other at different levels. Lord Bullingdon could not have seemed more helpless than at the end of the recital scene. But once order is restored, Barry's brutal victory spells defeat for his quest, which in turn is a victory for Bullingdon. The consequences of Barry's loss of self-control are revealed in a series of scenes. Alone, hands folded in resignation, Barry leans idly against the railing of a bridge on his estate. The camera slowly reverse zooms to envelop him in an elaborate, rigid pattern of stone architecture. Like Quasimodo in the final shot from the 1939 film adaptation of *The Hunchback of Notre Dame*, he is individual man trapped in a world contrary to his wishes. It is an impression the opposite of Alex's domination of the Korova Milkbar at the end of *Clockwork*'s first reverse zoom. Vivaldi's *Cello Concerto*, originally associated with Lady Lyndon's exile from Barry's affections, now echoes Barry's exile from society's elite. The music links this and subsequent scenes in a montage of dissolution.

At the club where Barry's campaign for a peerage began, his unspoken estrangement from the Earl of Wendover and all that Wendover represents, is finalized. Wendover is ushered to a table in the foreground of this one-shot scene. Barry, seated at a table in the background, appears as a smaller, duplicate version of the Earl. He still enjoys many of the privileges he did before the recital fiasco. But he has lost all hope of social advancement, as becomes painfully clear when he attempts to renew his friendship with his benefactor. No close-ups are employed here, because the characters' true feelings are masked behind polite formalities. Barry invites Wendover to his home for a game of cards. The Earl politely declines. Barry invites Wendover to join him at his table. The Earl politely declines, pleading expected company. The proof of Wendover's total rejection of Barry is revealed after Barry returns to his own table. Wendover tells the waiter he will be dining alone. There are no expected companions. And neither hesitation nor a change in tone of voice betray any shame for having lied to his former friend. The protagonist is no longer someone about whom there is no question.

A shot of Castle Hackton shrouded in fog reinforces an impression of Barry's fortunes provided by the narrator. "And a legend arose of his cruelty to his stepson." The fog conceals more than it allows us to see, just as the legend of Barry's cruelty constitutes a public impression that does not entirely square with what we have seen.

Inside the castle, we see another variation on a prior scene. Once the paying off of debts was a grim necessity serving Barry's quest for a peerage. It remains a grim necessity, but now without the promise of a future payoff.

Lady Lyndon occupies center screen. She no longer serves her husband's will, because her power to spend estate funds no longer holds the prospect of social advancement for him.

Confined to prison, *Clockwork's* Alex turns to the Bible for emotional escape. In *Citizen Kane*, the protagonist pours himself into his second wife's operatic career after his political ambitions are thwarted. Barry Lyndon, set adrift by genteel society, searches for fulfillment through Bryan. A reverse zoom shows them fishing from a boat in a picturesque stream. They and the water are almost as frozen in stillness as Lady Lyndon was in her bathtub many scenes earlier. In the next scene, Barry is seated on a couch, with Bryan on his lap, in medium shot. They happily discuss the boy's picture book. The camera then cuts to an extreme long shot of the same characters from a similar angle. The intimacy of a father-and-son conversation is suddenly placed in a visual context of institutional proportions. The "couch" on which they sit is in fact a long bench, designed more for large social gatherings than intimate diversions. Looming over them on the wall is an enormous painting depicting larger-than-life human figures elegantly posed and costumed, partly contradicted by the two slightly less-formal, living figures.

As proof of Barry's fidelity to genteel definitions of the good life, he resumes his quest for social prominence vicariously through his son. On manicured lawns, Barry instructs Bryan in the traditions of fencing and croquet. Returning to the soundtrack for the first time since Barry's duel with Captain Quin, Handel's "Sarabande" again conjures up an impression of the almost irresistible momentum of private passion bound to collective form, counterpointing the playfulness of the characters' demeanor. Barry's "thousand fond anticipations as to [Bryan's] future success and figure in the world," coming as they do on the heels of his own involuntary retirement from worldly matters, puts a slightly selfish spin on his devotion to the boy. He may yet master his social environment, just as Mrs. Barry sought to do through *him*.

Narration falls out of sync with the visual impression of Barry's new quest and into alignment with Handel's foreboding music: "But fate had determined that he should leave none of his race behind him. And that he should finish life poor, lonely, and childless." In effect a *temporal* reverse zoom, these words give us a broader view than what we see on screen. The seeds of Barry's future sorrow are sown in these otherwise happy scenes.

By encouraging his son to master adult activities, Barry inspires in him adult needs as well. As they ride horseback through the Lyndon estate, Bryan declares his burning desire to have a full-sized horse rather than a pony. Peer pressure from a friend reinforces this need. Thus far, Bryan has been spoon fed safe, scaled-down versions of adult realities (the sheep-drawn carriage, bedtime war stories, gentle thrust and parry with swords, et cetera). Now he presses Barry for the real thing. And Barry's fondness for his son, reinforced by his need to relive his own failed life through Bryan, makes the protagonist a very indulgent parent.

Negotiations with a neighbor over the purchase of a horse are cordial, unlike the transaction which led to the death of Barry's father. Mutual compromise results in an agreement between two gentlemen of somewhat contrary minds (one desires the highest possible price, the other the lowest). Barry instructs his groom not to reveal the purchase to anyone, especially Bryan, who is to receive the animal as a birthday gift. But after he and the horse's owner depart, the camera lingers on the groom and the horse, which will prove less than manageable components of Barry's plan.

The first glitch in Barry's plan is revealed at the Lyndon family dinner table. Barry is seated, appropriately, at the head of the table. Nothing disturbs the formal order of the meal until Bryan reveals knowledge of the horse. Loose talk among the grooms and stable boys has ruined Barry's birthday surprise. Bryan's sweet smile soon melts Barry's displeasure. Harmony restored between them, they look up together, as one, to face Lady Lyndon's contrary note of caution, spoken from off screen. Barry, suddenly reminded of his parental responsibility after lapsing into fond indulgence, echoes his wife's caution by threatening a whipping if Bryan rides the horse without adult supervision. Plan A spoiled, Barry reasserts a measure of control over the situation by introducing Plan B. Bryan is ordered not to visit his new horse until the appointed time. He is given a kiss and sent back to his chair. Dinner routine resumes as though nothing had disturbed it. But the "Sarabande" marches quietly on, grimly prophesying the next blow to Barry's plans.

It arrives during his morning shave, even as he appears a picture of physical health and material well-being. The background music ends when its messenger, Reverend Runt, arrives with news that Bryan has broken his promise and gone to see the horse. Though irritating, Bryan's disobedience is not yet alarming to his father, who calmly finishes shaving before attending to it. The extent of the catastrophe becomes evident to Barry only when, leisurely riding out to intercept Bryan, he encounters the badly injured boy being attended to by several grooms. One of the grooms secures Barry's abandoned horse as Barry rushes to the boy's side. Institutional order is automatically maintained, even in a crisis.

In a brief, slow-motion flashback, we see the accident that injured Bryan. The boy rides a horse much too big for him to control. They tumble to the ground, accompanied by a squeal of alarm that seems to emanate from both. It is a sickening sound, recollecting Sir Charles's heart seizure, HAL's swan song, and Alex's involuntary Ludovico belches.

The threat of punishment that Barry made at the dinner table dissolves in the wake of Bryan's injury, though the boy is not mature enough to comprehend the effect of circumstances on human perception. He pleads not to be whipped, which is the furthest thing from Barry's mind. On another level, Barry's perception, too, is narrow. He orders a servant to take his horse and fetch the doctor: "Whatever he is doing, he must come at once." Frightened and concerned, he understandably views his son's medical needs as more important than anyone else's.

A muted, funereal version of the "Sarabande" returns to the soundtrack as the scene shifts to Castle Hackton, where Bryan lies on his deathbed, flanked by his parents. Narration, in tune with the music, ponders the inadequacy of eighteenth-century medical science: "The doctors were called. But what does a doctor avail in a contest with a grim, invincible enemy." Of course, "invincible" is a relative term. Like the map of Africa in the schoolroom scene, the narrator's perspective is limited. "Fate" has a way of changing shape as the relationship of human beings to their environment changes.

An extreme close-up of two hands clasped, each adorned with ruffled sleeves — private emotion and collective fashion blend in one image. Bryan's head is swathed in bandages, his face discolored. Like Alex lying in a hospital bed after his "suicide" attempt, Bryan is emotionally empowered over his parents by the visible tokens of his physical weakness. Helpless to save their son, Barry and Lady Lyndon appear disheveled in their sorrow, out of step with the pristine order that usually surrounds and shapes them. Dialog between Barry and Bryan is a gentle duel between painful truth and comforting illusion. Barry, shielding himself as well as his son, denies the inevitability of death that Bryan senses is imminent. But although he sees right through his father's false show of optimism, Bryan finds security in an institutional safety net. An afterlife in Heaven is as real to Bryan as were his father's exaggerated, heroic tales of war.

Taking his parents' hands into his own, Bryan asks them not to quarrel any more because Lord Bullingdon once told him that quarrelsome people never get to Heaven. His plea for family reconciliation is somewhat ironic in view of the fact that he twice, if unwittingly, contributed to its breakup: first, by getting Bullingdon in trouble during the classroom scene, and second, by helping Bullingdon to disrupt Barry's recital. Barry's promise to Bryan may have its fulfillment in the subsequent duel scene with Lord Bullingdon.

Bryan distracts himself with his father's familiar war stories. His fear of death is thus soothed by idealized, safe *representations* of death. A similar situation occurs in *The Shining*, when Danny and Wendy Torrance seek emotional refuge from Jack's aggression by watching cartoon depictions of violence on television. Barry does his best to suppress his own grief and comfort his son by repeating the story he told many scenes ago, but he breaks down in tears halfway through. Along with his reaction to Captain Grogan's death, his tearful confession to the Chevalier, his apology to Lady Lyndon, and his assault on Lord Bullingdon, this is one of the few times we see Barry without a genteel mask.

Bryan's funeral procession is an extraordinary confluence of private passion and institutional ritual in full harmony. The "Sarabande" echoes that potent combination with increased volume and elaborate orchestration. The scene opens with a close-up of a small, white casket. A reverse zoom reveals the casket riding in the same miniature carriage, pulled by the same sheep, as at Bryan's eighth birthday party. In effect, the earlier shot is repeated under different circumstances, like the pan shots in *Clockwork* that introduce the Alexander household first before and then after Alex's assault. This time, Barry and Lady Lyndon trail behind instead of guiding the carriage from in front. Reverend Runt, positioned between Bryan's body and its mourners, is a symbolic intercession of institutional and/or divine power between the mourners and a tragedy they were helpless to prevent. Runt's are the only eyes not downcast in humble submission. In contrast to the predominant black of the mourners, he is dressed in white, signifying a triumph over death. Meanwhile, Lady Lyndon's sorrow is partially hidden by her veil. Barry, denied the veil, hides his grief behind a blank expression.

Barry withdraws from the wicked world by the same means the old Tramp did in *Clockwork*. But his relatively privileged *material* status, as opposed to the Tramp's, remains intact. The scene begins with a frontal shot of a door inside Castle Hackton. The door is bracketed by expensive vases and paintings. Through the door, held open for her, Mrs. Barry enters, accompanied by several male servants. The camera pans with them to where Barry sleeps, drunk, in a chair — a fallen king on his throne. The only sound is the clomping of the servants' shoes as they execute Mrs. Barry's instructions. She holds the candle that lights their way. Barry is gently yet unceremoniously hauled out of the room and off to bed. Shoeless, he looks as vulnerable as did Lord Bullingdon while being thrashed by Barry at the recital. The camera reverses direction and concludes the scene in its original position. In the space of a single shot we witness a change of royal administration at Castle Hackton. Mrs. Barry's act of compassion is also an act of appropriation. The door closes as quietly as it opened. It has been a most genteel power coup.

In the wake of Bryan's death, Lady Lyndon retreats to the security of religion and a renewed dependence on Reverend Runt. In this scene and the previous one, the narrator speaks in an understated tone of voice that counterpoints the visual evidence of inconsolable grief. Sometimes narration in *Barry Lyndon* illuminates what we see. At other times it is illuminated *by* what we see.

Mrs. Barry consolidates her power over the Lyndon estate by getting rid of what she sees as its greatest internal threat. Genteel order once again manifests itself in the precise ticking of a clock. In close-up, female hands hold financial documents. Earlier scenes have led us to presume they belong to Lady Lyndon. A reverse zoom reveals Mrs. Barry instead. Although she cannot legally spend estate funds, she appears very comfortable and efficient in her supervisory role. A steaming cup of tea lies at her right hand. Graham sits attentively at her left. A domestic Napoleon, Mrs. Barry's organizational skills allow her to "attend to all the ten thousand details of a great establishment."

In response to a summons, Reverend Runt quietly enters the room. Mrs. Barry sends Graham off on a mission elsewhere before acting against the clergyman. Isolate and conquer. She disguises her initial attack behind institutional masks of courtesy and duty. Recent financial strains on the estate make it necessary for her, "with the greatest reluctance," to dismiss Runt from his position. Complementing her dispassionate voice, her hands rest passively on the table in front of her.

Stunned by this unexpected statement, Reverend Runt nevertheless quickly recovers composure, nullifying his opponent's weapon by offering to remain at Castle Hackton without benefit of wages. Adding a moral argument, he insists he cannot in good conscience desert Lady Lyndon in her time of crisis. Mrs. Barry abandons her failed financial argument and attacks the root of Runt's ethical one. Her voice is slightly harsher, but the disintegration of decorum in this scene is gradual. She accuses Runt of unintentionally contributing to rather than alleviating Lady Lyndon's distress. In other words, Her Ladyship's recovery now *depends* on the chaplain's departure. Mrs. Barry's criticism may be valid, but her motive is suspect. Reverend Runt, shaken, defers the matter to the higher authority of Lady Lyndon herself, doing so "with the greatest respect" he does not actually feel for his adversary.

Dispensing with the sham of polite conversation, Mrs. Barry fiercely dismantles the chaplain's latest argument, and earns her first close-up of the scene, by pointing out that the power to decide estate affairs has been ceded to her. But her attempt to bolster her authority with a moral point ("My only concern is for Lady Lyndon") provides the frustrated clergyman with an opening for counterattack. Speaking boldly for the first time in the film, because his own security is at stake, he stands up and accuses his foe of being concerned only with Lady Lyndon's fortune. And he follows with a flood of perhaps legitimate criticisms he has obviously accumulated over the years but, for selfish reasons, has refrained from voicing until now. Like President Muffley arbitrarily cutting off an uncomfortable debate with General Turgidson, Mrs. Barry angrily terminates her conversation with Runt, ordering him to leave the estate by the next morning. He will, of course, comply.

Lady Lyndon, meanwhile, thrashes about her bedroom in a most ungenteel display of distress. We presume her behavior results from inconsolable grief over Bryan's death, until narration intrudes to paint a slightly different picture. Her pain is physical rather than emotional. She has attempted to commit suicide by taking poison. Repulsed by what he regards as excess, the narrator cruelly belittles her failure. Graham's arrival on the scene adds another layer of perspective. Shocked by what he sees, he interprets Lady Lyndon's distress differently than our initial impression and the narrator's subsequent redefinition. Only later do we become aware that Graham blames Her Ladyship's suffering on the Barrys. And that interpretation leads Graham, who appeared to be Mrs. Barry's passive tool in the previous scene, to take action which will eventually overthrow her rule at Castle Hackton.

Traveling to a neighboring estate, Graham meets with exiles Reverend Runt and Lord Bullingdon. As we join the scene, he has already delivered his disturbing account of Lady Lyndon and now sits passively, with head bowed. Runt sits at the other end of the table, also silent but far less charitable in his intentions. Between them, Lord Bullingdon browbeats himself into action with a series of self-accusations institutional in nature. In other words, he impels himself to do what his companions, for different reasons, want him to do.

The club where Lord Bullingdon confronts Barry is a comparatively shabby version of the elegant establishment where Barry hobnobbed with Lord Harlan and the Earl of Wendover. Barry's social status has slipped considerably, as, for whatever reasons, has that of his drunken companions. Into this moribund setting stride Lord Bullingdon and *his* two companions, bringing with them a sense of purpose contrary to the prevailing lethargy. All three carry walking sticks, recalling Alex and his droogs in *Clockwork*. With a mere nod of his head, Bullingdon posts his allies as guards at the door, then sets off to locate his quarry.

Bullingdon's search for Barry is followed by a backtracking camera, as was Alex's promenade through the Music Bootick. Both characters are fashionably dressed, though Alex to suit his own taste while Bullingdon conforms to prevailing style. In both scenes, the characters are surrounded by an indifferent environment, yet they respond differently to that challenge. Alex, his walking stick slung arrogantly over his shoulder, strolls confidently through the Bootick. *His* music dominates the soundtrack. Bullingdon looks nervous. He fiddles with his walking stick as if it were a pacifier instead of an instrument of command. And he is accompanied by the "Sarabande," which in part echoes the collective perceptions that push him toward his fate. Alex taps his stick three times on the floor to get attention from a sales clerk. Lord Bullingdon does the same to rouse Barry from his drunken stupor. But it is not enough. He must use his stick to lift up Barry's head so he can issue his formal challenge. "No gentleman can willingly suffer without demanding satisfaction" represents years of pent-up anger speaking through an institutional filter.

Promotional graphics for *Barry Lyndon* feature a pistol crossed over a rose — a synthesis of violence and elegance. That combination reaches its climax in the duel between Barry Lyndon and Lord Bullingdon, which is a variation on two previous duels. It begins with an extreme close-up of a pistol being loaded with a steel ball, by a hand in ruffled sleeves. The "Sarabande" carries over from the previous scene as both an echo and a critique of private passion interlocked with public ritual. Meanwhile, the cooing of pigeons adds an element of Nature divorced from both.

An extreme long shot places the duel within a large stone barn. Preliminaries to the duel are carried out by the combatants' seconds, while a neutral party named Sir Richard acts as overseer in this otherwise passionately partisan affair. He could be described as the master of ceremonies, except that ceremony is clearly *his* master and he its instrument.

Rather than skip the details of form by which collective man seeks to control and ennoble violent disputes between individuals, Kubrick explores and revels in them, because they are the voices through which his characters speak. Even the piece of cloth inserted between the iron ball and the pistol's hammer constitutes a layer of detachment between the antagonists. The ritual of a duel is equivalent to the elaborate safeguards Major Kong and his crew must pass through in order to unleash their hydrogen bombs, and the numerous bureaucratic signatures and countersignatures that formally validate Alex's transfer from Staja 84F to the Ludovico Centre.

As the younger man whose pride impels him to challenge a more experienced elder, Lord Bullingdon is to Barry what Barry was to Captain Quin. Yet the boy's obvious anxiety equates him more with Quin. And this time Barry *chooses* a pistol rather than accepting on faith one offered to him. The toss of a coin determines who will shoot first. The seconds and the overseer execute, inspect, and announce the results of that all-important step.

As the rivals take up firing positions, strictly proscribed by lines drawn on the ground (recollecting white lines toed by prison inmates in *Clockwork*), the illusion of alliance with their seconds diminishes. Bullingdon and Barry stand exposed to each other's wrath. The whole barn is incorporated into and redefined by their duel. Bathed in sunlight streaming in through narrow slits high up on the walls, and topped by a vaulted ceiling, the barn is metaphorically transformed into a cathedral of genteel faith, just as the cell block corridor in Staja 84F becomes a cathedral of government due process during the Interior Minister's visit in *Clockwork*.

Barry prepares to receive fire by turning sideways to reduce his exposure as a target — a remarkably modest form of self-defense, demonstrating the psychological power of a shared honor code that permits no more. But Lord Bullingdon fails to maintain equal self-discipline and squanders the advantage luck dealt him. Attempting to cock his pistol, he accidentally fires it. Pigeons take flight and mice squeal in startled reaction. Like the asteroids which pass silently by *Discovery* in *2001*, they are tokens of a Nature oblivious to the perceptions of man.

Bullingdon's demand for another first shot precipitates a conflict between private interest and collective procedure. One of Barry's seconds asserts his client's right to the next shot. Sir Richard agrees. Barry himself cannot properly participate in either the protest or the decision. Upon Sir Richard's pronouncement, one entire sequence of stylized steps is repeated, with the combatants in reversed roles.

Lord Bullingdon humbly submits to a resumption of a ritual that suddenly places him at a grave disadvantage. But his *in*voluntary reaction to the prospect of injury or death betrays his voluntary acquiescence, forcing him to abandon his appointed ground and retreat to the barn wall for support while he vomits. His situation recalls Alex's Ludovico-conditioned nausea, except that Alex's sickness preversely *furthers* institutional design while Bullingdon's *violates* it. Sir Richard and the seconds are embarrassed by his show of weakness. Precariously suspended between contradictory fears (of harm and of public disgrace), Bullingdon eventually resumes his ground and turns sideways to protect himself as best he can under the rules of the contest.

Barry's reaction to Bullingdon's pathetic condition may be a consequence of Bryan's dying plea for family reconciliation. But like Alex's display of compassion towards the old Tramp late in *Clockwork*, it goes unrewarded. He defies both self-interest and tradition by deliberately squandering his rightful advantage, firing his pistol into the ground. It is a brief, revolutionary act in a most unrevolutionary era. Lord Bullingdon is pleasantly surprised at his rival's refusal to shoot him, but like the old Tramp he is too embittered by past experience to forgive his enemy. He insists on taking the next shot. Barry looks a bit bewildered by this development, as though *his* disenchantment with the whole affair ought to be shared by his adversary. Nevertheless, he obeys the rules and resumes his defensive posture. After a moment of hopeful suspense, the ritual resumes its grim, fateful course.

Lord Bullingdon fires his pistol. Barry collapses with a strangled, ugly cry behind a pall of white smoke, his vulnerable, white-stockinged legs reminiscent of Bullingdon's at the recital. Like Mr. Alexander reintroducing Alex to Beethoven in *Clockwork*, this is revenge Bullingdon has anticipated for a long time. But unlike the emotionally crippled Mr. Alexander, Lord Bullingdon is not a committed sadist. While the other men rush to help Barry, the victor stands alone, awkwardly clutching his smoking pistol, now as empty as the genteel promise of satisfaction proved to be.

Barry is taken to a village inn and committed to the care of a doctor. His confrontation with Lord Bullingdon is not, after all, as uninhibited as the water hole battle in *2001*. But if the sound of a distant church bell signifies collective moderation, narration and action reveal the *limits* of institutional power. Barry's doctor is a model of dispassionate, efficient professionalism. Yet his skills are insufficient to save Barry's injured leg. Wiping the patient's blood off his hands, he discreetly distances himself from the suffering of a fellow human being. His two assistants do likewise, in their own ways. One winces and averts his eyes from the mess that was Barry's shin; the other lets go of Barry's hand — a contact Barry had used to fight off the pain caused by the examination. The protagonist is left to fend for himself. Upon learning that his leg must be amputated, he weeps over his unhappy fate. Then, as though embarrassed by his indiscretion, he averts his eyes in shame and fights back his tears.

In a coach thundering purposefully towards Castle Hackton, Lord Bullingdon plots the completion of his overthrow of the Barry dynasty. Graham and Barry himself are to be his principal tools for isolating Mrs. Barry from Lady Lyndon — the source of legal power fought over by all concerned. Graham, still a trusted pawn in Mrs. Barry's eyes, will seem a credible messenger. His account of Barry's injury will lure her away from the estate. Bullingdon adds, "Don't go into any unnecessary detail." His is a two-pronged strategy: to get rid of Mrs. Barry and to limit public knowledge of his undignified performance (and Barry's act of compassion) during the duel. "Unnecessary" is his euphemism for "embarrassing."

Reverend Runt remains a passive but interested observer in this scene. He smiles discreetly to himself as Bullingdon lists new restrictions to be placed on Mrs. Barry. From the clergyman's vantage point, Bullingdon and Graham are *his* instruments of revenge against a woman who exiled him from the Lyndon household. The present scene is the much delayed culmination of the partnership he slyly cultivated with Bullingdon many years earlier, during another carriage ride. Between those widely separated events, he accommodated quite comfortably to the Barry reign at Castle Hackton and virtually ignored Bullingdon's humiliation at Barry's hands.

The camera returns to an exterior view. In extreme long shot, the now tiny carriage rumbles across the vast and indifferent face of Nature at dusk. Though muted, the conflict between Man and Nature portrayed in *2001* lies just beneath the surface of *Barry Lyndon*.

At the inn, Mrs. Barry's situation is very different from the last time we saw her, confidently presiding over Castle Hackton. Then the camera reverse zooms to reveal a compensation for her loss. Barry, lying in bed, his stump of a leg wrapped in white bandages, is once again dependent on his mother's care. Bullingdon's victory has been less of a catastrophe for her than for Barry. Barry's situation superficially resembles Alex's after the "suicide" attempt in *Clockwork*. But Alex transforms his infirmity into a strategic advantage. Poor Barry finds no such opportunity. The only game left open to him, playing cards with his mother, is a mere idle diversion.

Lord Bullingdon delivers his surrender terms to the Barrys by way of Graham. Painfully aware of his duplicitous role in their downfall, the timid solicitor is a reluctant weapon against them. Mrs. Barry, who lost an estate but regained a needy son, greets the lawyer courteously. She may not even be aware of his treachery. Barry, however, fixes Graham with an accusing, intimidating stare even as he inquires politely about the solicitor's well-being. But Graham is only an intermediary, not a power broker. Neither Lord Bullingdon nor Lady Lyndon are within the reach of Barry's influence.

Graham disguises the grim purpose of his visit behind a mask of good manners. He sent a note in advance of his arrival, as though the impropriety of an unannounced visit holds any significance in the context of his mission. Unlike the parasitical Reverend Runt, Graham tries to do what seems right. But above all, he wishes to avoid confrontation. He is *Barry Lyndon's* answer to *Clockwork's* Pee. Perhaps not coincidentally, both characters are played by actor Philip Stone.

Lord Bullingdon's terms for a settlement with the Barrys are not draconian, as is often the case in *Clockwork* and *2001*, but they are harsh enough by genteel standards. Barry's fall from social grace, combined with the losses of a son, a wife, and a leg, and a return to dependence on his mother, is a terrible blow. He is granted a reasonably comfortable annuity of five hundred guineas. But the price is permanent exile from England and from Lady Lyndon. "Jail," a word Graham hesitates to use, is the threatened alternative. If Barry had any hope of maintaining the financial status quo, it disappears with his enforced separation from Lady Lyndon. And if, having given up his social ambitions in the wake of Bryan's death, Barry desires only the loving companionship of his wife, that too is denied him.

Barry's exit from the Lyndon stage is accompanied by the same music heard during his promising entrance, when he courted Lady Lyndon at the Belgian spa. Schubert's *Piano Trio* returns as an ironic echo of happier times. Subjectively linked now to Barry's misfortune, the music counterpoints the indifference of people on the street outside the inn from which he exits with his mother. But, even in defeat, the Barrys maintain decorum, concealing their sadness behind masks of stoicism. As Barry walks past a signpost, it becomes, in the illusion of two-dimensional perspective created by the camera, and only in the context of his troubles, a gallows — a symbol of institutional execution.

Reversing angle, the camera tracks from behind as Barry and his mother approach a waiting carriage. The power of this image is a consequence of its remoteness from its subject. Barry fades from our view almost anonymously (which is also *practical* for Kubrick, since the character is here played by a real amputee rather than the two-legged Ryan O'Neal). His downfall is conveyed indirectly, through the actions of his companions. A servant standing next to the coach nervously shifts his weight from foot to foot and wipes his mouth. He is unsure how to assist his crippled employer without causing offense. He reaches out tentatively to help Barry, then quickly withdraws his hand. Compensating for the crutches Barry discards as he enters the coach, Mrs. Barry and the servant reach out to support him. Our final, freeze-frame impression of Barry is of a figure receding into obscurity, pitied and propped up by his few remaining friends and employees. Narration compounds this impression by projecting it into the future. We learn that Barry returns to Ireland to recuperate, then travels to Europe to pursue his former profession as a gambler, with little success. Dave Bowman's mythical rebirth as the Star Child, and even the ironic resurrections of Dr. Strangelove and Alex, contrast vividly with Barry's disappearance from view — which we perceive indirectly, by word of mouth, rendering it even *more* anemic. In the end, we see Barry only as a ripple of memory in the affairs of other people.

The camera returns to Castle Hackton for the last in a series of family portraits. Schubert carries over from the previous scene, but now with the piano rather than strings at the forefront, echoing the shift in focus from Barry to Lady Lyndon, who for a time were in emotional harmony.

Graham, Lord Bullingdon, and Lady Lyndon are seated at a large table. Reverend Runt stands beside them. Fashionably attired and elegantly posed, they unconsciously mimic the figures in a huge painting on the wall above and behind them. Equivalent to the Flatblock mural in *Clockwork*, the painting depicts a collective ideal. Unlike Alex, however, the characters in *Barry Lyndon* conform to rather than rebel against that ideal. But not entirely.

At closer range we see a variation on three earlier scenes depicting the routine payment of debts. Documents are passed from Graham to Lord Bullingdon and finally to Lady Lyndon for her signature, while Reverend Runt observes with interest. Her Ladyship is surrounded by the separate concerns of three men who are dependent on her legal power yet supervise what she signs. Then, without a word spoken, routine is disrupted. Lady Lyndon is handed Barry's annuity check. She pauses, a pen poised gracefully in her hand, as her thoughts return to her life with him. The music, departing from its original form and delaying its resolution, falls into subjective sync with her private reverie. Music and imagery combine to create a moment of exquisite suspense. Lord Bullingdon, looking very adult and sober now in his new spectacles, appears dismayed at the ghostly return of an old rival. He glances at his mother with an expression suggesting both compassion for her and a selfish fear of the power Barry's memory may still hold over her.

Finally, Bullingdon leans towards his mother, disrupting her nostalgic trance. With a barely perceptible sigh, she resumes signing legal documents, though her face retains a wistful trace of sorrow. Whatever suffering Barry put her through, time and distance have softened. And whatever Barry gave her in terms of affection, happiness, and a sense of power cannot be compensated for by the three gentlemen surrounding her now. Nevertheless, Lady

Lyndon's lingering passion for Barry yields to the institutional forces in and around her.

Lush strings and broad piano strokes bring the counterpoint of private passion and collective decorum to a dramatic conclusion. Schubert, as modified by Leonard Rosenman and employed by Kubrick, now plays independently of any one character's perspective. The camera returns to its distant overview, providing a final portrait of genteel order restored to its pristine form. The music slows to a stop, echoing the written prologue. "It was in the reign of George III that the aforesaid personages lived and quarreled. Good or bad, handsome or ugly, rich or poor, they are all equal now." Individual and institutional perspectives, forces, and creations are all consigned to a common, apocalyptic fate. The date written on Barry's annuity check reads 1789 — the start of a revolution that changed the face of Europe and eventually toppled the social order and aesthetic style portrayed so lovingly and yet so critically in *Barry Lyndon*. Handel's "Sarabande" plays at full volume over the end credits, as a passionately formal dirge for the downfall of one character and the imminent passing of an Age.

In Kubrick's cinematic world, paradise is always qualified and temporary — a potential if enticing trap. The backward-looking gentility of *Barry Lyndon* may have been a tonic for him after the modern, futuristic, and often violent worlds of *Dr. Strangelove, 2001: A Space Odyssey* and *A Clockwork Orange*. In his next film, *The Shining*, Kubrick's protagonist will yield to the temptation of another privileged past, where sanctuary becomes nightmare.

CHAPTER 5

The Shining:
Unsympathetic Vibrations

And round about his home the glory
  That blushed and bloomed,
Is but a dim-remembered story
  Of the old time entombed.
                    — Edgar Allan Poe ("The Haunted Palace")

Kubrick's adaptation of Stephen King's 1977 novel, *The Shining*, pleased neither the author nor many of King's admirers. Major changes were made which bring the story into line with Kubrick's previous work, most of them elaborating on the interplay between various private and collective perspectives. For all of its initial family interaction, King's novel moves relentlessly toward the stock-in-trade of supernatural fiction, in which an undeniably demonic force exerts ever more influence over the lives of human characters, until it is defeated by means of a gimmick.

Kubrick's version certainly contains a supernormal phenomenon (the prescient vision named in the title), but it focuses on the encounter between the Torrance family, with its troubled past, and two overlapping environments: the Rocky Mountains and the Overlook Hotel. The mixture of characters and environments yields corrosive, then explosive results. Like *Dr. Strangelove's* War Room and *2001's* spaceship *Discovery*, the hotel is an emotional crucible. But unlike its predecessors, Overlook has a long history, perceived differently by each member of the Torrance family and by members of its staff. Kubrick and co-screenwriter Diane Johnson clearly delineate those separate points of view.

King's novel blurs such distinctions. Overlook's manager, Stuart Ullman, knows about Jack Torrance's drinking problem and declares he would have rejected Jack's application to be winter caretaker if not for the intervention of his own boss, Albert Shockley, who just happens to be Jack's old

Just a few requests

Please **DO NOT** write in the book.

Please **DO NOT** fold down the pages.

Please **DO NOT** leave sticky tabs, paperclips or bookmarks in the book.

Please **DO NOT** leave any personal items such as bank cards or receipts in the book.

Please **DO NOT** eat, drink or smoke over the book.

Thank you
for helping us
take good care of our books

National University Staff - Spectrum Library

drinking buddy. Two of Ullman's employees, Bill Watson and Dick Hallo-ran, openly discuss their contempt for Ullman. The film, on the other hand, emphasizes a collective spirit of polite professionalism as the arbiter of rela-tions between Jack and the hotel staff. Ullman is a model manager, appar-ently well liked by his employees. And Al Shockley does not exist in the film, eliminating a personal link between Jack and Ullman, who remains ignorant of Jack's history of alcohol abuse and domestic discord. A *second* institutional character, a doctor in Boulder, Colorado, is made aware of Jack's problem, but she knows nothing of the Torrances' plan to spend a winter alone at Over-look. She and Ullman see disconnected pieces of a dangerous puzzle.

In King's novel, young Danny Torrance discusses his deepest concerns and extraordinary power of insight with several strangers. In the film, he is defensive and secretive, even with Dick Halloran, who shares his ability to shine. Partly, this is because Kubrick portrays shining as a curse as well as a benefit to its possessor. During their private conversation about the hotel, Danny and Halloran each feel threatened by the other's ability to tap into his prescient fears. Later in the film, as Halloran travels from Florida back to Overlook on a rescue mission, he conceals from everyone he encounters the paranormal source of his concern about Danny. In the novel, his journey is aided by people whose shine allows them to sense his unspoken urgency.

King emphasizes emotional stress fractures existing within the Torrance family *before* their arrival at Overlook. The Torrance apartment in Boulder is a dump. Wendy has a superstitious dread of Danny's mysterious fainting spells. Jack is plagued by memories of his past abuse of Danny, swears fre-quently, and has a history of violent behavior independent of his drinking. Kubrick *hints* at the Torrances' pre-Overlook tensions. Their Boulder resi-dence is cluttered rather than shabby. Wendy is not superstitious. And Jack exhibits few signs of the alcoholism and violence to which he was prone in the past or of being haunted by their memory. Even after one month at the hotel, he and Wendy seem more like happy vacationers than besieged souls. Instead of portraying the Torrances on the verge of a family breakdown from the start, Kubrick plants tiny seeds of discontent in two specific deviations from the novel. Unlike her blond, beautiful, and fashionable literary coun-terpart, the film's Wendy is plain, a frowsy dresser, a poor housekeeper, and has a tendency to gloss over problems with platitudes. Yet she is by no means simple or stupid. We are made to see her partly through Jack's eyes, as a some-times irritating presence who does not measure up to his increasingly chau-vinistic, impossible ideal of a mate. Compounding his annoyance is her strong emotional bond with their son, which Jack eventually interprets as a con-spiracy against himself. In King's version, Danny is instead deeply attached to his father. In the novel, Danny is an exceptionally intelligent child with a large vocabulary. From his very first trance, he foresees virtually all of

Overlook's horrors, though he does not immediately comprehend everything he sees. The film portrays Danny as an ordinary boy with one extraordinary talent. His paranormal visions change and progress in response to the Torrances' developing situation at Overlook. And he copes with their terror by hiding behind his dispassionate alter ego, Tony, whose passivity he must later overcome in order to save himself from Jack's murderous assault. In other words, he must become a *normal* child again in order to survive a threat which his *super*normal vision warns him about long before the family reaches Overlook.

King's Overlook Hotel is a consciously malevolent force whose demonic agents physically manipulate and menace the Torrances. The fact that some of those agents appear to more than one member of the family suggests that they are not figments of any one character's imagination. In the film, none of these "supernatural" creatures overtly threatens or appears in the same form to more than one member of the Torrance family. Danny, Jack, and Wendy each make of Overlook and its past what he or she is equipped and inclined to make of it. The most virulent example of Overlook's supernatural malevolence in the novel is the aggressive behavior of its topiary. Kubrick replaces the topiary with a giant hedge maze, a passive institutional structure which favors no one and, depending on circumstances, serves anyone.

Like *2001, The Shining* features a small group of individuals confined to an artificial environment by an inhospitable natural environment. What happens to those isolated groups depends on the emotional and physical baggage they bring with them, what impact their confinement has on that baggage, and to what extent their own conscious will allows them to master the stresses that result.

*   *   *

A disembodied camera glides swiftly and soundlessly above a pristine mountain lake, giving us a purely subjective impression of effortless, unfettered mobility akin to Dave Bowman's journey "Beyond the Infinite" and Alex's Durango-95 excursion, except that it is independent of any particular technology or character.

The presence of the "Dies Irae," or "Wrath of God" theme, as background music adds a sinister note to the power of the disembodied camera. At the start of *Dr. Strangelove,* the combination of two aircraft refueling in midair and "Try a Little Tenderness" equates military technology with sex. Not until later in the film do we discover the origin of this linkage in the twisted mind of General Ripper. But whose godlike perspective do we share during the opening credits of *The Shining?* Surrounding the "Dies Irae" are weird fluttering sounds and wailing reverberations that suggest a supernatural presence. Later in the film we learn of Danny's unusual power of insight, referred to as shining. With hindsight, it appears that *his* is the power we share through the subjective camera.

The screen dissolves to an overhead tracking shot of a Volkswagen Beetle traveling along a winding mountain road cut through a forest of pine trees. The film's initial, purely subjective impression of unrestricted mobility overlaps and parallels a second, objective and more restricted example of mobility. Viewed from high above, the car appears small, the road narrow and confining, and the surrounding forest massive. As examples of technological power, the automobile and the road seem at best tenuous challenges to Nature.

Inching closer to the car with each passing shot, the camera passes alongside at a point where the road curves. Private, supernormal insight and collective technology travel side by side for a moment until the camera, following its own whim, sails straight beyond the guard rail and over a rocky ledge leading down to a lake. Free of technological limits, we navigate effortlessly where the car cannot safely go. The aesthetic effect of this imagery is an exhilarating sense of the power of the mind (paranormal or imaginative). But the "Dies Irae" puts a sinister spin on our impression of a power which will later prove unmanageable and dangerous.

At the upper end of the winding road stands the Overlook Hotel. A massive, gray, peaked building perched near the summit of a massive, gray, peaked mountain, Overlook, like spaceship *Discovery*, both defies and resembles Nature. A creation of collective man, it dwarfs the individual cars in its parking lot. But like *Discovery*, S.A.C., and the Ludovico Program, it will prove susceptible to appropriation and corruption by the individual.

The Shining's opening credits, like *Dr. Strangelove's*, contribute to the dramatic effect of the opening scene. Composed of streamlined, electric-blue lettering, they counterpoint the natural mountain scenery. As in *2001*, Nature and technology function as parallel yet distinct environments in relation to individual man. Unlike their staccato counterparts in *Clockwork* and *Barry Lyndon*, *The Shining's* credits roll by smoothly, harmonizing with the movements of camera and automobile while contrasting with the rugged, uneven landscape.

Caption cards are The *Shining's* only form of narration. Infrequent and brief, they contribute to dramatic effect by juxtaposition with events on screen and, more importantly, with each other. "The Interview" is a simple description of the traditional device by which institutional man examines the job qualifications of individual man.

The solitary journeys depicted in the first scene give way to a collective order in the second. The lobby of the Overlook Hotel is large, airy, and tastefully decorated in muted colors. Employees perform their routine duties quietly and efficiently. Stout pillars reinforce an impression of institutional strength and size. Entering the lobby, Jack Torrance fits into the collective pattern very nicely. To make a proper impression at his job interview, he is dressed in a suit and tie and is well groomed.

As with all other Kubrick institutions, Overlook features a formal chain of command, though it is comparatively relaxed. We track Jack's brief journey through the barriers between Overlook's manager and the general public, proceeding from desk clerk to secretary's outer office to Stuart Ullman's inner office. Respecting the symbolic significance of the latter, Jack stops and knocks before entering. As he hesitates in the doorway, we see framed pictures hanging on the wall on either side of him. Between them, framed by the doorway, is our first glimpse of Ullman's office. We see it as a thing once removed from us, neatly contained within the door frame. Then we enter along with Jack. The artificial frame recedes, and the office becomes an environment *in* which we and Jack function rather than an enclosed portrait we contemplate from a distance.

Stuart Ullman's office is a modest statement of collective authority when compared to General Ripper's in *Dr. Strangelove*. Various objects in the room give us hints of Ullman's personality and responsibilities. A name plate on his desk plus meritorious plaques on his walls reflect the conventional orderliness of his life. A barometer, a radio transceiver, and a Colorado state road map indicate his attention to weather, communication, and geography as major factors in Overlook's operation. A small American flag on his desk places Ullman, the hotel, and Colorado within an even larger institutional framework. The window behind him lets in sunlight from outside his personal domain. By contrast, Ripper *closed* the blinds in his office, transforming it into a private fortress against both outside interference and his own conscience.

When Alex was summoned to the Governor's office in *Clockwork*, he was compelled to stand at attention behind a white line painted on the floor. In welcoming Jack, Stuart Ullman sets aside other business and steps out from behind his desk to shake hands. He invests the hotel with a democratic rather than an autocratic atmosphere. Still, some formality and distinction of rank continue to operate. Ullman dispatches his secretary, Susie, to fetch coffee. There is no overt condescension in his manner, nor does she appear to resent the order. Nevertheless, a very old tradition of sexual stereotyping is laid out, barely visible, beneath the egalitarian surface of this first Overlook scene. And it is out of that and similar traditions that Jack's madness will take shape.

A dissolve lifts us out of the interview at a seemingly arbitrary point. Throughout the film the camera drops into and out of numerous situations, giving us a strong feel for each while generating a detached overview by juxtaposing them. Jack's interview at Overlook is split by a simultaneous scene in Boulder, Colorado. Like the isolated locations in *Dr. Strangelove*, each locale in *The Shining* develops its own pattern of logic. Later, the hotel itself will furnish numerous isolated settings in which individual characters engage in private dramas, which in turn affect their relations with each other.

An exterior shot of the Torrances' apartment building in Boulder counterpoints the first shot of Overlook. Nature in the city is less imposing. Inside the apartment, too, conditions are very different from what we saw at the hotel. Small, cluttered, and inelegant, it contrasts sharply with Overlook's immaculate, spacious, and decorous interior. Wendy Torrance matches her surroundings, at least in visual terms. This scene discreetly sets the stage for Jack Torrance's violent rejection of Wendy, Danny, and Boulder in favor of Overlook and its ghostly past.

Eating lunch together at the kitchen table, Wendy and Danny are separately entertained by two very different abstract representations of violence. Danny watches a *Road Runner* cartoon on television while Wendy reads a copy of J. D. Salinger's *Catcher in the Rye*. They share, albeit at different levels of sophistication, a comfortably detached experience of something that will become uncomfortably literal for them in subsequent scenes. By contrast, Jack Torrance will later embrace *without* detachment a story of violence from Overlook's past. Ironically, Wendy's novel has been misused by several real-life murderers in the same way Jack will misuse the tale of Delbert "Charles" Grady.

What Wendy and Danny do *not* share in this scene is a common anticipation of their upcoming stay at Overlook. Significantly, it is Danny who brings up the subject, though in a deceptively casual manner. "Do you really want to go live in that hotel for the winter?" is a statement of apprehension disguised as a question. Wendy's cheerful affirmative does not agree with Danny's feelings, so he disguises them further, rationalizing that since he has no playmates in Boulder, he gives up nothing by moving to Overlook. Wendy adds to our initial impression of Danny as a lonely child by asking what Tony, his make-believe friend, thinks about the trip.

Tony is presumably a substitute for the real playmate Danny lacks. Wendy addresses him as though he were a common childhood invention. Tony's deeper emotional roots in Danny are not revealed in this scene, but a few of his traits come to light. As Danny's alter ego, Tony is less emotional and less dependent on others. He addresses Wendy as "Mrs. Torrance" instead of "Mom," erecting a formal barrier between them. And he is less inhibited about expressing his opposition to the Overlook trip, though he is reluctant to give his reasons. Serving as a kind of fictional filtration device, Tony is the tougher-minded persona by which Danny can both explore and shield himself from the frightening insights brought to him by the power of shining. Tony's abstract nature is best illustrated by the childish symbols with which Danny associates him: a bent index finger and a low, croaking voice.

If Danny uses Tony to fend off unpleasant feelings, Wendy employs platitudes and a patronizing tone of voice to do the same: "Well, let's just wait and see. We're all gonna have a real good time." The first line suspends judgment about the hotel. The second replaces that suspension with optimism. She does not take Tony's misgivings seriously. And so Danny buries them, just as Jack and, to a lesser extent, Wendy keep their troubled emotions buried, until the absence of conventional social inhibitions at Overlook unleashes them.

Overlook's assistant manager, Bill Watson, is a reflection of his boss. After obligatory greetings all around, the men take their appointed places for the interview. Jack and Bill are seated opposite Ullman, formally separated from him by his desk and the authority it represents. But their conversation is shaped not so much by their respect for Ullman's authority as by the habitual deference all three men display toward the collective sense of decorum that regulates their behavior toward one another. Watson and Ullman appear relaxed. Jack, who is under institutional scrutiny, is slightly less so, nervously rubbing his leg.

Part of the ritual of getting acquainted is to define each other by occupation. Ullman introduces Jack as a schoolteacher. Jack corrects him: "*Formerly* a schoolteacher. I'm a writer." Obviously the distinction is important to Jack, whose self-esteem is linked to his profession. He distances himself from and belittles his teaching job by relegating it to the status of financial prop for his chosen career. Judging from their lack of reaction, Ullman and Watson make no such distinction.

A man evidently very content with his *own* profession, Ullman smiles and nods his approval of Jack's qualifications for the caretaker job. A recommendation by Ullman's subordinates in Denver reinforces that assessment. The Denver people are no less instruments of Ullman's will than is Bill Watson, who is assigned to take Jack on a tour of the hotel after the interview.

Through Jack's inquiry as to why the hotel is closed during the winter, we learn something about the vision of Overlook's original owners. Winter sports, Ullman reveals, were not as popular in the old days. As an institution, the hotel spans generations of owners, employees, guests, and fashions. And in those overlapping layers lie numerous contradictions, running parallel to which is the conflict between Man and Nature. For example, Overlook does not cater to the *current* popularity of winter sports because snow-blocked mountain roads make it economically unfeasible, as Ullman explains with his hands hanging limp in a mild gesture of helplessness.

As caretaker, Jack is employed to protect the hotel from Nature's encroachment while the regular staff is away — a role roughly equivalent to HAL's on board *Discovery*. And like HAL, Jack will be adversely affected by the circumstances of his assignment. Ullman warns him of the danger of "cabin fever." Jack takes advantage of this warning to bolster his qualifications for the caretaker job, redefining "tremendous sense of isolation" as "five months of peace" ideally suited to his plan for writing a book. Institutional and private needs appear to be in perfect harmony. And in response to Ullman's prudent inquiry about the reactions of Wendy and Danny, Jack assures him they will love Overlook. Smiling, Ullman accepts this statement at face value, but we have already seen evidence of Danny's misgivings about the hotel.

Perhaps because it involved a catastrophic breakdown of collective order at Overlook, Ullman is reluctant to discuss the cabin-fever incident in which Charles Grady, the hotel's winter caretaker in 1970, murdered his wife and children with an axe. Like President Muffley trying to tell Premier Kissoff about a nuclear attack on Russia, he alternately acknowledges and minimizes the horror. Ullman admits that Grady passed all of the standard institutional tests by which unfit job applicants should be weeded out, just as General Ripper passed the psychological screening referred to in *Dr. Strangelove*. On the other hand, Ullman distances himself from the tragedy by pointing out that it was his predecessor who hired Grady. Even his reference to Grady's first name as "Charles," which does not square with the name given the character later in the film, suggests that Ullman is not entirely familiar with the facts of a case he would probably like to forget.

Bill Watson, too, seems embarrassed by the Grady incident. But Jack, a writer in search of a story, is intrigued by it, encouraging Ullman to tell more. Currying favor with his new boss, Jack tells him that Wendy, a "confirmed ghost story and horror film addict," will be thrilled when she hears about it. In Ullman's eyes, Wendy must seem the perfect wife of the perfect candidate for the caretaker job. The scene ends with a shot of Ullman, Jack, and Bill all smiling at each other after having successfully navigated some mildly turbulent waters.

Returning to the Torrances' Boulder apartment, the camera creeps up on Danny in the bathroom, standing at the sink, talking to Tony. Clashing with that sober activity are collective images of childhood fun: cartoon characters on the hallway walls and on Danny's shirt. Complementing Danny's mood are the long, monotone pulses of the background music, from Krzysztof Penderecki's "The Awakening of Jacob." The music's Biblical title adds definition to the scene. Translating from the Hebrew into "He overreaches," it parallels Danny's unusual insight into other people, places, and events. He overreaches in this scene by conjuring up Tony's paranormal revelations about Overlook as casually as he stirs up water in the sink. Tony is both the name Danny gives to the source of his unusual insight and the emotional filter through which that insight must pass before it reaches Danny's conscious mind. Through Tony, Danny learns that Jack has gotten the caretaker job and will soon phone home to inform Wendy. Both revelation and prediction prove accurate, straining the boundaries of coincidence. The nature and extent of Danny's supernormal vision are, like the nature and intentions of alien intelligence in *2001*, never spelled out by Kubrick. Danny's shine makes him an advanced type of human being akin to the Star Child. But the Star Child was a gloriously generic, metaphorical idealization of the potential for human growth. Danny is a *specific* character possessed of a great but unwieldy power that sometimes proves to be a handicap.

Speaking with Wendy by telephone from Overlook's lobby, Jack slouches against the check-in counter, relieved of the need to perform for his interviewers. Nearby, a bellhop stands at attention next to one of the sturdy pillars, still in performance mode. On a more personal level, Jack's conversation with Wendy is outwardly affectionate, clashing with the foreboding background music linked to Danny's shine, which anticipates the evil effect Overlook will have on them.

The camera returns to Danny in the bathroom, where he converses with his own reflection in the mirror, which he calls Tony. Tony finally relents and allows Danny to shine on Overlook. What he gets is vivid but disorganized imagery forming an ominous puzzle. An elevator disgorges a slow-motion torrent of blood that sweeps aside neatly arranged lounge furniture and throws up obscene red stains on walls painted institutional white. That image is interspliced with a brief shot of identical twin girls with vacant facial expressions. Then Danny sees himself, presumably in the future, his mouth wide open in a mute scream. Danny anticipates a terror to come but not its specific source. Before he learns more, the horror of what he has seen so far overwhelms him emotionally. He blacks out.

Danny's power to shine has limits. *We* have an idea who the girls in his vision might be, thanks to information disclosed during Jack's interview. Danny cannot clearly identify their connection to Overlook. On the other hand, the elevator doors in Danny's vision are unfamiliar to us until later in the film, when we see their like at the hotel.

The twins in Danny's vision do not quite square with Ullman's description of Charles Grady's daughters being of different ages. Kubrick refrains from objectively confirming one interpretation or the other, thereby involving us in a subtle conflict between different vantage points.

Subjective music concludes with Danny's blackout, displaced by a voice speaking from *outside* the boy's point of view. The camera awakens to find him lying on his bed, being examined by a doctor. Wendy looks on, hugging herself in an unconscious effort to control her anxiety. The doctor is dressed casually but in subdued colors — a careful balance of informality and formality that preserves her aura of professional detachment yet keeps her from appearing too remote. Her calm voice is intended to put Danny at ease so that she can coax information out of him.

Her examination of Danny is both physical and verbal. Careful questioning eliminates suspicion of a tumor or epilepsy and targets Tony's role in

Danny's blackout. In close-up, Danny's inexpressive face is juxtaposed with the jolly teddy-bear pillow lying beside him and a happy portrait of Bugs Bunny on his shirt — two more images of childhood out of tune with the image of one very troubled little boy. He plays cat and mouse with the doctor, revealing little information about Tony. "He's a little boy that lives in my mouth," he concedes. Wendy redefines her son's oddly internalized companion in more conventional terms, as an "imaginary friend," thereby making Danny seem more normal. The doctor accepts that explanation and prudently refrains from probing further against Danny's wishes. But she asserts a measure of control over the boy by telling him to remain in bed for the rest of the day. Then she adjourns to the living room with Wendy to discuss Danny's situation out of his earshot.

The conversation between Wendy and the doctor unexpectedly develops into another cat-and-mouse affair. Sensing Wendy's repressed concern, the doctor assures her that Danny's blackout, though mysterious, is probably a one-time incident, and that, in the unlikely event of another seizure, they have recourse to a standard battery of medical tests which can pinpoint the cause. Stuart Ullman likewise relied on his standard resources of evaluation ("our people in Denver") to evaluate Jack — to his regret, as it will turn out.

From the doctor's point of view, the house call should now end. But Wendy's continued agitation (trembling hands lighting a cigarette) alerts the doctor to the possibility that there is more to be learned about Danny's case. Twiddling her thumbs to control her own curiosity, she deftly questions Wendy until she uncovers Tony's possible origin. Each probe provides new clues, which in turn help shape new questions, until a dirty little family secret is exposed. Wendy reluctantly reveals Jack's problem with alcohol and how he "unintentionally" dislocated Danny's shoulder while drunk. The focus of institutional scrutiny, originally applied to Danny at Wendy's request, suddenly expands to the Torrance family as a whole, to Wendy's discomfort. Struggling with conflicting loyalties, Danny's most devoted protector finds herself defending the man who injured him. So eager is she to minimize Jack's guilt, and perhaps indirectly her own as well, that she transfers some of it to Danny, whose irresponsible behavior allegedly triggered Jack's violent outburst. Finally, Wendy wraps up the unsavory story with a happy ending. Jack has sworn off alcohol. But the scene concludes with a shot of the doctor sitting in polite silence yet looking far from reassured. Unfortunately for Wendy and Danny, she is not one of the professional judges of character Stuart Ullman consults before approving Jack's application to be caretaker.

"Closing Day" begins with a variation on the disembodied camera once again gliding effortlessly over a mountainous landscape, then falling into stride with the Torrances' VW Beetle on the road below. The synthesized background music, by Wendy Carlos and Rachel Elkind, consists of big descending chords, like instruments in an orchestra warming up before a performance. Fragments of sound crisscross, generating brief sympathetic vibrations which echo the film's juxtaposition of characters and of characters with environments.

The music follows the camera down to ground level where it echoes subconscious forces at work in the Torrance family as they travel toward Overlook. Traces of family discord peek through conversation that is otherwise casual and innocuous. The stationary camera gives us a view of Jack's reactions that neither Danny nor Wendy share.

Wendy begins the conversation by casually noting how different the atmosphere seems at high elevation. There is nothing foreboding about her comment, yet it unwittingly touches on the matter of environmental impact on human perception. Jack's reply is equally casual but contains a slight hint of annoyance, which is enhanced by their son's entry into the conversation. Danny complains of hunger. Jack is unsympathetic, pointing out that he should have eaten his breakfast. Wendy resolves this minor conflict by promising to get Danny something to eat at the hotel. Jack listens without apparent reaction as his parental admonition is undermined by his wife.

Wendy is inadvertently responsible for the next tiny rift between herself and Jack. Her casual inquiry about the Donner Party sparks a dialog between Danny and Jack on the subject of cannibalism. Wendy, ever protective of Danny, mildly rebukes Jack for elaborating on such a topic. Danny reassures her that he learned all about cannibalism from television. Grinning, Jack then appropriates Danny's remark to mock both his son's naive presumption and his wife's overprotectiveness. Coincidentally, the Donner Party incident, an historical event that has become a collective myth, echoes what the Torrance family will later experience at Overlook.

The camera returns to its high-flying perspective, tracking the Torrance's Volkswagen and its potentially volatile cargo through broken clouds. The fading background music associated with their journey lingers briefly into the next scene, where it counterpoints the local, institutional sounds and sights of closing-day routine inside Overlook. A departing employee cheerfully bids goodbye to her boss, whom she addresses as *Mr.* Ullman. Though a casual atmosphere pervades the hotel, distinctions of rank and power remain subtly in force.

The consummate host, Ullman slides effortlessly from a discussion of travel plans with Bill Watson to a warm greeting of the new caretaker. The consummate manager, Ullman keeps everything on schedule (after all, he has an airplane to catch) without appearing to rush it. He personally takes charge of Jack for a grand tour of the hotel, while Bill is shuffled off to attend to the Torrances' luggage. Yet we see no overt evidence of arrogance in Ullman or resentment in his employees.

The Torrances' tour of Overlook is also *our* tour, once removed. A partly subjective camera travels with the characters through the hotel's rooms and corridors, but it also observes them from a discreet distance, allowing us to see more than they do. On their way to the Colorado Lounge, the group steps out of an elevator identical to the one we saw earlier in Danny's shine. Instead of disgorging a sea of blood, it opens to reveal a congenial group of people. But the emotional baggage Jack and Wendy carry deep within themselves creates, in the context of winter isolation, a potential for violence that Danny has foreseen in symbolic form.

The Colorado Lounge is a huge, elegant public room that dwarfs its occupants, to their delight. Its large "halo" light fixtures, hanging from the ceiling, are tokens of collective order and grace, like *Barry Lyndon's* chandeliers and *Dr. Strangelove's* fluorescent halo. A large American flag hangs over the entrance. The routine of closing-day clean-up and departure supplies a background hum of activity that gives Overlook the feel of a functioning institution. Later, in the *absence* of such activity, Overlook acquires the haunted atmosphere of an institutional ruin.

While escorting his guests through the Colorado Lounge, Ullman acquaints them, and us, with two different aspects of Overlook's past. Geometric patterns in the Lounge decor are based on Apache and Navajo motifs. In its long history, the hotel, a creation of predominantly European culture, incorporated elements of Native American culture into its structure for the gratification of wealthy and, at least in Overlook's early days, very likely *non*-Native American patrons.

Ullman also expounds on Overlook's less-visible charms. "In its heyday it was one of the stopping places for the jet set, even before anybody knew what a 'jet set' was." He playfully acknowledges the anachronism (there were no jets in the 1920s) of his own description of the past, which exists now only in memory and in relics. "In its heyday" implies, perhaps unwittingly, that Overlook's prestige as an institution was greater in days gone by, when the social hierarchy was more rigidly defined. Political leaders, movie stars, and especially foreign royalty (the most distant and therefore most impressive) makeup a glamorous past that captivates Wendy. Ullman's description, "all the best people," takes us back to Lord Wendover's definition of people "about whom there is no question" in *Barry Lyndon*. Tangible evidences of Overlook's past are numerous photographs hanging on walls throughout the hotel. Jack remains silent while his wife gushes over that past. But her passion is superficial and safe. His will turn out to be fanatical and dangerous.

Danny's second shine comes upon him unbidden, unlike his first. The music of Gyorgy Ligeti's "Lontano" emerges on the soundtrack as a seismic register of that experience even before Danny is consciously aware of it. Initially he is absorbed in a game of darts in Overlook's game room. A reverse zoom surrounds him with various institutional objects. Then the camera zooms in to a close-up of his face as he is overtaken by a paranormal vision. In Boulder he *summoned* such a vision. This time it arises independently of his will.

From Danny's vantage point we see the same twin girls from his earlier trance. But this time they seem more objectively real. They appear visually aligned with a red fire alarm on the wall behind them. And for Danny they function in an analogous manner, as his *private* warning of danger. But he cannot clearly discern what they portend. Their ominous silence frightens him. A sphinx-like face on a wall poster behind the girls resembles the "face" on Heywood Floyd's space shuttle in *2001*. Like advanced technology to individual man in the earlier film, the power of shining is to Danny a double-edged sword, empowering yet also potentially damaging. Before departing, the twins exchange a conspiratorial look, sharing a secret not yet accessible to Danny.

Elsewhere, Ullman introduces Wendy and Jack to their assigned living quarters in the staff wing of the hotel. Along the way, he says goodbye to two more departing employees, referring to them as "girls" while they address him as "sir." The exchange is casual and friendly but reveals an underlying social hierarchy. Until this point in their tour, the Torrances have been treated as guests. Now, without deviating from his courteous manner, Ullman gently puts them in their proper place. Even the term "quarters" denotes subservience.

Through Kubrick's mobile camera, we both share in and observe Jack and Wendy's first impressions of their rather spartan living quarters. Ullman describes it in enthusiastic salespeak, emphasizing its dubious virtues. Jack and Wendy collaborate with him to maintain an appearance of mutual satisfaction. The "small bedroom for your son" (Ullman) is "perfect for a child" (Jack). The "nicely self-contained" kitchen and master bedroom (Ullman) are "cozy," says Jack as he gives the mattress a pointlessly feeble push.

At the end of the scene, the camera becomes subjective from the point of view of Stuart Ullman, whose disembodied voice becomes a rather abstract, generic embodiment of institutional authority. The Torrances look ill at ease with their hands passively tucked in their pockets, suppressing their disappointment as they politely agree with Ullman's favorable assessment of the apartment. As during Heywood Floyd's conversation with Russian scientists, a collective spirit of decorum conceals but does not erase private differences of perception.

As he entered the apartment with Wendy and Ullman, Jack cast a discreet backward glance at two young and attractive female employees in the corridor. Like other subtle hints of his yearning for something better, this one later develops into a dangerous quest. Jack's wandering eye, innocent enough now, eventually becomes a full-blown rejection of Wendy in favor of Overlook's charms.

Outside the hotel, the Torrances are shown Overlook's hedge maze, a mammoth reconstitution of Nature by collective man for the entertainment of guests. Ullman reveals that Overlook was built over an old Indian burial site, in the face of actual Indian attacks. His casual manner reduces a once passionate cultural conflict to a trivial footnote in history. Nevertheless, he adds yet another layer to the hotel's past, which will figure, at least on a metaphorical level, in relations between Wendy and Jack.

Concluding his tour of the hotel grounds, Ullman acquaints the Torrances with a snowcat parked outside the garage. A large vehicle with broad steel tracks instead of wheels, the snowcat is a prudent institutional safeguard making it possible for the Torrances to travel the otherwise impassable road to Sidewinder during winter if the need arises. But like the CRM 114 recall code option in *Dr. Strangelove*, it presumes a unanimous desire to maintain a link between isolated individuals and distant society. Jack Torrance, like General Ripper before him, will find it to his personal advantage to subvert that emergency link.

Back inside the hotel, and leaving behind whatever disappointment they felt about their assigned living quarters, Jack and Wendy are ushered into the fabulous, recently redecorated Gold Ball Room. With each stop along the tour, we get a new angle of perspective on the hotel. Overlook is a composite of institutional fragments from different eras. Like the unannounced Soviet Doomsday Device in *Dr. Strangelove*, it is a somewhat uncoordinated and contradictory whole.

Wendy, doing a little dance step, speculates on the great party she and Jack could have in the Gold Ball Room. Ullman points out that all liquor has been removed from the premises, for insurance purposes another subtle reminder that the Torrances are employees, not guests. By coincidence, however, institutional policy in this case harmonizes with private interests. Jack reveals that he and Wendy don't drink. Ullman is pleased by this surprising accord, which makes his job less unpleasant. But he is ignorant of the reasons for the Torrances' abstinence, which we learned about earlier in the film and which if, known to Ullman, might undermine his confidence in Jack's suitability to be winter caretaker.

Standing beside the empty Ball Room bar, Jack, Wendy, Ullman, and Bill Watson makeup a collection of varied perspectives. They are joined by head chef Dick Halloran and Danny, who, like the addition of two new pieces to a chess board, expand and modify the overall arrangement. Danny secretly craves the security of his parents in the wake of his traumatic encounter with the mysterious twins. Bypassing Jack to accept Wendy's embrace, he obviously prefers the comfort of his mother. Jack asks him, "You get tired of bombing the universe, son?" referring to what might be a typical childhood diversion available in Overlook's game room. Like the sports team logo on

Danny's jacket, Jack's question counterpoints the far-from-ordinary experience that Danny actually had there. But Danny conceals that experience from
everyone around him.

With a bald head, bowed legs, and an easy manner of speech, Dick Halloran might have supplied stereotypical black comic relief in old Hollywood
movies contemporaneous with Overlook's so-called heyday. In *The Shining*
he displays intelligence, insight, compassion, and courage. Like Wendy, he is
much more than initially meets the eye. But at Overlook their social rank is
rather precariously balanced between old and new sensibilities.

Under Ullman's direction, the group splits up into smaller units. Halloran, Wendy, and Danny (black man, woman, and child) are sent off to sur-
vey the kitchen, while Ullman and Bill Watson show Jack (three adult, white
males) the rest of the hotel. There is nothing overtly sinister about this
arrangement. But the vague *outline* of an older, less egalitarian social order
occasionally shows through modern, democratic sensibilities.

The hotel kitchen is, in its own way, as imposing as the public rooms
we have seen. The camera backtracks with the characters, giving us a sense
of what Wendy and Danny experience as they wend their way between aisles
laden with utensils, scrubbed and neatly stowed away for the winter. Numerous safety devices, warning signs, and a time clock attest to the supervisory
role of institutional man.

Holding on to Danny's hand for her own security as well as his, Wendy
is understandably intimidated by the size and complexity of it all. Her comparison of the kitchen to a maze requiring a trail of breadcrumbs to navigate
it unwittingly foreshadows the physical and emotional disorientation she and
her family will experience throughout Overlook.

Halloran's public relations skills prove equal to Ullman's as he puts his
guests at ease. After making two incorrect guesses as to Wendy's familiar name
(she was introduced to him as Winifred), he diplomatically praises the correct one as the prettiest. He has also thus erased one barrier of formality
between them.

If the Donner Party is a classic example of one particular hazard of isolation from society, the Torrances obviously do not face quite the same danger. Overlook's walk-in food lockers are stocked with supplies far beyond the
needs and, as Halloran discovers, the tastes of one, small, middle-class family.

Halloran's miscalculation of Wendy's name is offset by his unaccount-
able knowledge of Danny's nickname, Doc. Reluctant to explain how he knew
about it without hearing it previously, he evades Wendy's curiosity by hiding behind his institutional assignment. Guiding his guests into a second food
locker, he recites in ritual fashion its inventory of supplies. But parallel to
this institutional recitation for Wendy's benefit, he briefly communicates on

a paranormal and intensely personal level with Danny. In close-up, the boy appears stunned by Halloran's telepathic message, the content of which is friendly while the manner of its transmission is disturbing. The sound of Halloran's voice, along with the return of "Lontano" as background music (previously established as a subjective echo of paranormal experience), counterpoints the rather comforting sight of familiar corporate brand names (including another Native American reference) on the food containers behind Danny and the familiar sports logo on his jacket.

Outside the food locker, Ullman, Jack, and Bill rejoin Wendy, Danny, and Halloran. And once again, the hotel manager sorts out a new arrangement of the characters, apologetically confiscating Wendy and Jack and leaving Danny alone with Halloran. While communicating with the boy telepathically, Halloran offered Danny ice cream to divert his attention from the shock of discovering a soulmate. He now repeats that bribe in a conventional, less disturbing manner and is doubly careful to seek permission from Danny's parents. Danny is sufficiently comfortable now to accept the offer, which in turn reassures Wendy enough to leave her precious son in Halloran's care. It is a strategically savvy performance by Overlook's head chef.

Wendy and Jack depart with their arms around each other in a display of mutual affection. Separation from Danny removes a primary source of emotional conflict between them. Coincidentally, that same separation serves Halloran's wish to forge a more intimate relationship with the boy. Stuart Ullman's larger, institutional reason for splitting up the group just happens to harmonize with Halloran's private agenda and the cause of marital contentment.

As Ullman's group walks through one of Overlook's service corridors, Wendy notes the closing-day activity around them. Ullman comments, "By five o'clock you'll never know anybody was ever here." Wendy adds, "Just like a ghost ship, huh?" Everyone shares a chuckle, reducing the eerie prospect of isolation to safe dimensions, in the same way Ullman, Jack, and Bill Watson diminished the unpleasantness of the Grady tragedy. But, as the scene ends, the camera stops tracking the group and watches them, from an emotionally detached perspective, walk away. As a result, we feel less and less amused and more uneasy at the prospect of being isolated at Overlook.

In the absence of outside interference, Halloran tries to break through Danny's defensiveness. The boy's mouth is stained with ice cream. He has accepted the bribe and is now expected to return the favor. Camera angles make Halloran look big and intimidating yet both characters fold their hands passively on the table in front of them. Faint sounds of kitchen clean-up activities occurring off screen counterpoint their intensely private conversation.

Under Halloran's careful, soothing interrogation, Danny reveals more about his relationship to Tony than he has to anyone else. He discloses that Tony's revelations come to him as though in a dream. When fully conscious, he cannot remember everything, probably because, unlike his alter ego, he cannot bear to. Halloran pumps Danny for paranormal insights about Overlook to add to his own. But that initiative backfires when Danny turns his shine on his inquisitor, sensing Halloran's own fear of the hotel. The camera registers that strategic shift by assuming a neutral angle that eliminates Halloran's visual dominance. The head chef now becomes defensive and secretive, fearing the disclosure of his own paranormal insights as much as Danny did Tony's.

Tentatively, in their developing spirit of friendship and trust, Halloran reveals his impressions of Overlook. But, whether shielding himself or Danny from their disturbing nature, he filters them through a safe analogy drawn from his own profession. Events from the past, he explains, can leave traces of themselves behind, like "burnt toast," which only people who shine can recognize. And he admits that some of the events in Overlook's past were not good. Danny cuts through Halloran's soothing voice and gutless simile to expose the root of his companion's fear. "What about Room 237?" Halloran feigns ignorance, but in the face of Danny's persistent curiosity he turns aggressively defensive. He denies that there is anything special about Room 237 — but by forcefully ordering the boy not to enter 237, he indirectly acknowledges that there is.

Unlike Mrs. Barry's during her confrontation with Reverend Runt, Halloran's highhandedness with Danny is motivated by compassion. But by trying to get at the boy's paranormal knowledge of Overlook in the first place, he inadvertently alerts Danny to some vague but sinister significance about Room 237. And that knowledge plays an important role in future relations within the Torrance family, which in turn will have a great impact on Halloran's own well-being.

In *2001* we joined the *Discovery* Mission to Jupiter three months into its voyage, at which point there were few outward signs of emotional strain among the crew. The Torrance family's stay at Overlook is joined in progress, one month after it begins, with even fewer symptoms of stress.

A variation on spaceship *Discovery*, Overlook is an artificial world set in counterpoint to the natural wilderness around it, yet sharing some of Nature's aesthetic qualities. It both shields the Torrances from and mimics the landscape surrounding it. A thin thread of smoke drifts up from its chimney — a token of the small and vulnerable lives inside. Outside, nothing else disturbs the stillness of a crisp autumn morning.

Inside Overlook, there is a striking counterpoint between private and institutional order. Wendy wheels a breakfast cart through the hotel lobby. Dressed in a robe and slippers, her hair unkempt, she is out of tune with her surroundings. The formality that governed the Torrances' attire and demeanor in Stuart Ullman's presence has, in his absence, yielded to the informality of their existence at home in their Boulder apartment. On the other hand, the hotel's spacious elegance inflates the dimensions of their domestic routine, just as military weapons and strategy inflated the private quirks of many characters in *Dr. Strangelove*. The cart Wendy uses to transport breakfast is no ordinary tray, and her journey from the kitchen to the bedroom is a long and scenic trek.

Overlook's remote location isolates the Torrance family from society at large. *Within* Overlook, size and distance isolate the Torrances from *each other*, encouraging each of them to forge a separate relationship with the hotel. Danny, tracked by a partly subjective camera, rides his tricycle through parts of the hotel, redefining various corridors and rooms as an elaborate racetrack. Traveling through utility corridors to the Colorado Lounge and back again, Danny transforms into a single circuit areas of Overlook that would ordinarily serve separate functions. For example, it is unlikely that a hotel guest would enter a service corridor or that an employee would be allowed full use of the Colorado Lounge. But in the absence of hotel management, Danny unites these distinct areas to serve a revised function. To the Torrance family, Overlook is a deserted, unsupervised institution largely thrown open to their private whims.

Danny's trek through the Colorado Lounge is also an acoustical lesson in the ironic interplay of individual and institution. As he passes over alternate stretches of carpeted and hardwood floor, the sound made by his tricycle wheels is alternately muffled and amplified. Institutional environments may either dilute or accentuate the activities of one person. In another sense, Danny's ride is analogous to Frank's shadowboxing jog around *Discovery's* sphere. Both are attempts to generate a semblance of purpose and endeavor, even competition, in an emotional void.

Upstairs, the Torrances' assigned living quarters are a slice of middle-class modesty inside a modern-day palace. Inside the apartment, we see Jack asleep in bed as Wendy enters. The camera reverse zooms until we realize we are seeing Jack as reflected in a large mirror, while Wendy appears both in the mirror and directly. Reflections are a recurring theme in *The Shining*. As *indirect* vantage points, they sometimes clarify and sometimes confuse. As viewed directly, Wendy appears an attentive wife to Jack. But, as viewed in the mirror, she hovers rather oppressively over him, which is how he will increasingly see her. The camera reverses its movement and zooms in on the reflection of Jack as he looks at himself in the mirror. He sticks out his tongue, poking fun at his own image. As the film progresses, he is less and less able to see himself with any such emotional detachment.

At the end of one month, Jack and Wendy view their stay at Overlook as a vacation from the ordinary cares of life. They seem relaxed, refreshed, and happy. Even Danny gets some enjoyment out of the hotel he was reluctant to occupy. A rustic painting over his parents' bed offers a picturesque idealization of the natural wilderness that surrounds Overlook. Yet the Torrances' troubled past lurks just beneath the surface of their tranquil present. Jack wears a monogrammed T-shirt that reads "notgnivotS" as reflected in the mirror. But, when seen directly, it reads "Stovington," which clarifies its identity. Stovington is the name of a college in Vermont, where the family's domestic problems, we learned in Boulder, first turned violent. Beneath the monogram is the imprint of a large bird of prey — a fanciful collegiate metaphor for power, but, in the present context, a harbinger of Jack's potential for violence, which is rooted in memories of Vermont. This symbolic echo of Jack's pre-Overlook discontent intrudes on the otherwise friendly dialog between husband and wife.

Jack brings the vacation atmosphere to an end by announcing his decision to return to work on his long-delayed writing project. An old-world burden, brought from Boulder, intrudes on what has been virtually a second honeymoon. Jack confesses that he has no good ideas yet for his project. Typically, Wendy trivializes his writer's block, just as she trivialized Danny's misgivings about Overlook earlier. But her efforts to reassure Jack inadvertently have the opposite effect. Munching away on "eggiwegs and lomticks" of bacon, Jack acts and sounds a bit like *Clockwork*'s Alex as he gently mocks her sugary optimism. A slight tension creeps back into their relationship.

After this brief sour note, harmony returns as husband and wife discuss their reactions to the hotel. Wendy confesses to some wariness when they first arrived. Jack, on the other hand, felt immediately at home. Thus far, the hotel has been for him an escape from his failures as a writer, a husband, and a father. But his attraction runs even deeper, verging on the mystical as he describes a strong feeling of familiarity with the hotel, as though he had been there before. Or is it that Overlook, with its potent echoes of privilege and glamour, supplies what Jack wants but has never had, just as Bible stories provided Alex with an imaginative escape route from prison? No longer reminded of his subservient status by Stuart Ullman's presence, Jack is free to appropriate Overlook for whatever use he wants, just as Danny appropriates it for a racetrack.

A teacher as well as a creative writer, Jack is reluctant to give himself up to intoxication. Just as he mocked Wendy's simplistic view of his writer's block, he pokes fun at his own attraction to the hotel, as though to reduce its influence on him. The scene ends with Wendy and him sharing a laugh about it. They have never seemed more in tune or comfortable with each other. From this point on, events will push them further and further apart, until they become bitter, violent enemies.

Trouble in paradise begins when Jack returns to work on his novel. The *sound* of that trouble erupts on the soundtrack before the laughter and smiles of the previous scene have faded. Loud bangs from off screen accompany a close-up of an unattended typewriter containing a mostly blank piece of paper. The camera slowly reverse zooms, adding details to the initial image. Surrounding the typewriter are pencils and cigarettes, the traditional tools of a writer. But no writer is in sight. Beyond the typewriter and the large, polished table on which it incongruously sits are strewn magazines and newspapers. Obviously Jack has been doing research for his novel. But some part of the creative process has failed him. As the camera frame widens, we identify the setting as the Colorado Lounge. Jack, far from his typewriter (another case of isolation, this time of a character from himself), repeatedly hurls a rubber ball against a wall. His action cuts across the grain of linear alignment established by the typewriter, chandeliers, furniture, and a grand staircase at the far end of the room, all of which contribute to a visual sense of collective order. The energy Jack wants to channel into his novel finds temporary release in a purely physical act, which, like Danny's tricycle ride, is aurally magnified by institutional surroundings.

Like Wendy wheeling a breakfast cart through the lobby, Jack is aesthetically out of sync with his surroundings. His clothing is casual, almost sloppy. And his use of a decorative wall as a backboard is one measure of the diminution of collective authority over his behavior. He would not indulge his frustration in such a manner if Stuart Ullman were present.

Jack's return to work nudges Wendy and Danny closer together in a mutual effort to ward off loneliness and boredom. Lady Lyndon and Lord Bullingdon forged a similar alliance during Barry's absence. Outside the hotel, mother and son are visually dwarfed by both institutional and natural environments. Their voices sound thin and distant in the mountain air. Their game of tag is less a competition between them than a mutual weapon against solitude.

Tag yields to the diversion of Overlook's hedge maze. As Wendy and Danny enter that maze, the camera lingers on a large sign outside. The sign features a diagram of the maze. In effect, it is the guide and solution to a mammoth puzzle designed to amuse hotel guests. The diagram is an abstract representation of what is already an abstract reshaping of Nature. Like General Turgidson's Big Board, the diagram yields an impression of clarity and mastery through visionary detachment. That such an impression is partly an illusion becomes strikingly evident when the camera cuts to Wendy and Danny inside the hedge maze and tracks with them as they encounter one confusing dead end after another. Wendy takes Danny by the hand so they don't get separated. Just as horror films in general take viewers close to an experience of terror without committing them fully to it, the hedge maze allows its guests to feel lost but not necessarily trapped.

Accompanying Wendy and Danny through the hedge maze is Bela Bartok's *Music for Strings, Percussion, and Celesta*, an unsettling piece that counterpoints their sense of fun. Coincidentally, the Bartok composition dates from approximately the same period as Overlook's so-called heyday — the period between the World Wars. Kubrick employs Bartok to create a mood and to conjure up a dead era whose sensibilities lurk within Overlook.

A forward-tracking shot of Wendy and Danny walking through the hedge maze for fun dissolves into a parallel shot of Jack ambling through the hotel's maze-like lobby in frustration, searching for a new outlet for his dammed creative powers. Bartok now echoes rather than counterpoints the character's mood. Jack slams his rubber ball against the lobby floor, ceiling, and wall, angrily striking out in three dimensions against his emotional confinement. But, increasingly, he sees Overlook as his escape from rather than a place of confinement. Discarding his rubber ball to search for a more satisfying substitute for his abandoned typewriter, he wanders through the hotel lobby, passing by several of Danny's toys strewn on the floor, likewise discarded in favor of other diversions. Then he chances upon a table-top replica of the hedge maze. The now subjective music builds to a kind of vortex, sucking us into Jack's point of view. The camera cuts to a purely subjective, overhead, zoom-in shot of what we assume to be the model. But we see and hear the tiny, moving figures of Wendy and Danny inside the maze. Jack's creative imagination combines physical reality with abstract representation, giving him, and us, a brief impression of godlike power over his wife and son, who are reduced to the equivalent of mice in a laboratory maze. The sense of masterful, comprehensive overview we got from the maze diagram in the previous scene is duplicated and modified by Jack, who gives it a sinister slant.

The camera doubles back to Wendy and Danny inside the actual hedge maze. They have reached the central court and seem pleased with their achievement. Bartok's music once again plays counterpoint to the characters. The same institutional facility (maze), in two different guises (actual maze and replica), simultaneously serves different characters in very different ways.

The title card "Tuesday" signifies nothing by itself. But, in conjunction with the previous title card, it implies a quickening pace in the flow of events at Overlook. Jack's decision to go back to work is the catalyst for change. A distant, peaceful view of the hotel registers none of that change.

Torrance family portraits in this scene reveal three isolated characters, beginning with Wendy, who struggles to open a restaurant-size can of fruit cocktail. The camera reverse zooms, placing Wendy's modest preparations for a family meal in the visual context of Overlook's massive kitchen. She has transformed a large table designed for preparing rather than serving meals into a more intimate setting for her small family. Three place settings are positioned close together at one end of the table. Occupying what amounts to a fourth place setting, and in effect blocking off the empty stretch of table to the right, is a television set broadcasting the news. TV breaks the hotel's oppressive silence and provides a comforting link to civilization. Ironically, its role as pacifier clashes with the content of its broadcast: news of a woman missing from a hunting trip with her husband in the wilderness, and the forecast of an approaching blizzard. The announcer's dispassionate and glib manner clashes with the seriousness of what is reported.

While his mother is occupied in the kitchen, Danny rides his tricycle through guest room hallways in another part of the hotel. Bartok's music returns to the soundtrack, counterpointing Danny's mood at first, then falling into sync with it as he stops to look at the door of Room 237, which moments earlier had been just an insignificant feature of his racecourse. Thanks to Halloran's reluctant revelation earlier, it now looms over him in a partly subjective, low-angle shot. He regards it with a mixture of fear and curiosity, the latter proving stronger. Glancing around to make sure he is not being watched, Danny approaches the forbidden door and tries to open it. Like his father, the boy takes advantage of isolation to defy institutional authority.

At the far end of the corridor hangs a red fire alarm — an institutional safety device and a metaphorical echo of Halloran's warning to stay out of Room 237. Though Danny ignores his friend's warning, he is prevented from entering the room by a locked door and by his own, internal, paranormal alarm. The camera cuts away briefly to his unsettling vision. By shining on the twins while trying to enter Room 237, Danny adds his own fear of Overlook (the twins) to the fear (of 237) he sensed in Halloran. He returns to his tricycle and races down the hall. No longer riding just for the fun of it, he flees a dreaded unknown. The camera, remaining stationary, does not participate in his flight. For a moment it and we *become* that dreaded unknown.

The third movement of this Torrance family sonata is a portrait of Jack in splendid isolation, apparently working on his novel in the Colorado Lounge. We enter the Lounge by passing through an opening in a wall covered with framed photographs from the hotel's fabled past. Jack, framed by the doorway, appears for a moment as just another picture out of that long history. Above his head hangs one of the hotel's round light fixtures, like a royal crown. But from a different camera angle, we get an ominous, symbolic hint of what may be occupying Jack's creative imagination. Visible behind him are the features of an elevator similar to the one in Danny's first shine. Its "eyes" frame Jack's head, which is situated where the elevator doors would be — the same type of doors from which a torrent of blood poured out in Danny's vision.

The camera cuts back to its prior position, recapturing the majestic symmetry of Jack's private sanctuary, which is then spoiled by Wendy's arrival. He stops typing. Wendy's dress, moccasin-like shoes, and black hair give her the vague appearance of a Native American woman. And for the first time in the film, Jack treats her as an inferior. The racial analogy in their conflict is an oblique reference to Overlook's and America's institutional past.

Though her hands are passively stuffed into her pockets, Wendy arrives as an intruder in Jack's world, unaware that he has staked a private, territorial claim to the Colorado Lounge. He conceals his literary work from her view. The only visible clue to its content is an open scrapbook full of newspaper clippings, possibly concerning the Delbert Grady incident. The extent to which relations between husband and wife have deteriorated comes as a complete shock to Wendy. Pleasurable small talk, such as they enjoyed up in their apartment, is no longer possible. Jack interprets her casual remark about the approaching storm as an annoying request for him to do something about it. Still unaware of the intensity of his hostility, Wendy tries to kid him into a better mood. He *chooses* to take offense at that attempt. Inhibitions that earlier kept him from openly expressing his dislike of her are dissipating. And in a deserted Overlook, there is no one else to reinforce them. Jack's expressions of anger and contempt are tempered a little by fitful attempts at self-restraint. Malevolent grins, head slaps, paper tearing, exaggerated typing, and verbal sarcasm (all indirect acts of aggression aimed at Wendy) are countered by averted eyes, a shrug, a clearing of the throat, and the smoothing of hair.

In the absence of outside authority, Jack redefines the Colorado Lounge as his throne room, then banishes Wendy from it as if she were a lowly peasant. So passionate is his declaration of sovereign rights there that he literally runs out of breath in his rush to define and then redefine them. The Colorado Lounge is now his equivalent to Alex's locked bedroom in *Clockwork*. With a regal wave of his hand he dismisses Wendy from his presence. His use of profanity during this encounter marks his sloughing off of one, albeit trivial, layer of collective restraint that governed him earlier. The camera returns to the position it occupied when Wendy entered. The scene's original outward appearance is restored. But in emotional terms there has been a radical change.

The title card "Thursday" indicates a further acceleration, from weeks to days, in the pace of significant developments at Overlook. Expelled from Jack's world, Wendy consoles herself with her son's. She and Danny play a game of tag outside the hotel, as they did earlier. But the environment has changed. Heavy snow now blankets and obscures everything. Piled high on the roof and creeping up the outer walls, it has all but buried Overlook's once imposing facade. Outside, at least, Nature has overwhelmed and redefined the hotel. Nevertheless, Wendy and Danny adapt well to the blizzard, incorporating it into their game of tag by adding a snowball fight. The hotel snowcat sits outside the garage, implying recent use. It, the characters' heavy winter clothing, and the warm, well-provisioned interior of the hotel are all resources that render the storm a relatively manageable phenomenon, at least in physical terms.

Ligeti's "Lontano" rises on the soundtrack, echoing the overwhelming whiteness of the snow and playing against Wendy and Danny's spirit of fun.

But when the camera cuts to a shot of Jack inside the Colorado Lounge, the music seems to fit *his* mood. Dressed in black, standing stock-still, Jack appears absorbed in a private fantasy, the passion of which is reflected by a fire in the Lounge fireplace. Behind him, on the wall, we see a symbolic array of nearly all of Overlook's influences on him. A slow zoom-in to Jack's face takes us closer to his private reverie. Unlike Danny's paranormal visions, we get no subjective glimpse into Jack's mind. But the cruel pleasure of his classic Kubrick glare hints at the nature of his daydream. His unshaven whisker stubble suggests a further slide away from social norms established in earlier scenes. He would not have shown up for the Ullman interview with whisker stubble on his face. In a different situation, whisker stubble could just as easily be interpreted as a token of *liberation* from stifling social conformity. Only in the context of Jack's growing hostility towards his family does the stubble seem an ominous harbinger of change.

"Saturday" propels us another two days forward into the Torrance family's odyssey through a winter at Overlook. Another remote establishing shot of the hotel illustrates a significant change in Overlook's relationship to Nature. Barely visible through the falling snow, it now appears a fragile and precious outpost of humanity. Only from *inside* does it seem like a prison, where cabin fever is beginning to take a toll on the inhabitants.

Another series of isolated family portraits commences. Jack sits in the Colorado Lounge, presumably typing his new novel. But out in the lobby his wife is clearly uncomfortable with *her* situation at Overlook. Behind the front desk she works the telephone switchboard to contact the outside world for the first time since the Torrances arrived. Visible nearby are numerous, thick telephone directories — further evidence of an impressive communications network that the individual often takes for granted until circumstances highlight its importance. In *Dr. Strangelove*, Captain Mandrake almost saved the world from nuclear obliteration by means of a pay phone. But that same network fails Wendy now. The blizzard has disrupted telephone service.

Wendy walks briskly and purposefully from the front desk to Stuart Ullman's office, looking nothing like the ignorant child Jack made her out to be in the Colorado Lounge. But the cigarette in her hand betrays her nervousness, as it did in Boulder, and her buckskin jacket reinforces the metaphorical role of enemy she is being forced to play in Jack's Overlook production.

Inside Ullman's office, Wendy employs a citizen's band radio to circumvent broken telephone lines. Identifying herself as KDK-12, she contacts the nearest U.S. Forest Service Office, appropriately designated KDK-1 because it is a *center* of institutional power and information. A uniformed ranger answers her call, confirming her suspicion about the downed telephone lines. Snow that previously enhanced her game of tag with Danny is now an inconvenience, if not yet a threat. Wendy prolongs the phone call, engaging the ranger in small talk to relieve her solitude, which is aggravated by the howl of the storm outside. Recognizing the shift from business to chitchat, the ranger politely nudges the call to a conclusion, leaving Wendy with a promise of easy future access to him by telling her to keep her radio switched on all the time.

While speaking to the Forest Service, Wendy casually props one of her feet against Ullman's desk — an unwitting and trivial violation of the decorum that governed her behavior in Ullman's presence. Thus, Wendy simultaneously solicits and defies collective order.

Music *anticipates* Danny's situation as he rides his tricycle elsewhere in the hotel. The camera, too, foreshadows danger, initially tracking the boy from a distance, picturing him small and vulnerable, before joining him at close range as he veers from corridor to corridor. Florid wallpaper in the hotel's staff wing should alert him to what lies ahead, because it matches the wallpaper in his previous vision of the twins. But he fails to recognize it and is therefore taken by complete surprise when he encounters them, standing hand in hand at the far end of a hallway. We alternately share in his shock and scrutinize his reaction.

As they do in each successive appearance, the twins add to their identity. For the first time they speak: "Hello, Danny. Come and play with us." But the creepy, other-worldly tone of that otherwise welcome invitation renders it menacing. Worse yet, one paranormal image is split by another from a different time. The girls' invitation is juxtaposed repeatedly with the sight of their butchered, bloody corpses lying in the same corridor. An offer of companionship thus becomes an invitation to death.

Danny reflexively withdraws from the horror by covering his eyes with his hands. Then he peeks out between his fingers at the corridor, which now appears empty. His tactic works, suggesting that his monsters are self-generated. But he still looks bleary eyed and haunted, like Dave Bowman after his epic trip into the Unknown. Though alerting him to danger, Danny's strange power is also an emotional burden. Changing his voice and facial expression, he calls on his emotional thermostat for reassurance. Tony reduces the horror of the dead girls to manageable dimensions: "It's just like pictures in a book, Danny. It isn't real." But Danny's fear is not entirely dispelled. Tony's unruffled facial expression partly reverts back to that of a frightened little boy as Danny casts a final, wary glance down the hallway.

Two more days pass. A television screen shows an excerpt from the 1971 film *Summer of '42*. The camera slowly reverse zooms, adding layers of context to the central image. The television picture is surrounded by the blizzard, visible through large windows in the background. The muted howl of wind competes with dialog from the movie. Impressions of the storm are, in turn, framed and held at bay by the sturdy architecture of Overlook's lobby.

Three distinct layers of environment (the storm, the hotel, and society at large as represented by the telecast) are juxtaposed.

Retreating further, the camera brings Danny and Wendy into the picture. Physically sheltered from the storm by Overlook, they in turn employ the television as an emotional shield against the deserted hotel. Though almost any program could have served as a diversion, the choice of *Summer of '42* furnishes a loose analogy to the situation of the Torrances. A budding romance between characters played by Gary Grimes and Jennifer O'Neill results from their separate but complementary needs. Older woman and younger boy meet in the absence of her husband, who was killed in a war. Jack's absence, for very different reasons, strengthens the bond between Wendy and Danny. *Summer of '42* postulates a healthy if bittersweet encounter set in the idyllic isolation of an island cabin. *The Shining* offers a more dangerous alternative in which the conveniently absent third party stages a violent return.

Less interested in the movie than is his mother, Danny requests permission to retrieve a toy from the apartment upstairs, where Jack is sleeping. Wendy is reluctant to let him go, but equally reluctant to expose him to her fear. So she invents a safe, phony objection, insisting that Jack needs his rest and must not be disturbed. Danny forces the issue until she gives in. But, to enhance his safety, she tells him to make as little noise as possible and to hurry back because it is almost time to eat. Lunch is *not* her real concern.

The only "loud" thing about Danny's entrance into the apartment is the incongruously jolly figure of Mickey Mouse imprinted on his sweatshirt. The haunting moan of the storm seems to penetrate further and further into Overlook with each passing scene, coincidentally reinforcing the background Bartok music that echoes Danny's anxiety about encountering his father — whose instability the boy's shine alerted him to long before Wendy tried to conceal it from him.

Instead of sleeping, Jack sits, staring, on the edge of his bed. Frozen awake by emotional contradictions brewing inside him, he slowly turns his head to look at his son. From a position near Jack, we see Danny in the distance looking small and vulnerable, surrounded by two images of Jack, one of them a reflection in a mirror. In looking at Danny, Jack seems to interact with his own reflection. To an ever greater extent, Danny and Wendy are becoming fictional projections of Jack's own guilt, anger, frustration, and despair.

The encounter between father and son yields conflicting impressions. Jack's attempts to show affection for Danny are unwittingly undercut by his grotesque mannerisms. Danny, meanwhile, passively yields to his father's whims, trying not to upset him but also gently probing for Jack's feelings about the hotel while keeping his own hidden. Expressing fondness for Overlook, Jack adds, "I wish we could stay here forever and ever and ever," echoing the twins' ghoulish invitation. Danny's shine anticipated the direction of Jack's thoughts and emotions by way of his own counterparts — the dead Grady girls. His next question arises out of his insight into what happened to the twins: "You would never hurt Mommy or me, wouldja?" Jack, however, interprets it according to his own perspective, which is different from Danny's. "Did your mother ever say that to you?" is more a statement of suspicion than a question. Danny's denial satisfies him, for the moment. But a seed has been planted. Jack's feelings of guilt over the injury he once inflicted on Danny is being given Wendy's face. Like Halloran's interrogation of Danny, the boy's of his father backfires.

Two more days pass. The storm continues. An overhead close-up shows Danny playing with his toy cars and trucks on the floor in one of the hotel's guest wings. His godlike perspective recalls Jack's overhead view of the hedge maze replica many scenes ago. But whereas the music of Bartok echoed the power of Jack's dark vision, Penderecki's "The Awakening of Jacob" counterpoints Danny's lightheartedness — until his playtime is interrupted.

The camera reverse zooms to place Danny and his pretend roadway within the larger, maze-like pattern of the carpet. A subjective shot becomes an objective shot. Then, mysteriously, a white billiard ball rolls into the frame from off screen, traveling along a strip of carpet Danny's imagination had redefined as a road. Intruding on his playtime, the ball may be something from Danny's own mind, of which he was unaware and therefore does not control. Like the last paranormal appearance of the twin girls, it takes him by surprise, counterpointing the comfortably familiar Apollo imprint on his sweater.

Danny's first assumption is that the ball came from his mother, who has been his only playmate since the film began. A red fire alarm on the wall behind Danny is a prudent institutional safety device, but useless in his present situation. He walks in the direction from which the ball came until he encounters the unlocked, open door of Room 237. The lights inside are on. Danny calls out, "Mom, are you in there?"

Who unlocked Room 237 remains a mystery. "The Awakening of Jacob" suggests that we have entered another of Danny's paranormal visions, each of which reveals more than its predecessor. The billiard ball is his own curiosity, luring him into a revelation for which he is not emotionally prepared. Disobeying Halloran's order, Danny enters the forbidden room. We do so with him via a subjective camera. Then that camera transports us elsewhere before we see what awaits inside. Subsequent events suggest that Danny's keen perception has plugged into Jack Torrance's concurrent nightmare, which, as we later discover, involves a threat to the boy's life.

The family status report shifts to Wendy. Dressed in work clothes, clipboard in hand, she inspects the hotel boilers. Unofficially, caretaker duties have shifted from Jack, who is increasingly preoccupied with private concerns, to Wendy, who is more conscientious about duty.

"The Awakening of Jacob" carries over from Danny's paranormal episode and counterpoints Wendy's routine maintenance work. Unknown to her and to us, the music foreshadows an overreach other than Danny's. Cries of alarm filter down to Wendy through Overlook's maze of corridors. She gradually sets aside her institutional task for a private concern. The faintness of the cries and the amount of time it takes Wendy to identify and act on them are measures of the great distances, physical and emotional, separating the Torrances within the huge hotel.

The source of the cries is Jack, slumping unconscious at his writing table in the Colorado Lounge. He has fallen asleep while typing and, in turn, fallen prey to a nightmare. Creative energy that should be channeled through his typewriter and into fiction finds release elsewhere. He calls out in alarm. While dreaming, Jack is less inhibited than when he is conscious, yet his conscience rebels against the violent content of that dream. His inarticulate protests are analogous to the various fire alarms and warning signs on display throughout the hotel and are viscerally echoed by the music.

Tracked by the camera, Wendy answers Jack's alarm signal. He awakens. Disoriented, he drools on the floor — a brief loss of motor control in keeping with Kubrick's policy of not glamorizing his character's exhibitions of weakness. Jack glances around in wild-eyed confusion. Visually, he is hemmed in by the writing table that looms over him. Writer's block, we eventually learn, is still a major cause of his frustration. On the other hand, a row of historical photographs on a wall far behind him figuratively points a way out of his creative dead end. They follow a stairway leading up to other regions of the hotel, where other possibilities await him. As an institutional structure, Kubrick's Overlook resembles Giovanni Battista Piranesi's *The Prisons*. Each chamber contains numerous exits which hint at liberation yet merely lead to other places of confinement. Dave Bowman eventually frees himself from *his* self-made prison. Jack Torrance cannot escape the grasp of Overlook and tries to trap two other people there with him.

Wendy's arrival draws a curious response from Jack. She comforts him, but his first reaction to the sight of her, before he regains full control over his faculties, is one of disgust. He is still too immersed in the emotions of his dream to see her as a compassionate ally rather than a repulsive victim. But his disgust quickly passes. Recoiling from the moral horror of it, Jack confesses to Wendy his as yet only imagined crime of murdering and mutilating her and Danny. Emotional burdens of Jack's past and present resolve themselves, if only in a dream and under protest, in violence modeled after a piece of hotel history — the Grady tragedy. Neither Jack nor Wendy are aware of the connection.

The last time Wendy entered the Colorado Lounge she did so, unwittingly, as an intruder. Jack all but threw her out and told her not to return. This time her presence harmonizes with his desire to escape from a self-generated nightmare. Their reconciliation is analogous to that of Barry and Lady Lyndon, which occurred in the absence of Lord Bullingdon. Though circumstances in the two films differ, Danny's arrival in the Colorado Lounge proves as disruptive as Bullingdon's appearance at a recital proved to be in the earlier film. The camera tracks with the boy as he enters the Lounge. For the first time since they were left alone at Overlook, all three family members appear in the same place at the same time, bringing with them all of their accumulated emotional baggage.

From our position behind Danny, we cannot see details of what he brings to the gathering. And from the other side, Wendy is too far away to see them as well. Preoccupied with Jack's problem, she tries to shield Danny from it and to shield Jack from their son's ill-timed intrusion. Telling Danny that his father just has a headache reduces Jack's condition to something ordinary and safe. Wendy tells her son to go play in his room, then leaves Jack's side to reinforce that command when Danny does not obey. "I'll be right back," she reassures her husband. But when she approaches Danny and notices his injury, she reasons, incorrectly, that Jack is responsible for it. Her promise to "be right back" evaporates. Suddenly she is no longer her husband's ally. What began as a shot of Danny in the foreground, while Jack and Wendy huddled together in the background becomes a shot of mother and son in the foreground with Jack isolated in the distance. Subjective music revives on the soundtrack, but this time it is linked to Wendy's point of view rather than Danny's. Later, when mother and son depart, it plugs into Jack's.

After his traumatic experience in Room 237, Danny seeks out his parents for security, not because he wants to drive a wedge between them. Entirely by accident he enters in this scene as an agent of destruction, shattering the family's last chance for a peaceful reconciliation. Staring vacantly and sucking his thumb, he cannot verbally describe what he experienced in 237. Therefore Wendy draws her own conclusion about the bruises on his neck, constructing a false explanation rooted in previous family experiences. In an earlier scene, Danny aggravated Jack's resentment of Wendy by speaking. In this scene, he aggravates Wendy's suspicion of Jack by *not* speaking.

The camera reverses position to a partly subjective shot from behind Jack. Wendy and Danny appear as far-off allies as she accuses Jack of injuring their son. Now it is *Jack* who cannot speak, failing to challenge Wendy's false impression. His prior confession about the content of his nightmare, which helped break through the emotional barrier he previously erected between them, now fuels her suspicion of him, in effect creating a new barrier. Wendy angrily flees the Colorado Lounge with Danny in her arms. As

A brief chance for family reconciliation turns sour as Wendy Torrance (Shelley Duvall) mistakenly blames husband Jack for injuries to their son, Danny (Danny Lloyd).

he sits helpless on what was his throne, Jack's expression of perplexity changes to one of anger. There is no objective evidence that he is directly responsible for what happened to Danny in Room 237. On the other hand, Wendy's assumption that he is, based on Jack's past behavior and recent dream, is not unreasonable.

The confluence of the Torrances' separate perspectives at this particular time dooms their future relations. Failure of communication is a common Kubrick theme, and the Colorado Lounge scene is a prime example of it. None of the characters involved consciously promotes or benefits from the misunderstanding that occurs. And the pity of it is that the same ingredients which produce that misunderstanding hold a great potential for family healing. A golden opportunity is sadly lost, as it was in *Clockwork* when Alex offered some spare change to the old Tramp.

After the rare convergence of all three Torrances in the Colorado Lounge, the family splits up again. Wendy and Danny go off in one direction, Jack in another. Looking angry and unkempt, he strolls through an elegant corridor and into the Gold Ball Room, following the same route as during Stuart Ullman's guided tour but under vastly different circumstances. Muttering something about "me" and "you," a stark characterization of the basic conflict between the Self and the Other, he spasmodically lashes out with his arms in anger. The music in this scene remains subjective, consisting of two layers: one, a steady note of high emotional tension, and the other an almost seismographic register of Jack's physical outbursts.

The maze that is Overlook opens up new possibilities at every turn. With the simple flip of a light switch, the Gold Ball Room becomes a vibrant new haven for Jack. Everything in the place has a golden, rather abstract appearance. But in addition to the absence of guests and the anachronism of his own sloppy appearance, Jack's illusion of paradise is marred by the lack of liquor. He bellies up to an empty, untended bar and pleads rhetorically for a drink. Having one would violate the pledge he made to Wendy after injuring Danny. But insurance safeguards mentioned earlier by Stuart Ullman coincidentally reinforce that pledge. Jack complains to himself, "God, I'd give anything for a drink," and covers his eyes with his hands to blot out the unpleasant reality of empty liquor shelves behind the bar. Danny used the same method to escape his unpleasant vision of the murdered twins. One character sees too much in Overlook, the other not quite enough. When Danny peeked out between his fingers, the gory image of death was gone. When Jack looks up, he likewise sees something more to his liking. But rather than escape a product of his own mind, he manufactures one to replace a reality that does not please him. Background music attuned to Jack's mood fades out and is displaced by the moan of winter wind. But while the soundtrack shifts into an objective if complementary mode, imagery becomes increasingly subjective.

During his nightmare in the Colorado Lounge, Jack was torn apart by violently opposing emotions. When he now declares rhetorically, "I'd sell my goddamn soul for just a glass of beer," the stage is set for another internal confrontation. He lowers his hands from his eyes, looks straight into the camera, which is aligned with a mirror behind the bar, and greets a bartender named Lloyd. We assume he is talking to an imaginary, invisible bartender. But a change in the camera angle reveals a visible Lloyd standing in front of a fully stocked liquor case as radiantly lit by the "light of heavenly grace" as Alex's sex object on the Ludovico stage in *Clockwork*. And when the camera pulls back, Lloyd and Jack, or character and author, appear together in the same shot. Subjective and objective impressions become intertwined and confused.

Lloyd is a composite drawn from two different sources: Overlook's glamorous heyday and Jack's private past. Immaculately groomed and costumed, speaking respectfully and with professional detachment, Lloyd seems to hail from the old school, when servants knew their place. Through him, Jack cultivates the illusion of a privileged life in Overlook's class-conscious past. But in addition to being a product of Jack's desires, Lloyd also bears the stamp of Jack's *fear* of unrestrained desire. His Mephistophilian features are drawn by the stubborn critic in Jack that is not yet consumed by anger, frustration, and wish-fulfilling fantasy. Lloyd first appears in front of the mirror where Jack's reflection should be. Though it becomes less and less apparent to him, Jack is conversing with himself. And just as he employed sarcasm to intimidate Wendy, he uses it now to mock the fantasy he both needs and fears. "A little slow tonight, isn't it?" challenges the reality of that fantasy by pointing out the absence of other patrons in the room. Lloyd, however, remains unflappable. An adult male who lends passive support to Jack's resentment of Wendy and Danny, the bartender is a perfect ally for his creator's darkest urges. With Lloyd, Jack indulges in the most shameless, chauvinistic and simplistic assertions on a variety of topics.

Jack refers to the liquor now available to him as "white man's burden," which is an ambivalent literary nod to Rudyard Kipling and the Victorian notion of Europe's duty to civilize the "uncivilized," nonwhite world. It foreshadows the racism that will later color Jack's relationship with Dick Halloran. But it also suggests that Jack, for the moment, recognizes booze as something of a curse. In either case, Jack lifts his glass of bourbon in defiance of Wendy, Danny, Stuart Ullman, and his own better judgment. The intense pleasure of his fantasy is written on his face as he tastes his first drink in five months. His upturned eyes and facial expression recall Alex's during fantasies of sadistic violence. Lloyd slyly extends Jack a line of credit for the liquor. He is, in part, an instrument by which Jack deflects his own guilt about drinking and other matters. He is to Jack what the Doomsday Machine, HAL, and the Ludovico Technique are to their respective masters — a tool that eventually gets out of hand.

Through conversation with the bartender, Jack reduces some of the painful issues in his life to manageable terms. He relegates Wendy to the status of "old sperm bank," diminishing any moral challenge she might make to his authority. Lloyd agreeably distills Jack's views into the hoariest of male clichés: "Women. Can't live with 'em. Can't live without 'em." Jack compliments the bartender on his wisdom, but the sarcasm in his voice suggests that part of him still recognizes crap when he hears it.

With Lloyd's soothing help, Jack picks away at unpleasant memories until he reaches the wound that Wendy so rudely reopened in the previous scene. The depth of Jack's guilty feelings about dislocating Danny's arm is evident from his tortuous attempts to excuse his violent behavior. At first, he denies hurting the boy. Then, blaming Wendy for reminding him of it, he admits doing so. It is obvious that, with or without Wendy's contribution,

Jack has never forgiven *himself* for the incident. Wendy is made to bear the burden of guilty feelings he cannot face.

"I did hurt him once, okay," is an admission of responsibility spoken so broadly, with hands outstretched in an exaggerated gesture of innocence, that it is as much an attempt to minimize as to acknowledge the incident. And Jack's subsequent description of the dirty deed is a ludicrous clash of understatement and sudden outbursts of anger in which he comes close to reenacting the crime. Academic, scientific jargon usually applied to inanimate phenomena renders his dislocation of Danny's shoulder into a painless abstraction. But the critic still alive in Jack compels him to mock the absurdity of his own defense.

Out of the same objective portion of the soundtrack on which is heard the muted howl of the blizzard, which coincidentally reinforces Jack's fantasy, now comes the sound of Wendy screaming, which has the opposite effect. As she enters the Ball Room, we see Jack seated at the bar, facing forward, as though still engaged with Lloyd. But neither the bartender nor the liquor is visible to us, suggesting that both are products of Jack's imagination. Only when Wendy touches his shoulder does Jack emerge from his fantasy.

Carrying her son's baseball bat (a toy redeployed as a weapon), Wendy tells Jack that a "crazy woman" in one of the rooms tried to strangle Danny. The boy's delayed explanation of the bruises on his neck causes Wendy to revise her opinion of Jack. Instead of accusing him of child abuse, she now recruits him for the traditional role of family protector.

In *The Shining* television is a collective instrument of communication, connecting the individual to society at large. It was part of Wendy and Danny's routine in Boulder. At Overlook, it has helped them combat feelings of isolation. Now, in sunny Florida, it connects vacationing Dick Halloran to events back in storm-ravaged Colorado.

A slow reverse zoom neatly frames a television newscast between Dick Halloran's reclining feet and a pair of table lamps in his bedroom. He peers out at the world from the comfortable confines of his private sanctuary. A reaction shot of his face illustrates the dispassionate nature of his attention. Like General Turgidson barricaded in his bedroom in *Dr. Strangelove*, Halloran's personal contentment does not easily yield to external concerns. A news story about Colorado's blizzard does not of itself move Halloran, but it seems to trigger his paranormal insight, which, like Colonel Puntridge's phone call to Turgidson, alerts him to trouble. And, judging by his facial expression, the intensity of his shine overwhelms him.

If Halloran's bedroom is in some respects analogous to Turgidson's, it also shares something with Alex's in *Clockwork*. Portraits of nude African-American women in alluring poses grace the walls. Though compassionate and even heroic in his actions on behalf of Danny and Wendy, Overlook's head chef is not immune to the same natural urges which in Alex and Jack Torrance become virulently chauvinistic.

Our return to Overlook's Room 237 involves a complicated synthesis of separate perspectives that is difficult to sort out. We enter the room through a purely subjective camera. But subjective from whose point of view? Halloran's, shining all the way from Florida? A cut-away shot of Danny, sitting up in bed and helplessly absorbed in another paranormal episode, suggests another possibility. "The Awakening of Jacob," linked to Danny's previous entry into the forbidden room, returns to the soundtrack. But overlapping the music is a heartbeat which began with Halloran's shine on events at Overlook.

The art deco splendor of 237's decor harkens back to Overlook's heyday. Penetrating the mystery one layer further than we did earlier, we enter a bathroom that is an art deco shrine. At the far end of the room is the bathtub, half concealed by a shower curtain. Does Danny's "crazy woman" lurk behind it? Is this a bizarre reversal of *Psycho's* shower scene? A reaction shot informs us that it is Jack, in response to Wendy's plea, who has entered Room 237. His is a third vantage point overlapping those of Danny and Halloran, who shine on the event from afar. The contradictory expectations of all three characters mingle as a figure steps out from behind the shower curtain, in dreamlike slow motion.

At first, Jack's *desires* shape what we see. The mysterious denizen of Room 237 is an attractive young woman. The metaphorical incarnation of Overlook, she moves in a smooth, sophisticated manner and has a cool facial expression the opposite of Wendy's. Jack, initially influenced by Wendy's report of what Danny encountered in 237, is pleasantly surprised. His wariness changes to grinning lust.

Beautifully illuminated from overhead, the woman is framed within a proscenium arch formed by a decorative green stripe on the wall behind her. When Jack moves forward to join her under the light and inside the green arch, the camera remains stationary. A subjective shot thus becomes partly objective — only *partly* because the woman remains a product of Jack's fantasy. The camera's new detachment allows us to see the marriage of individual and institution as imperfect. The slovenly Jack makes an incongruous lover for the embodiment of Overlook's stylish, elitist past, just as he seemed unsuited to the lavish Gold Ball Room and its bartender.

When Jack and his ideal woman embrace and kiss, the camera cuts to a close-up of them. Jack's eyes are closed; he is blinded by pleasure. On the soundtrack, musical alarms go off, echoing the concerns of Danny and Halloran. Only when Jack opens his eyes and sees himself and his Overlook lover *in*directly, as reflections in a mirror across the room, do he and we view his fantasy as a nightmare instead of a wish fulfillment. Subjectively, the camera pans in the direction of Jack's critical gaze. What was a beautiful young woman is now a rotting old corpse. Brought to life by Jack's fascination with the hotel, the spirit of Overlook is transformed into a hideous, mocking omen by a part of Jack that still fears being seduced by the hotel's charms. Pursued by this monster, with ghoulish laughter and open arms, Jack backs out of his fantasy just as he scared himself awake from his dream of murdering Danny and Wendy.

The camera crosscuts to Danny, shining on Jack's activity from his own bedroom. Jack's flight from one apparition of Overlook is interspliced with images of a similar but not quite identical apparition: a dead, decaying old woman rising up from the bathtub, presumably to strangle Danny. For a moment, father and son share a dread of the hotel. Or do they? Are we seeing Jack's tour of Room 237 through the filter of Danny's shine, and perhaps Danny's in turn through Halloran's? Jack's experience of 237 may be twice removed from our perception of it. How much of the rotting corpse is *Halloran's* contribution to this mix of perspectives?

Like Danny's, Halloran's paranormal insights are limited. So he employs an institutional tool, the telephone, to supplement them. But the phone lines to Overlook are down due to the storm. So, like President Muffley and Wendy Torrance, Halloran pursues alternate routes to his goal.

In the Torrances' Overlook apartment, Wendy wears a sweater with Indian motifs on it, reinforcing the historical parallel of her antagonistic relationship to Jack. But when Jack returns from his exploration of Room 237, he seems at first more an ally than an enemy. As he enters the apartment, we see both Jack and his reflection in a mirror on the wall. Like the temptress in 237, he has a double personality. He reassures and comforts Wendy, but there is madness in his method.

In the Colorado Lounge, Wendy and Danny unwittingly ganged up on a vulnerable Jack. Now he quietly maneuvers to divide them, closing Danny's bedroom door, discrediting the "crazy woman" story the boy told earlier, and suggesting that Danny caused his own injuries. Meanwhile, the terrified boy eavesdrops on his parents' conversation. A paranormal warning, typically abstract and convoluted, flashes subjectively on the screen. "Redrum" ("murder" spelled backwards and with a reversed letter), scrawled in red on a door, is disguised just enough to blunt its emotional impact.

Jack's attempt to drive a wedge between mother and son by explaining Danny's injuries as self-inflicted backfires when Wendy, accepting that explanation, concludes that Danny must be gotten away from Overlook, which is the foundation of Jack's security. Danny's bloody vision of a hotel elevator anticipates his father's reaction by seconds. Jack turns on Wendy, accusing her of plotting to ruin his life. Stunned by his sudden change of attitude, she cannot defend herself. As Jack storms out of the apartment, he glances malevolently at the camera, which stands directly between him and Danny's bedroom. If Wendy is Jack's immediate foe, Danny is the more deeply rooted demon — a living reminder of Jack's failure as a father. By its positioning, the camera momentarily makes us the target of Jack's hatred. Reunited by the fiction of Room 237's "crazy woman," the Torrances once again split apart as a result of their conflicting interpretations of her. Wendy, overwhelmed by the confusion of it all, sits crying on her bed. On the wall behind her hangs the now bitterly ironic portrait of Nature that once matched her experience of Overlook as a paradise.

Striding through a service corridor and accompanied by a backtracking camera, Jack sweeps tidy stacks of utensils to the floor. Previous neglect of his caretaker duties has degenerated further into outright vandalism. Yet Overlook's glittering past serves him as a means of escape from his private troubles. And its charms become ever more seductively convincing. This time, unlike Lloyd, they arise unbidden, which is to say independently of his will but not of his desires. From Jack's vantage point, the hotel lobby appears littered with party favors and the air is filled with period music. Thousands of miles away, Halloran solicits the help of the same government agency Wendy contacted earlier. The only difference between the U.S. Forest Service in this scene and an earlier one is that Halloran is served by a different ranger than was Wendy. The uniform and the professionalism remain the same. The ranger promises to contact Overlook for Halloran using his CB radio.

Back at Overlook, Jack strolls towards the Gold Ball Room, just as he did several scenes ago. But this time the corridor is fogged with cigarette smoke and permeated by a song from the 1920s entitled "Midnight with the Stars and You." Each time Jack fantasizes about the hotel's past, he creates a more detailed and convincing version. Jack glances inside the Ball Room entrance and away from a mirror on the wall opposite. The last time he looked *into* a mirror, in the bathroom of Room 237, it gave him a detached and critical view of the hotel's corrupting influence on him. This time he ignores self-examination in favor of self-indulgence.

Inside the Gold Ball Room, the decor described by Stuart Ullman as of recent vintage remains unchanged, yet the room is full of patrons in fancy period costumes from the 1920s. A more jarring anachronism is Jack, whose sloppy appearance clashes with everything and everyone around him. But because this is *his* party, literally his creation, no one seems to mind. He is greeted with deference by the doorman and gleefully soaks up the festive atmosphere.

During Jack's previous visit to the bar, the matter of payment for drinks was deferred. This time Jack comes prepared to pay in cash, which precipitates a subtle crisis between him and Lloyd. The bartender insists, "Your money's no good here. Orders from the House." So the "House" is now dictating the terms of Jack's fantasy. A metaphor for Overlook, the "House" is

Jack Torrance (Jack Nicholson, left) mocks his own fantasy world, presided over by demonic bartender Lloyd (Joe Turkel).

that part of Jack which desperately needs the illusion of liquor and of membership in elite society. The more conscientious part of Jack tries to maintain control over that need. "I'm the kinda guy likes to know who's buying the drinks, Lloyd." The bartender, in an act of self-preservation, refuses to reveal the buyer. If Jack's fantasy dies, so does Lloyd. The very foundation of Jack's grand illusion is threatened by this internal debate between fragments of his increasingly divided mind. Faust challenges Mephistopheles, then blinks. Jack relents.

Reveling in but not yet completely *of* Overlook's glamorous past, Jack lumbers inelegantly across the dance floor. Then an anonymous waiter, sidestepping one of the other patrons, bumps into him, spilling a drink over his cheap jacket. It is a trivial accident, but there is a hidden significance to this encounter. Having just lost a battle of wills to Lloyd, Jack is about to suffer the same at the hands of yet another of his fanciful characters.

Playing tolerant superior, Jack forgives the waiter for his clumsiness. He even dubs his new character "Jeeves," a stereotypical name for manservants back in the hoary old days of high society, as depicted in countless movies and novels. And as they head for the "gentlemen's room" to wash out the stain, Jeeves plays along with that class distinction. "That doesn't matter, sir. You're the important one," is music to Jack's ears, physically punctuated by Jack patting Jeeves on the back and leaving white stains on the waiter's black uniform. As they exit the Ball Room, Jack announces grandly, "Of course, I intend to change my jacket this evening before the fish and goose soiree." Still convinced he is master of his fantasy, he feels free to mock it. The waiter adds, "Very wise, sir. Very wise." Apparently Jack has only to speak of an event in order to make it part of the itinerary in his dream world.

In terms of decor and atmosphere, the lavatory is as far removed from the Gold Ball Room as the Ball Room is from the Torrances' spartan apartment upstairs. Though not yet aware of it, Jack has stepped out of one period from Overlook's past and into another. Jeeves, still playing a 1920s waiter, cleans the stains from his master's jacket. Then Jack is shocked to learn that the waiter's real name is Delbert Grady. The 1920s have become 1970. The muted strains of "Home," filtering in from the Ball Room, are a haunting echo of a period Jack did not realize he had left, until now. Cutting closer to the characters, the camera gives us a series of reverse-angle shots that render Jack and Grady mirror images of each other. Jack even checks Grady's reflection in a mirror over the sink. And he addresses the former waiter as *Mr.* Grady, much more respectful than Jeeves, even though Grady still performs his humble clean-up task.

Regaining composure, Jack tries to reassert dominance over his fanciful creation. Forearmed with knowledge of Grady's crime, he cruelly forces the caretaker to acknowledge it. He takes the cleaning towel from Grady's hands, stripping Grady of his innocent identity as Jeeves and imposing on him the identity of murderer. But Grady chooses a different role for himself than Jack would have him play. Though probably a creation of Jack's imagination, Grady embodies emotional forces Jack does not fully control. In an increasingly self-assured voice, Grady first denies having any recollection of his alleged crimes, then slyly reverses roles with his tormentor: "I'm sorry to differ with you, sir, but you are the caretaker. You've *always* been the caretaker. I should know, sir. I've always been here." The fiction of Jack's privileged status within Overlook's golden past is shattered. One of Jack's own creations turns on him and puts him in his place, just as Stuart Ullman did, if more subtly, when he introduced the Torrances to their humble living quarters. In a series of alternating close-ups, Grady's head appears in front of a mirror that would otherwise contain Jack's reflection.

Looking shabby and nervous next to the formally attired, eerily calm Grady, Jack wilts under Grady's merciless probe into his domestic troubles. Soon he is a helpless child, hanging on to whatever train of thought Grady introduces into their conversation. The process by which Grady imposes his identity and history on Jack is precise and unhurried. *He* is now the author of a story, while Jack passively accepts his assigned role in it. Eventually Jack comes to regard Grady as his ally against the treachery of Wendy and Danny. A fragment of Jack himself, Grady is less interested in humbling Jack for the cruel pleasure of doing so than in appropriating Jack for his own purpose, which is to say for Jack's *repressed* purpose, revealed earlier during Jack's homicidal nightmare. Grady is to Jack on an individual level what Dr. Strangelove is to President Muffley on an institutional level — a subordinate whose power of action is dependent on that of his superior. And again like Strangelove, Grady's conquest of his superior is insidious. When Jack describes Danny as "a very willful boy," Grady redefines him as "a rather naughty boy." Any defiance of Jack's paternal authority must be wrong. Danny's distant ally, Dick Halloran, is reduced to "a nigger cook." By the time the co-caretakers get around to discussing Wendy, Jack is a mass of twitching energy waiting to be given direction and purpose by his alter ego.

Grady patiently nudges Jack towards a final solution to the problem of an unruly family, using his own past as an example. "But I *corrected* them, sir. And when my wife tried to prevent me from doing my duty, I *corrected* her." "Corrected" is a grotesque euphemism for hacked to death, while "duty" invests the deed with false institutional legitimacy. By previously reminding Jack of his subservient status as caretaker in Overlook's social order, Grady deprives him of an easy escape from his real problems. Frustrated again, Jack must solve his *present* troubles, using Grady's 1970 crime as a guide, before being allowed admittance to Overlook's elite social circle of the 1920s.

If Grady is only a figment of Jack's imagination and not an independent, demonic entity, how can he know about the paranormal contact between Danny and Halloran? Perhaps something Halloran said in his conversation with Danny provides a clue. Halloran commented that most people have the power to shine but either do not realize it or refuse to believe it. If Jack is one of those people, he may have stumbled upon his ability to shine through his alter ego, Grady, just as Danny did through Tony. Possibly Jack has intercepted Danny's paranormal distress signal to Halloran just as Danny once tuned in on Halloran's fear of Room 237. Or, to look at the situation from an entirely different angle, maybe the story unfolds as a product of Jack's literary fiction from the point at which he tells Wendy he should get back to work on his writing project, in which case Grady is master only of Jack's fictionalized self, while Jack the author remains in overall control. But, like the power of shining and the meaning of *2001*'s monolith, the nature of Overlook's ghostly inhabitants remains a mystery never fully explained by Kubrick.

Delbert Grady is played by actor Philip Stone, who portrayed Pee in *Clockwork* and Graham in *Barry Lyndon*. Like those earlier characters, the caretaker at first appears to be weak and easily dominated. But, unlike Pee and Graham, he reverses that strategic situation.

In the family's apartment upstairs, Wendy pacifies herself by smoking a cigarette and by verbalizing her contingency plans for escaping Overlook with Danny. The snowcat, the Forest Service and the CB radio in Ullman's office are essential ingredients in her scenario. Meanwhile, downstairs, Jack anticipates her plan and sabotages it. By removing components from the radio, he silences the Forest Service's attempt (on behalf of Halloran) to contact the Torrances. Juggling those components in his hand, he savors the power they represent. The annoying sound of a ranger's voice is replaced by, for Jack, the comforting howl of the storm. Like General Ripper sealing off Burpleson Air Force Base, Jack isolates his family from contact with the outside world. But, throughout this scene, we hear a heartbeat on the soundtrack, implying that Danny is aware of his father's malevolent actions.

Speaking to Dick Halloran in Florida, the ranger whose voice Jack silenced explains in conventional terms his inability to contact Overlook. The family must either have turned off the radio or is too far away to hear it. He does not realize that one member of the family does not wish the other two members to communicate with him.

The title card "8 a.m." indicates an acceleration in the pace of events, from weeks to days and now to hours. This counterpoints the impression of slow and steady change in family relations as provided by the film's editing, which skipped over the first month of the Torrances' stay at the hotel.

Pursuing an alternate route to Overlook, Halloran travels by airliner from Florida to Denver. The word Continental is printed on its fuselage, adding another recognizable corporate name to those on food containers in Overlook's kitchen locker. "Continental" is an accurate description of the power of institutional transportation which makes it possible for one man to pursue his private agenda across the country in a matter of hours. The private, visceral, heartbeat link between Halloran and Danny overlaps the whine of jet engines which allow Halloran to answer the boy's distress call. Inside the aircraft, Halloran sits absorbed in his own thoughts. The camera reverse zooms to bring into view other passengers, each preoccupied with his or her own concerns. Halloran breaks out of his reverie to ask a flight attendant when the aircraft will arrive in Denver. Subjective music echoing his passionate paranormal link to Danny counterpoints this brief, casual conversation.

At Overlook, we get a surprising impression of restored stability. From behind, the camera observes Jack typing in the Colorado Lounge. He seems to have returned to work on his novel. The absence of both heartbeat and subjective music reinforces our visual sense of normalcy. Is it possible that this brief scene gives us our first truly objective view of events since Jack began writing his story? If so, then much of what we saw before it and all of what we see after it is the product of Jack's fiction.

Halloran's plane lands at the Denver airport, in the middle of a winter storm. Red warning barriers with flashing lights guide the huge aircraft onto an obscured runway, beyond which lies danger. Durkin's Service Station, located in Sidewinder on the road from Denver to Overlook, is pounded by the same storm. Posters lining its walls advertise brand name services and products, once again emphasizing the presence of a collective network. For Halloran, who telephones (another link in the chain) the garage from Denver, Durkin's is a necessary bridge between himself and Overlook, as was Continental Airlines. He asks Larry Durkin, a personal friend, about road conditions and the use of a snowcat to travel up blocked mountain roads. But he does not share with Larry his paranormal insight into the trouble at Overlook. Even a friend might not believe such a tale. Instead, Halloran fabricates a plausibly conventional excuse for his trip to the hotel, claiming that Stuart Ullman ordered it. In effect, Halloran lies to one friend in order to help another, illustrating yet again the communication gaps that isolate characters from one another.

On the wall behind Larry Durkin is a television showing cartoons. Though the sound is turned down and it is largely ignored by customers, TV's mere visual presence provides a measure of reassurance and connection for refugees from the blizzard.

Halloran's drive from Denver to Sidewinder in a rented car (another institutional resource contributing to his rescue mission) is an adventure in itself, yielding a variety of impressions. A backtracking shot of his car traveling along an icy road conveys both the vehicle's power and the treacherous conditions it must overcome. We see the car from outside, but we hear what the driver hears from *inside*. The comic banter of two radio announcers helps dispel Halloran's anxiety, as watching a movie on television did for Wendy and Danny at Overlook. The camera then cuts to inside the car, where Halloran, dressed in protective winter clothing, peers out intently at the treacherous road ahead. The radio announcers, though still in cheerful voices, now dispense official weather bulletins that are less than comforting. Among those bulletins is word that Denver's Stapleton Airport may soon close, confirming the fragility of the transportation network that has gotten Halloran this far.

Another change in camera angle gives us a partly subjective view, from Halloran's vantage point, of the eerie world outside the car. The scene of an accident is marked by flashing lights, a patrolman signaling caution to drivers, and the huge, ghostly image of an overturned truck on top of a crushed Volkswagen Beetle. These mechanical corpses are grim testaments to the limits of technological power. It could just as easily be Halloran's vehicle under the truck. And the fact that the demolished car is a Beetle metaphorically brings the Torrance family into the equation. Halloran is attempting to prevent a tragedy no less violent than the one he has just come upon.

Sequestered in their sanctuary within Overlook, Wendy and Danny again employ television as a diversion from their worries. But Wendy is able to rise above her fears by acting to improve her son's situation. She tries to prepare him for her necessary departure but cannot get past his unresponsive alter ego, Tony, who in emotional terms does not need her. On her way out of the apartment, Wendy grabs Danny's baseball bat. Two contradictory impressions of violence, one visual and the other aural, overlap each other. Sounds of stylized violence emanating from a *Road Runner* cartoon on television soothe Danny's fear of *real* violence lurking elsewhere in the hotel. Meanwhile, Wendy employs Danny's bat, designed for play, as a shield against the threat of violence she is about to face.

Wendy last entered the Colorado Lounge in aid of her distressed husband. This time she arrives in fear of him. Previously she called out his name to reassure him. Now her calls are like radar, sent out to locate an enemy. The sound of the storm raging outside reinforces her anxiety and therefore works in Jack's strategic favor.

Wendy glances at what Jack has written in the typewriter and is horrified to see a single sentence, an otherwise meaningless cliché, obsessively repeated. "All work and no play makes Jack a dull boy" is Jack's madcap way of compensating for a bad case of writer's block. But what makes it frightening is the sheer *volume* of his desperation, which belies the phrase's lighthearted tone. An entire ream of paper is devoted to the same sentence, which is arranged in various literary forms, from prose to poetry, but devoid of literary content.

The camera cuts away from Wendy to a wall of photographs behind her. A dolly left takes us into an open doorway, through which we see Wendy in the distance, with her back to the camera and looking like just one more portrait in Overlook's historical gallery. Then Jack enters the frame in the foreground, and the shot becomes subjectively his. As he now sees her, Wendy is little more than an abstract character out of Overlook's past. She has become Delbert Grady's interfering wife.

Distracted by the troubling sight of Jack's writing, Wendy is now vulnerable to attack from behind. But instead of taking advantage of that vulnerability, Jack makes his presence known because he wishes to terrorize her before killing her. And he achieves his goal, transforming their conversation into an emotional weapon against her even as she physically yields ground to him. So confident is Jack that any topic of discussion can be turned to his advantage that he lets Wendy choose it.

Jack and Wendy's slow dance of intimidation across the Colorado Lounge is shown in alternating subjective shots from both of their vantage points, intercut with shots of Danny upstairs, eavesdropping on his parents' confrontation by way of shining. Their dialog overlaps and sometimes counterpoints what and how we see. One moment it aligns with the subjective camera and against the character on screen; the next, it aligns with the character on screen and against the subjective camera. Meanwhile, background music registers emotions felt by *both* characters.

Fear robs Wendy of much of her power to speak, which plays into the hands of her articulate husband. Every feeble attempt on her part to reason with Jack is twisted into a barb against her. Knowing that Wendy is avoiding the subject of Danny's welfare in order not to antagonize him, Jack brings it up himself, because he *wants* to vent his anger and increase her terror. And he draws out that process for sadistic gratification. Verbal repetition and elaboration allow Jack to build his anger to a crescendo. On the surface, his words suggest a rational, compassionate attitude. But his tone of voice is viciously sarcastic. Because Wendy is by now almost too frightened to speak the dialog Jack assigns her, Jack becomes her prompter as well as her tormentor. After all, if she cannot perform, he cannot enjoy the full mastery of his production.

When he finally coaxes Wendy into admitting that she thinks Danny should be taken away from the hotel as soon as possible, Jack mocks her by repeating her words with exaggerated emphasis. Then he challenges the morality of her proposal. Punctuating his cruel logic with finger pointing and violent hand gestures, Jack transforms Wendy's maternal concern about Danny into a lack of concern about himself. In effect, he forces her to choose between them.

Finally, Jack adds an institutional argument to his arsenal. Wendy's desire to leave Overlook becomes a violation of the sacred social contract he made with Stuart Ullman. In this, he echoes Pee's excuse for not allowing Alex to return home in *Clockwork* and HAL's excuse for killing the *Discovery* astronauts in *2001*. And like HAL's, Jack's rationale is absurd. It is Wendy, not Jack, who has tended the hotel boilers. The institutional prop that Jack calls to his defense is the same one he has increasingly neglected and even defied ever since Ullman's departure from Overlook.

Reduced to abject terror, Wendy momentarily forgets about her son's welfare and begs only to be allowed to leave the Colorado Lounge and return unharmed to her upstairs sanctuary. Unfortunately, Jack now lays imperial claim to the entire hotel. Her previous banishment from the Lounge is superseded by a sentence of death.

Closing the physical gap between himself and Wendy (both are now visible in the same shot), Jack toys with her by word and gesture. He reaches for her, then holds up his hands in a mock expression of innocence. He assures her in a sugary voice that he will not hurt her, then adds, "I'm just gonna bash your brains in." Only Danny's baseball bat stands between Jack and his victim. He reaches out to deprive her of it, and she hits him on the wrist.

Pain and anger make him careless. He lunges at her, and she clouts him on the head. He falls backwards down the stairs, unconscious.

The camera starts the next scene in partial alignment with Jack as he regains consciousness and moves mysteriously across the hotel floor. Beginning with a medium close-up and then cutting to a more distant, revealing shot, the camera mimics Jack's reawakening to his surroundings. Wendy is dragging him across the floor of the kitchen, which was defined as her domain when Stuart Ullman shuffled her off to it in Halloran's care. Her familiarity with its facilities now proves to be a strategic advantage. On the other hand, her fear of Jack's return to consciousness makes an almost undecipherable puzzle out of the lock on the food locker where she hopes to imprison him. She solves that puzzle and locks him inside just as he regains mobility. But his appearance of physical recovery is premature anyway. The pain from putting weight on his unexpectedly injured ankle causes him to lurch into a pile of boxes — a little lesson in the illusion of power, which is then replayed on the other side of the door. Wendy backs away from the locked door as though to reestablish the safety zone which Jack violated in the Colorado Lounge. She bolsters her meager sense of security by appropriating a large kitchen knife — one of the group of knives that metaphorically threatened Danny during his conversation with Halloran. Like the pods in *2001*, the knives indiscriminately serve different masters at different times.

Unable to attack Wendy physically, Jack falls back on his rhetorical skills, first trying to intimidate her into releasing him, then appealing to her conscience. An extreme low-angle shot of him leaning against the inside of the food-locker door yields a demonic impression of a man consumed by rage, reminiscent of Mr. Alexander sitting outside his bathroom door in *Clockwork*. Both characters must overcome that rage in order to formulate a plan of action. Jack pleads with Wendy to take him to a doctor, which in view of his reaction to her similar plea on Danny's behalf is blatantly hypocritical. Compassionate by inclination, Wendy is moved by his appeal, which is acoustically rendered more plaintive by the same door that imprisons him. But she holds her ground, announcing her intention to take Danny to Sidewinder and *then* return with a doctor.

From the prison to which Wendy confined him, Jack joyously curtails Wendy's freedom of movement by telling her to check out the snowcat, which is her sole means of escape from the hotel. Precautions Jack took *before* the Colorado Lounge confrontation now shape events *after* it, despite the fact that he fared poorly *during* it. Savoring his surprise advantage over Wendy, he taps lightly on the locked door with his fingers, in effect playing a tune of victory on the instrument of his defeat. At the same time, he clutches in his other hand an instrument (the door-lock release) that might be the key to his freedom — a key whose power he does not yet recognize, if indeed it has any. It all depends on whether or not Wendy has engaged the bolt lock on the outside of the door, which would override Jack's instrument.

Outside the hotel, Wendy confronts a spectacularly daunting environment. Moving out from under the main entrance overhang, which for one shot confines that environment within an artificial frame, she appears small and fragile against the snow-covered landscape. Even Overlook's massive facade has been transformed and abstracted by the storm. Music linked to Wendy's recent confrontation with Jack realigns itself now to include her confrontation with Nature.

The hotel garage door stands open, allowing snow to "gain a foothold," as Stuart Ullman once described Nature's threat to Overlook. Also open is the snowcat's hood, revealing that Jack has "gained a foothold" in the engine. Wendy is shocked to discover that he has cut the vehicle's distributor-cap cables. In one hand, she holds the kitchen knife, her weapon of choice against Jack. In the other, she holds the useless distributor cap, Jack's chosen weapon against her. Rook takes pawn. If Wendy has contained Jack within the food locker, he has trapped her within the larger prison of Overlook.

Musical bangs associated with Wendy's rude discovery counterpoint deceptively peaceful shots of Overlook and then of Jack, curled up on the food locker floor, asleep. A soft knock on the door awakens him, but he returns to consciousness in slow stages. A reverse zoom expands our point of view just as regaining consciousness expands Jack's. Reacting first to physical sensations, Jack touches his aching head. Then, in response to another knock, he calls out Wendy's name in an almost friendly tone of voice. For a moment he is distracted from his rage towards her. Then the twisted logic of that rage reasserts itself.

Delbert Grady speaks to Jack from the other side of the locked door, which alters the quality of his voice just as it altered Jack's for Wendy. It is a disembodied, spectral voice speaking as though from a great distance — most likely from deep within Jack himself. We never see Grady in this scene as he reignites the homicidal flame in Jack, now diminished by fatigue and pain, that he originally ignited in the Gold Ball Room lavatory. And to do so he employs the same sarcasm that Jack used, at various times, to keep Grady, Lloyd, and Wendy in line. Speaking for himself and for other imaginative characters from Overlook's past, Grady accuses Jack of not having "the belly for" murder. It is interesting that Grady figuratively locates the source of Jack's inspiration, and therefore his own habitation, in the stomach, which is also where Danny houses Tony during periods of tension. Grady and Tony serve their respective creators in similar capacities. Through Grady, Jack voices repressed resentment of Wendy and Danny and also sits in harsh judgment on himself. By accusing Jack of cowardice, the self-indulgent part of Jack that he calls Grady seeks to maneuver the *whole* personality to execute a violent, final solution to his domestic problems. By the end of the scene, Jack is ready to resume that crusade.

Jack's release from the food locker, like Grady's knowledge of Danny's paranormal contact with Dick Halloran, is another mystery. Jack looks at the door and grins knowingly as we hear it being unlocked, off screen. Has the significance of the emergency release mechanism, if indeed it has significance, finally dawned on him? Or is his liberation due to outside, supernatural intervention?

Halloran's journey by snowcat from Sidewinder to Overlook is a variation on his previous trip from Denver to Sidewinder, and it is presented in a similar sequence of shots. Blizzard has a different meaning high up in the mountains than it did on the highway below. The road is no longer even discernable under monstrous snowdrifts. Only a vague clearing between stands of pine trees marks the route to Overlook. Viewed from a distance, the snowcat is dwarfed by Nature. There is no highway patrol to call upon here, nor the companionship of radio announcers. Halloran is alone now. From inside the snowcat we look out, with its driver, at a bleak snowscape illuminated by headlights. Some of the large trees have been knocked down by other forces of Nature. Like Overlook's snow-covered facade, they are great ruins which testify to the power of chaos encroaching on order, and they mirror the chaos threatening to overwhelm the Torrances inside the hotel. Jack's autumn joyride through these same mountains is far behind us now. In deep winter this environment is aesthetically closer to Nature portrayed in *2001*. More than ever, Halloran's determination to reach Overlook seems courageous and compassionate.

After first envisioning and then verbalizing his paranormal alarm "Redrum," Danny now acts more decisively to convey that warning to his mother, who lies asleep on her bed. But he is caught in a dilemma. Tony's existence makes it possible for Danny to cope with what would otherwise be emotionally unbearable. Yet Tony is of necessity dispassionate, fiercely self contained, and shrinks from contact with other people. Danny repeats his message of doom over and over, but, as spoken through Tony's subdued voice, it is insufficient to rouse Wendy. So he devises other means of broadcasting the danger. The camera follows him around the room, matching Tony's frustratingly slow pace as he does so.

Danny appropriates Wendy's knife to transmit his warning about Jack, just as she previously appropriated his baseball bat for protection against Jack. Then he employs Wendy's lipstick to write "Redrum" on the bathroom door. But even three variations of the same alarm (verbal, written, and symbolic) fail to do the trick. What happens next is an extraordinary display of willpower by the boy. In order to warn his mother of impending danger he breaks through the protective shield that is Tony and *shouts* "Redrum" loud enough to wake Wendy. The fact that his alarm succeeds only a moment before the danger arrives, and therefore does not materially affect the outcome of events, should not obscure the fact that Danny has liberated himself from a *part* of himself, which is the kind of victory Jack will not achieve over *his* alter ego — Grady.

Waking up with a scream, Wendy is confused by the mix of impressions that greets her. The sight of Danny standing beside her, holding a knife and hollering "Redrum," is disconcerting. She prudently disarms the boy before hugging him protectively. Then she sees a reflection of "Redrum" in a mirror. Detachment helps clarify perception as "Redrum" becomes "Murder." But before she can ponder its implications, the reality it prophecies crashes in on her.

Sloughing off the slowness of Tony's movements, the camera plugs into the emotions and actions of Wendy, Danny, and Jack as they once again converge on the same spot. While Jack hammers at the apartment door with a fire axe (intended by institutional man for life-*saving* rather than life-taking), Wendy retreats with her son into the bathroom, which becomes their fortress within a fortress. Danny clings to his mother, as dependent on her now as he was on Tony moments earlier. Wendy discards her useless knife and focuses her efforts on a small window leading outside the hotel which Jack now claims as his exclusive domain.

Throughout the film, Nature plays a significant yet ambivalent role in the lives of the Torrances. Aesthetically remote from human confrontations occurring inside Overlook, the world outside nevertheless affects their outcome. A huge snowbank turns a perilous second-story drop from bathroom window to ground into a gentle slide. Ironically, ice caused by the same storm clogs the window, preventing Wendy from making a similar escape.

Penetrating the outer barrier of Wendy's fortress at the same time Danny escapes, Jack presses his face to the splintered hole he has made in the door and announces, "Wendy, I'm home," mocking a line spoken by many fathers in many TV situation comedies. Twisting collective clichés for his own amusement, Jack casts himself as a preverse variation on *Father Knows Best*. Then, advancing on his wife's second line of defense, he adopts the fictional role of the Big Bad Wolf, transforming the abstract violence of a fairy tale into a real threat. He even supplies the dialog for intended victims — Wendy and Danny as the Little Pigs. But even as he expands and embellishes his power, a pronounced limp caused by the ankle injury he suffered in a previous battle with Wendy betrays his own vulnerability.

Wendy abandons the window that failed her (though not her son), takes up the knife she previously abandoned, and cowers in a corner of the bathroom, behind the door Jack assaults from outside. In a beautifully conceived tight shot, Wendy literally tries to press herself into the wall that stands between her and Jack. Her knife looks small and inadequate compared to the axe blade repeatedly smashing through the door. And her involuntary screams of terror are syncopated with Jack's concussive blows, no doubt pleasing him, as the Alexanders' cries of pain pleased Alex in *Clockwork*. After carving himself an opening into Wendy's tiny sanctuary, Jack transforms it into a ghoulish variation on a television icon — Ed McMahon introducing Johnny Carson on the *Tonight Show*. Only a few scenes ago television provided *comfort* to Wendy.

When Jack's hand replaces his axe blade through the shattered door, as he reaches in to undo the lock, Wendy's useless knife suddenly becomes useful again. She slashes that hand, and he painfully withdraws it. The same slashing, subjective music that accompanied his verbal assault echoes her physical counterattack. It plays no favorites. Outside, Halloran's snowcat approaches Overlook. Inside, the sound of that approach disrupts the confrontation between Jack and Wendy. Three very different points of view (sound implying Halloran's) collide at a critical moment. But if the sound of the snowcat momentarily rescues Wendy, it also dooms Halloran by betraying his presence to an enemy he has not yet identified.

After the apartment scene, the four characters roam Overlook in isolation from one another except during brief, violent encounters. The same storm that aided his escape from the bathroom drives Danny back into the hotel to escape the cold. He takes refuge in a service-corridor cabinet. A tracking camera follows Jack through the kitchen. Visible in the foreground are many dormant institutional machines. Jack's ankle sprain diminishes his movement yet aesthetically *enhances* his aura of menace. He shambles forward like Kharis, the vengeful Egyptian mummy brought back to life in several 1940s horror films.

Upstairs, Wendy is still haunted by thoughts of Jack lurking on the other side of the shattered bathroom door, even though he is long gone. When she summons enough courage to flee her breached sanctuary, fear diminishes her capacity to deal with the lock she formerly employed to keep Jack out. Frustrated, she hacks at the lock with her knife, which proved so useful against Jack a few minutes earlier but is useless now. At last she solves the puzzle by other means.

As Halloran approaches Overlook's main entrance, the only visible clue to trouble is the door left ajar by Wendy when she went to check on the snowcat. Inside, the hotel becomes ever more maze-like with Halloran's arrival. We follow Jack as he plods down a corridor unfamiliar to us. Somewhere off in the distance Halloran calls out "Hello." Only when Jack stops at a point overlooking the hotel lobby, from an angle we have not experienced before, can we situate both him and the unfamiliar area from which he has just come.

We join Halloran elsewhere. When he turns a corner and enters the lobby, the partly subjective camera following him also becomes partly *objective*, because we can anticipate the approximate location of the danger awaiting him — the spot where Jack stood overlooking the lobby just moments earlier. Sure enough, Jack leaps out from behind the last pillar on Halloran's right and slams his axe into the startled man's chest, through thick layers of a coat that served him well against winter cold but cannot protect him now.

Three distinct yells ring out in ironic harmony. Jack's howl of brutal triumph mixes with Halloran's scream of shock and pain, which in turn triggers an empathetic scream of horror from Danny, who shines on the event from an adjoining corridor. A single incident yields three aesthetically similar yet emotionally different reactions.

A medium close-up of Jack, looking grotesquely happy as he digs his weapon deeper into Halloran's chest, takes its place alongside other Kubrick portraits of unrestrained egotism: Barry Lyndon flailing away at Lord Bullingdon, Alex pounding on Billyboy, Moonwatcher exulting over the conquest of a waterhole rival, and Private Pyle savoring his murder of Sergeant Hartman (*Full Metal Jacket*). Rising from his first kill, Jack is a frightening image of a man suddenly released from *all* inhibitions, of private conscience as well as collective rule. He is at once a free man and a slave to his own aggressive urges. His former capacity for self-criticism has been extinguished. Penderecki's "Utrenja" echoes his fanaticism on the soundtrack. Banging wood blocks reinforce the visual violence, while the vaguely defined chant of human voices lends an aura of almost religious conviction to what Jack sees as Overlook's collective support for his crusade of extermination.

Danny's paranormal insight again proves to be as much a handicap as an asset. His scream lingers a moment longer than its two counterparts, betraying his location to Jack. The boy must flee his discovered hiding place, but though Jack looms as much larger and more powerful in a tracking shot of both characters, Jack's ability to give chase is noticeably hampered by his injured ankle.

Wendy's assent to Overlook's upper regions is accompanied by the same hushed chanting we heard after Jack's murder of Halloran. For her, too, the hotel has come to life, but with monsters instead of allies. She half whispers/half shouts the name of her son in a self-defeating attempt to locate him without betraying her own location to Jack. Then, for the first time in her life, Wendy shines, suggesting that Danny's ability is inherited. Perhaps it is no coincidence that both characters experience shining for the first time after an emotional upheaval: Danny after Jack dislocated his shoulder in Vermont, and Wendy in the midst of chaos at Overlook.

Having previously expressed her fascination with Overlook's glamorous "jet set," Wendy now encounters two of their number under less appealing circumstances. From a hallway she sees two party revelers engaged in oral sex in one of the guest rooms. She flees in terror from her vision, as Danny did from his first vision of Overlook and even as Jack did from his encounter with the temptress in Room 237.

Meanwhile, Danny seeks refuge outside the hotel, behind Halloran's snowcat. He prefers winter's cold to Jack's fury. Jack, however, illuminates Danny's new hiding place by activating Overlook's battery of outside lights. Robbed of the cover of darkness, Danny deserts one sanctuary for another, leaving the snowcat for the hedge maze. Pursuing the boy, Jack likewise deserts *his* sanctuary. Leaving behind the warmth of Overlook and the visual containment of its main entrance overhang, Jack appears vulnerable against a massive backdrop of snow, even though his black silhouette conveys menace and fanatical determination. Releasing one hand from his axe, he clutches his chest in an involuntary display of physical strain.

Inside the maze, the camera alternates its point of view, stalking Danny and then being pursued by Jack. The boy's previous familiarity with the maze gives him a strategic advantage. But fickle Nature returns the advantage to his father. Danny's footprints are clearly visible in the snow, allowing Jack to track him. The same element that made possible Danny's safe descent to the ground from a second-story window now betrays him. But Jack, too, is betrayed by Nature. Calling out to his son, Jack transforms what would ordinarily be a father's reassuring voice into a terrifying threat of harm. By increasing Danny's fear, he increases his own pleasure. But the expression on Jack's face fluctuates between malevolence and pained exertion. Hobbled and ill clad, he is a predator with large teeth (the axe) but no insulating fur.

Inside Overlook, Wendy stumbles through the kitchen utensils Jack smashed to the floor earlier. Then she stumbles upon a much more disturbing example of Jack's violent deviance. We already know about Halloran's murder, yet it comes as a surprise even to us to discover, along with a stunned Wendy, his bloody corpse around the next corner, which unexpectedly returns us to the lobby. Trembling badly, she edges away from the body. But in the midst of her effort to evade a literal horror, she is overtaken by a paranormal one. Screaming, Wendy anticipates danger behind her, which is often the place from which we expect danger to approach. She turns to face it, the camera following her lead. And there stands another creature from Overlook's past.

Like Danny's twins, Wendy's hotel guests become more terrifying with each appearance. Unlike his mute companions upstairs, this one speaks to her. Smiling, he raises his glass of liquor and observes cheerfully, "Nice party, isn't it." But he does so with blood streaking down his forehead. As with the twin's invitation to Danny, "Come and play with us," there is nothing frightening about what he says. But the *circumstances* of his saying it render it so. Wendy's subsequent flight from her own vision of Overlook's past is juxtaposed by direct cut with Danny's continued flight from Jack, who has imaginatively recast Danny, Wendy, and himself as characters from that same past.

Rounding yet another corner, Wendy is confronted by yet another paranormal vision of horror. The same hotel lobby which moments earlier appeared well lit is now, from a different angle of perspective, dark and populated by skeletons in formal attire and various, casual poses. Even further removed from her ideal of a "jet set" than were her two previous visions, this one contains an image straight out of her beloved horror films and ghost stories. And the fact that Halloran's body is no longer visible where it was suggests that what we see now is in Wendy's mind.

Instead of being chased by Jack through the maze, the camera now often observes him from behind, and at a greater distance, emphasizing his slowing pace and indecision. Meanwhile, Danny recognizes the betrayal of his own footprints and takes steps to correct it. He carefully backtracks in those footprints, then steps out of the passageway he was following and wipes out the evidence of his departure. In other words, he manipulates Nature to his own advantage rather than passively accepting its fickle strategic handouts.

Still wandering the hotel in search of her son, Wendy turns yet another corner in that maze and is overwhelmed by yet another paranormal shock — all occurring too late to do her any good. Hers is the same bloody elevator vision that Danny has had numerous times throughout the film. Under the present circumstances, however, it is just one more emotional roadblock for Wendy to overcome.

Inside the maze, Danny hides behind a snow-encrusted hedge while Jack pursues the boy's footprints in the adjacent passage. Puffing for air, his eyes flashing hate, Jack is confused by the abrupt disappearance of those footprints. He bellows out Danny's name, as though to command the boy's presence by sheer force of will. Danny, crouching only a few feet away, refuses to answer. Subjective music echoes both Jack's yell and Danny's silent rejection. An evil grin crosses Jack's face. Guided by some private light, he hobbles off purposefully in a new direction. And this time he is careful not to call out Danny's name, therefore not to betray his own location. But, in extreme long shot, he is dwarfed by a harsh environment he is poorly equipped to navigate. When Danny emerges from his sanctuary, we see, from his vantage point, the same view of the corridor in which Jack disappeared. But this time the impression is different. From the boy's perspective, not knowing where Jack might be lurking is almost as terrifying as previously knowing that Jack was right behind him.

Danny doubles back towards the maze entrance, using as a guide the same footprints by which Jack tracked *him*. Elsewhere, the camera tracks Jack through, for him, unfamiliar passageways containing no clues as to Danny's whereabouts. The slowness of his pace is juxtaposed with the swiftness of Danny's.

Escaping the confusion and terror of Overlook, Wendy tracks her son's escape route outside. When she sees him emerge from the maze, she tosses aside her knife and rushes to him, her relief and joy at seeing him unhurt momentarily displacing her fear of Jack. Two such extreme and extremely different passions cannot coexist in the same mind at the same time. And like films about war, horror films often deal in emotional extremes which are difficult to appreciate from a broad perspective of comfortable detachment.

Like some great monster succumbing to the vast forces arrayed against it, Jack and his rage grind to a slow, dramatic halt. He can barely move now, calling out incoherently between gasps for air, while outside the maze his intended victims *run* towards the snowcat. Halloran's rescue mission has succeeded, though not in the way he anticipated.

Wheezing and reeling, Jack finally stumbles and falls. He struggles back to his feet. The camera scrutinizes him coolly from a distance, then closes in on him like a fascinated observer, if not a hungry predator. His silhouette is outlined by the pitiless glare of the lights *he* activated in his pursuit of Danny. All of the natural and institutional phenomena that formerly served his interests now seem to conspire against him, as they did against Alex when he returned to the home of Mr. Alexander in *Clockwork*. In the distance we hear the snowcat's engine — technology employed in *defiance* of Jack's will. Kubrick flirts with the horror film cliché of an escape vehicle which, for whatever monstrously ill-timed reason, malfunctions. But in this instance the monster is in no position to take advantage of it. Outside the maze, the glare of the snowcat's headlights illuminate Wendy and Danny's escape route out of Overlook, in contrast to the maze lights which illuminate Jack's imprisonment.

Jack's final burst of ranting is unintelligible, directed perhaps at the entire, uncooperative world outside himself. The snowcat's departure leaves him alone, trapped in the same prison to which he confined his wife and son when he imagined them inside the table-top replica. Music returns to the soundtrack, but now as a reflection of Nature rather than of Jack, who is too exhausted to raise his voice above a babble. A piercing, icy whine mixes with and reinforces the sound of winter wind that cuts through his inadequate clothing. Like HAL's death in *2001*, Jack's is drawn out and disturbing rather than quick and morally comforting. Finally he collapses, resting against the wall of his prison.

Cut to a frontal medium shot of Jack the next morning, he is frozen in the same posture he fell into at the end of the previous shot. On the soundtrack, the transition is made by a brittle glissando — the musical approximation of freezing to death. Jack's face is a frozen mask of malevolence, yet he feels nothing anymore. Winter has gotten a foothold in Jack, reducing him to an abstract ruin, destroying consciousness while perpetuating the *appearance* of passion.

The Shining's last scene is an ironic, one-shot variation on the first shot in *A Clockwork Orange*, which began with a close-up of Alex and then dollied back to reveal a collective order sympathetically arranged around him. This time the camera begins with an impression of collective order, then dollies *forward* to reveal the protagonist as a small detail assimilated within that larger whole. Starting in the lobby, the camera glides forward towards a group of framed photographs on the far wall, in the corridor leading to Jack's beloved Gold Ball Room. White sheets draped over lobby furniture suggest that time has passed since the Torrance family occupied the hotel. Has Overlook been closed as a result of their tragedy? In any case, the camera takes us back to Overlook's heyday, revived on the soundtrack by "Midnight with the Stars and You" and on screen by old photographs. We zero in on an idealized portrait of a past that Jack has flirted with since the film began. Successive dissolves bring that past closer and closer, revealing more detail each time.

The subject of the central photograph is an elegant and festive social gathering in the Ball Room, featuring hotel guests dressed in early 1920s fashion. Everyone is smiling. Jack is among them, front and center. Dressed like his companions, clean shaven, a drink in hand, he is finally "Home." No longer does his sloppy appearance clash with his idyllic fantasy of Overlook's past, as it did in previous Ball Room Scenes. And the Ball Room itself appears in its original form, before the recent redecoration. Jack's smile is wholehearted, untainted by the mockery with which he once maintained a degree of emotional detachment from the hotel's charms. Perhaps the photo illustrates Jack's final, delirious impression of himself before he died, in the same way Rosebud and all that it stood for was the last retreat of the protagonist in *Citizen Kane*. One of the hotel guests standing near Jack gently grasps his waving arm, as though to restrain his contact with the outside world. Unlike Barry Lyndon, Jack Torrance attains harmony with his social environment at the end of the story, but only on the level of private delusion. In literal terms it costs him his life, and therefore it cannot be directly compared to the attainments of Dr. Strangelove, Dave Bowman, and Alex.

The photograph depicting Jack and his new/old friends is captioned "Overlook Hotel, July 4th Ball, 1921." Jack has retreated to a distinctly American past, at a moment of national celebration just a few years after a victorious World War and nearly a decade before the Great Depression. *The Shining*, in its characters' perceptions and attitudes, is a distinctly *American* nightmare.

"Midnight with the Stars and You" carries over into the closing credits but ends before they do. As the last credits roll by, we hear polite applause followed by the vague sounds of a party breaking up. Like the morning after Alex's perversely exhilarating night of ultraviolence in *Clockwork*, Jack's intoxication with Overlook yields, at least for us, to the inevitable hangover. The demonic spell is broken. The party is over.

CHAPTER 6

Full Metal Jacket:
Semper Infidelis

> If I belong to a party, I am for my party; to an army, for my army; to a
> State, for my State.... That's the only truth. The opposite you may tell
> to children of eighteen.
> — Napoleon Bonaparte, *The Mind of Napoleon* (Herold, 5)

Gustav Hasford's *The Short-Timers*, like Anthony Burgess's *A Clockwork Orange* and William Thackeray's *Barry Lyndon*, is narrated by its protagonist. Private Joker is our tour guide through the twin hells of Marine Corps basic training and combat service in Vietnam. And from the beginning he is dedicated to becoming a hardened soldier, relishing the challenges heaped on him by superior officers, fellow marines, and the enemy, facing them all down with either threats of or actual violence. In addition, he courageously risks his life to rescue a wounded comrade. And, as a combat journalist for the Marine Corps newspaper, he exhibits no ethical qualms about faking photographic evidence for propaganda purposes.

The only reservation Private Joker has about being a marine is accepting a leadership role, which would entail selectively inflicting on other soldiers the hell he is so willing to endure himself. Hasford's novel reaches its dramatic climax when the protagonist finally shoulders the terrible responsibility of assuming leadership of his squad in order to get them through a desperate situation.

Full Metal Jacket, Kubrick's adaptation of *The Short-Timers*, portrays Private Joker's crisis of conscience in different terms. Throughout most of the film, the protagonist is an emotionally divided character: half committed to being a hard marine, but equally determined to maintain some critical distance from that role. Like *The Shining*'s Jack Torrance, he employs sarcasm both to fight and to serve his temptation to unconditional commitment. And his moment of personal crisis in the film occurs when circumstances conspire to erode his independence.

285

Private Joker's pared-down narration in *Full Metal Jacket* is sardonic, cynical, and dispassionate, coming to us from his hardened perspective at the very end of the film, after the emotional toll of combat forces him to embrace unequivocally the collective spirit of the Corps. At that point he shields himself with an indifference not unlike that of Danny Torrance's alter ego, Tony. As a result, Joker's narration sometimes clashes with the passions of his onscreen persona, especially when those passions include fear, revulsion, or remorse.

Like Burgess's *A Clockwork Orange*, *The Short-Timers* portrays an institution rampant with violent abuse. Master Gunnery Sergeant Gerheim inflicts savage discipline on his new recruits, and he is in turn stabbed by one of them. *Full Metal Jacket* portrays a more structured and restrained Marine Corps, where violence is more selectively employed as a teaching tool. Like the Chief Guard in Kubrick's *Clockwork*, Sergeant Hartman is a conscientious professional, meting out punishment with theatrical flair but also impersonally, to achieve an institutional goal rather than to feed his own sadistic impulses.

In their respective combat scenes, too, Kubrick's film is more restrained than is Hasford's novel. Attempted rape, cannibalism, and superhuman feats of fighting skill are featured in *The Short-Timers*. The marines in *Full Metal Jacket* are brutal and tough, but, like all Kubrick characters, they are vulnerable and occasionally, when overcome by terror or pain, pathetic.

Two types of violence emphasized rather than muted in *Full Metal Jacket* are sexual and racial bigotry, both of which are incorporated into and transformed by Marine Corps basic training. On the one hand, Marine Corps reeducation makes comrades out of strangers and even potential enemies by desensitizing racist language, even turning it into a token of respect and affection. On the other hand, sexist language is employed to make anything female a universal metaphor for weakness. And since there are no women among the marines portrayed, there is no risk of alienating them from their comrades. Racism and sexism crisscross during two scenes in the film that have no counterparts in the novel: Joker and Rafterman's street-corner encounter with a Vietnamese prostitute and the Lusthog Squad's encounter with a Vietnamese prostitute and her ARVN pimp.

*   *   *

Johnny Wright's "Hello, Vietnam," heard over *Full Metal Jacket*'s opening credits and first scene, is a classic slice of American country music, in the style of Hank Williams. A homespun lament for soldiers on their way to fight in Vietnam, the song is a touching if simplistic ode to the individual's sacrifice for his country's cause. Juxtaposed with the music is a visual montage depicting a sacrifice somewhat different than that referred to in the song's lyrics. In addition to their sweethearts, new recruits at the Marine Corps Parris Island training camp give up their hair. In shot after shot, man after man is shaved nearly bald by an anonymous barber wearing a white smock, like those worn by Ludovico scientists in *Clockwork*. The unusual mix of music and imagery, recollecting the midair refueling scene at the start of *Dr. Strangelove*, transforms Johnny Wright's lament into a *mock* lament for the recruits' loss of cosmetic distinction. Obviously the Corps does not consider that distinction trivial. Like Alex's check-in at Staja 84F, basic training at Parris Island begins with a deconstruction process, to be followed by a reconstruction along new lines and for a specific purpose. "Hello, Vietnam" becomes, in its visual context, the ironic flip side of "Hair," a Vietnam-era song that celebrated its title subject as a symbol of liberation from traditional authority. In another context, Kubrick's use of "Hello, Vietnam" is ironic because the song implies a quick transition from civilian life to combat service, whereas the film spends much of its time depicting the long and complicated process by which a civilian becomes a soldier. The many basic-training scenes portray what necessarily comes between "Goodbye, darling" and "Hello, Vietnam." The film's very title is a metaphorical description of that difficult transformation.

Judging from their facial expressions, the new recruits find their loss of hair somewhat disconcerting. The exception is Private Leonard Lawrence, whose silly grin suggests enjoyment. We later learn that Lawrence is, by inclination, a follower. His sense of self is less keenly developed, and so he is less troubled by regimentation. Ironically, of all the new recruits he proves the least capable, physically and psychologically, of coping with the severe training regimen. The Corps, it seems, *requires* a strong ego as raw material to be broken down and reconfigured into a soldier. With Lawrence (later rechristened Private Pyle), Sergeant Hartman must start from scratch, creating an ego before he can reshape it to a collective end. And that difficult process will fail, disastrously, resulting in a deviant, malevolent grin that mocks the smile on Lawrence's face in the present scene. And there is an ironic parallel between *Full Metal Jacket* and *The Shining* in that regard. Jack Torrance's *isolation* from society triggers the same lethal consequences that collective *indoctrination* will have on one recruit who cannot properly absorb it. Identical results proceed from opposite influences acting on very different characters.

The marine barracks occupied by Sergeant Hartman's platoon combines the spartan look of Staja 84F's admissions room with the institutional dimensions of Overlook's lobby. White, evenly spaced pillars support the ceiling. New recruits, standing at attention, evenly spaced and stripped down to their white underwear, are being reconfigured to support the mission of the Marine Corps. Regimentation is the first, but *only* the first, step in that process.

Sergeant Hartman, immaculately uniformed, with a chest full of medals, combines the roles of *Clockwork*'s Chief Guard (traffic cop), Chaplain (spiritual guide), and Dr. Brodsky (psychiatrist/physician) into one. The high priest of collective order, Hartman holds nearly all the advantages in various duels with the unindoctrinated minds and bodies of his new recruits. Methodically and efficiently, he turns their civilian psychological baggage against them. *His* point of view and his metaphors will echo again and again in *their* speech, long after he passes from the scene.

Prowling the spotless barracks floor as he harasses the new recruits, Sergeant Hartman unites the contradictory extremes of cruelty and emotional detachment. As an instrument of the Corps, he employs verbal and physical abuse to achieve an institutional goal, presumably without feeding his own sadistic impulses. Significantly, we never see Hartman out of professional character in a private, unguarded moment. His address to the men is well rehearsed and makes no room for debate. The camera backtracks with him, conveying his power in the manner of Alex strolling through the Music Bootick and Dr. Taylor pushing her cart of instruments through hospital corridors in *Clockwork*.

After losing their hair and being stripped and re-dressed in Corps-issued apparel, the recruits are verbally redefined. They are no longer civilians. They are not yet marines. They are "pukes," with the rights and privileges of neither. Hartman's task is to restructure their perceptions as well as to condition their bodies. Part of that effort consists of repetitive lessons in marine-speak, which distils and simplifies the English language to a few amplified analogies to power and weakness, or good and evil. The result is a more systematic variation on the banal languages of General Ripper, Alex, and Jack Torrance, in which all human relationships are described in terms related to sexual intercourse, bodily functions, and inanimate objects. And in Hartman's language, ideas are sometimes less important that the aesthetics of pure sound.

The Marine Corps deliberately overturns the proprieties of its parent culture. Sergeant Hartman is authorized to use slurs of all types in his attempt to break down the civilian identities of his recruits, reducing them to a common denominator before rebuilding them into "ministers of death praying for war." All pukes are referred to as "ladies," which in Hartman's lexicon signifies submissiveness, incompetence, and weakness. Distinctions based on racial, regional, or national heritage are retained only for the purpose of insult — certainly not for building pride. In Hartman's institutionally anointed hands, bigotry is merely a tool for manufacturing marines and is therefore ostensibly cleansed of any immorality. The Sergeant is at once the worst of racists and not a racist at all, in the same way *Clockwork's* Dr. Brodsky is and is not a sadistic torturer. And it is this contradiction between private and institutional vision, combined in one person for the purpose of achieving a collective goal, that Kubrick relentlessly questions.

An African-American recruit rechristened Private Snowball by his drill instructor is expected to formally acknowledge Hartman's strange new world order by making obligatory gestures of submission. Not only is Hartman empowered to humiliate his recruits, they are compelled to accept his insults with respect and even enthusiasm. "Sir! Yes Sir!" is their mandated reply to all questions from a superior. This *doubles* the formal show of respect the Chief Guard demanded of Alex and other prisoners in Staja 84F. One can only imagine the supreme confidence such constant reinforcement must inspire in Hartman, who will, however, eventually suffer the consequences of his inability to control every element of his carefully constructed scenario, just as President Muffley, Soviet Doomsday engineers, Ludovico advocates, Redmond Barry, and Jack Torrance paid dearly for *their* oversights.

Hartman's verbal attack on Private Snowball is interrupted from the opposite side of the barracks by another recruit's sarcastic impersonation of John Wayne, the popular civilian personification of Hartman's warrior mentality. Like Alex mocking the Chief Guard's military gait at the Ludovico Centre, Joker undermines Hartman's dignity and authority. Not only does Joker render his superior's bombastic performance cartoonish, he reveals his own divided attitude towards the warrior mentality Hartman tries to instill in all new recruits. "Is that you, John Wayne? Is this me?" suggests an objective/subjective split in the face of Hartman's demand for total commitment. The drill instructor does not help his own cause by hopping around like an enraged child, searching for the culprit. He mistakenly targets a Texas recruit whom he renames Private Cowboy and whose short stature he insults.

Cowboy is rescued from Hartman's onslaught by Joker's confession of guilt. Joker then becomes the focus of Hartman's wrath, but his self-sacrifice on behalf of a comrade marks him, in Hartman's mind, as promising marine material. Private "Joker," as he is rechristened, is severely punished for his transgression. But, in time, his reckless courage will elevate him in rank above the thoroughly conformist Private Snowball.

Hartman's dressing down of Joker makes use of the recruit's own sarcasm. Every weapon in the arsenal of individual man must be turned against its source. Yet by figuratively offering Joker his sister for sexual pleasure, Hartman extends a weird sort of compliment. Reckless courage must be slapped down hard but not eradicated. It must be tempered with discipline so that it will be useful to the Corps. After returning Joker's verbal volley, Hartman raises the stakes of their confrontation, and simultaneously shatters any lingering amusement Joker might be feeling about the Sergeant's theatrical performance, by punching the new recruit in the stomach, dropping him to his knees. From the camera's subjective point of view, we share in Joker's involuntary submission to Hartman's authority. He forces Joker to acknowledge that he joined the Marine Corps to *kill*, depriving the reluctant warrior of any civilian shield of innocence. By demanding to see Joker's "war face," Hartman also compels Joker to act out a caricature of marine toughness that Joker's initial remark satirized. To the recruit's rhetorical question, "Is this me?" Hartman forces him to answer with a resounding "Yes!" Joker becomes John Wayne. And his performance in that compulsory role fails to impress the director of this little production: "You didn't scare me! Work on it!"

Cowboy's reprieve is brief. Presuming that a young man from Texas would be sensitive to an accusation of homosexuality, Hartman savagely attacks that point of weakness. Regional affiliations and attitudes are regarded as obstacles to marine solidarity, but also as sources of emotional leverage for the purpose of reeducation. No doubt Hartman would trash old John (*Sands of Iwo Jima*) Wayne himself if he saw it as a strategic opening into the emotional makeup of his trainees.

Private Joker rode to the rescue of fellow recruits Snowball and Cowboy. A fourth recruit is *amused* by Cowboy's humiliation and is therefore an even bigger target for Hartman's anger. Marine indoctrination is not successful as long as one recruit remains indifferent to the fate of another. In his effort to wipe the grin from the face of Private Leonard Lawrence, Sergeant Hartman modifies two insults he used on Cowboy. He exploits Lawrence's large size, labeling him "fatbody," and the coincidence of his sharing a name with the famous Lawrence of Arabia to suggest that he is homosexual. And he reinforces the latter charge by insulting the Marine Corps' brother service — the United States Navy. A sense of exclusivity and superiority is so essential to the molding of marine identity that *nothing* outside the Corps is immune from ridicule.

Unfortunately for Hartman, Private Lawrence's sense of self identity is so poorly developed that it is a difficult target to locate. His silly grin persists, and with it so does ours. So Hartman pulls rank and *orders* Leonard to lose it. But Lawrence, who possesses little self-discipline, cannot obey even though he wants to. His pinched, involuntary grin continues to undercut Hartman's authority. So Hartman redefines their relationship by way of an analogy. He rechristens Lawrence as Private Pyle, after a character from a 1960s television comedy about marine life. Tall, ungainly, slow witted and good natured, Gomer Pyle functioned week after week as a comic foil to his flustered drill instructor, Sergeant Carter — the popular, safe image of a marine disciplinarian. Hartman, with his head and cap thrust aggressively forward and up at the taller recruit, recalls the image of Sergeant Carter furiously battling Pyle's genial incompetence. Why would he introduce an analogy that makes himself look like such a fool? Kubrick, too, must have recognized the comic pitfalls inherent in the portrayal of a frenetic drill instructor. The punch line to Hartman's little joke comes quickly and rudely. After creating certain expectations in the minds of his recruits by comparing one of them to Gomer Pyle, he undercuts the analogy by demonstrating that, unlike Sergeant Carter's, *his* bite is far worse than his bark. He eliminates Pyle's height advantage by forcing him to his knees, then makes Pyle choke him-self on his (the Sergeant's) hand. Viewed in a tight shot of Pyle's head and upper body, Hartman's hand appears as an anonymous extension of institu-tional authority, presumably free of the corruption of personal cruelty. And by making Pyle place himself in the Sergeant's choke hold, Hartman begins the process of internalizing marine discipline within his recruits. Gasping for air, his silly grin now gone, Private Pyle is no longer amused by the drill instructor. A shot of Hartman's face as he punishes Pyle strongly resembles a close-up of Dim, in police uniform, looming sadistically over a kneeling Alex in *Clockwork*. If Sergeant Hartman enjoys his violent exercise of power over his victim, he does a much better job than Dim of masking it within the confines of his institutional task. Whatever the case, in this first barracks scene, Sergeant Hartman, mixing ridicule and physical violence, defeats his new recruits in a battle of wills, transforming their various attributes and even their chosen weapons (such as Joker's sense of humor) into servants of his own cause.

Scattered among the training scenes at Parris Island are a series of back-tracking shots of Platoon 3092 jogging along camp streets. Like the refrain of a song, these interludes are recurring exercises in uniformity of movement, accompanied by marine chants containing crude internal rhymes. Sergeant Hartman, trotting alongside yet apart from his men, firmly directs these pro-ductions. The first chant he leads introduces sex as a measure of power. Mama asking papa for sex is equivalent to the recruits, already cast as "ladies" in the previous scene, welcoming the rigorous physical training meted out to them by their drill instructor, who takes the role of "papa."

A second hymn, to marine endurance, overlaps a sunset silhouette of recruits humping it over an obstacle course. Imagery and sound create an abstract, anonymous impression of marine dedication. Then the chant of Hartman's platoon shifts gears, targeting an enemy (Ho Chi Minh) with a sexual insult. Recruits are trained to respond to basic, uncomplicated urges as a shield against ideological confusion.

Marine basic training, especially in its early stages, demands absolute obedience, no matter how trivial the order may seem. During rifle maneu-vers, Private Pyle is momentarily confused about where to shoulder his weapon. Hartman pounces on this small lapse of attention, imposing a false interpretation on it in order to advance his own, larger cause. By asking if Pyle knows his right from his left, to which Pyle of course replies in the affirmative, Hartman transforms the recruit's momentary confusion into a deliberate defiance of authority. For the Sergeant, accidents are the most seri-ous impediment to a soldier's ability to carry out his assigned mission; much more so than Joker's open defiance in the barracks. By redefining all accidents as *choices*, Hartman implies that they can be prevented by an act of will.

General Mireau expressed a similar idea in Kubrick's *Paths of Glory*. But Mireau employed it for obviously selfish reasons. Hartman seems a more valid proponent of the notion that all things are subject to a soldier's will.

Unfortunately, Pyle has not yet mastered his own emotional reactions, much less rifle drill. For him, Hartman is still Sergeant Carter, carrying on like a comical bantam rooster. Another silly grin erupts spontaneously on the big recruit's face. Hartman erases it with a hard slap. Shock, humiliation, and a trace of anger replace the grin. *This* Private Pyle, unlike his television namesake, is not immune to shame. And shame is one of Hartman's greatest weapons against incompetence and disobedience. Unlike Ludovico scientists who wished to squelch Alex's rage, Hartman *needs* Pyle to feel rage so that he can channel it for Marine Corps use. Pyle must become, in Hartman's evangelical lingo, "born again hard."

As further punishment for his "willful" nonconformity, Pyle is in the next scene separated from the platoon, whose group identity is strengthened with each arduous experience they share. And his exile is stripped of any rebellious romance. Compelled to suck his thumb, with his pants down around his ankles, Pyle trots along behind the group like a child struggling to keep up with adults. The effectiveness of Hartman's punishment is measured by *our* amusement at Pyle's situation. But Pyle's fellow recruits are not permitted to enjoy their comrade's humiliation, the way a British Army unit enjoyed first Redmond's and then Toole's in *Barry Lyndon*. Hartman's task is, after all, to forge a collective unit in which each member takes responsibility for his comrades.

If Pyle is reduced to infantile status for his sins, Sergeant Hartman exercises parental authority over the entire platoon. Bedtime is the same for everyone and is not negotiable. The ritual of lights out includes a bizarre marine variation on the traditional, civilian bedtime prayer. Stripped down once again to their underwear, the men form a straight line parallel to the barracks' white pillars and a row of overhead lights. Outwardly they makeup a perfect institutional symmetry. Hartman sermonizes to them about the relationship between a marine and his weapon. "You're married to this piece, this weapon of iron and wood. And you will be faithful." Women, already reduced to sexual metaphors for weakness, are replaced by rifles as objects of romantic fidelity — shades of *Dr. Strangelove* and its infusion of sexual meaning into the weapons and politics of nuclear warfare. But Sergeant Hartman's purpose in forging such a relationship is more deliberate and controlled than were the tortured sublimations of General Ripper. The drill instructor takes advantage of his recruits' isolation from women in order to channel their frustrated passions into the vital (especially in combat situations) care of their rifles.

A poster on the barracks wall reads, "Pride Builds Men." Like Hartman's various pronouncements, its message is clear, concise, and simple — almost simpleminded. No complications or ironies, symbolic or otherwise, are permitted within the confines of Parris Island, which is nothing less than a laboratory for deconstructing individuals and reconstructing them into marines. Only by investing new recruits with the collective tenets of the Marine Corps will they stand a chance of surviving the emotional and physical challenges of war in a foreign land. Remaining stiffly at attention, the men are put to bed alongside their rifles and compelled to recite in unison a declaration of fidelity to it: "I must master it as I master my life. Without me, my rifle is useless. Without my rifle, I am useless.... We are the masters of our enemy. We are the saviors of my life." "We/our" and "we/my" unite marine and weapon into a single identity.

Prayer concluded, Hartman exits, firing two parting gender insults at the recruits and their guards, whom he regards as unfinished, weak-minded, and weak-bodied marines. Having been displaced by rifles in the Sergeant's reworked notion of a marriage, women are reduced to the level of an unflattering analogy.

The task of mating recruit to weapon carries over into another field drill. And again it is Private Pyle who fails to measure up. Cowboy earns a relatively mild rebuke for improperly handling his rifle. "This is not your daddy's shotgun!" aims at divorcing the recruit from his civilian past and replacing an old parental figure with a new one. Pyle's mistake, however, draws heavier fire from Hartman simply because he has already been established in the Sergeant's mind as a special problem.

The next scene opens with a frontal medium shot of Sergeant Hartman, in full uniform, leading his platoon, in their underwear, through yet another rifle drill, this time inside the barracks. "This is my rifle/This is my gun. This is for fighting/This is for fun" is spoken as they march with one hand holding their rifles to their shoulders and the other grabbing their crotches. "Rifle" and "fighting" signify a marine's weapon. A slow reverse zoom reveals that "gun" and "fun" are equated with a recruit's genitals. Hartman drills into their heads the sober distinction between professional work and private recreation. After the romantic analogy he made during bedtime prayer, he now differentiates between serious and trivial sex. Killing and risking death is, obviously, serious sex. And although the confusion between sex and aggression never becomes as insanely literal as in *Dr. Strangelove*, marines in later scenes make frequent combat references to sex, while their sexual encounters with Vietnamese prostitutes contain language more suited to battle. There is perhaps an unavoidable price to pay for tapping into one passion in order to reinforce another.

As the routines of basic training settle into a drill montage, background music by Abigail Mead (a.k.a. Vivian Kubrick, the director's daughter) begins as a subjective echo of Sergeant Hartman's lyrical voice. It reinforces our sense of harmony as the recruits refine their martial skills. Later, as the camera picks out flaws in that collective order, the juxtaposition of music and imagery becomes ironic. Though Kubrick seldom if ever fully embraces his subjects, he often infuses them with aesthetic vitality, even when he questions their morality.

Predictably, it is Private Pyle whose substandard performance disturbs the harmonious whole. He performs miserably in pugil-stick combat with a fellow recruit. Staged within a circle formally marked out with tires, this exercise is a piece of educational theater designed by the Corps, directed by Hartman, featuring proscribed competition and weapons for the contestants and virtually proscribed reactions from other members of the platoon who watch. The setting and action resemble Redmond's fistfight with Toole. But this time institutional man (Hartman) dictates not only the form but also the *purpose* of combat.

The next challenge is a set of uneven wooden bars over which the recruits must hoist themselves. The first few men make it over quite easily, if not to Hartman's complete approval, which he withholds as a matter of principle. Praise is something pukes are seldom permitted to taste. Pyle cannot navigate even the first bar, and he falls to the ground. Shot from a slightly low, oblique frontal angle, his belly pushes out from under his sweatshirt, while a handheld camera empathizes with his exertion. Kubrick intends us to feel both the cruelty of Sergeant Hartman's relentless harangue and the unattractiveness of Pyle's failure to overcome a challenge he is being conditioned to accept as the only measure of self-worth.

Hartman's reaction to Pyle's incompetence is again to ridicule his presumed lack of willpower. A marine makes his own destiny. He does not rely on God or Chance to do it for him. Hartman also takes aim at Pyle's lack of motivation, crudely suggesting that the prospect of sex would motivate him to succeed. In other words, the sexual urge is a powerful motivator which Pyle has thus far been unable to channel into the tasks assigned to him by Hartman and the Corps. And yet the determined expression on Pyle's face as he tries again and again to hoist his bulk over the first bar implies that he *is* giving his best effort, perhaps because Hartman has convinced him that failure to pass a test proves he is not. Hartman may truly recognize Pyle's physical limitations and may be employing the fiction that force of will is directly proportionate to triumph over any obstacle in order to push his recruit beyond those limitations. Thus, Pyle's failure in this scene is also Hartman's failure. Meanwhile, other platoon members observe Pyle's difficulties with mandated passivity. It is not their place to react to anything, except when and in the manner dictated by their drill instructor.

While Platoon 3092 is put through its paces, other platoons in training are visible in the background, giving us a sense of the larger Marine Corps machinery required to maintain a production line of fresh soldiers. Sergeant Hartman looms so hugely in the lives of 3092 recruits that he sometimes seems to be the sole embodiment of Marine Corps authority. He even refers to the Marines as "*my* beloved Corps." But his claim is only one of many.

The next confrontation between Hartman's ideal of what a marine should be and what Private Pyle is occurs at the chinning bar. And again, the Sergeant's displeasure falls on someone else first. After numerous chin-ups, Private Joker fails to deliver "one [more] for the Corps" and earns Hartman's rebuke. "I guess the Corps don't get theirs" typically describes a recruit's performance in sexual terms. No matter how many chin-ups Joker does, his drill instructor will demand one more. This exam has no passing grade, or at least none the teacher is willing to share with his students.

If Hartman links a recruit's performance at the chin-up bar to his virility, Private Pyle is virtually impotent. He cannot do a single chin-up, at which Hartman feigns astonishment as the most effective means of embarrassing the recruit. Pyle is made an *extraordinary* exception to the general rule of unsatisfactory performances. He is deliberately set apart from Joker, who merely failed to satisfy a higher standard of competence.

In the next scene, Hartman sits astride the top rung of a high obstacle, observing his recruits climb up one side and down the other. As usual, the only approval he grants is the absence of verbal abuse. Private Pyle, fearing heights, freezes at the top rung. Furious at his unwillingness to swing his leg over that rung, Sergeant Hartman tells him to get off the obstacle entirely and threatens him with a marine variation on Social Darwinism. "I'm gonna rip your balls off so you can't contaminate the rest of the world!" is the flip side of what Hartman, only half in jest, told Private Joker on the occasion of Joker's foolish display of courage. "You can come over to my house and fuck my sister!" was a backhanded compliment. Pyle, on the other hand, is a species slated for extinction. And, to the sexual reference, Hartman adds a racial one by declaring that he will transform Pyle into a proper marine, "if it short dicks every cannibal on the Congo," which is a stronger version of Major Kong's "if it harelips everybody on Bear Creek." Marine language in *Full Metal Jacket* is a first cousin to the highly decorative nadsat of Alex and his contemporaries in *Clockwork*.

On a forced march along a country road, Pyle lumbers along, gasping for air, supported on one side by Joker. On the other, Sergeant Hartman harasses him to do better by equating exhaustion with sexual arousal, attempting to transform pain into pleasure in the mind of his faltering recruit. Meanwhile, the rest of the platoon runs on ahead. They are an increasingly disciplined unit, able to function with less supervision and greater efficiency than Pyle. From their ranks, Hartman has solicited Joker, whom he has already identified as a recruit willing to sacrifice himself for a comrade, as an ally in his battle against Pyle's incompetence. Joker is Pyle's physical crutch in this scene, while Hartman supplies emotional motivation.

The last of the training montage scenes consists of a single shot of Platoon 3092 slogging through a field of mud. Slow-motion cinematography and a frontal camera angle abstracts and heightens the effect of their shared ordeal. Private Pyle is back with the group. When he stumbles and falls, he is helped back up by his comrades. In fact, everyone supports each other in this powerful image of solidarity under pressure. Background music, with its intoxicating martial cadence and sense of progressive development, is modified by the remote sound of synthesized trumpets, which, like the slow-motion cinematography, aesthetically encourages us to see the action with some detachment. Forced to wallow in muck, the men visually become one with their challenging environment. A uniform gray covers everyone, erasing individual identity even more effectively than did marine barbers in the film's first scene. Each man takes responsibility for the progress of the entire platoon.

Like the fluorescent lights that stagger to life at the flip of a switch, the recruits of Platoon 3092 snap automatically to attention when Hartman rouses them out of sleep with a stick and a garbage can. Orders for the day include chapel service for most. Joker and Cowboy are to remain behind and clean the head so thoroughly that "the Virgin Mary herself would be proud to go in there and take a dump." Religion is incorporated into and modified by Hartman's Marine Corps perspective, just as is every other civilian phenomenon. Private Joker's admission that he does not believe in the Virgin Mary challenges this odd marriage of convenience between Christianity and the Corps. Hartman tosses aside his trash can in a loud, theatrical display of outrage. From garbage receptacle to alarm clock to instrument of intimidation, the can has been a remarkably versatile tool. Joker's lack of conventional faith constitutes an unmastered element in Hartman's world. Blasphemy earns Joker a hard slap across the face, arousing humiliation and anger which he must repress. And, like many other Kubrick characters, he is ugly in his weakness. Hartman offers him an opportunity to change his mind and perhaps escape further punishment with a false show of contrition. *Clockwork*'s Chief Guard would have been satisfied with such empty conformity. But Hartman, like Dr. Brodsky, is more ambitious, and Joker is smart enough to recognize a trap. With the closed symmetry of a barracks window frame visible in the background, Joker stands by his original statement, correctly believing that a retraction will earn him even greater punishment for vacillating. True enough, Sergeant Hartman is a marine first, a Christian second, with a clear distinction in his mind between their separate priorities. He summons and fires Private Snowball as squad leader, then appoints Joker in his place. "Private Joker is silly and ignorant, but he's got guts, and guts is enough." Conventional piety is less important to the Marine Corps than is unwavering fidelity to a principle, however "silly" or "ignorant," in the face of tremendous pressure to recant. Such strength of will can be tapped into and molded by the Corps. Mindless, passive obedience cannot. Joker's reward for proving his fortitude is, predictably, more responsibility — another challenge. Assigned to tutor Private Pyle in proper marine ways, Joker serves as an extension of Sergeant Hartman, who has neither the time nor the inclination to nursemaid a single recruit who cannot keep up with the platoon's overall progress.

The film's second drill montage is a variation on the first. This time basic training proceeds on two separate and, in some respects, contrasting levels. Joker and Pyle drill by themselves in the foreground while Sergeant Hartman and the rest of Platoon 3092 occupy the background, just as earlier the activities of 3092 were set against a backdrop of other platoons. A *personal* story now develops within the broader, collective drama. Isolation from the platoon allows Joker to obtain results that Hartman failed to get. The discordant incompetence of Pyle's performance in the earlier montage gives way to his slow but steady progress in this one. Joker even restores his pupil's civilian first name (Leonard) as a show of respect. Pyle's silly grin returns, but as a token of affection for and gratitude towards Joker rather than as a challenge to Hartman's command. Pyle learns to take apart, clean, and reassemble his M-14, lace his boots properly, conquer his fear of heights on the obstacle course, make his bed regulation neat, and maneuver his weapon properly in parade drill.

Part Two of the second training montage shows Pyle's reintegration into the platoon. Remedial classes are over. With slow-motion cinematography emphasizing his coordination, Pyle successfully navigates a water obstacle in tandem with two fellow recruits. Then he marches in step at the front of the platoon, with Hartman walking alongside, subjecting him to close but apparently approving scrutiny. As the platoon shifts their rifles from left to right shoulders, the camera sweeps across them in the opposite direction, emphasizing the smoothness of their movement — and no disruption by Pyle. Hartman has successfully incorporated Joker's compassion into an overall training process that rejects compassion as a tool. In other words, he transforms what is to him foreign, even contemptible, into a useful ally.

A reverse zoom away from targets on a rifle range settles on Hartman lecturing on the finer points of killing. The camera movement, placing the mechanical aspects of marksmanship into a broader context, parallels Hartman's talk, which likewise moves beyond the simple matter of accuracy achieved through practice to the more complicated, emotional aspects of taking a life. The recruits of Platoon 3092 sit gathered around their drill instructor like Boy Scouts at camp. The relationship is similar, but the lessons being taught and learned are different. Private Pyle is smiling again, this time with the contentment of being a respected member of the team.

Hartman declares that if a soldier is to survive in combat he must harness his killer instinct. The romantic devotion between recruit and rifle cultivated earlier, in order to motivate him to take proper care of his weapon, is now *de*emphasized in order to make the point that it is "a hard heart that kills." Unlike *Clockwork's* Ludovico advocates, who aimed to create robotic pacifists, the Marine Corps seeks to amplify the passion and refine the skills of aggression. To describe killer instincts as "clean and strong" is to speak of a *lack* of moral impediments to killing. The only restraint on those instincts is to be supplied by the Corps in the form of target selection. The arrogance of that collective power over the minds and bodies of individual soldiers is evident in Hartman's absurd declaration that marines are not allowed to die without permission.

During an exercise run along camp streets, the recruits chant, "My Corps! Your Corps! Our Corps! Marine Corps!" The individual recruit is figuratively made both subject and master of the institution. Compare this relationship with the one described in the Prisoners' Hymn 258 in *Clockwork*, which offers only a depressing submission to rather than participation in collective power.

Stripped down again to their underwear, standing at attention atop their footlockers like statues on pedestals (recall the statues in *Barry Lyndon*), the recruits of Platoon 3092 are inspected by Sergeant Hartman for personal hygiene and tidiness of personal property. Following a pattern established in previous scenes, Hartman points out minor defects as a matter of routine before settling on Private Pyle as the major offender. He has left his footlocker unlocked. Ironically, in an institutional environment where the individual retains little privacy, Pyle is vilified for not keeping his personal property secured, thereby encouraging thievery. To illustrate the potential consequences of Pyle's oversight, Hartman dumps out the footlocker's contents the way a ruthless foe might challenge a careless marine's unsecured combat position. Strangely enough, Private Pyle's first violation makes it possible for the Sergeant to uncover a second. Pyle has hidden inside his footlocker a forbidden jelly doughnut taken from the mess hall. If Pyle had locked the container, as per general order, Hartman would not have discovered his unauthorized doughnut and would have remained unaware of Pyle's lack of self-discipline with regard to sweets. Pyle's initial misdeed therefore serves institutional interests by uncovering a greater sin.

The comic ghost of *Gomer Pyle's* hysterical Sergeant Carter threatens once again, after a long absence, to undermine Hartman's aura of authority. So much fuss over one jelly doughnut. But as in the film's first barracks scene, Hartman forces the Carter analogy beyond the bounds of humor. In one striking shot, Joker appears between Hartman and Pyle. As a tutor appointed by Hartman to teach Pyle to be a proper marine, he has failed. Hartman's criticism of the entire platoon's failure to give Pyle proper motivation is in

Sergeant Hartman (Lee Emery) transforms a forbidden jelly doughnut into a symbol of shame for Privates Pyle (Vincent D'Onofrio, left) and Joker (Matthew Modine, center).

particular aimed at Joker. But the Sergeant's harshest punishment is reserved for Pyle. Parading the incriminating doughnut in front of the outwardly expressionless but inwardly shamed platoon, Hartman collectivizes Pyle's guilt. The process of isolating each recruit from his civilian past, so evident in the film's earlier scenes, has been superceded by the building up of a group identity. And now it is time for the platoon as a whole to take responsibility for the performance of each member. The recruits are ordered to do push-ups while chanting their love of the Corps (every challenge must be accepted as a chance to prove one's worth) as penance for the dishonorable behavior of Private Pyle. Gone are the slaps and punches with which Hartman initially punished deviance and incompetence. This time he inflicts a much deeper wound, made possible only by the spirit of fraternity cultivated in previous scenes. Hartman's crowning victory over Pyle's uncontrolled appetite is achieved when he transforms an object of desire into one of disgust. He forces Pyle to eat the forbidden jelly doughnut while the rest of the platoon is punished for it. In a revealing long shot, the men do their push-ups at Pyle's feet. What superficially looks like a posture of respect, if not reverence, is in fact one of shame. Pyle is made to feel bad because he does not share in his comrades' punishment. *His* pleasure is *their* pain. With a meticulous piece of stage direction, Sergeant Hartman does to Pyle's appetite for sweets what Ludovico scientists do to Alex's excessive appetite for violence in *Clockwork*.

Resented by his platoon brothers in the aftermath of the jelly doughnut episode, Private Pyle is more than ever dependent on his tutor and only friend, Joker. "I need help," he pleads. He looks at Joker with near reverence while being taught the rudiments of dressing himself properly. Out on the training field, Pyle is once again the shamed outcast, sucking his thumb off to one side while the platoon is put through its paces. No longer is it a privilege to get out of hard work. But the illusion of this scene is that Pyle's status within the platoon has simply regressed to an earlier stage of alienation. In fact, the platoon's collective mentality has changed under Hartman's direction. Transgressions once purely an issue between Pyle and Hartman are now also an issue between Pyle and his teammates, who have internalized their drill instructor's strict moral standards and increasingly take responsibility for the discipline of their own.

The proof of this transformation is a terrifying, claustrophobic scene of ritualized retribution set off from surrounding scenes by blackouts. Although the emotional groundwork was laid out for it, nothing quite prepares us for the bizarre act of violence that now occurs. The scene begins, in typical Kubrick fashion, with a close-up that reveals only a small portion of what will gradually develop. Moonlight through a barracks window casts an ethereal glow over a white bar of soap being silently wrapped in a white towel by anonymous hands. Soap is a cleaning agent. Platoon 3092 is about to ritually cleanse itself of dishonor. The makeshift club is tried out on a mattress.

Elsewhere, Joker lies awake in his bunk, one hand resting on his head and the other on his heart — one of several images in the film suggesting an internal conflict. Joker is both a personal friend to Private Pyle and a squad leader responsible for the larger welfare of the group. Whatever qualms he has about what is going to happen, Joker initiates the ritual by getting out of bed and standing beside Pyle. The other recruits quietly assemble, like ghostly avengers, around their sleeping victim, whose large stomach protrudes from under a regulation undershirt too small to contain it. In a swift, concerted action Pyle is gagged, bound to his bunk, and beaten with soap clubs wielded by his comrades. This is a marine "blanket party," which is no party for its victim. The aural violence of both punishment and suffering is deliberately smothered. Yet the overall impression is far more disturbing than anything Pyle suffered at the hands of Sergeant Hartman, whose role as disciplinarian is now internalized in each member of the platoon. Ironically, it is possible that the recruits who punish Pyle in this scene channel into their violence the repressed anger they feel toward the leader who has inspired them to do so. After all, his humiliation of them has been only slightly less than his humiliation of Pyle.

The last to punish Pyle is Joker, who is torn between sympathy for the victim and duty to the platoon as a whole. He hesitates. Cowboy urges him on. Pyle makes a counterappeal with his eyes — the only avenue of expression left open to him. In order to overcome the power of that appeal, Joker must tap even deeper into his sense of collective retribution than did his comrades. Playing Brutus to Pyle's Caesar, he hits Pyle more times and with greater force than anyone else. Joker's betrayal shatters his special relationship to Pyle and completes Pyle's emotional isolation from the platoon. As the avengers slink back to their bunks, Pyle hugs his bruised body and cries for himself. Bawling like a child, he seems grotesquely out of place in a Marine Corps barracks. But his wailing has the power to torment Joker, the leader of the opposition, who lies in his bunk cupping his hands over his ears. He has not yet found, as Hartman once described it, his "hard heart."

Before removing the gag from Pyle's mouth, Cowboy whispers, "Remember, it was just a bad dream, fatboy!" The blanket party is not officially sanctioned or even acknowledged by the Marine Corps, yet it is a logical extension of Hartman's indoctrination. Platoon 3092 disciplines one of its own under cover of darkness, unsupervised by higher authority and in a ritualized manner that lends it an aura of collective legitimacy. Background music reflects the scene's duality. Part of it mimics the calm, steady breathing of sleep, metaphorically echoing Cowboy's phony claim that the whole episode is just a dream. But another part emulates the martial music of training episodes in which the platoon's solidarity was forged. In other words, the music of sleep is challenged by a haunting reminder of marine honor turned against itself.

The routine of basic training returns as though the blanket party had never occurred. Private Pyle resumes his place in the ranks, apparently restored to the good graces of his drill instructor and his comrades. Sergeant Hartman leads a ritual chant of collective devotion and combat bravado. But a zoom-in on Pyle reveals chilling counterpoint. In earlier scenes, Pyle was often separated from the group as punishment for his mistakes. This time, the camera exposes a flaw *within* what is otherwise a harmonious whole. Pyle does not participate in a chant of "Blood! Blood! Blood!" and "Kill! Kill! Kill!" Looking grim and introspective, he has separated *himself* from the platoon. Ironically, his nonparticipation in a ritual ode to violence is more frightening than his comrades' enthusiastic participation. Their performance is a piece of theater under strict institutional control, while his brooding silence suggests a growing, private rage independent of that control.

For the first time in the film, camera angle and choice of lens render Private Pyle's large size imposing rather than comic. The Marine Corps cap on his head looks too small to contain his deviant, unspoken thoughts. Previously it just looked ill fitting. And unlike Pyle's weakness for sweets, Sergeant Hartman fails to notice a lack of discipline potentially far more dangerous.

A lesson in marine traditions of marksmanship excellence is fashioned by Hartman into a question-and-answer session that incorporates two infamous examples from civilian life: University-of-Texas-tower mass murderer Charles Whitman and Lee Harvey Oswald, President John F. Kennedy's alleged assassin. The fact that only one recruit (a native Texan) is familiar with Whitman while the entire platoon knows about Oswald illustrates the nature of fame. Whitman killed *many* people but remains a relatively obscure public figure because none of the victims were famous. Oswald, who possibly killed *two* people, is known to almost everyone because of the notoriety of one of them. Therefore, in spite of his lower body count, Oswald is more valuable to Hartman's lesson than is Whitman.

Private Snowball triggers laughter in the ranks by confusing the words "depository" and "suppository." Hartman cuts that laughter short because it does not serve his purpose. By identifying Oswald and Whitman as former marines, he elevates their deeds from the deviant actions of deranged individuals to admirable examples of military training. Technical skill is divorced from civilian society's legal and moral judgment.

While Hartman extols the violent proof of marine skill, the camera zooms in on Private Pyle, who listens with more passionate concentration than do the other recruits. With upturned eyes in the Kubrick tradition, he is a portrait of aggressive self-absorption. If Hartman transforms a violent slice of civilian history into a clinical example of Marine Corps marksmanship, Pyle, in his embrace of that example, restores to it the passionate deviance it originally had. And in the process we get a glimpse of Pyle's *real* "war face."

Announcing Christmas religious services, Hartman delivers a sermon of his own, revising traditional Christian views on the relationship between God and Man. "God has a hard-on for marines because we kill everything we see. To show our appreciation for so much power, we keep heaven packed with fresh souls!" Typically, violence and power are translated into sexual terms. According to the Sergeant's creed, God, the free world, and the Marine Corps are allies in a crusade against communism. But the pecking order within that alliance is vague. "You can give your heart to Jesus, but your ass belongs to the Corps!" In Hartman's weird vocabulary, "ass" is equivalent to "soul." Fidelity to the Corps supplants fidelity to God, the free world, or anything else.

As Hartman's disciplinary role becomes internalized within the recruits, his part in basic training becomes less active and more supervisory. In the barracks, he watches the men clean and reassemble their rifles. The symphonic clicking of rifle components is proof of the Sergeant's efficient instruction. But as the camera sweeps across Hartman's orchestra, we hear the quiet, slightly discordant sound of Private Pyle talking affectionately to his weapon. What he says is barely audible. It is his *manner* of saying it that conveys to us his undisciplined passion for his weapon. In his romantic outpouring, he repeats the word "clean." The platoon's concern with cleaning away Pyle's stain on its collective honor, resulting in the blanket party, manifests itself *in* Pyle as a fixation on the condition and operation of his rifle, which echoes his desperate need to clean away the shame of his humiliation.

Perhaps because of their previous closeness, which was mandated by Hartman, Joker is the only character to sense danger in Pyle's odd behavior. In a subjective close-up from his vantage point, Pyle appears in profile, his head an imposing, pug-faced mask of self-absorption. The childishness that seemed so pathetically out of place during the beating he took from his comrades now seems to be a token of his invulnerability to collective authority. His face is equivalent to Jack's writing ("All work and no play makes Jack a dull boy") in *The Shining*.

The barracks of Platoon 3092 are reduced to spartan simplicity and antiseptic cleanliness — a condition which the Marine Corps, through Hartman, seeks to duplicate within the minds of its recruits. The fewer and more orderly the ingredients, physical and emotional, the easier they are to control — or so the theory goes. New recruits are isolated at Parris Island, away from the complexities and distractions of civilian life. Privates Joker and Cowboy find themselves in turn isolated from the platoon and from Sergeant Hartman's supervision when they are assigned to mop the lavatory. There they are relatively free to speak their minds without fear of censure. The lavatory, by the way, is a comic illustration of contrary needs reconciled. The individual's physiological needs are addressed, but with a lack of privacy favored by the Corps.

Joker reveals to Cowboy his suspicions about Pyle's mental instability, which he describes in military jargon as Section Eight. Apparently forgotten is his moral anguish at betraying a friend in the name of platoon solidarity. So slight is his concern about Pyle now that in the next breath he casually announces he wants to have sex with Cowboy's sister, again employing a colorful marine metaphor. And Cowboy's reply illustrates the strengthening hold of platoon solidarity on *him* as well. Instead of being offended by Joker's request, he is agreeable. Under Sergeant Hartman's tutelage, what were once regarded as insults have been transformed into tokens of affection.

Though judged a potentially dangerous deviant by Joker, Private Pyle progresses nicely in the eyes of his drill instructor. On the rifle range, he displays the sort of marksmanship Hartman praised in the examples of Whitman and Oswald. In the next scene, he accurately quotes a general order from the basic training manual, earning Hartman's rare praise for doing so, after Joker *fails* to do the same, receiving a tongue-lashing and twenty-five pushups as punishment. For the first time in the film, Pyle is not the biggest foulup in the platoon. Incidentally, Hartman does not monitor Joker after ordering the push-ups. He knows, at this late stage of basic training, that Joker's internal sense of discipline will do the job for him.

Speaking in a flat tone of voice, coming from a distant future when Joker has fully embraced his marine identity, narration confirms the hardening process we have been watching. "Ready to eat out their own guts and ask for seconds" is hyperbolic Marine Corps rhetoric for welcoming danger, fear, and pain as chances to prove one's self. For the first time, we see the recruits looking like combat soldiers, in full battle gear. Charging towards the camera, displaying their "war faces," the recruits look very different from an earlier portrait in which they struggled awkwardly together through a sea of mud. They have grown "beyond the control of their leaders" because esprit de corps has become second nature and self-sustaining in them. As the narrator explains, the Corps wants to build "indestructible men — men without fear" — except, of course, fear of dishonor, which is the emotional foundation of that indestructibility.

Promoted by Sergeant Hartman from "maggots" to "marines," the men of Platoon 3092 cut the umbilical cord of basic training. The whole process has been a rebirth equivalent to a religious conversion — an attempt to eradicate and/or reshape everything the men brought with them from civilian life. Hartman's benediction begins in the barracks, then overlaps a series of graduation ceremony shots in which the new marines, in full dress uniform, strut their stuff for the edification of family and friends, for whom this colorful, superficial, inoffensive display is everything. The day-to-day realities of basic training, or of subsequent combat duty, are not for civilian consumption. Hartman's disembodied verbal blessing on the soundtrack is in its own way an equally idealized vision of what it means to be a marine. "The Marine Corps lives forever. And that means *you* live forever" is a promise of immortality through the marriage of individual and collective identities. Backed by a stirring rendition of the Marine Hymn and images of the graduation ceremony, Hartman's description of power and order on a grand scale is as appealing as it is absurd.

Duty assignments handed out by Hartman to his men are like diplomas distributed at a civilian graduation. They signify the earned right to pass on to bigger and more prestigious responsibilities. The more dangerous the job, the more honor accompanies it. Private Pyle makes it into the Sergeant's beloved infantry. In frontal close-up, he wears the same self-absorbed, aggressive glare he did during the marksmanship lecture. Lost in a private fantasy of fulfillment having nothing to do with his official assignment, he fails to answer Hartman's roll call. The Sergeant, in turn, fails to recognize Pyle's inattention as a sign of dangerous nonconformity.

Private Joker reasserts a measure of independence from Marine Corps solidarity by choosing to become a marine journalist. Such a soft assignment earns Hartman's contempt. "You think you're Mickey Spillane?" is both an insult aimed at Joker and perhaps a clue as to Hartman's reading habits. Spillane's crime thrillers are hardboiled stories about tough guys doing tough things in tough situations. But *writing* about being tough is, in Hartman's view, a far cry from *being* tough. Joker compounds his offense by mentioning that he used to write for his high-school newspaper. The specter of civilian life raises its ugly head in Hartman's exclusively marine domain.

Same setting, different circumstances. Night transforms the barracks into a haunted variation of itself, as during the blanket-party scene. But this time it is collective order that sleeps unaware while private deviance rises to the surface. Performing "fire watch," Joker is an unarmed, token representative of the former, patrolling the barracks for unauthorized activity. Pausing between opposing doors leading to Sergeant Hartman's quarters and to the lavatory, he is figuratively caught in a tug of war between his own heart, which sympathizes with Private Pyle, and his head, which rationalized the blanket party as necessary for the platoon's welfare. In more practical terms, he is caught in the middle of a struggle between the contrary and, in this instance, irreconcilable perspectives of individual (Pyle) and institutional (Hartman) man.

Hearing a disturbance in the lavatory, Joker enters and finds a soul in Hell, a man pulled apart by contradictory loyalties within himself. Private Pyle sits slumped on a toilet seat, as compelling a portrait of powerlessness as Kubrick has projected. Dressed only in his underwear, he looks exposed and vulnerable. In emotional terms, he lacks the shield of self-discipline and group identification that Hartman has tried to instill in him. Joker's flashlight illuminates his face, disrupting his private torment and turning his rage and self-loathing outward. Pyle flashes a nasty, cheerless grin that chillingly mocks the silly Gomer Pyle grin he wore at the start of basic training. The only thing the two expressions have in common is that both are spontaneous and involuntary. Matching his joyless smile is his friendly, yet creepy, greeting of Joker. Like Jack Torrance speaking to his son Danny in their Overlook apartment, Pyle's speech is distorted by agitation. He is pathetic and unpredictable at the same time, like a wounded animal — an animal with sharp teeth and claws, it turns out. Beside him stands Charlene, his rifle. Between his legs, he methodically loads an ammunition clip. Replying to Joker's cautious inquiry as to whether or not the ammunition is live, Pyle announces loudly, "Seven six two millimeter, full metal jacket," punctuating his words by snapping another bullet into the clip. The film's title comes into play here. Individual marines are to the Marine Corps what bullets and rifles are to the individual marine — tools by which power is greatly magnified. "Full metal jacket" refers to the hard steel casing which shields a bullet and allows it to penetrate its target without shattering on impact. Basic training likewise aims to insulate recruits against the physical and psychological rigors of combat. In metaphorical terms, Private Pyle is a bullet without a steel jacket — a killer without proper discipline. Instead of anchoring his private passions in the rigid discipline of the Corps, Pyle makes his basic training skills serve those passions. Similarly in *Dr. Strangelove*, General Ripper's institutional authority and sense of duty became enslaved to his sexual fears.

Joker tries to manage the situation by appealing to conventional, institutional logic. If Hartman finds Pyle and him in the lavatory with live ammunition, they will both be "in a world of shit," the traditional marine metaphor for serious trouble. Pyle, however, overrides that definition of trouble with one of his own. "I *am* in a world of shit!" may seem amusingly literal because Pyle is sitting on a toilet. But his manner of saying it is not. Joker's idea of trouble involves individual man violating collective order. Pyle's, on the other hand, is a *private* hell where he is punished by his own demons. He has mastered his body and his rifle, to Hartman's satisfaction, but he has not conquered the shame of his humiliation by the platoon. Instead of Pyle being defined by the spotless, spartan, collective environment of the lavatory, the lavatory is defined by Pyle's inner torment as a place of emotional chaos.

Jumping to his feet, Pyle gives a spirited and flawless performance of rifle drill and prayer, but in an inappropriate setting and time. His lack of clothes reflects his lack of proper institutional containment. Attaching the ammunition clip to his weapon, he violates yet another regulation. Sergeant Hartman, meanwhile, confronts the noisy aberration in his latrine like the outraged minister of institutional order that he is. Playing divide and conquer, he first orders the other, curious recruits back to their bunks before entering the lavatory. Then, in typical fashion, he deals with the two principle transgressors in his kingdom. Joker is his first target because he is responsible for maintaining order in the barracks while the Sergeant sleeps. Only when Joker alerts him to the seriousness of Pyle's violation does Hartman alter his aim. Unwisely, however, he does not change his blunt tactics. Standing ramrod straight, his posture commands respect but, his lack of uniform does not. Ironically, being dressed only in underwear *enhances* his opponent's aura of rebellious aggression. Pyle looks much larger and more powerful now than does his stripped drill instructor, who tries to compensate for the disadvantage with sheer volume and bravado. He tries to berate Pyle into backing down, mocking the idea of psychological problems rooted in childhood experiences. Marines simply do not permit such obstacles to interfere with their performance of duty. This is the same argument he used with Pyle in earlier scenes. But the circumstances are radically different. Backing down from a challenge now would merely *increase* Pyle's self-hatred.

Hartman orders Pyle to surrender his weapon. Pyle, grinning and gasping grotesquely at the pleasurable thought of overcoming his greatest obstacle to happiness, responds by shooting Hartman in the chest. We see the impact from Pyle's point of view, in slow motion, the way we saw Alex's revenge against his droogs at the Flatblock marina in *Clockwork*.

Ominously, Pyle's focus of revenge shifts to the ex-friend who betrayed him. Joker stands frozen in terror, his only defense a lame appeal to "Go easy, man." But unlike Jack Torrance in *The Shining*, Private Pyle retains a spark of compassion and a little critical detachment from his own passions. His powerful physique goes limp. He lowers his rifle. In a limited sense, Pyle triumphs where Joker, the superior marine, failed. Though reluctant to do so, Joker gave in to peer pressure and participated savagely in the blanket-party beating of Pyle, who now restrains himself from taking revenge on his former friend and tutor. Instead, Pyle's anger turns inward again. Slumping back down on the toilet seat where he began the scene, he blows out his brains, passing brutal judgment on himself rather than on Joker. A moment after violently defying institutional authority, he carries out what would surely be its sentence on him.

Like the blood gushing from the elevator door in Danny Torrance's paranormal visions of Overlook, Private Pyle's blood obscenely stains the pristine white walls of his orderly institutional environment. But just as Jack Torrance's violent actions were shaped partly by Overlook's violent past, Pyle's killer instinct was encouraged and exploited by the same authority figure who eventually becomes its victim.

Part One of *Full Metal Jacket* chronicles, among other things, the failure of Marine Corps indoctrination with respect to Private Pyle. Part Two chronicles the gradual, ironic *success* of that same indoctrination with respect to Private Joker. A fade to black concludes the basic training sequence, where Kubrick presented in loving detail the collective full metal jacketing of marine recruits ultimately bound for Vietnam. Without that lengthy portrait of the indoctrination process, the behavior of American soldiers in subsequent combat scenes cannot be fully appreciated. Into each new, challenging situation the marines carry with them a set of tools (physical and emotional) imparted to them by their drill instructors.

Private Pyle was an aberration who failed to make it through basic training. He is one example of the violent deviance that director Francis Ford Coppola relentlessly pursued into the officially off-limit jungles of Cambodia in his 1979 film *Apocalypse Now*. Pyle never made it that far. The horror at the end of Private Joker's journey through combat hell resides in his involuntary commitment *to* rather than defiance *of* conventional military order.

Following the example of Part One, Part Two opens with a song that overlaps and redefines the imagery it accompanies. Nancy Sinatra's "These Boots Are Made for Walking" is a song about betrayal and revenge. Our first visual impression of Vietnam is a long shot of a busy street corner in Da Nang. Stepping into that low-angle shot, which then becomes a partly subjective tracking shot, is a Vietnamese prostitute. She does not actually wear a pair of boots, but the song's lyrics speak for her, at least on a metaphorical level. The rocky romance Nancy Sinatra sings about is roughly analogous to the relationship between Americans and South Vietnamese during the war. "Boots," like most other period songs heard in *Full Metal Jacket*, is an apolitical song that acquires political meaning only in the context of the images it accompanies, and even then it contributes a discordant sense of American provincialism at odds with visual impressions of Vietnam.

Private Joker and fellow marine journalist Rafterman (Platoon 3092 has broken up, but in a larger sense *all* marines are brothers) negotiate with the prostitute for her services. She offers to be their "girlfriend," but the encounter is hardly romantic. Joker gives her a friendly hug but at the same time warns his companion that some whores serve the Viet Cong while the others have tuberculosis. "Make sure you only fuck the ones that cough." Under these bizarre circumstances, disease becomes a desirable quality because it implies the absence of an even greater evil. Meanwhile, the prostitute must accommodate to her somewhat hostile customers by speaking their language, which puts her at a strategic disadvantage.

This encounter takes place against the backdrop of a huge billboard featuring the grinning face of a Vietnamese man. Almost a caricature, that face reflects the mistrust of American soldiers for their South Vietnamese allies, even in the heart of a "friendly" city. Validating their suspicions, the marines are attacked by a young Vietnamese male who steals Rafterman's camera. Though only mildly hostile, this initial encounter illustrates the fact that American soldiers serving in Vietnam occupy a world unfamiliar, confusing, and often hostile to them.

Like Jack Torrance in *The Shining*, Private Joker uses sarcasm to battle various enemies, including an unfriendly ally. When the young thief celebrates his victory over the Americans with a brief exhibition of martial arts skill, Joker mocks him with a comic display of his own, reducing the intimidation factor of his enemy. Juxtaposed with this duel, in the background, is an elegantly attired, white-gloved traffic cop. Looking like a holdover from French colonial days, he maintains order over passing automobile traffic but obviously has no control over street-corner crime. Meanwhile, Joker is juxtaposed with a commercial portrait of Jesus Christ. In some ways, Americans viewed themselves as saviors in the Vietnam War. But Joker's mocking martial arts pose clashes with that saintly image of self-sacrifice.

Joker and Rafterman's stroll back to the Da Nang marine base features another symphony of conflicting verbal and visual elements. Joker expresses admiration for the thief who stole Rafterman's camera, echoing Sergeant

Hartman's praise for the marksmanship of Whitman and Oswald. But he also refers to the thief as that "little sucker," echoing a bias stemming from the same institutional source. Rafterman, meanwhile, is trapped between his implanted marine need to prove himself in combat and his contempt for the people he is officially defending. His determination to "get out into the shit" wars with his disgust for the South Vietnamese, who "shit all over us every chance they get." Some types of "shit" are more conducive to self-esteem than others. Marine Corps indoctrination fills Rafterman with enthusiasm for combat even in the absence of a compelling political justification for the personal risk.

The Da Nang marine base is a haven of Americanism in a foreign land. Joker and Rafterman walk past a group of soldiers playing basketball. Rafterman smokes a conspicuously American brand of cigarettes. The words "U.S. Marine Corps, Da Nang" sit astride a pagoda-like structure at the main gate. Aesthetically, at least, the Marine Corps dominates its alien environment.

Military journalism is in some ways an oxymoron. The Marine Corps newspaper, *The Sea Tiger*, is to the Corps what the Corps is to the American government — an institution within an institution; an institution with inherent differences from its parent, whom it must accommodate in order to justify its existence. The conflict between journalistic detachment and loyalty to the Marine Corps and its mission is humorously proclaimed in our first glimpse inside the Da Nang press hut. Articulate, relatively easygoing and cynical, Lieutenant Lockhart, the soldier/journalist in charge, looks more like a television anchorman than a marine officer. On the wall behind him hangs a banner that reads, "First to go, last to know. We will defend to the death our right to be misinformed." — a far cry from the "Pride Builds Men" poster in the Parris Island barracks of Platoon 3092. Marine reporters harbor few illusions about their lowly status within the Corps. But in spite of their mockery, they dutifully yield to their institutional parent.

The first press hut scene demonstrates how the traditional function of journalism in a free society is appropriated and modified by the Corps. *The Sea Tiger* staff must coordinate, edit, and even re-create a large mass of war impressions, to the satisfaction of several diverse audiences, including top brass, combat grunts, and civilians back home. The hut walls and conference table are littered with objects (from Charlie Brown, sword in hand, giving *his* war cry, to an insolent Mick Jagger) that, taken together, makeup a cultural grab bag of impressions and attitudes with which Americans entered the Vietnam War.

Journalism as practiced at *The Sea Tiger* involves selecting and tailoring war-related news to suit conflicting audiences. Obviously accustomed to this sort of compromise, Lockhart is glib to the point of lyrical grace as he orchestrates the next issue. His personal sense of power and contentment, as exercised through his collective assignment, depends on formulaic pre-dictability rather than on the surprise of hard investigation. His job is to contain, not expose. Rumors of an enemy attack during Tet, the Vietnamese lunar New Year, are dismissed as paranoia. Employing typical racist and cultural slurs, Lockhart expresses contempt for the Vietnamese and their hitherto predictable behavior during Tet.

Entertainment notes for the upcoming issue are to include some revealing, but not *too* revealing, photographs of Ann-Margret at a U.S.O. show. Characteristic of marine-speak, Lockhart's description of the assignment is both sexist and colorful. Explicit pictures of Ann-Margret are for the edification of sex-starved marine grunts. *Restrictions* on that explicitness are a concession to higher military authority, which must answer to the civilian sensibilities of *its* institutional superiors. Another such concession is a story about the Lawrence Welk television show — something of little interest to grunts but which lends the Corps a public image of wholesomeness.

The role played by the enemy in official marine news coverage of the war is paradoxical. One story tells of an NVA soldier who deserted from his unit after reading American propaganda pamphlets, appealing to readers who still believe in a political justification for the war. Lockhart even changes the enemy's designation, from North Vietnamese Army "regular" to "soldier," in order to make him more human and less abstract. On the other hand, stories about enemy soldiers killed in battle bolster morale among the American combat soldiers. The enemy is valued as either a living convert to the American way of life or a lifeless testament to American military superiority. And the "journalists" who contribute to that propaganda campaign do not quibble much about the authenticity of their material. Euphemisms are freely employed to soften the brutality of U.S. military actions. "Search and destroy" becomes, by directive from higher authority, the less specific and less violent "clean and sweep." On the other hand, enemy kills are often *embellished*, even fabricated, in order to placate the grunts. An unproductive patrol reported by Private Joker becomes, without evidence to back it up, a confirmed kill. In effect, Lockhart rewrites Joker's unsatisfactory story, inserting a happy ending. But the Lieutenant reveals a *second* propagandistic agenda beneath the first. By making the dead NVA soldier an officer, he panders to American grunts who resent their *own* commanders and get revenge vicariously through surrogate targets. If Private Pyle had survived basic training and served in Vietnam, he might have read Joker's rewritten article and fantasized about the death of Sergeant Hartman. Battle lines implied in this scene cut across political and cultural distinctions.

Joker, retaining some of his civilian notions of what a reporter should be, resents the falsification of his story. But he challenges Lockhart in terms of marine-defined self-esteem rather than of journalistic integrity. Referring sarcastically to his superior as "sir," he suggests the Lieutenant go on a few combat missions and gather his own kill confirmations. In other words, he questions Lockhart's manhood in front of the entire unit, the way Redmond and Toole questioned each other's in front of their regiment. There is a bit of Sergeant Hartman in Joker's choice of attack. But Lockhart brushes it off with equal bravado, transforming his own weakness (lack of combat experience) into an asset (proof of his intelligence), and doing so in colorful marine-speak. Still, Joker has obviously touched on a vulnerability felt by all marine journalists.

From inside the marine base, we see fireworks exploding in the distance, outside the base — visual tokens of the Vietnamese Tet celebration. Joker's dispassionate narration trivializes the foreign holiday by recasting it in familiar, irreverent, American terms. On the soundtrack, the pop song "Chapel of Love" further domesticates Tet. Contempt for Vietnamese traditions is one way the marines shield themselves emotionally from the alien culture that surrounds and often threatens them.

"Chapel of Love" continues as the camera cuts to inside the press hutch, where it echoes a distinctly *American* drama of faith. Conversation among the journalist/soldiers gathered in the hutch revolves around their experiences in combat rather than their achievements as reporters. Joker starts the ball rolling by remarking, "I gotta get back in the shit." From the opposite side of the barracks, a fellow reporter, nicknamed Payback, makes fun of Joker's pretensions to toughness and stakes a more valid claim of his own. Joker then falls back on his liberal defense, reviving his John Wayne impression to mock combat machismo in general, thereby undercutting Payback's superior claim. Joker's tactics are further evidence of his conflicting desires to be a born-again-hard marine and yet maintain a critical distance from that identity.

For reasons of his own, a third member of the group, named Chili, aligns himself with Joker and against Payback, just as an anonymous third party gave support to Redmond's assault on Toole. Payback retaliates with a slur on Chili's Spanish-American heritage, then defends his prior claim by infusing it with a certain mystique. He speaks of a "thousand-yard stare" possessed by all true combat soldiers. By insisting that he is the only man present who has such a stare, Payback becomes a challenge to the entire group. A fourth man joins in the verbal assault on Payback, and with a racial slur equivalent to Payback's. Only the marines' overriding collective identity makes it possible for them to exchange such insults without becoming true enemies. Sergeant Hartman and other drill instructors successfully transformed such volatile language into expressions of fraternity.

Pictured at the center of this debate is Rafterman, lying on his bunk. Of the reporters present, Rafterman has perhaps the least combat experience. Ashamed of that fact, he takes no active part in the debate. His position would be indefensible. And like the Ludovico Auditorium spotlights that shine on Alex in *Clockwork*, the overhead lights that illuminate him in this scene are tokens of a pitiless collective scrutiny, operating both internally and externally.

The hutch lights, and with them all debate on the subject of combat experience, flicker off when the remote sounds of Vietnamese ceremonial fireworks become the uncomfortably close sounds of enemy gunfire. Combat comes to the journalists as base sirens cry out in institutional alarm. The attack on the Da Nang marine base is typical of the Tet Offensive in that the enemy confronts Americans on territory previously presumed to be secure. Jungle warfare was never more than an endless series of firefights in which territory often changed hands from day to night. But the cities and the big American military installations in South Vietnam were thought to be almost unassailable, rather like Pearl Harbor before the Japanese attack in World War II. Joker, Rafterman, and Payback take up defensive positions near the main gate. Forgotten now are false displays of bravado. Joker confesses, "I ain't ready for this shit," to which a colleague adds, "Amen." Yet Joker's first real exposure to combat is somewhat muted. Shielded by the fortified walls of a concrete bunker, he views the approaching enemy almost like an audience watching a movie.

A "Stop" sign at the main gate now seems a ludicrously inadequate token of institutional order, as did numerous safety devices at the Overlook Hotel in the context of Jack Torrance's homicidal rampage. Yet the NVA soldiers prove extremely vulnerable to marine machine gun fire, falling like targets in a shooting gallery. Joker, firing his weapon with abandon, grows ever more confident of his power and security. He even smiles. Maybe he *is* ready for combat. Neither he nor any of his companions are injured in this scene. A peace-symbol button, illuminated by the flames of battle, shines prominently on Joker's flak jacket. It is his modest, abstract defiance of the war and of the marine combat mentality. But Joker's *face*, illuminated by the same flames, betrays his enjoyment of battle, at least as experienced from the relative safety of a concrete bunker.

Next morning the camera tracks with Joker and Rafterman as they walk across the base, past the bullet-pitted main gate. In the foreground, captured and wounded enemy soldiers file past in the opposite direction. Almost in silhouette, they are visually prominent, yet beneath the notice of the two marines. Different aspects of imagery (size and camera movement) operate in counterpoint. The shot is reminiscent of one in *Metropolis*, where the looming black shapes of underground workers, injured in the explosion of a huge machine they were forced to operate, file past the small white figure of young Fredor, aristocratic heir from a privileged social class that lives above ground. Fredor is as much a stranger to the workers as the marines are to the

Vietnamese. But Fredor is saddened by the workers' plight and eventually joins in a crusade to liberate them. Joker and Rafterman, in contrast, are oblivious to the nameless, faceless enemy, whose visual prominence in the tracking shot is ironic. After all, sympathy for the enemy could be detrimental to their own welfare.

The shocking surprise of the Tet Offensive reduces *The Sea Tiger* hut and staff to chaos and confusion. While Lieutenant Lockhart briefs his men on the overall situation, the camera circles nervously opposite him, giving us a panoramic view of the room and its jumbled contents. The hut now seems less a clearinghouse than a log jam. In addition to the tools of a journalist's trade, the conference table is heaped with combat gear. Joker's peace button is offset by hand grenades hanging from his chest—a visual legacy from *Dr. Strangelove*'s Colonel "Bat" Guano.

Rather than admit the folly of his earlier prediction regarding Tet, Lockhart vents his embarrassment by complaining about the enemy's deceitful exploitation of the traditional holiday ceasefire. His comfortable, predictable routine has been disrupted—and so have many of America's presumptions. Enemy suicide squads have invaded the U.S. Embassy in Saigon. The marine base at Khe Sanh is on the verge of being overrun. Popular CBS News anchorman Walter Cronkite will soon announce his opinion that the war cannot be won. And in the midst of this collective crisis, Joker resumes his personal duel with Lockhart, using Tet as *his* sword. "Sir, does this mean Ann-Margret's not coming?" mocks what had been the Lieutenant's unshakable faith in predictable routine. Feeling more vulnerable as a result of Tet, Lockhart retaliates more forcefully than he did earlier. But he masks that retaliation in the deceptively dispassionate cloak of duty, giving Joker a dangerous combat assignment and ordering him to remove his offensive peace button.

It is just possible that Joker, desiring a combat assignment, *maneuvers* Lockhart into sending him to Phu Bai, even though the Lieutenant intends it as punishment. But Joker fails to anticipate that Rafterman will take advantage of that maneuver in order to advance his own burning quest to acquire combat credentials, which Joker refused to help him get earlier. Lockhart grants Rafterman permission to accompany Joker to Phu Bai. Joker's objection to that approval merely reinforces the Lieutenant's decision. Thus Joker manipulates Lockhart to get what *he* wants; Rafterman uses that confrontation to get what *he* wants; and Lockhart takes advantage of the disagreement between Joker and Rafterman to get what *he* wants. And all of them do so within the context of their official duties.

The helicopter ride from Da Nang to Phu Bai is the first in a series of brutal combat lessons for Joker and Rafterman. Occupying the rear compartment with them is a doorgunner gleefully and randomly firing his weapon at Vietnamese on the ground below. He channels his private sadism into an institutional task that lends itself to violence. Viewed from his vantage point, the victims fall in lyrical waves, emotionally remote but aesthetically pleasing. This is another variation on the film-audience experience, with its inherent capacity for selective emotional involvement combined with safe detachment. Referring to his targets as "dead gooks killed" the doorgunner enhances his pleasure by the redundancy of "dead" and "killed," and by inflating their number with dead water buffalo. He is Alex playing "hogs of the road" with other drivers in *Clockwork*. Making a joke of his country's political rationale for the war, he explains his criteria for target selection: "Anyone who runs is a V.C. Anyone who stands still is a well-disciplined V.C." In other words, the situation for his victims is a catch-22. And when Joker questions the ethics of his action, the doorgunner disarms that attack by deliberately misinterpreting it as an inquiry about strategy. "How can you shoot women and children?" Joker asks. "You just don't lead 'em so much," the doorgunner replies. With calculated irony, he adds, "Ain't war hell!," his grin implying the opposite. He is Dr. Strangelove, albeit at a much lower level of institutional power.

Cutting back and forth among the doorgunner and the two journalists, Kubrick's camera creates the impression of a three-way debate on the topic of random killing. The doorgunner is an enthusiastic advocate, relishing his role as hired gun. Joker retains a journalist's skepticism on the matter, criticizing the doorgunner's indiscriminate choice of targets. Counterpointing that criticism is the "Born to Kill" Joker has scrawled on his helmet. Like the handwritten messages on two hydrogen bombs aboard Major Kong's B-52, "Born to Kill" is a personal embellishment of institutional hardware. But Joker's private message is mixed. "Born to Kill" is offset by his peace button. Together they makeup his comment about the discordant nature of human desire.

Rafterman provides a third "voice" in the debate. Gagging with nausea, he is, unlike the more dispassionate Joker, sickened by the doorgunner's homicidal joy. Or does he merely suffer from airsickness, which gives him the *appearance* of moral disgust? Whichever the case, by the end of the film Rafterman will rival the doorgunner as an enthusiastic proponent of killing.

The sadistic doorgunner tells the reporters they ought to do a story about him. But as a grotesque perversion of America's official motive for fighting in Vietnam, he does not quite conform to Lieutenant Lockhart's earlier description of the types of stories done by *The Sea Tiger*.

Walking along the road to Hue with Rafterman, Joker discovers one strategic advantage to his otherwise dubious status as a marine journalist. Trying to locate his basic training buddy Cowboy, he solicits information from a lieutenant named Schinoski, whose cooperation increases the moment he discovers what the two strangers do. Nicknamed Mr. Touchdown, no doubt by his drill instructor, Schinoski makes sure the reporters know his full, civilian name as well, in case they want to mention him in a story. The private lure of fame momentarily overshadows the collective sense of duty.

In long shot, we see an American military convoy moving up the road towards Hue, the scene of battle. To the right of this column, in the grass, Vietnamese refugees stream silently away from the combat zone. Physically separated by a canal ditch, the two officially allied columns move in opposite directions, with little or no communication between them. Imagery reflects a fundamental difference in outlook. Officially espousing the cause of freedom but emotionally trained to view combat as a stage for proving self-worth, the marines march on Hue. The Vietnamese refugees, largely indifferent to a liberation that is only a dim abstraction to most of them, seek merely to survive the fighting. But if the South Vietnamese refugees elicit little or no compassion from the marines, enemy soldiers do. "Charles definitely got his shit together" is a compliment from one grunt to another, regardless of political differences. Self-discipline and determination are things a marine can admire, even in a deadly foe. Lack of same can arouse contempt, even for an ally. "Charlie" is at least an improvement on the more generic "gook."

Viewed in close-up, Joker's grim facial expression contrasts with the "Born to Kill" on his helmet. A reverse zoom reveals the cause for his disgust. An open mass grave contains South Vietnamese civilians killed by NVA soldiers who tricked them to their deaths. Accompanying background music is vaguely Oriental in flavor and unsettling in effect, with heavy drums beating out a broken rhythm analogous to the random artillery fire of battle, not at all like the invigorating, familiar martial music heard during basic training scenes. Joker's dispassionate, war-weary narration states a fundamental truth about human existence in a war zone: "The dead only know one thing. It is better to be alive." Actually, the dead know nothing. The living, *pondering* death, appreciate the value of being alive

The pit and its gruesome contents play visual counterpoint to Joker's subsequent conversations with two marine officers. The first is Lieutenant Cleves, whom Joker asks for details about the massacre. The Lieutenant perks up when he learns that his otherwise unwelcome guests are reporters. His attention is rather ghoulishly divided between describing mass murder and smiling for Rafterman's camera — affability and self-interest set against a backdrop of collective horror. He makes sure the reporters know his real name and his home town.

The personal priorities of Lieutenant Cleves are abruptly displaced by those of a marine colonel whose pride, like Sergeant Hartman's, is passionately wedded to his profession. There is no room for divided loyalties in his world, so he challenges Joker's mixed message of peace button and "Born to Kill." Lieutenant Lockhart did the same, but strictly out of *personal* revenge

Private Joker (Matthew Modine, right) advertises his own emotional duality ("Born to Kill" on his helmet and peace button on his chest) while on patrol with the less divided Animal Mother (Adam Baldwin).

for Joker's insult to *him.* "You'd better get your head and your ass wired together, or I will take a giant shit on you" is a typically worded marine threat of punishment for deviance. Joker tries in vain to justify his mixed symbolism with a reference to the psychological theories of Carl Jung. But this is like Alex pleading moral enlightenment to Dr. Brodsky. Wrong audience. Obviously the Colonel has never heard of Jung. As the soldier of superior rank, he simply imposes his own, preferred metaphors on the debate, reducing war to a grab bag of sports analogies, racial slurs, and political evangelism. Joker must "jump on the team" in order to participate in the "big win," which involves liberating the "gooks" from themselves so they can become "American." Judging by the lime-covered, white-faced Vietnamese corpses in the background, that crusade can be fatal to its intended beneficiaries. And, according to the Colonel, it can only be achieved by the unquestioning, undivided loyalty of U.S. marines.

Joker and Rafterman locate Cowboy's platoon inside a bombed-out pagoda courtyard. Round doorways are a distinctly foreign architecture. But the marines of First Platoon, who have rechristened their unit the Lusthog Squad, make themselves at home in the ruins of an alien world. Cowboy shaves at an improvised sink, while his buddies relax amidst the debris. The camera strolls into this setting of chaos and serenity to the music of "Woolly Bully," an American song that seems to defy the Vietnamese imagery and boldly contradicts the background music that echoed Joker's disorientation in the previous scene. It is a protective jacket of sound that helps keep out doubt, confusion, and fear.

In an unwitting tribute to Sergeant Hartman's training, Joker and Cowboy reaffirm their friendship with affectionate insults. But the warm reception is not unanimous. If Joker's journalist status proved a strategic advantage with Lieutenants Schinoski and Cleves, it yields the opposite with a tough Lusthog Squad member nicknamed Animal Mother. Like Hartman, Mother is unimpressed by soldiers who opt for soft assignments. He immediately challenges Joker's combat credentials. Joker responds, as usual, with his John Wayne impression, mocking the enemy's macho attitude, as he did Hartman's and Payback's. Animal Mother threatens to escalate the conflict from words to fists. Refusing to back down, because he cannot without losing face, Joker transforms Mother's threat into a return insult. A low-angle close-up gives Animal Mother a pair of bull-like "horns" derived from the background pagoda structure. Horns are also referred to in "Woolly Bully," which has by now become Mother's anthem. Big, athletic, wrapped in ammunition belts that form a literal "full metal jacket," he appears to have the advantage.

In *Barry Lyndon,* Redmond's army regiment enjoyed and encouraged his confrontation with Toole, which was prevented from turning physical only by the intervention of a superior officer. Similarly, the marines of the Lusthog squad are at first amused by Joker's face-off with Animal Mother. But when the confrontation threatens to become violent, they themselves intervene rather than rely on higher authority to do so. As was demonstrated by the blanket party for Private Pyle, marines are trained to maintain order among themselves. Curiously, however, while Eightball restrains Animal Mother and Cowboy holds back Joker, Rafterman stands off to the side and rather callously scrutinizes the combatants for signs of weakness. Of the soldiers gathered in this scene, he is the least indoctrinated in the notion of collective responsibility. Moments later, Eightball and Animal Mother sit down together. Mother comments to his African-American companion, "Thank God for the sickle cell," referring to a disease that usually attacks black people. Smiling, Eightball accepts the insult as a token of friendship. But later evidence suggests that this marine tradition disguises a *genuine* racism on the part of Animal Mother.

Like Joker, many of the soldiers in First Platoon have embellished their helmets with personal statements, reflecting a wide variety of perspectives and loyalties. One wears a crucifix, adding God to the fight against communism. Another declares, "I'm hard," which merely apes Marine Corps mythology. "Blood Type 'O'" mocks the grunt's assigned role as living target. But it is more a sardonic statement of bravado in the face of danger than a criticism of the Corps or the Vietnam War. "Nam Sucks," making no distinction between North and South, undercuts the political justification for America's participation in the war. But since marines are trained to welcome the challenge of combat as a chance to prove their worth, who needs a political excuse? Cowboy wears a rebel flag on his helmet, ironically harkening back to a rebellion against the government he and the Marine Corps now serve.

Animal Mother's helmet features a phrase similar to that of the despised newcomer, Joker. "I Am Become Death" is Mother's appropriation of scientist Robert Oppenheimer's appropriation of Hindu scripture to describe the atomic bomb he helped create. Calling on the spectral imagery of nuclear annihilation, Animal Mother magnifies his own power as a killer by equating himself with collective man's highest achievement in technological destruction. At a higher level of institutional authority, Mother could be another General Ripper. But if he is dangerous, he is also, under certain circumstances, admirable. Eightball assures Joker that "under fire, Animal Mother is one of the finest human beings in the world. All he needs is somebody to throw hand grenades at him for the rest of his life." Or to state the same thing from a different perspective, without the Marine Corps and the Vietnam War, Animal Mother is an angry, bullying, violent racist.

If combat makes comrades out of potential enemies in the case of Animal Mother and Eightball, Crazy Earl uncovers a much stranger example. Lifting the cap off a soldier slumped next to him — a figure that until now appeared to be just another member of the platoon — Earl introduces a dead NVA soldier in respectful terms as "my bro." Admiration and contempt, even love and hate, intermingle in a marine logic that can respect only what resembles itself. "After we rotate back to the world, we're gonna miss not having anyone around that's worth shooting." This ironic remark blends alienation (if the "world" is America, Vietnam is the foreign equivalent of the moon, Jupiter, and the Unknown in *2001*) with nostalgia (Crazy Earl feels more at home with a respected foe than with contemptibly weak American civilians). But Earl's "bro" is dead. His comment, "I love the little commie bastard," is eerily reminiscent of Jack Torrance's remark about Danny ("I love the little son of a bitch"), whom he tried to kill, in *The Shining*.

The entry of American marines into Hue is orderly but tense. The camera tracks with the Lusthog Squad, matching their cautious pace. They are welcomed to enemy-occupied territory by the same, smiling Vietnamese-billboard caricature we saw on a street corner in "friendly" Da Nang. The image of Vietnam in the minds of many of its liberators is singular. *None* of the natives are to be trusted. The barrel of an American tank seems, in one shot, aimed at that billboard.

Lieutenant Schinoski leads his men into the battle zone but follows the protective lead of the tank — a part of *his* full metal jacket defense. Visible in the same shot as they walk in loose formation are Joker and Animal Mother, looking very much alike. Momentarily forgotten is their earlier dispute. The inscriptions on their respective helmets are now complementary boasts of their power to destroy, yet the apprehension on their faces belies their written war cries.

Enemy shellfire cuts through layer after layer of institutional protection, striking Schinoski with shrapnel. He collapses to the ground and dies in a sickening display of muscle spasms and blood. Other marines hit the ground as one when the shelling begins. A series of frontal close-ups captures the unanimity of their fear, despite the boasts on some of their helmets. Discipline and training, however, render their recovery swift and automatic. Crazy Earl, second in command, quickly takes charge while another soldier gives medical aid to Schinoski, though to no avail.

Profiting from his predecessor's fatal mistake, Crazy Earl leads his men in a renewed, but more cautious, zigzag advance on the enemy. A handheld camera low to the ground tracks with them, mimicking their movements as they pick their way through the burning wreckage of Hue. Ominous, vaguely Oriental music returns to the soundtrack as an echo of the alien environment that threatens to overwhelm them.

As proof of that danger, one soldier peers around the corner of a building and pays the ultimate price for exposure. He is shot by an enemy whose exact location is unknown. Other marines open fire on the general area of offense, their bullets and grenades scarring buildings in an impressive but inefficient display of technological superiority. Crazy Earl is delighted when he picks off a few NVA soldiers crossing an open space between buildings up ahead. But several make the hazardous trip successfully while he reloads his weapon. Face-to-face encounters with the enemy are scarce, and so are clearcut victories. Combat neophyte Rafterman, meanwhile, can barely control his weapon — the camera with which he is supposed to take combat photos.

Crazy Earl's somewhat misplaced elation is echoed on the soundtrack by the familiar, upbeat song "Surfin' Bird," which displaces the unfamiliar, unsettling music from earlier. Like "Woolly Bully," "Surfin' Bird" is a triumph of rhythm over lyrical content. The song carries over into the next scene, where it helps define a new situation. The first "bird" we see is a helicopter, which leads the camera into a new battle scenario. Tanks pound the invisible NVA, while marines huddle behind a stone wall for protection. Music falls into sync with and mocks the awkward movements of a television camera crew as they pan over the marines, trying to condense the whole experience of war into a single shot. Meanwhile, the soldiers they film are emotionally divided between an indoctrinated contempt for journalism and a private desire for fame. They simultaneously show off for and make fun of the TV crew's endeavor.

Cowboy dubs the TV production *Vietnam: The Movie*. His comrades flesh out a hackneyed script full of colorful character types drawn from countless war movies and novels. But in their sarcastic descriptions, the marines reveal a little of their true feelings about Vietnam. Joker casts himself as John Wayne. Eightball, perhaps criticizing the role of African-American soldiers in the war, assigns himself the subservient role of a *horse*. Animal Mother is given the part of a rabid buffalo, befitting his nickname and his passionate commitment to victory. In turn, he puts the "gooks" (making no distinction between North and South Vietnamese) in the unenviable role played by Native Americans in many Hollywood westerns.

The Lusthog Squad's lighthearted mockery of the television camera and, by implication, its civilian audience is abruptly displaced by a very different perception of war. Comic informality yields to solemn formality, beginning with a grim, subjective, overhead shot of two dead marines, Schinoski and Hand Job, from the vantage point of their comrades, gathered in a circle around them. This is a makeshift funeral service, for family members only. No outsiders allowed. The camera reverses its position to give us a low-angle view of the survivors from the imaginary perspective of the deceased. Each survivor delivers a eulogy in turn. The wreckage of their hostile environment looms above them as they do so. Each man draws from his collective resources what he requires to manage his sorrow and fear of death. Most offer conventionally pious words of comfort, emphasizing fraternity, relief from suffering, and the possibility of an afterlife. Animal Mother, however, violates that respectful tone. "Better you than me" puts the victims at an emotional distance. Rafterman tries to reintroduce reverence by observing that at least the dead men died for a good cause. But Animal Mother undercuts him, replacing the cause of freedom with what he regards as the more realistic cause of personal gratification and survival.

Cowboy expands on but also softens Mother's irreverence, telling of Hand Job's unorthodox attempt to get out of the Marine Corps on a Section Eight by excessive masturbation. Yet there is an edge of respect in his voice, as though he admires the sheer audacity of Hand Job's outrageous effort to achieve an admittedly personal and unmarinelike goal.

In a subsequent series of *individual* television interviews, the marines of First Platoon are more subdued, intimidated, and stilted in their remarks. But as they grow more comfortable in front of the camera, their comments become less guarded and more revealing. Creative editing breaks up and splices together various interview fragments, juxtaposing different points of view, some of which progress while others do not.

Animal Mother and Cowboy tentatively move towards an open expression of contempt for their ARVN allies. The bolder of the two, Mother finally declares, "We're shooting the wrong gooks." But after expressing admiration for the born-again-hard NVA, he contradicts himself by advocating an all-out bombing campaign on North Vietnam, which exceeds official limits placed on military operations in Vietnam. Animal Mother cannot respect people who are less dedicated and aggressive than himself (ARVN), yet he feels compelled to challenge and conquer those who are (NVA). Catch-22 again. Cowboy, meanwhile, amends Mother's open resentment of ARVN cowardice by expressing a dislike of Vietnam because it is environmentally so different from his native Texas.

Crazy Earl's interview pursues the same logic he expressed previously. Regardless of America's political reasons for fighting in Vietnam, he belongs there because the challenge of combat defines him as a man. By contrast, Doc Jay overtly criticizes the war by mimicking President Johnson's false assertion that he would not send American boys to do the job Asian boys should do. Eightball echoes Doc Jay's criticism of the government in a different way, referring to the Vietnamese who flee the war as "poor dumb bastards," but implying that such a disparaging description is better suited to the American soldiers trying to force freedom on them at any price.

Perhaps because they are the least experienced in combat, Rafterman and Joker furnish the most superficial and defensive remarks. Consumed by his need to be taken seriously as a battle-hard marine, Rafterman offers an embarrassing ode to the Marine Corps — its efficiency as a killing machine and its superiority to its allied rival, the Air Cavalry. His false bravado echoes that of Generals Faceman and Turgidson as they debated the relative combat skills of their respective services while ignoring a far more serious challenge in *Dr. Strangelove*. Joker, meanwhile, supplies vacuous liberal counterpoint, mocking the role of killing machine that he agreed to play when he joined the Marine Corps. What Rafterman aspires to be, Joker feels uncomfortable being. For the TV camera, Joker has removed his "Born to Kill" helmet but retained his peace button, pandering to his own civilian sensibilities by concealing his more aggressive urges. But the grenades hanging from his flak jacket undermine his flaunted antiwar symbolism and words.

Isolated from one another during their interviews, the Lusthog Squad reassembles as a united front for their encounter with an ARVN pimp and his young prostitute. Far from the intimidating scrutiny of television cameras, they are freer to express the hostility they hinted at during their interviews. This scene takes place in front of the same deserted movie theater where the interviews were staged. Like the derelict casino in *Clockwork*, the empty movie theater contributes to an analogy between the arts and real life. The marquee in front of the building advertises a film entitled *The Lone Ranger*. To the far left of that title appears an image of Tonto, the Lone Ranger's faithful companion. A fictional portrait of the relationship between European Americans and Native Americans, the Lone Ranger and Tonto are an idealized alliance of different races and cultures. The American/South Vietnamese alliance on display *outside* the theater is somewhat less ideal.

Lounging on chairs in front of the theater, the marines react to the Vietnamese in the casual, semidetached, sometimes arrogant manner of an audience reacting to images on a movie screen. Their perspective is roughly analogous to that of Alex and his droogs watching Billyboy's gang assault a girl on the stage of the derelict casino.

Both Vietnamese in this scene wear dark glasses, hiding their emotions from American harassment. But because they are soliciting money from the marines, they must compromise their security. The pimp removes his glasses and makes a sales pitch in broken English. The prostitute, with her pimp serving as go-between, retains her glasses and her indifferent, defiant posture.

The marines ridicule the pimp for being Vietnamese and an ARVN soldier, the prostitute for being Vietnamese and a woman. Haggling over the price of services to be rendered, Cowboy offers to trade the pimp ARVN rifles, "never used and only dropped once." More than a simple business deal, this is a war within a war, fought behind "friendly" lines and between "allies." The pimp is in no position to retaliate in kind. His only payback is to take the marine's almighty dollar. To do that he employs his own countrywoman as bait.

The pimp lowers his price, and Eightball steps forward to claim the girl. But this triggers two more conflicts: one with the Vietnamese and one within marine ranks. Speaking through her pimp interpreter, the prostitute refuses to service the black man because she assumes he is too big for her — racial prejudice in reverse. Though this particular prejudice flatters his ego, Eightball has no intention of sacrificing a good time to a backhanded compliment. He offers the girl visual proof that she is in no danger. Satisfied, she withdraws her objection. And she gives her approval *directly* to Eightball, in *English*. Intrigued by Eightball, she lowers her defenses a bit and dispenses with the services of her mediator.

Before Eightball and the prostitute can consummate their business deal, Animal Mother intervenes to claim first go at her. He, for one, is not amused by the myth of black sexual superiority. If his reference to the prostitute as "meat" is insulting, even more so is his racist comment about Eightball, perhaps too insulting to be interpreted as a marine token of affection. A civilian prejudice predating basic training threatens marine solidarity. Other members of First Platoon defuse Animal Mother's racial slur with an affectionate chorus of obscenities. Individual conflict is suppressed. Collective order is preserved. But in the course of this one scene, numerous layers of conflict and alliance have been exposed: national, sexual, and racial.

First Platoon's last patrol through the wreckage of Hue is *Full Metal Jacket*'s version of Dave Bowman's journey "Beyond the Infinite" in *2001*. Like Da Nang, Hue is a visual cacophony of American and Vietnamese symbols. But unlike Da Nang, it is also a deserted ruin that dwarfs the American soldiers who patrol it. The camera tracks with them, encouraging us to experience their anxiety. Narration informs us that military intelligence reports a North Vietnamese pullout from the area. First Platoon has been sent in to confirm that report. But in order to cover a wide area, they must split up, becoming isolated and vulnerable individuals. And it is as a lone soldier that Crazy Earl falls victim to an enemy who exploits his emotions.

In the wreckage of a building, Earl spots a child's stuffed toy — an object completely at odds with its grim surroundings. Carelessly diverted, he picks it up. The booby trapped toy explodes and kills him. The NVA turned his sentiments against him, just as Alex exploited the compassion of the Alexanders in order to gain access to their home.

Crazy Earl's death results in Cowboy's promotion to squad leader. Joker congratulates his best buddy with an affectionate marine insult. One man's downfall can be another man's path to power, even when they belong to the same team. The situation itself generates emotional and moral contradictions.

The platoon reunites under Cowboy's command to continue their patrol. And just as Wendy Torrance sought information and reassurance from the Forest Service, Cowboy seeks it from higher command via a two-way radio. There is little else, aside from each other, for the marines to cling to for support in this wasteland. But, again like Wendy, Cowboy and his men will have to make do without assistance from headquarters when their crisis arrives.

Crouching behind a low concrete wall for protection, the marines stop in front of a towering block of bombed-out buildings. With Eightball's requested help, an unsure Cowboy concludes that the squad may be lost, which means that, contrary to expectations, they may no longer be in an area of Hue evacuated by the enemy. From a beer ad on the wall of a building behind them, a Vietnamese youth appears to be looking over Animal Mother's shoulder. Nearly all things Vietnamese in *Full Metal Jacket* are divorced from their native context and viewed by us as American soldiers might view them. Metaphorically, the painted youth is the enemy the marines suspect might be lurking ahead of them. Meanwhile, the visual presence of the squad behind him, awaiting his next order, places enormous pressure on Cowboy to make the right decision. And his situation is not improved when Joker, ever the inquisitive journalist, asks if they are lost, inadvertently undermining his best friend's fledgling authority. Cowboy angrily tells him to shut up.

Eightball recommends a change in direction to get back to where they should be. Tragically, that recommendation seals his own fate. Cowboy sends him on a reconnaissance mission to explore unfamiliar territory ahead. Before departing, Eightball employs typically colorful marine language to shield himself from fear, replacing the protective concrete wall with a verbal one. "Put a nigger behind the trigger" is a short, snappy piece of internal rhyme containing a racial slur that, by marine definition, serves Eightball in the opposite manner. There is no indication that Cowboy's choice was racially motivated or that Eightball sees it that way. But in a broader, historical context, Eightball's battle cry echoes the fact that a disproportionate percentage of American soldiers in Vietnam *were* black.

As viewed by the camera from behind the wall, Eightball appears dwarfed by the massive, burning, sinister block of buildings up ahead. Walking into an empty square in the midst of those buildings, as a consequence of his own recommendation, Eightball stands completely exposed to enemy fire. For the first time in the film, the camera switches to a subjective point of view vis-à-vis that enemy. The sniper's rifle barrel points through a jagged hole at the distant marine — an image very similar to one in *Barry Lyndon* during a battle between Prussian and opposing forces. We do not see the sniper. We only see what and how he sees, from a perspective emotionally remote from his target.

Eightball is signaling his comrades to join him (one of many strategic mistakes in this scene) when the sniper fires. The camera cuts instantly to a close shot of the victim, recording in agonizing slow motion the impact of a bullet on his body and mind. Distorted sound and imagery reflect the emotional impact of his injury on the rest of the squad, who are as physically removed from him as is the sniper but who cannot be indifferent to his plight. Ironically, Eightball's situation triggers conflict within the platoon *because* of their fraternal devotion to him. At first they respond as one, blasting away impressively but ineffectually at the unseen enemy. In almost every military encounter in *Full Metal Jacket*, the NVA get off the first shot, drawing a massive but scattershot reply from frustrated marines.

As squad leader, Cowboy must assess the strategic situation, of which Eightball's predicament is only one factor, more objectively than do his men. With great difficulty, he gets them to stop firing and conserve precious ammunition. Then he contacts headquarters to request tank support to flush out what he believes is a strong enemy force up ahead. The problem is time. His suspicion of an enemy ambush dictates that the platoon sit tight and wait for the tank. But Eightball's cries of distress work on the squad's indoctrinated sense of fraternal responsibility to press for an immediate rescue mission. Cowboy must ignore the desperate pleas of a subordinate *he* put in danger if he is to prevent what he views as an even greater disaster. Two contradictory facets of basic training collide in him. He must master his own feelings, as well as those of his men, if he is to do his job well. His predecessor, Crazy Earl, died because of a failure to do likewise.

More bullets rip into Eightball's body, causing more agonizing cries and exacerbating Cowboy's crisis of command. It is as though the sniper were using his first victim as a weapon to lure more victims into his web. Finally Doc Jay rebels, disobeying Cowboy's orders and charging to Eightball's rescue. The rest of the squad, including Cowboy, provides covering fire, until Cowboy manages to reassert control over them.

Doc Jay meets the same fate as Eightball. Severely wounded, he cannot help but add his voice to the conflict of loyalties, replacing that of his dead comrade. Cowboy's predicament gets even worse when headquarters tells him there will be no tank support. Cursing higher command, he makes the extremely difficult decision to evacuate the area, deserting Doc Jay and Eightball in order to save the rest of the squad from the massive enemy attack he anticipates. But this time it is Animal Mother who mutinies, cursing his timid comrades and vaulting the protective wall, accompanied by a tracking camera. Undeniably courageous, he is for a moment and in a limited context the living embodiment of the John Wayne myth. As with Major Kong, Kubrick would have us admire and empathize with him even as we recognize his flaws.

Animal Mother follows Doc Jay's defiant lead, but he possesses enough of Cowboy's strategic detachment to go about it in a smarter way. Instead of exposing himself rashly to sniper fire, he remains behind a sheltering building and asks Doc Jay where the sniper is located. Displaying incredible willpower, Doc Jay points the way, then dies in a resulting hail of bullets. His assistance to Animal Mother costs him his life, which defeats the goal of Mother's rescue mission.

Armed with knowledge that there is only a single sniper, Animal Mother signals the rest of the platoon forward. His revelation contradicts Cowboy's suspicion of a large enemy ambush. Cowboy was wrong, if understandably so. Somewhat contritely, he leads a portion of the platoon forward. Joker and Rafterman, who for different reasons than Cowboy need to prove themselves in combat, insist on going with him.

Cowboy is the first to pay for his courage. Sheltered from enemy fire by the side of a building, he neglects to account for a gaping shell hole that gives the sniper visual access to him, just as Bowman and Poole failed to lock HAL out of their secret strategy conversation in *2001*. Cowboy takes a bullet in the chest. Animal Mother then transforms that same hole into a gun portal, blasting away at the sniper's fortress. A commercial sign on the roof of that fortress reads "My Toan," which approximates "My Town" in English. This is as much a territorial conflict as the waterhole confrontation in *2001*. Mother's gunfire destroys the sign but not the sniper.

Surrounded by his comrades, Cowboy is a marine to the last. He dies struggling to master his pain and terror. "I can hack it!" echoes Sergeant Hartman's declared mandate to weed out all *non*hackers from his platoon. Joker, meanwhile, frantically tries to rally his dying friend with a typical marine expression of affection: "You're my favorite turd." But it is not enough to save Cowboy, who dies coughing up spit and blood. Like Frank Poole's lifeless body rotating in outer space, Cowboy is a pitiable figure of human vulnerability.

One by one, members of Cowboy's squad stand up and detach themselves from him. Joker is the last to do so. For Animal Mother, who has been tending to business elsewhere, sorrow translates automatically into a desire for revenge. His call for payback catches Joker at just the right moment. After seeing things differently during much of their time together, the two marines are, for the time being, of like mind.

With Animal Mother in charge, the remaining squad members mount a carefully coordinated and strategically smart offensive. Inside the sniper's building, they split up to cover more territory. The camera tracks with Joker. Scraping, disturbing music subjectively echoes his disorientation and vulnerability. This is *his* journey "Beyond the Infinite" as well as into his own heart of darkness. The sniper's lair flickers with infernal firelight. Joker manages to infiltrate it without being detected. But when he tries to shoot the unsuspecting enemy, his rifle produces an impotent click. Joker fails one of Sergeant Hartman's basic training lessons by being unfaithful to his "lover." His weapon either jams or is empty. Even worse, his failure alerts the sniper to his presence. She turns and fires her weapon, pitting the stone pillar he cowers behind. Tossing aside his useless rifle, Joker reaches for a back-up pistol, which looks about as inadequate vis-à-vis the sniper's weapon as Wendy Torrance's knife appeared to be vis-à-vis her husband's fire axe during the bathroom attack scene in *The Shining*.

The revelation that the sniper is a young woman comes as a surprise. The marines' until-now largely rhetorical war on women becomes literal and reaches a climax in this scene. The only other women in the film thus far have been Vietnamese prostitutes, who were ridiculed both for their nationality and their gender. The implied vengeance of "These Boots Are Made for Walking" is almost realized by the sniper. Private Joker has flirted with chauvinism ever since he entered basic training, but he has also displayed a contrary attitude, as when he criticized the helicopter doorgunner for shooting women and children. That perilous balancing act is about to be challenged to the fullest.

Joker's salvation comes from, of all people, Rafterman. When they departed on this mission, Lieutenant Lockhart made Joker responsible for Rafterman's safety. That relationship is now reversed. Blindsided, the sniper is cut down by a hail of bullets. Savoring his new role as combat veteran (or,

in the words of the Lusthog Squad, "life-taker" and "heartbreaker"), Rafterman scours the area for other enemy soldiers, striking exaggerated marine
poses to impress himself. For him, this has been a joyous opportunity to fulfill
a dream, a triumph over self-doubt. For Joker, on the other hand, it is something very different.

Members of the squad gather around the fallen sniper, each bringing his
own perspective to the situation. None of them pays much attention to Rafterman's high-pitched celebration, which is counterpointed by somber background music that echoes Joker's subsequent soul-searching dilemma — the
same music heard during Private Pyle's blanket party.

Flickering firelight illuminates the separate but interlocked hells experienced by Private Joker and the sniper. Except for Rafterman, all of the marines
are surprised to discover the identity of their foe. They speak about her in
typically chauvinistic terms but with little conviction in their voices. In spite
of the rhetorical disrespect for women they were taught in basic training, they
do not easily give up their lingering civilian perspectives.

Terrified, in agony and dying, the sniper fights to maintain self-control,
just as Cowboy did earlier. When Cowboy ordered the platoon to abandon
two wounded comrades, Animal Mother rebelled. Now it is Mother who
orders a withdrawal and Joker who protests. He cannot leave the dying girl
to suffer alone. The sniper herself exacerbates this confrontation between
authority and morality by pleading, in English, to be shot. Animal Mother
appropriates that request and transforms it into a challenge of Joker's ethical
challenge to *him*. "If you want to waste her, go on, waste her." The pressure
is put squarely on Joker. This is the culmination of Mother's earlier challenge,
"You talk the talk. Do you walk the walk?" This is what it means to face real
combat. Is Joker what Animal Mother *used* to be?

Vivid close-ups convey to us the parallel suffering of Joker and the sniper.
His original desire to avenge the death of his best friend mixes with and
becomes morally inseparable from his compassion for Cowboy's killer. Opposite emotions push him towards a single, violent resolution. And just as he
forced himself to participate in the collective punishment of Private Pyle,
Joker has to work himself up to a fever pitch of passion in order to overcome
doubt and revulsion. Background music echoes his growing agitation. Other
squad members scrutinize his performance closely, increasing the pressure on
him. Cruelest of all is Rafterman's callous smirk. He cannot imagine that
what *he* did to the sniper (shooting her to save a friend) was so much easier
than what now faces Joker.

After much internal debate, Joker shoots and kills the sniper. The "Born
to Kill" on his helmet has never seemed emotionally less appropriate, even
though he has just fulfilled its literal meaning. Tension gradually drains from
his face and from the subjective background music, like water from an

unplugged sink. This almost mechanical impression of involuntary release is reminiscent of Dave Bowman's arrival in his genteel sanctuary in *2001* and the burned-out light bulb sound and imagery concluding Susan Alexander's misguided operatic career in *Citizen Kane*. Trapped in contradiction, Joker stands looking down at the object of his revenge and his mercy. Rafterman, meanwhile, makes an incongruous, ignorant, and cruel remark about his friend's distorted facial expression. But the other squad members have a keener appreciation of Joker's ordeal. Donlon, speaking for them, observes in a quiet, even awed voice, "Hardcore, man. Fucking hardcore." Or maybe "Hard Corps" is the more appropriate interpretation. In marine-speak, astonishment and admiration can be expressed in language more commonly associated with pornography. Most of Joker's comrades realize that he has faced and overcome one of the most obscene challenges of combat. But at what cost to himself?

The last scene in *Full Metal Jacket* is a joyous/ironic fusion of private and collective perspective that has strong parallels in Kubrick's earlier films. Private Joker, pushed beyond the limits of his capacity to juggle contrary loyalties, gives up the fight and commits wholeheartedly to the Marine Corps. His narrator persona, speaking from an emotionally insulated and even hackneyed marine perspective, reduces First Platoon's last patrol, including the death of a best friend and a major transformation for himself, to a routine passage in a soldier's diary. Violence, horror, death, and a radical shift in outlook are masked and muted beneath a few colorful phrases. It's just another day in the life of a marine grunt.

In extreme long shot, we see the men of First Platoon walking together past the burning ruins of Hue, at dusk. In *Clockwork* Alex whistled his way contentedly through the equally ugly world of municipal Flatblock 18a Linear North at dawn. The marines bolster themselves with a chorus of the Mickey Mouse Club song: a civilian, children's ode to solidarity appropriated for use by soldiers in combat. The marines have successfully adapted to life in Hell, transforming the destruction visible behind them into a triumphant demonstration of their own power to overcome any challenge they encounter. The difference between *this* infernal impression and the sniper's firelit lair is Joker's reaction to it. What was Hell is now Home.

The camera begins this scene in a somewhat detached mode, then catches up to the platoon, tracking with Joker, Rafterman, and Animal Mother as they march in tandem, singing their sardonic platoon anthem. Smiling, Joker is no longer troubled by doubts. "I'm in a world of shit … yes. But I am alive. And I am not afraid" is his final pronouncement. Joker and his narrator alter ego are at last of one mind. And it is a mind at peace with itself.

The camera slows down, letting the platoon pass away into the distance and giving us a little detachment from Joker's unquestioning embrace of the

Corps. Played over the closing credits is "Paint It Black" by the Rolling Stones. Roughly equivalent to Alex's "Singin' in the Rain" in *Clockwork*, it echoes Private Joker's ironic triumph over the chaos in and around him. Combining musical elements from both West and East (if not specifically Oriental), the song also forms an aesthetic bridge between the upbeat, distinctly American tunes and the brooding, vaguely Oriental background score heard earlier in the film. Private Joker, the closet peacenik who, for whatever private reasons, chose to explore other aspects of his nature by enlisting in the Marine Corps and fighting in Vietnam, has finally learned to stop worrying and embrace the carnage around and within him. Semper Infidelis has yielded to Semper Fidelis.

CHAPTER 7

Eyes Wide Shut:
The Waking Dream

...In every human being there exist, as the primary cause of dream-formation, two psychic forces ... one of which forms the wish expressed by the dream, while the other exercises a censorship over this dream-wish, thereby imposing on it a distortion.
— Sigmund Freud, *The Interpretation of Dreams* (223)

Outwardly, Kubrick's *Eyes Wide Shut* is a faithful screen adaptation of Arthur Schnitzler's novella, *Dream Story*. Aside from a change in locale from 1920s Vienna to 1990s New York, much of the action and dialog is the same. Describing his main characters' afterthoughts about the flirtations they experienced during a masked ball, Schnitzler writes of "the treacherous illusion of missed opportunities" which haunts them, and presumably all of us on occasion. (Schnitzler, 177). Time and again, our imagination runs wild with speculation about what *might* have been or even with revised interpretations of what actually was. The human inclination to reconfigure reality for its own ends is a notion that fits in well with all of Kubrick's work. How to bring *Dream Story* dramatically alive on film and infuse it with his own aesthetic sensibilities was Kubrick's challenge. More often than not, the task came down to details — and no one sweats the details more than Kubrick.

One aspect of Kubrick's fictional worlds is a keen portrayal of the dichotomy between professional duty and personal agenda. Just as many of the characters in *Dr. Strangelove* use their public powers to further private goals, Dr. Bill Harford deceptively employs his identity as a physician to access information and material which advance his personal desires. And so, in their own ways, do the amorous hotel desk clerk and balding costume shop proprietor upon whom he works his professional magic. But unlike most of the characters in *Strangelove*, Bill's exploitation of his professional status sometimes occurs to a consciously benevolent end, as when he tries to help friends whom he may have gotten into trouble. In Schnitzler's original story, there is less delineation of this professional/personal duality.

In the novella, Albertine's cruel dream of infidelity and spousal crucifixion is complicated by husband Fridolin's admirable display of fidelity within it. Thus, we get to see her internal dream censor at work. In the film, Bill neither proves his fidelity nor is crucified in Alice's dream. This is perhaps because Alice is awakened before the dream plays itself out. By waking his wife in mid-dream, *Bill* functions, if unwittingly, as her censor.

Most of the subtle changes between novella and film involve the character of Bill Harford, originally Fridolin. Though both are basically decent men, Bill is, at least to begin with, more naive and tentative in his thoughts and actions. Unlike Fridolin, he does not respond to his wife's admission of fantasized infidelity with a similar confession of his own. By focusing instead on Bill's shocked reaction to Alice's revelation, Kubrick emphasizes the husband's initial lack of emotional awareness (including self-awareness), which sets the stage for his overreaction during the sexual odyssey that follows. He must experience firsthand the risks and agonizing contradictions of infidelity (real or imagined) before he can be as open with himself and his wife as she has been with him.

Bill seems totally surprised when Marion Nathanson declares love for him while grieving over her dead father. Fridolin, on the other hand, long suspected Marianne's romantic attachment to him and is a little bolder about getting together again with her later in the story — likewise during their respective encounters with the costume shop owner and his daughter. Bill is too shocked to openly display much arousal or outrage; Fridolin, though he, too, avoids sexual involvement, is less so. And during the orgy, Fridolin is more forceful about defending himself and his mysterious savior than is Bill, who is emotionally overwhelmed by it all. Only later, with hindsight, does he regret his timidity and feel guilty about his savior's fate.

Two small changes between novella and film emphasize Bill's subconscious motivations early on during his sexual odyssey. Fridolin and a prostitute named Mizzi consciously refrain from having sex after coming close to doing so. In contrast, Bill and Domino have already begun to make out when a telephone call from Alice interrupts them and breaks the mood. If this is a dream, Bill is not aware that he has conveniently censored his own pleasure.

In Schnitzler's story, Fridolin encounters his old friend, Nightingale, entirely by chance in a coffee house where the latter plays piano. In the film, they meet for the first time much earlier, at Ziegler's party. By later on seeking out Nightingale at the Sonata Cafe, Bill vaguely searches for adventure to soothe his frustration about Alice. Nightingale, representing a more exotic, freer lifestyle, is for Bill a potential avenue to that adventure.

The character of Victor Ziegler, added to the film by Kubrick and co-screenwriter Frederic Raphael, is not in the novella. Ziegler is the lying, hypocritical, misogynistic adulterer that Bill Harford *could* become if he indulged his sexual fantasies to the fullest over a long period of time. He is to Bill what Strangelove is to President Muffley and Charles Grady is to Jack Torrance. Harford's final encounter with Ziegler, in Victor's sumptuous billiards room, is a confrontation with his own demonic self, a last temptation to absolve himself of all responsibility for the consequences of his careless actions. By refusing to give in to Ziegler's insidiously self-serving logic — in other words, by not becoming another Ziegler — Bill gives himself at least a chance of saving his marriage with Alice by admitting everything to her. By contrast, Ziegler's marriage remains a sham. After telling so many stories in which his main characters *fail* to overcome their worst inclinations, Kubrick finally portrays a hard-fought, if qualified, success.

* * *

During Stuart Ullman's guided tour of Overlook's staff wing in *The Shining*, Jack Torrance discreetly casts a lustful backward glance at two of the hotel's departing female employees. Only with hindsight does that trivial action betray his growing discontent with Wendy, his wife. After Ullman and his staff depart Overlook for the winter, that discontent, along with frustration at his lack of success as a writer, his forbidden desire for alcohol and his guilt over injuring his son Danny, triggers fantasies of an alternate lifestyle. These fantasies are encouraged by the opulent decor and colorful history of the empty, snowbound Overlook.

Dr. William Harford embarks on a similarly obsessive and dreamlike odyssey in *Eyes Wide Shut*, after his wife's confession of an adulterous fantasy prompts him to get back at her in the same fashion. But like Jack, Bill's commitment to wish-fulfillment is complicated by his own fears and moral reservations. By occasionally mocking the anachronisms within his own fantasies and making monsters out of his allies, Jack tries, with decreasing success, to keep his fantasies in check. What we experience with Bill Harford is a fitful series of sexual encounters offering a wide range of erotic possibilities but never quite living up to his expectations. Unable to rid himself of his internal censor, Bill is finally able to step back from the brink of disaster in a way that Jack cannot.

The Shining contains hints of supernatural forces at work (if only on a metaphorical level) in the lives of the Torrance family. In addition, being trapped in a deserted hotel during a raging blizzard fuels their troubled imaginations. By steeping us in Jack's progressively more convincing fantasies, Kubrick makes it difficult for us to distinguish between reality and unreality. *Eyes Wide Shut* is set in and around New York City. No demons. No profound sense of isolation from society. No extreme weather. If there is an aesthetic catalyst for the sexual fantasies of Bill and Alice Harford, it is the colorful Christmas lights which illuminate almost every location in the film.

Bill Harford's sexual odyssey seems objectively real, yet it possesses the logic of a dream, logic which at times stretches the credibility of a literal interpretation. And I suspect the tension between these two perspectives was deliberate on Kubrick's part. The film's very title is an oxymoron, suggesting a confusion of wakefulness and sleep. By blurring the distinctions between dream and reality, Kubrick reminds us how easily these can influence and even displace each other. Bill's nocturnal prowlings through New York City are facilitated by yellow taxis so visually prominent that they become dream metaphors, transporting the protagonist from one fantasy to another. *Eyes Wide Shut* treads a risky dramatic path which is bound to disappoint many viewers, including some who are predisposed to like Kubrick's work. It is the only one of the seven films discussed in this study which does not portray a dominant, narrowly-defined institutional or natural environment in which the lead characters struggle for survival and happiness. Instead, the film's various settings serve as externalizations of the inner lives of a less-than-happily married couple. New York City, or Kubrick's re-creation of it, becomes their dreamscape. Whatever its critical fate in years to come, *Eyes Wide Shut* is easily Stanley Kubrick's most intimate work.

One thing Kubrick's last film has in common with its predecessors is a strong sense of the roles that chance, coincidence, and misperception play in the fortunes of its characters. Just like Bill Harford, we are frequently given an impression only to have it challenged or overturned. And in the final analysis, there are some things about which we can draw no definitive conclusions. In short, real life can be as difficult to figure out as a dream. But then, confounding our expectations is Kubrick's stock in trade. Even the pre-release publicity surrounding *Eyes Wide Shut* led many people to anticipate a story of unrestrained eroticism, if not outright pornography. Perhaps anticipating that anticipation, Kubrick begins his film with a brief peep show, a few seconds of a famous and gorgeous movie star undressing. But the "sexiest movie ever" turns out to be a *cautionary* tale of desire, jealousy, revenge, and regret.

The first image we see in *Eyes Wide Shut*, after the opening credits, is Nicole Kidman removing her clothes. At first we know nothing about her character, including her reason for getting undressed. She is just a beautiful, naked movie star. Married or single, perhaps even man or woman, it is difficult *not* to get an erotic charge out of this scene. For a moment, Kubrick would have us be what Bill and Alice Harford will prove to be, susceptible to sexual temptation and therefore to its equally passionate counterpoint — jealousy. There is nothing particularly extreme or ominous about this first impression. We are not Norman Bates peeking through a hole in the wall at Marion Crane, torn between lust and homicidal rage. We are simply intrigued and aroused.

The sirens of passing police cars wail outside the apartment building of Bill and Alice Harford. Inside, the married couple gets ready to leave for a party at the home of a friend. They are, as most of us would be, oblivious to the anonymous crisis signaled by the passing siren. They are insulated from events outside their private realm, just as General Turgidson tries to be in his mirrored bedroom in *Dr. Strangelove*, or like Mr. and Mrs. Alexander in *Clockwork*. But Turgidson seeks isolation even from the woman who shares that sanctuary with him, retreating to the bathroom to take care of business. Bill and Alice have been married for nine years. Their private lives have become so intertwined that he thinks nothing of walking into the bathroom while she sits on the toilet. Nor does she seem bothered by it. By this simple action, plus the typical messiness of a family bathroom, Kubrick creates an unobtrusive impression of everyday marital intimacy.

Also contributing to that impression is the scene's dialog, beginning with Bill asking his wife if she has seen his missing wallet. For perhaps the hundredth time in their marriage, she tells him where it is. Then she informs him of their babysitter's name, which he has also forgotten. They are a team, with Alice routinely compensating for her husband's absentmindedness. He takes much for granted, as many people do in a long-term relationship. Sitting on the toilet, Alice asks Bill if she looks okay. Without even glancing at her, Bill tells her she looks beautiful, as always. His compliment appears to be the product of long habit rather than true feeling. Not a lie, exactly, but more a pro forma than a profound token of love. And Alice, *mildly* chastising her husband for it, knows that she is being taken for granted.

Reinforcing our impression of a marriage that, while superficially happy and successful, has succumbed a little to passionless routine is the background music: Dmitri Shostakovich's "Jazz Suite Waltz No. 2" begins with the opening credits and carries over into the first and second scenes. In the style of Kurt Weill, the music has a vaguely cynical flavor, mocking the Harfords' slightly jaded marriage with its rigid dance rhythms. Presumably the characters are unaware they have fallen, emotionally speaking, into a rut. *We* feel superior to them. But we get a little surprise. Background music turns out to be *local* music when Bill switches off the stereo. For the two characters on screen, the sardonic waltz was a source of pleasure, not a critical comment on the state of their marriage. In addition to reminding us that one thing can serve different people in different ways, Kubrick subtly leads us to question the reality of what we see and hear. Our initial impressions are frequently modified or even reversed.

Whatever the state of their marriage, the Harfords seem devoted parents to their seven-year-old daughter, Helena. Exhibiting a balance of fond indulgence and prudent responsibility, they allow her to stay up and watch *The Nutcracker* on television, but deny her permission to stay up until they get home from the party. Perhaps in honor of her beloved *Nutcracker*, Helena is dressed in an angel-wing costume. And it is as an angel that her parents undoubtedly perceive her. At no point in *Eyes Wide Shut* is the child's relationship with her parents explored to the extent of Danny's with Jack and Wendy in *The Shining*. She never becomes a source of contention between her mother and father the way Danny does.

Unlike the Torrances, the Harfords are materially well off. Their Central Park West apartment far outshines Jack and Wendy's humble Boulder residence. Filled with an eclectic assortment of art objects, it resembles a museum. Nothing is overtly made of the fact that Alice is a former art gallery manager who now stays home to care for her daughter, but it is not unreasonable to suspect that she has brought her former profession home with her. Even Bill's medical office is filled with paintings possibly selected by his wife. Is it a coincidence that Alice, like *The Shining's* Jack Torrance, who is more obviously frustrated about his profession, initiates the dispute that will later threaten to break up her marriage?

Judging by the size and opulence of their residence, Victor Ziegler and his wife, Ilona, occupy a position of social prominence considerably greater than do the Harfords. But despite their smiles and easy cordiality, there is an almost imperceptible hint of disunity within their marriage as they greet Bill and Alice. Victor lavishly praises Alice's beauty, which prompts Ilona to comment, with a smile, that he does the same for *all* women. Nothing more is made of this incident, and Ilona never again appears in the film. But later revelations about Victor's behavior and attitude towards women in general suggest that his wife is aware of his infidelities.

After making polite, conventional small talk with their hosts, Bill and Alice form a united front against the crowd of strangers surrounding them. Questioning why they came to the party in the first place, they agree that it was a matter of social obligation. At the beginning of this scene, they seem to be on firmer ground, emotionally speaking, than do the Zieglers. But their affectionate, almost conspiratorial solidarity is broken, innocently enough, when Bill spots an old classmate from medical school playing piano in the hired band. Alice leaves him in order to go to the bathroom. They agree to get back together later at the bar, unaware that their temporary separation will generate other alliances and will eventually endanger their marriage. How easy it is to unwittingly slide from one situation into another that contradicts it.

Bill hooks up with Nick Nightingale to reminisce about old times. Like the rest of the band, Nick is dressed in a white suit jacket. Bill's is black, like those of other male party guests. As the camera backtracks with them, sharing their private pace and conviviality, we are made conscious of the social inequity between them. Yet their former acquaintanceship, in college, was as equals. They interact now as old buddies, despite their very different fortunes in life. Both have wives and children. But Nick has had to leave his family back in Seattle in order to pursue work as a jazz pianist. We do not know the state of his domestic affairs. But there may be a hint of trouble in his reply to Bill's inquiry as to why he walked away from a career in medicine. "It's a nice feeling. I do it a lot." Has he walked away from his marriage and family as well? By comparison, for the moment, the Harfords' marriage appears to be more stable.

Meanwhile, Alice waits for her husband at the bar, as promised. A little bored and a little tipsy (after all, these are not her friends, and she is here because of her *husband's* social obligation), she is more open to the rather obvious sexual advances of a strange man than perhaps she would otherwise be. Sandor Szavost, a suave, middle-aged Hungarian, tries to impress her with a pick-up line referencing the ancient Roman poet Ovid. Alice transforms his effort into an insult by criticizing that same poet. But Sandor is persistent, and Alice, as though on a whim, does not turn him away. Despite his sophisticated manner and speech, Sandor is nothing more than a sexual predator — another Clare Quilty at the high-school dance in *Lolita*. He is no match for Bill Harford. But he is a stranger, his attraction to Alice is flattering, and he catches her at a weak moment. So she plays along.

The Ziegler residence is aglow with Christmas lights and awash in popular love songs played softly by a jazz combo. These aesthetic ingredients create a richly seductive atmosphere for Alice's mild flirtation with Sandor. The camera tracks intimately with them as they whirl dizzily around the dance floor, caught up in the superficial magic of the occasion. With decreasing subtlety, Sandor makes his pitch for sex. His cynical view of marriage is that it makes deception a necessity for both partners. He makes no pretense of offering Alice love and devotion. He just wants a quickie with her up in Victor's deserted sculpture gallery.

Intercut with Alice's flirtation is Bill's with two pretty young women, both models, who latch onto him. Double-entendres flow freely from both sides, though Bill appears slightly more awkward at flirtation than either his partners or his wife. Nevertheless, he obviously enjoys it. And when interrupted by one of Victor's servants requesting his presence upstairs, Bill leaves his admirers with a promise to return and continue their game. It is not certain that he would have refused their sexual invitation to visit "the rainbow's end" (another linkage of color and sex), but neither is it certain he would have accepted.

Late during her dalliance with Sandor, Alice spots her husband nearby, shamelessly flirting with the pretty, attentive models. There is no obvious concern or jealousy in her facial expression, just observation, to be stored for later contemplation and strategic use. In fact, when Sandor soon thereafter makes his lewd proposition, Alice awakens from her flirtation, as though from a dream, and rejects him. "I Only Have Eyes for You" plays softly in the background, echoing her devotion to Bill. Though both husband and wife toy with infidelity in this scene, neither seems inclined yet to take the plunge. But that is obviously not the case with Victor Ziegler, who has adjourned to the upstairs bathroom with a prostitute.

In terms of decor, the upstairs bathroom harkens back to both Alex's bedroom in *Clockwork* and to the bathroom in Room 237 at the Overlook Hotel. Like the former, it features an unflattering portrait of a naked woman, a portrait whose owner views women *solely* as sexual objects. Like Overlook's Room 237, it is luxurious and painted largely in green, and it contains a naked woman other than the illustration on the wall. Upon entering, Bill finds Victor getting dressed after having sex with a beautiful prostitute named Mandy, who lies slumped and nude in a chair, semiconscious from a drug overdose. Victor is concerned only with getting the girl back on her feet and out of his home, so she doesn't ruin his reputation. Bill, by contrast, displays both cool professional efficiency and genuine compassion as he examines Mandy, warns her soberly that she might not survive another overdose, advises her to seek out a drug rehabilitation program, and informs Victor in no uncertain terms that the patient must remain where she is for another hour or so and then be taken home, not pushed out the door. Like Redmond Barry rescuing Captain Potsdorf from a burning building in *Barry Lyndon*, Bill's compassion is spontaneous. And as with Barry, it will reap (or *apparently* reap) a reward for him later in the film.

But if Bill treats Mandy far better than does Ziegler, he is also, as a friend, willing to accommodate Victor's wishes by telling no one else about the prostitute. And, in this context, the romantic music seeping into the bathroom from the party downstairs generates another parallel to *The Shining*: Jack Torrance and Delbert Grady discussing their mutual domestic problems, and possible violent solutions thereto, in a rest room while romantic music seeps in from a party in the nearby Gold Ball Room.

After an evening of unconsummated flirtation at the Ziegler party, Bill and Alice make passionate love in their own bedroom back home. Who do they *imagine* their partners to be? Naked, they embrace, fondle, and kiss each other while standing in front of a large mirror. Both initially glance at the reflected image of their lovemaking. But while Bill refocuses attention on his wife's gorgeous body, she seems more intrigued by their reflection). Is she thinking of Sandor? More spectator than participant, sex becomes for her an abstraction, half pornography. Meanwhile, Chris Isaak's "Baby Did a Bad Bad Thing" plays on the soundtrack, conveying the intensity while hinting at the dangerous volatility of the couple's desires and fantasies.

Alice Harford (Nicole Kidman) is more interested in watching her erotic reflection in the mirror than in making love with her husband, Bill (Tom Cruise).

Despite the use of this scene in pre-release publicity for the film, Kubrick does not linger long over it. After observing Alice's repeated glances away from her husband and toward their reflection in the mirror, the screen slowly fades to black, Alice's wayward eyes lingering in our minds as it does so.

Just as the camera crosscut between Bill's and Alice's separate flirtations at the party, it now crosscuts between his professional routine at the office and her domestic routine at home. The Shostakovich Waltz returns, suggesting an element of boring predictability about each. Bill greets his employees pleasantly, but more from habit than from real affection. As he examines a woman who is nude from the waist up, neither doctor nor patient betray any hint of sexual arousal. But then they wouldn't, would they? Later, Bill examines a boy and an older man. Meanwhile, at the apartment, Alice dresses Helena. They share bathroom space while Alice applies deodorant to her underarms and checks its effectiveness with a sniff— routine and intimacy on display, side by side. Later, mother and daughter wrap a Christmas gift. The box, reflecting Alice's former profession, is illustrated with the name and work of a famous painter. She *has* brought her work home with her. A shot of Alice and Helena seated at the dinner table, mother reading a newspaper while daughter watches television, echoes an early impression from *The Shining* in which Danny watches cartoons while Wendy reads a book, except that Alice looks more bored than does Wendy.

That evening both Bill and Alice seem tired after getting through their repetitious, daily routines. As if to spice up the end of the day (just as Alex did with an injection of Beethoven's *Ninth*), Alice retrieves some marijuana hidden in a Band-Aid can in the bathroom medicine cabinet. Not surprisingly in a Kubrick film, an institutional container (like the S.A.C. safe on board Major Kong's B-52) yields a *private* cargo (like Kong's cowboy hat).

Smoking pot in bed, Bill and Alice begin foreplay. All seems cozy and agreeable until Alice bluntly inquires if Bill "fucked" the two women he flirted with at the Ziegler party. Bill truthfully denies doing so, but he does his cause no good by mentioning that the women were professional models. Pursuing the matter further, Alice asks him where he disappeared for awhile during the party. No doubt she draws a parallel to her own flirtation, when Sandor asked *her* to disappear with him for awhile so they could have sex. Bill explains that he went upstairs to tend to Victor, which is at best a half-truth. But in keeping his promise to a friend by not mentioning the prostitute, Bill undermines his credibility with Alice.

Sexual foreplay continues even as the Harfords slip and slide into a full-blown marital argument. Two patterns overlap as one slowly displaces the other, in the manner of Lord Bullingdon disrupting his mother and stepfather's concert in *Barry Lyndon*. The argument between Bill and Alice develops as a series of strategic moves and countermoves that gradually get out of hand. Bill casually retaliates against Alice's mild accusation of infidelity by inquiring about her flirtation with Sandor. "What did he want?" Bill asks. Her inhibitions diminished by marijuana, just as they were by alcohol at the party, Alice replies aggressively, "Sex, upstairs." Somewhat less uninhibited, Bill tries to nip their dispute in the bud by being very tolerant: "I guess that's understandable." Bad tactic. Alice interprets his tolerance as an insult, and from that point forward, figuratively speaking, he digs his own grave.

As the bedroom scene begins, the embracing couple in the foreground is bathed in a warm, sensuous, yellow glow, while in the background the bathroom is bathed in blue light. When Bill makes the mistake of being overly tolerant of his wife's flirtation, she breaks off foreplay, leaves their bed, and retreats towards the emotional cool of the bathroom. Later, as her coolness turns to anger, she crosses the bedroom and appears within the vibrant red arch of window drapes, while yellow and blue hover nearby. A variety of emotions are at work within her.

When Bill comments that because of his wife's beauty it is understandable that a stranger would want to have sex with her, he opens up a Pandora's Box of emotions. Initially, Alice is offended by the implication that the only reason a man would want to be with her is for sex. More than likely, that is not what Bill meant. All of his statements in this argument are poorly thought out and invariably get him into deeper trouble. Like Jack Torrance willfully and cruelly misinterpreting Wendy's comments during their argument about Danny in the Colorado Lounge, Alice willfully and vindictively misinterprets (or *over* interprets) what her husband says.

By defending his specific remark with a general statement about "what men are like," Bill makes himself vulnerable to a similar charge. Since he is a man, he must have wanted to fuck the two models simply because they were beautiful. Backtracking, he qualifies his general statement with exceptions. He did not want to have sex with the two models because he loves Alice, because they are married, and because he would never lie to or hurt her. This all sounds very clichéd, convenient, and unconvincing. Bill may believe it, but he doesn't seem to feel it.

Once again, Alice turns her husband's own words against him. She reasons from his argument that he refrained from committing adultery only out of "consideration" for her, not because he didn't really want to. She then expands her point to include potentially adulterous situations and to question his professional ethics as a doctor. When Bill examines a naked woman, does he never get aroused or fantasize having sex with her, and vice versa? Bill rebuts by pointing out that the circumstances of a medical examination preclude such emotions, and besides, "Women basically don't think like that." Like a poor chess player, he does not anticipate the long-term disadvantages of a move he makes for short-term gain. Alice resents having her own desires taken for granted despite having just accused Bill of an *excess* of lust. Laughing hysterically at her husband's naiveté, and because smoking pot has made her a bit silly, she sternly lectures him on female sexuality. Then, to hammer home her point, she confesses to a fantasy she once had about a naval officer whose path she and Bill crossed while on vacation.

The detail and lugubrious intensity of Alice's fantasy, enhanced by the dreamy, sensual yet melancholy background music of Jocelyn Pook, has the desired effect. Kubrick alternates close-ups of Alice telling her tale with frontal close-ups of Bill reacting to it. With his black hair, dark eyes, and grim facial expression, Bill joins a Kubrickian gallery of passionate portraits, including General Turgidson, Dave Bowman, Alex, Mr. Alexander, Barry Lyndon, Jack Torrance, and Private Pyle. He no longer takes his wife for granted. But by making her husband jealous, Alice opens up her own Pandora's Box of emotions, which will threaten consequences far beyond the goal she presently has in mind.

Though it is remotely possible that Alice exaggerates her sexual fantasy, or even makes it up out of thin air in order to make Bill jealous, the aesthetic power of her recollection (and Kidman's performance) suggests otherwise. A chance encounter with a naval officer with whom she never even spoke develops into a sexual obsession so intense that she would have given up her marriage and her family for just one night of pleasure with him. Throughout Kubrick's work, triumph and disaster often turn on a whim — a moment's inspiration or carelessness — Alex attacking his rebellious droogs at the Flatblock marina, then dropping his guard against them in front of Catlady's house. With as little long-range foresight as her husband, Alice acts for short-term gain.

Strangest of all the emotional ebb and flow in this scene is the final part of Alice's fantasy. It is the only part of her confession that is not calculated to arouse jealousy in Bill. Instead, it reveals things about herself which even she does not fully understand. She claims that while fantasizing about making love to her naval officer, she felt closer to her husband than ever before, experiencing a love for him both "tender and sad." Like a classic Freudian dream, wish-fulfillment is tempered by an internal censor. Ironically, physical infidelity inspires emotional fidelity. But her unexpected tenderness does not register with Bill, who is consumed by the jealousy she wanted him to feel in the first place. In a close-up of his face, the sensuous yellow of the wall behind him is modified by the angry red of the headboard, which matches the angry red of the curtains that framed Alice. They are swimming in a river with many contradictory currents.

Like so many moments of crisis in *Eyes Wide Shut*, the Harfords' argument is interrupted by a telephone call. Bill is summoned to the home of a patient who has died suddenly. Professional duty displaces a private dispute. But private dispute will soon begin to color professional duty, to the extent that the two will be difficult to distinguish, much less separate.

William Harford's sexual odyssey begins in the back seat of a yellow taxi, on the way to the home of Lou Nathanson. He cannot help reflecting on what Alice said, picturing his wife having sex with her mysterious naval officer. Recurring, subjective, black-and-white glimpses of that passionate encounter convey to us Bill's imaginary re-creation of it. Progressively more revealing, those snippets are the film's only examples of unrestrained, unselfconscious sex. Every other sexual encounter, including the Harfords' stand-up affair in front of a mirror, features at least one barrier or counterpoint. In Bill's jealousy-fueled imagination, there is no evidence of the "tender and sad" love Alice claimed to have felt for him while fantasizing about another man.

One particular shot in *The Shining* of Jack Torrance fantasizing something nasty (the camera does not reveal what) shows him wearing a black sweater. Throughout his sexual odyssey, Bill is clothed in black, and he has black hair. He is a grim, rather *formal* figure of fantasy indulgence who never looks very comfortable at it.

Christmas trees and lights appear virtually everywhere in *Eyes Wide Shut*, even in the bedroom of a dead man. In keeping with Dr. Harford's attire, everything is sober and proper and conventional as he makes his way to Lou Nathanson's room, where daughter Marion grieves. Like Heywood Floyd and his Russian counterparts in *2001*, or Jack Torrance, Stuart Ullman, and Bill Watson during the job interview in *The Shining*, a collective sense of propriety governs behavior and, to a degree, masks private feelings. Bill puts his hand on Lou's head and seems to pray, a formal gesture of respect. He assures Marion, extrapolating from her account, that her father died peacefully in his sleep. But even if he didn't believe it, it is the sort of thing many physicians would say to a distraught survivor, just to be kind.

Bill and Marion divert their thoughts from death, briefly, with small talk about her impending marriage to boyfriend Carl and their move to Michigan. Eventually, however, that facade of placid politeness breaks down. Emotions overwhelm propriety. Marion sobs openly. Bill moves closer to comfort her. Then, shockingly, she kisses him on the mouth and confesses her love for him. Like Alice willing to sacrifice her marriage for a one-night stand with a stranger, Marion claims she would give up her life with Carl just to be near Bill, even without a commitment from him.

From the moment of the kiss, this scene follows a double logic. Marion's confession of love, occurring in the midst of a very different emotional crisis that erodes her normal inhibitions, is a believable example of previously concealed passion rising to the surface. We all have our secrets. The inappropriateness and suddenness of Marion's declaration makes us, who see it from an emotional distance, uncomfortable. We would rather laugh at or discredit it than accept its possibility. Compare Marion's emotional breakdown with that of Redmond Barry when confronting the Chevalier de Balibari for the first time in *Barry Lyndon*.

In the context of Bill's vengeful sex odyssey, Marion's declaration of love may be his angry reaction to Alice's flirtations, real and imagined, with adultery. Like Sandor, Marion speaks with a foreign accent. And like Alice and her naval officer, Marion is willing to sacrifice everything to be with Bill.

Not yet emotionally ready to cheat on his wife, Bill pulls away from Marion and rationalizes away her declaration of love as a byproduct of grief. But he lets that kiss linger for a moment before doing so. Wish-fulfillment and censorship contend with each other, if not on even terms.

Carl's arrival disrupts Bill's furtive dalliance with Marion. A university professor of mathematics, Carl's social status is roughly equivalent to Bill's. Both have black hair. Like Bill, Carl seems to be a nice guy, compassionate and soft spoken. In dream terms, he is that part of Bill that disapproves of a sexual encounter with Marion. By way of contrast, Lloyd the bartender, in *The Shining, encouraged* Jack Torrance's worst inclinations. Yet Jack dressed Lloyd in subtly demonic clothing, at least making an attempt to warn himself of the bartender's evil influence.

With Carl present, Bill and Marion return to the conventional, polite, and restrained behavior they exhibited at the start of the scene. Both of the guilty parties unconsciously wipe their lips, as though to get rid of incriminating evidence. But romantic tension remains. As Carl escorts Bill out of the room, Marion starts to protest, then restrains herself when Bill discourages her illicit romantic urge by saying a firm good night.

Earlier in the scene, Marion comments on her father's death: "I think I was more afraid of how it was going to happen than of the death itself." In other words, *imagination* can frighten us, or by like token intrigue us, as much as, if not more than, the thing itself. Clearly that was the case with Alice and the naval officer about whom she fantasized. And so it is with Bill and *his* fantasies, which are a reaction to hers.

Out on the street, the camera backtracks with Bill as he walks along the sidewalk. Frustrated and angry, he slams his fist into his other hand while again imagining Alice in the arms of her naval officer. This shot is reminiscent of a furious Jack Torrance walking down a hallway towards the Gold Ball Room after Wendy accuses him of injuring Danny in *The Shining.* Through the fantasized characters of Lloyd the bartender and Grady the caretaker, Jack taunts himself to seek revenge on his wife and son. Bill Harford's taunting comes at the hands of a group of young men he encounters on the sidewalk. Bragging about their sexual exploits as they approach, they knock him down and challenge his manhood as they pass by. To quote Alice Harford from the end of *Eyes Wide Shut,* "whether they [are] real or only a dream," the angry, arrogant, vicious young men echo and aggravate Bill's worst impulses as he reacts to powerful feelings of jealousy and self-doubt. Like virtually all of Bill's encounters on this and the following night, his confrontation with the gang of thugs is both temptation and warning.

Angered by the gang's challenge to his manhood, still upset about his wife's fantasized infidelity, and now aroused by the sight of a man and a woman making out in public, Bill cannot resist temptation when he encounters a prostitute on a street corner. He puts up a token fight. But she is gorgeous, friendly, and intelligent — a dream come true. After a double entendre for an appetizer, he is ready for the main course. The door to her apartment building is painted bright red: red for arousal, but also for caution.

Domino's apartment is shabby and messy but glows with Christmas tree lights. After the matter of payment is settled, she sets no time limit to their fun. And judging from her book collection, she is very well read. She *must* be a dream. Romantic mood music completes the scenario. Bill and Domino are about to do the deed when, just in the nick of time, he gets a call from Alice on his cell phone. Bill lies to his wife about where he is and what he is doing, hiding behind his professional mask. But Alice's monstrously ill-timed or wonderfully convenient (depending on one's perspective) interruption pricks Bill's conscience just enough to end the encounter prematurely. In dream logic, Bill's internal censor has struck again.

Polite and considerate as always, Bill insists on paying Domino in full for services not rendered. Domino, being his idyllic vision of prostitution, accepts his change of heart graciously and tries to decline the money. He insists she take it. Only later, in retrospect, will this encounter take on less than idyllic, potentially lethal, dimensions.

Resuming his nocturnal wanderings, Bill seems surprised to find himself outside the Sonata Cafe, where Nick Nightingale is performing. But is this encounter really coincidental, or has Bill unwittingly sought out his old friend? Is this a literal encounter? Or does Bill, unhappy with his own life, invent a walk on the wild side through an old friend who has already confessed to him that he *likes* the feeling of walking away from things?

Bill enters the brilliantly lit nightclub just as Nick and his jazz combo are playing their last number of the evening. In other words, on a *literal* level, Bill's life is about to be altered in a major way by an encounter he almost misses.

Initially, the two old friends restrict their conversation to conventional small talk, comparing notes on families and careers. But from the latter topic comes an indiscreet revelation by Nick that develops into another stop along Bill's sexual tour. Like a kid sharing a secret with his best buddy, Nick tells Bill about a mysterious moonlighting job in which he plays piano at orgies while blindfolded, at locations revealed to him only an hour before his performance. Like all great collective endeavors in Kubrick's films, these secret orgies fall short in their execution. Security is breached when Nick's blindfold comes loose and he glimpses the beautiful women involved. His sniggering disclosure about those women just happens to complement Bill's determination to cheat on his wife. When Nick gets a phone call informing him of the address and password for tonight's gathering, Bill kindly holds a napkin in place so he can write down the information. But Bill's consideration, though typical, in this instance serves a selfish purpose. To Nick's dismay, Bill presses him for the orgy's address, time, and requirements for admission. Only under the implied threat of being followed does Nick reluctantly provide that information. Attempting to be considerate even as he exploits his friend, Bill assures Nick that he will arrive at the orgy separately and will make no mention of Nick to its organizers.

Marion Nathanson was Bill's first, tentative, and relatively passive exploration of sexual revenge. The more alluring Domino, along with her unmistakable offer of sexual gratification, was a bolder stab at adultery. The prospect of sex with *many* beautiful women promises a much grander fulfillment of his desires. But what he anticipates and what he gets, or dreams, are two very different things.

In order to participate in the secret orgy, Bill requires a costume and a mask. And to fulfill his private wish, he again takes advantage of his professional status. Arriving at the Rainbow Fashions Costume Shop long after closing time, he rings up its presumed owner, a former patient, to ask a favor. But his old patient has moved out of town, so he must deal with a stranger named Milich. Like the acquaintances who took advantage of Barry's need to acquire expensive possessions in order to impress society's elite in *Barry Lyndon*, Milich holds out for a two-hundred-dollar bonus before opening his shop for Bill. Once again, money facilitates wish-fulfillment.

There is something eerie about the costume shop at night, with its dressed-up manikins foreshadowing the ideal body shapes, masks, and rigid movements of participants in the orgy that Bill will later attend. But that impression is purely metaphorical. On a more practical level, the shop is just a means of getting into that orgy. In danger of being too late to attend, Bill is slightly frustrated by Milich's desire to take personal advantage of Harford's professional credentials (asking for advice about hair loss), even though Bill tried to do the same thing by hitting up a former patient (Milich's predecessor) for a favor.

Inside one of the costume storage rooms, Milich discovers his young daughter having sex with two middle-aged men. Appearing to be morally outraged, Milich chastises the girl and threatens to have the frightened men arrested for corrupting a "deranged" minor. He locks them in the storage room pending further action. The scantily clad girl, meanwhile, seeks protection from her father by latching onto Bill. Before being sent off to bed, she whispers something lewd in his ear. Bill is shocked. But if her proposal is just another variation on his wide-ranging odyssey of sexual indulgence and revenge against Alice, Bill's *conscious* mind appears more horrified than intrigued. Clare Quilty and Lolita are the ghosts behind this encounter. But Bill Harford is, as of yet, nowhere near Quilty's level of sexual perversion. He does not possess Humbert's ability to rationalize a sexual relationship with a young girl.

Bill's determination to attend the orgy is fueled by yet another imaginary scene of Alice's infidelity as he rides in a taxi taking him to a secret location in the country. That ominous ride, with the cab's headlights fitfully illuminating trees on either side of the road, recollects Dick Halloran's snow-cat ride to Overlook in *The Shining*. Both journeys prove to be much more dangerous than the characters anticipate.

Once again, money is a great facilitator for Bill. He pays the cab driver much more than the meter reads, then gives him half of a torn hundred dollar bill and promises him the other half if he will wait until Bill returns. On a literal level, his action is practical. After all, he has traveled far out of the city and has no way to get back on his own. In dream terms, Bill leaves himself an escape route just in case the orgy does not turn out to be what he hopes.

The estate's heavy iron gate is lit by overhead lamps piercing the gloom of night and guarded by two large men in suits. Symbolically, this is the entrance to Hell. But the guards are most gracious and civilized in appearance, rather like Lloyd in *The Shining*. The password "Fidelio," the title of Beethoven's only opera, opens the gates to sexual fantasy. Ironically, "Fidelio," implying fidelity, serves the cause of *in*fidelity, just as Beethoven's "Ode to Joy" was made to serve various and contradictory causes in *Clockwork*. But Bill is not Alex. His fantasy is shaped by *mixed* emotions. What part of him anticipates to be a bacchanal turns out to be, perhaps due to his internal censor, a chillingly *non*erotic spectacle in which impersonal sex feels more like ritual sacrifice.

Like the red doorway to Domino's apartment, a red car takes Bill from the main gate to a palatial house where the orgy occurs. Again, color signifies both thrill and danger. The parking lot outside the house is filled with limousines. Though he possesses enough money to manipulate a costume shop proprietor and a cab driver, Bill is clearly out of his socioeconomic depth here. A stranger in a strange land, he is like Redmond Barry passing through Prussian territory after deserting from the British Army. Once inside the house, he dons his mask and cape to preserve his anonymity. But like Redmond unwittingly betraying himself to Captain Potsdorf, he cannot sustain the charade. Unlike Redmond's, however, Bill's self-betrayal may be a subconscious act of self-preservation.

The large chamber where the orgy begins is transformed into a kind of cathedral of evil by its ancient architecture, by music, and by the ritual that occurs within its walls, much as the site of Barry and Lord Bullingdon's duel in *Barry Lyndon* and the prison cell-block corridor in *Clockwork* acquire extrinsic definition by events which occur in them. Jocelyn Pook's somber music, which as *local* music is both a part of and a critical comment on the orgy, reinforces our impression of ritual sacrifice. Everyone gathered is robed and masked. The high priest is draped in red and wields a scepter. When he bangs that stick on the floor, it produces an exaggerated sound, just as Danny's tricycle wheels sounded louder than normal when he rode over uncarpeted stretches of wood floor in Overlook's Colorado Lounge. Institutional settings can either exaggerate or diminish the influence of individual man. Arranged in a circle around the high priest are a submissive group of women who, at his signal, stand and disrobe. Nude from the waist up, they are rendered anonymous by face masks. Tall, lanky, and firm, they conform to an abstract ideal of feminine beauty. They even *move* like models on a runway, in a silky smooth, artificial manner. In their own way, they are sisters to the Korova plastic figures and the Ludovico stage temptress in *A Clockwork Orange*. Not so much real women as they are abstract projections of someone else's sexual desire, they are equivalent to False Maria in *Metropolis*.

Two masked figures observing the ritual turn and nod in Bill's direction. Has he been recognized as an interloper? If so, his fascination with the incredible spectacle before him dulls his appreciation of danger. He is as much slave to lust as are the masked women.

At the command of their master, the women ritually kiss each other. Or, to be more precise, their *masks* kiss, which renders the contact doubly impersonal. Then they are dismissed to pair off with various masked patrons in the audience. Not a word is spoken. One of them links up with Bill, strolling off with him in the silent promise of adulterous and vengeful fulfillment. But without removing her mask or altering her studied stride, the woman becomes a nonpuppet, an *individual*, a real person, warning Bill of the danger he faces if he doesn't leave immediately. In dream terms, his victim becomes his potential savior by breaking through the silence he imposed on her. In a sense, she is equivalent to the attractive, sexually accommodating siren who appears to Jack Torrance in Overlook's Room 237 and is then transformed into the rotting corpse of an old woman whose mocking laughter drives him out of the room and, if only temporarily, out of his dangerous fantasy. But Bill's heroine is subject to the rules of the house. She is soon taken away by another eager, masked admirer. Her elegant, outwardly cool backward glance at Bill as she climbs the stairs with her new companion reiterates her warning without violating the aesthetics of the role she plays in the orgy. But Harford is still too captivated by what he sees to heed his censor.

A traveling camera accompanies Bill on a tour of the house's many rooms, which, in their size and ornate décor, resemble the interiors of *Barry Lyndon*. Each room features a sexual variation performed by one or more of the sacrificial women and one or more of the patrons, observed by a crowd of people awaiting their turn to perform. All retain their masks. Solemn, arabesque music by Jocelyn Pook plays on the soundtrack. Equivalent in dramatic function to Rimsky-Korsakov's *Scheherazade* during Alex's extravagant Biblical sex fantasy in *Clockwork*, Pook's music nevertheless echoes the protagonist's contradictory emotional reaction to what he sees. The orgy is superficially exotic, but also terrifying, even profoundly sad. Late in the scene, "Strangers in the Night" plays as local music in a room full of dancing strangers: some naked, some clothed, but all anonymously masked. The song may tell of love at first sight; imagery, however, portrays the concept of "stranger" in literal terms. There is no romance here — just impersonal coupling.

In the American release of *Eyes Wide Shut*, the sex acts witnessed by Bill are partially hidden behind computer-generated human figures. This was apparently a concession to the desire for an R rather than an NC-17 rating. The film is not greatly damaged by that compromise, but the audience's emotional identification with Bill during these traveling shots is somewhat diminished. We are not *quite* allowed to experience the shock of what he experiences.

The masked figure who nodded to Bill and recognized him as an uninvited guest sends one of the masked women to proposition him as he watches others engaged in sex. And he seems willing to take her up on it until his secret benefactor intervenes, escorting him out of the room and warning him yet again of danger. Simultaneously aroused by and grateful to her, he asks her to leave with him. "That's impossible ... it could cost me my life and possibly yours," she replies. In dream logic, it is also impossible because it would allow Bill both fulfillment of his illicit wishes *and* escape from the danger they pose to him. He cannot have it both ways.

Both fulfillment of and escape from his dream are precluded when Bill is separated from his would-be guardian, lured downstairs under false pretenses and put on trial by the high priest in front of the assembled guests. Upon confirmation that he crashed the orgy without an invitation, Bill is forced to remove his mask, thus revealing his individual identity in a situation where scandal could ruin his career. Then he is ordered to remove all his clothes, which implies not only a loss of personal dignity (he is not, after all, being invited to have sex with other naked people) but possibly threatened with unspecified bodily harm. Torture? Mutilation? This bizarre crowd seems capable of anything.

Scared and helpless, Bill is rescued from his predicament by his protector's sudden, convenient return and offer to sacrifice herself for his safety. The formality of this action seems more dreamlike than realistic. A different yet plausible interpretation of events is offered later in the film by Victor Ziegler. But his motivations are suspect, so we must decide for ourselves. In symbolic terms, the compassionate woman is a Christ figure, sacrificing herself for Bill's sins, of which she is also a victim. Conscientious as usual, he expresses concern about her fate. But the high priest refuses to discuss the matter, and he threatens dire consequences for Bill and his family if Bill pursues it any further. And so if Bill has distorted his own fantasy by thwarting his desire for sexual revenge on Alice, he conveniently provides himself with an escape route, then complicates that escape with a burden of guilt.

Returning home late after his nearly catastrophic brush with infidelity, Bill looks in fondly at his sleeping daughter, hides his rented costume in a locked cabinet, and goes to his bedroom, where he finds Alice in the midst of her own wish-fulfillment dream. She seems to be having a good time until Bill awakens her, which is equivalent to Wendy waking Jack out of his homicidal nightmare in *The Shining*. And like Jack, Alice confesses to her spouse what, in the light of full consciousness, terrifies rather than pleases her. And that confession, like Jack's, will have bad consequences.

Frightened and ashamed, Alice seeks reassurance in physical contact with her husband, asking him to lie down beside her, then stroking his hair as she relates her dream. The beginning is innocent enough, with the two of them inexplicably wandering naked through a deserted city. But for some reason Alice is ashamed and terrified, blaming Bill for her situation. When he leaves to find her clothes, her dream takes on a new direction. She lies naked in a garden, feeling wonderful. Then her naval officer, from a previous fantasy, arrives. Has she conjured up her own variation on the old Garden of Eden myth, complete with Adam, Eve, and the snake? The officer (snake) laughs at her, mocking her. Before long, however, they are having sex, which then becomes an orgy, providing Alice with numerous partners. Curiously, her dream resembles Bill's fantasy (or reality, whichever it was), except that she is less inhibited and therefore pursues her sexual whim further than he was able to.

In the dream, Bill returns. Alice, knowing that her husband sees her cheating on him with multiple partners, laughs at him in a deliberate effort to humiliate and hurt him. This is the "fun" she was having when he woke her up. Crying, Alice is horrified at her own capacity for selfishness and cruelty. Bill tries to soothe her by reassuring, "It's only a dream." But like his attempt to belittle their respective flirtations at the Ziegler party, this one ignores what it does not understand. And the less-than-forgiving look on his face belies his comforting words.

Alice's wish-fulfilling dream suggests that she still resents being taken for granted by her husband. She is not aware of the fits of jealousy and the sexual fantasies they have inspired in him. Only *his* confession of guilt, late in the film, can balance out that emotional equation.

Guilt and concern drive Bill to search for Nick the following morning. Unable to find him at the Sonata Cafe, he tries the nearby Gillespie's Cafe, where he uses his professional status deceitfully in order to pursue his private agenda. "To be perfectly honest" is a bald-faced lie but told in a compassionate cause. He tells a waitress that he is Nick's doctor and that he has some important test results he needs to communicate immediately. Properly motivated, she overrules her own ethics and gives him the address of Nick's hotel. The fib Bill tells in this scene is equivalent to Dick Halloran lying to friend Larry Durkin in order to facilitate a rescue mission to Overlook. Deceit is not always wrong or selfish — just *most* of the time.

Bill repeats his performance, or a variation of it, for the hotel desk clerk, who has a private agenda of his own. He is obviously attracted to Bill, flirting with him as he relates information about Nick, who returned to the hotel early that morning, looking bruised and battered and accompanied by two tough-looking men. "They weren't the kind of people you'd like to fool around with, if you know what I mean." Betraying his feelings for Bill, the clerk appears self-conscious about the potential double meaning of his words. But Harford is oblivious to the clerk's semantic gymnastics. For him the salient part of their conversation is that Nick looked injured, frightened, tried unsuccessfully to slip the clerk a note, and left the hotel with the men who brought him.

In the context of Bill's ongoing, dreamlike sexual odyssey, the hotel clerk represents a homosexual option the protagonist does not consciously acknowledge, any more than he will the possibility of sex with an adolescent in the next scene. Instead, he uses Nick, who may or may not have been roughed up by agents of the orgy's organizers, to punish himself with guilt for indulging his forbidden, adulterous sexual fantasies at the orgy.

Bill returns his orgy costume to the Rainbow Shop. But his attempt to conceal incriminating evidence from Alice is not wholly successful, just as the orgy organizers were unable to keep Nick in the dark with a blindfold. The mask is missing. On a practical level, the price he pays for that oversight is minor. Milich just tacks on another twenty-five dollars to the bill. But the emotional cost will prove more substantial.

To Bill's and our great surprise, Milich's daughter and the two older men who had sex with her the night before exit from the back of the store. Milich behaves cordially towards them. Bill, concerned about the girl, asks Milich about his earlier threat to have the men arrested for corrupting his daughter. But it seems that Milich is prostituting her and that his objections the night before were not moral but financial. His daughter and her customers were screwing around behind his back, after hours and without paying for services rendered. In other words, Bill's and our earlier impression of Milich's relationship with his daughter was completely wrong. Like Joe, the lodger in *Clockwork*, the proprietor's show of moral outrage was nothing more than a cover for a selfish agenda of his own. To make matters worse, he now offers *Bill* a chance to have sex with his daughter. But that is one sexual adventure the protagonist flatly rejects.

Continuing visions of Alice and her naval officer, however, prevent Bill from abandoning his odyssey altogether. In order to pursue a private agenda, he cancels his professional appointments for the day and drives to Somerton Estates, the scene of the orgy. What exactly is his motivation here? Is he concerned about Nick Nightingale and the woman who saved his life? Or is he still intrigued by the prospect of random sex? Whichever, he is thwarted by a locked, cold blue iron gate and a note, delivered to him by a silent stranger, which warns him again, in simplistically dreamlike terms, to make no further inquiries into the matter. Gyorgy Ligeti's grim "Musica Ricercata II" reinforces both the formality of the exchange and the sense of lurking danger imparted to Bill. This almost ritualistic scene is, on one level of interpretation, an internal struggle between Bill's fear for his own welfare (the locked gate and the written warning discourage his curiosity) and his nagging concern for the friends he endangered by his reckless actions.

Obsessive jealousy pollutes any sense of normalcy for Bill at home. He arrives there while Alice is helping Helena with her homework at the dining table. Helena begs for a puppy for Christmas. It *should* be a warm scene, especially when Bill goes to the kitchen to get a beer and then looks back at his wife and daughter through the doorway. A subjective camera, from his point of view, slowly zooms in on them. But overlapping and contradicting it is the vocal memory of Alice's dream confession the night before. She and Bill exchange smiles through the open doorway. But *his* smile is false. There is no such thing as *totally* uninhibited communication between two people, even if they love each other — if for no other reason than that an individual is never totally consistent in his or her *own* thoughts and feelings.

Still haunted by the image of Alice and her fantasy lover after returning to work, Bill embarks again, if tentatively, on his fantasy of revenge. He pursues the *safest* variation first, telephoning Marion Nathanson. But Carl, the censor, answers, so Bill hangs up without identifying and incriminating himself.

The next, somewhat more dangerous, alternative is Domino. Bill arrives at her apartment with a pizza in hand. A pizza is more suited to a fun evening with a girlfriend than to a business transaction with a prostitute. Harford just can't help being a nice guy, most of the time. But instead of Domino, he encounters her roommate, Sally, who lets him in because he is handsome and because Domino told her how nice he was. Sally discreetly checks out his physique and flirts with him as they enter the kitchen.

Bill may have arrived with a gift of friendship, but it is sex he really wants — any port in a storm of jealousy. He brazenly unbuttons Sally's blouse, with her cooperation. But then she pours cold water on their brief encounter. Whether acting as Bill's internal censor, on a dream level, or out of self-preservation, on a literal level, she reveals that Domino just that morning got back blood test results indicating she is HIV positive. Not only does this disclosure put a damper on Bill's sexual desire in this scene, it also kills his desire in retrospect. Had he and Domino not been interrupted by Alice's telephone call, Bill might now be fatally infected with HIV. And Sally, not knowing for sure if Bill and Domino have had sex, prudently fends off her own attraction to him. She and Bill revert to safe, conventional small talk in order to evade the shocking news about Domino, just as Bill and Marion did in the presence of her dead father in an earlier scene.

Full of contradictory feelings, including anger, desire, guilt, and fear, Bill wanders the streets of New York. Spotting a man following him, he assumes it is an agent of the people who warned him not to investigate the orgy, maybe even a hired assassin. At one point, Bill and his shadow stop and stare at each other. Has Bill become as paranoid as General Ripper? Or is the specter that stalks him *real*? Frightened, Bill tries to escape his mysterious stalker by fleeing in a taxi, which has been his mode of transportation into and out of so many other dreamlike situations. But for the first time in the film, the taxis do not heed Bill's call. He is trapped in this particular nightmare, where he is either threatened with retribution for his sins by his own conscience or menaced by the external evil of other people.

Pursuing an alternate avenue of escape, just as Alex did through Bible stories in Staja 84F, Bill stops at a newsstand and buys a newspaper. His pursuer stops too, then finally walks on by. The danger has passed. But Bill's ordeal has not. From out of the instrument of his emotional escape (the newspaper) comes his next nightmare. Retreating to the safety of a public coffee bar, he sits down to read his newspaper. In it he sees an article about the drug overdose of an ex-beauty queen named Amanda Curran, who presently lies in a hospital in critical condition. Is she the woman who rescued Bill at the orgy? And is this the price she was made to pay for that sacrifice? Ligeti's doomsday piano strokes return to the soundtrack. Neither Bill nor we can escape their relentless message of guilt.

At the hospital, Bill again takes advantage of his status as a physician, and again it is in a noble cause. Posing as Amanda Curran's doctor, he learns that she has died. In the hospital morgue, he grieves over her lifeless, nude body. Lying on a slab slid out of a stainless steel drawer, she appears as vulnerable and is as pitiable as the astronauts who died in their hibernation chambers in *2001*. She might also be compared to the sad image of Lady Lyndon, pale and frozen with sorrow, seated in her bathtub in *Barry Lyndon*. "Because it could cost me my life and possibly yours" overlaps on the soundtrack, recollecting the line spoken by Bill's protector at the orgy. There is no doubt he believes the dead woman to be that protector. "Grey Clouds," a delicately mournful piano piece by Franz Liszt, echoes his sorrow. He bends over her body as though to kiss her forehead out of respect. But he stops short (the camera pulling back too), either repulsed at the thought of kissing a corpse or overcome by shame at his responsibility for her death. The interpretation is up to us.

Though Bill's outpouring of grief is sincere, it may be rooted in a delusion. He assumes not only that the dead woman in front of him is the same woman who saved his life earlier, but also that her sacrificial act was exactly what it appeared to be. The latter assumption is challenged, though not quite disproved, in the next scene.

A summons from Victor Ziegler reaches Bill over the telephone (as do so many disruptions and invitations in *Eyes Wide Shut*), lifting him out of his gloom as he walks down a hospital corridor, crying over Amanda Curran's fate. He joins Ziegler in Victor's billiards room: a symmetrical paradise filled with expensive objects oozing wealth, privilege, and tradition. On one level, Ziegler is a man of high social stature, seeking to preserve his public reputation and retain the trust of his corrupt peers (the organizers of the secret orgies) by persuading Bill to keep his mouth shut and stop inquiring into recent events. In another sense, however, Ziegler is Bill's desperate, self-serving escape route from the mountain of guilt he has accumulated during his sexual odyssey. He provides Bill with logical reasons to believe he caused no harm to Nick or Amanda, and that the man following Bill intended no harm either. In the latter role, he serves Bill rather like Lloyd the bartender serves Jack Torrance in *The Shining*. In either role, Victor is evil. He is, like Charles Grady to Jack Torrance, what Bill Harford could become without much difficulty.

Very cautiously, Victor raises the delicate subject of the orgy. He discloses only as much information as he thinks necessary to accomplish his purpose, which accounts for the slowness of the dialog in this scene. At first Bill denies even being at the orgy, until Ziegler undercuts him by revealing that he was there, too, and saw everything that happened. Then, for every self-incriminating interpretation of events Bill offers, Victor supplies an antidote. Bill blames himself for Nick Nightingale's troubles. Victor blames *Nick* for *Bill's* nightmare, which is understandable, since Victor owes Bill a favor for keeping quiet about the prostitute who overdosed in his bathroom. Victor claims that Nick was merely roughed up a little, then put on an airplane to Seattle, where he is probably "banging his wife right now." This colorful little speculation is meant to reassure Bill, but it also reinforces our impression of Ziegler's misogynistic tendencies. He would fit right in with Jack Torrance and Lloyd trashing the "old sperm bank." And like the Interior Minister in *Clockwork*, Ziegler is a satanic temptor and manipulator, motivated purely by self-interest rather than concern for a friend.

By admitting it was he who hired the mysterious man who followed Bill through the streets of New York, Victor helps alleviate Bill's fear of retribution by the orgy organizers. So civilized and polite on the surface, Victor even apologizes for the action. But this is counterpointed by his not-so-subtle hint that Bill faces far greater danger than he realizes if he doesn't stop his

Bill Harford (Tom Cruise) is tempted to absolve himself of responsibility for his selfish actions by his amoral acquaintance, Victor Ziegler (Sydney Pollack), in Victor's lush billiards room.

investigation immediately. The people who organized and participated in the orgy are so high on the social ladder that Bill would be astonished to know their names, which Victor prudently refuses to disclose. As in *Dr. Strangelove*, private perversions presumably infect even the highest ranks of social power and prestige.

In order to soothe Bill's guilt about the woman who sacrificed herself to save his life, Victor first reveals that she was a common hooker. But when this fails to do the trick, because Bill is not contemptuous of women just for being prostitutes, he switches tactics, undercutting the sacrifice itself. He claims that everything that happened to Bill during the orgy trial, including the intervention that apparently saved his life, was faked in order to scare him into silence. Therefore, the woman was never in any danger. In rebuttal, Bill shows him the newspaper article about her drug overdose and tells him about her subsequent death. Ziegler responds with a plausible explanation. The hooker was an addict who overdosed *after* she was safely returned home following the orgy. As further evidence, Ziegler claims she was the same prostitute Bill treated for a drug overdose, and warned of the danger of future overdoses, at the party a few nights earlier.

Piece by piece, Ziegler discredits Bill's logic of guilt. But Bill remains unconvinced. As a final reassurance, Victor puts his arm on Bill's shoulder and says, "Life goes on. It always does, until it doesn't." This piece of cheap, shallow cynicism, offered so casually that it loses some credibility on style points, is equivalent to Lloyd's comment, "Women. Can't live with 'em. Can't live without 'em," in *The Shining*. But unlike Jack Torrance, Bill Harford does not buy into it. Earlier in the scene, he declined an offer to play a game of billiards on Victor's large, vibrantly red (another symbolic mixture of temptation and warning) table. In *Clockwork*, by contrast, Mr. Alexander yielded to the temptation to make use of Dolin's pool table (political agenda) for personal gain.

Returning home after another exhausting night, Bill again wanders through the family's quiet apartment, taking stock of his life and beginning to appreciate what he could so easily lose. As he walks by the Christmas tree, he switches off its lights. This otherwise trivial action signals, on a symbolic level, the end of his disappointing wanderlust. For the first time in the film, there are no dazzling holiday lights illuminating the action.

Bill enters his bedroom. Next to the head of his sleeping wife, on his own pillow, lies the mask he lost. Perhaps he subconsciously forgot to return it to the costume shop so that Alice would find and question him about it. Or maybe he left it behind by accident. In either case, it is for him a potent symbol of his attempted infidelity and his reckless endangerment of Nick Nightingale, Amanda, even his wife and daughter. Upon seeing it, he breaks down in tears and confesses all to Alice, who takes him in her arms. He finally reciprocates the painful admission she made following her cruel dream of infidelity several scenes earlier. It has taken him a long time to catch up.

Cut to the following morning. The emotional cost of Bill's confession is painfully evident in the initial close-up of Alice, whose red-rimmed eyes, exhausted facial expression, and lit cigarette attest to her ordeal. It would have been too easy to end the film with Bill locked in Alice's reassuring embrace. But infidelity, even in a dream or a fantasy, can be hurtful and damaging. There is no guarantee that the Harfords' marriage will survive it.

Bill weeps silently on the couch nearby. Neither character speaks, until Alice comments that their daughter will soon be up and expects her parents to take her Christmas shopping. Alice thus introduces a sense of family routine to the scene — a routine that once seemed rather dreary but is now therapeutic — infused with rejuvenated passion and value. As in so many of his films, Kubrick returns at the end to an impression from the beginning, but under radically altered conditions.

The final scene of *Eyes Wide Shut* occurs in a department store lavishly decorated for the holidays. With Helena out of earshot, Bill asks, "What do you think we should do?" Alice's reply is both an answer to that question and perhaps a comment, by Kubrick, on the ambiguous nature of what we have seen and heard during the film. "Maybe we should be grateful that we've managed to survive through all of our adventures, whether they were real or only a dream."

Easy certainty is no longer a part of the Harfords' marriage, though Bill still yearns for it. "Are you sure about that?" he asks Alice in reply to her remark. But her answer is a comment on the ambiguous and complex nature of truth. "Only as sure as I am that the reality of one night, let alone that of a lifetime, can ever be the whole truth." Bill catches her drift towards uncertainty and adds, "And no dream is ever just a dream," which overturns an earlier remark he made about Alice's adulterous dream being insignificant. He no longer takes such things for granted.

Alice sounds a note of cautious optimism: "The important thing is we're awake now, and hopefully for a long time to come." Bill, however, can't resist being romantically optimistic one more time. "Forever?" he asks hopefully. But Alice will not follow him down that path. She has always been wiser about the emotional facts of life than her husband. Instead, as therapy for their wounded marriage, she recommends that they "fuck" as soon as possible. This would seem to be a shocking ending to *Eyes Wide Shut* because it returns, very bluntly, to sex as a solution for problems arising out of sexual obsession and jealousy. Yet it makes good sense. Throughout the film, Alice and Bill have fantasized about having sex with *other* partners. Even when they made love together in front of a mirror it was, for Alice, watching their reflection, a fantasy of something *else*. Now, frightened by the recent consequences of obsessive fantasizing, Alice seeks comfort and reassurance in the *physical* act of love with *her husband*. She has transformed something so cheapened by fantasy (especially by the orgy scene) into an act of healing. But it took a long time and much suffering to reach that point. If Alex's final line in *Clockwork*, "I was *cured* all right," is grimly ironic, Alice's startling recommendation is ironic in a more positive sense.

The return of the Shostakovich Waltz during the final credits tempers the optimism of the final scene just a little, suggesting a return to the routine, boredom, and emotional blindness we observed in the Harfords' lives at the start of the film. But maybe, like the return of "The Blue Danube" Waltz during *2001*'s final credits, Kubrick is merely returning us to the jumping-off point of a dangerous odyssey, to make of it what we will. If so, we embark with his warning in hand.

* * *

The seven film odysseys discussed in this study are as different from each other in some ways as they are similar in others. Never repeating settings or time periods, they nevertheless *all* depict worlds in which motivations and circumstances are multifaceted and contradictory. After all, even the writing of this book was prompted, if I can judge, by a variety of motives: a strong and enduring fascination with Kubrick's work, the desire for a little notoriety (at the risk of criticism), and perhaps even a need to compensate for the frustrations and disappointments of everyday life.

Through his manipulation of image and sound, Kubrick is our relentlessly inquisitive, empathetic, yet skeptical guide through the multilayered worlds he portrays on screen. His inclination to embrace and emphasize contradictions inherent in the human condition, rather than reconcile or eliminate them in the final reel, often render his work unsettling, disappointing, and even infuriating for some audiences. Few of us would pop a Kubrick movie into the video player in order to validate a singular point of view, such as the triumph of love over hate or good over evil, or the righteousness of heroic effort. And sometimes we need that validation. Kubrick takes us through too many twists and turns to make it a smooth ride. After a triple dose of *Lolita, The Shining* and *Eyes Wide Shut*, we might yearn for the predictable happy ending of a traditional romantic comedy. And repeated viewings of *2001* might send us scurrying for the shelter of *Star Wars*. But after a little sugar-coated reaffirmation, some of us can't help returning to the inseparable sweet-and-sour served up by Stanley Kubrick — to, for example, the contradictory mix of critical scrutiny and compassion in the agonizing close-up of Private Joker after he kills an enemy sniper in *Full Metal Jacket*. Whether confounding our expectations or undercutting our inclinations, Stanley Kubrick encourages us to feel and see more than we sometimes want to.

Selected Bibliography

Arendt, Hannah. *Eichmann in Jerusalem: A Report on the Banality of Evil.* Revised and enlarged edition. New York: Penguin, 1964.

Botting, Douglas. *From the Ruins of the Reich: Germany 1945–1949.* New York: New American Library, 1985.

Bryant, Peter. *Red Alert.* New York: Ace, 1958; report, 1963.

Burgess, Anthony. *A Clockwork Orange.* New American Edition. New York: Ballantine, 1990.

Ciment, Michel. *Kubrick.* Trans. by Gilbert Adair. New York: Holt Rinehart and Winston, 1982.

Clausewitz, Carl von. *On War.* Trans. by J. J. Graham. Anatol Rapoport, ed. Harmondsworth: Penguin, 1981.

Freud, Sigmund. *The Basic Writings of Sigmund Freud.* Trans. by A. A. Brill, ed. New York: The Modern Library, 1965.

Friedman, Thomas. *From Beirut to Jerusalem.* New York: Doubleday, 1989.

Herold, J. Christopher. *The Mind of Napoleon.* New York: Columbia University, 1961.

Kagan, Norman. *The Cinema of Stanley Kubrick.* New York: Grove, 1972.

Mostert, Noel. *Supership.* New York: Alfred A. Knopf, 1974.

Nelson, Thomas Allen. *Kubrick: Inside a Film Artist's Maze.* Bloomington: Indiana University Press, 1982.

Nietzsche, Friedrich. *Thus Spoke Zarathustra.* Trans. by R. J. Hollingdale. Harmondsworth: Penguin, 1976.

Phillips, Gene D. *Stanley Kubrick: A Film Odyssey.* New York: Popular Library, 1975.

Schnitzler, Arthur, Stanley Kubrick, and Frederic Raphael. *Eyes Wide Shut: A Screenplay, and Dream Story.* New York: Warner, 1999.

Skinner, B. F. *Walden Two.* New York: Macmillan, 1976.

Tillion, Germaine. *Ravensbruck.* Trans. by Gerald Satterwhite. Garden City: Doubleday, 1975.

Walker, Alexander. *Stanley Kubrick Directs.* New York: Harcourt Brace Jovanovich, 1972.

Index